A P... ...STORY OF SCOTLAND

CHRIS BAMBERY is a writer, broadcaster, TV producer and founding member of the International Socialist Group in Scotland. He is the author of *Scotland: Class and Nation* (1999), *A Rebel's Guide to Gramsci* (2006) and *The Second World War: A Marxist History* (2013).

A PEOPLE'S HISTORY
OF SCOTLAND

Chris Bambery

VERSO
London • New York

First published by Verso 2014
© Chris Bambery 2014

The moral rights of the author have been asserted

1 3 5 7 9 10 8 6 4 2

Verso
UK: 6 Meard Street, London W1F 0EG
US: 20 Jay Street, Suite 1010, Brooklyn, NY 11201
www.versobooks.com

Verso is the imprint of New Left Books

ISBN-13: 978-1-78-168284-5
eISBN-13: 978-1-78-168285-2 (US)
eISBN-13: 978-1-78168-654-6 (UK)

British Library Cataloguing in Publication Data
A catalogue record for this book is available from the British Library.

Library of Congress Cataloging-in-Publication Data
Bambery, Chris.
A people's history of Scotland / Chris Bambery.
pages cm
Includes bibliographical references and index.
ISBN 978-1-78168-284-5 (alk. paper) – ISBN 978-1-78168-285-2 (ebook)
1. Scotland–History. 2. Scotland–Social conditions. 3. Socialism–Scotland–History.
I. Title.
DA760.B36 2014
941.1–dc23
2014002213

Typeset in Adobe Garamond Pro by Hewer Text UK Ltd, Edinburgh, Scotland
Printed and bound by CPI Group (UK) Ltd, Croydon, CR0 4YY

Contents

ONE

Scotland Emerges

Imagine you are travelling up one of the great sea lochs that penetrate far into the interior of the Scottish Highlands. Say, Loch Linnhe, which leads to the Great Glen stretching north-east to what is now Inverness. You are in a party of four or five in a canoe, and other canoes are being paddled behind. Men, women and children are travelling together. Physically the lochs, glens and mountains you see around you are the same as today, but with one important difference: they are covered in a dense forest. For this is Scotland 11,000 years ago.

The last Ice Age has come to an end and the great glaciers have retreated. The forests abound with red and roe deer, elk, wild cattle, boars, bears, wildcats and wolves. In the trees live pine martens, polecats and a variety of birds. The seas and rivers are alive with fish and shellfish. This is what has brought you here. Over the summer you will set up camp and feed on the wildlife, before sailing south to escape the winter. You have no fixed home because you travel constantly in search of game to hunt, or fruits, nuts and other foods.

Hunter-gatherers were the first settlers in Scotland we know anything about. It is likely they were not the first humans here because we know people had reached Britain before the glaciers overran most of the island. The ice, however, destroyed all trace of these earlier humans. The hunter-gatherers were a highly mobile people, doing their rounds of seasonal sites. You can imagine them moving between these favourite spots, taking delight in the locations and joy in discovering new sites with an abundance of food. There were no monarchs, priests or other leaders; people pooled their skills and knowledge. For the first and last time they were living in relative accord with nature.

Flint tools have been found on Ben Lawers in Perthshire and at Glen Dee (a mountain pass through the Cairngorms), demonstrating that these people travelled inland, probably keeping to the high ground above the deep forest. At a rock shelter and shell midden at Sand, near Applecross in Wester Ross, facing across the sound to Skye, excavations have shown that around 7500 BC people had tools of bone, stone and antler, and were living off shellfish, fish and deer. They used pot-boiler stones as a cooking method, made beads from seashells and used ochre pigment and shellfish to make purple dye.

They were sophisticated in their ability to track the changing moon, and with it the tides and the turn of the seasons. In the summer of 2013 archaeologists reported a find in Aberdeen where a group of twelve pits appeared to mimic the phases of the moon, allowing their creators to track lunar months over the year. It was thought that the first means of measuring time had been created in Mesopotamia about 5,000 years ago, but this new discovery predated that by thousands of years. The leader of the project, Professor Vince Gaffney of the University of Birmingham, noted, 'The evidence suggests that hunter-gatherer societies in Scotland had both the need and sophistication to track time across the years, to correct for seasonal drift of the lunar year and that this occurred nearly 5,000 years before the first formal calendars known in the near east.'[1] Even as these hunter-gatherers arrived in Scotland, agriculture was being developed in the Nile Delta and on the banks of the Tigris and Euphrates rivers in modern-day Iraq. The first traces in Britain of communities that farmed to some degree, made pottery and buried their dead in formal and elaborate tombs date back to 4000 BC. New arrivals from the east brought innovations in techniques for growing food and domesticating animals, but the existing evidence suggests this movement of people was not an invasion. They seemed to have settled down with the natives. Neither was there any dramatic conversion from hunter-gathering to farming. The two co-existed for some considerable time.

Yet, as farming communities evolved, humans started to build shelters of wood and then stone, in settlements such as the one excavated at Skara Brae in the Orkneys. Farming gradually led to the destruction of the great forest that covered Scotland, for use as timber and to clear the way for pasture and crops. This coincided with, and may have contributed to, the cooling of the climate, which increased deforestation, created peat bogs where trees had once stood and rendered much of the uplands infertile.

As pressure on the land grew, boundaries were laid down as farming communities marked out their fields and pastures. They developed the skills to produce pottery and learnt how to polish and grind stone, techniques used in the making of axes to chop trees, and in the preparation of animal skins to provide clothing and waterproof shelter, and to cover timber-framed boats. Trade began to develop, as we know from axes found in Scotland from as far afield as Cornwall and the Lake District.

By around 2500 BC, grand monuments started to dot the landscape – henges with their standing stones and great ditches and burial mounds. Where once people had been buried together, these structures were now reserved for the great and the good, as is evident by the relative riches that accompanied the dead to the world beyond. The building of burial chambers and standing stone circles indicates that a process of societal differentiation was already taking place. Arguments would soon break out between communities in moments of scarcity and vulnerability. Wars began to occur.

With war came the emergence of warriors: strong men charged with protecting the community, its crops, animals and harvest. Over time they would emerge as chiefs or even kings. In other words, a class system was emerging.

Until this development, children had probably been brought up collectively; now the responsibility fell on the mother. Further, where women and men had once been equals, now the priests and chiefs were male. This was what Friedrich Engels called the 'world historic defeat of the female sex'.[2]

By the late Stone Age period there were established settlements where people grew grains and barley, raised sheep, cattle and, increasingly, pigs, while continuing to exploit the natural resources around them. Farming also relied on communal effort to hoe, sow and harvest.

Around 2500 BC, bronze began to be smelted from copper and tin, and it was used to make weapons, tools, armour and jewellery. The tin had to be imported from Cornwall, and only the wealthy who had access to surplus food and livestock had the means to trade for it. The arrival of bronze, then iron, around 1000 BC (at the same time as the wheel), would have increased class division. A ruling, warrior class had a virtual monopoly of the new metals.

During this period the territory of modern Scotland was made up of tribes or clans. Warfare, particularly feuding and raiding, were endemic. Chieftains built hill forts, brochs (those strange beehive-like towers) and crannogs, artificial islands on a loch which were easily defended. We have no direct knowledge about the lives of the ordinary people, because they left no records that have come through to us. It would be left to an alien force to give us some inkling of what this society had been like.

'They Create a Desert and Call It Peace'

As the Roman Empire extended itself into what is now England and Wales, it began to encounter people beyond its northern frontier. By the first century AD, the Romans had given the name Caledonia to the country beyond the Solway Firth and River Tyne, meaning 'the woods on the heights'. But by then most of southern and central Scotland was deforested. Having established control of the province of Britain, the Romans were inevitably drawn northwards.

In AD 80, a Roman army stood ready to battle a Caledonian army at Mons Graupius, somewhere in north-east Scotland (the battlefield has still not been identified with certainty). These were tribes who lived north of the Forth and Clyde valleys. The tribes to the south were not under Roman control but had been absorbed through trade. Those to the north would prove resistant to any such integration.

The Roman historian Tacitus, who happened to be the son-in-law of the commander Agricola, identified the Caledonian leader as Calgacus, the 'swordsman'. In Tacitus's account of the preparation for battle, Calgacus tells his men that the Romans '. . . create a desert and call it peace'. It's a pretty good description of Roman or any other imperial occupation, and the words have echoed down through the ages.[3]

In fact, Tacitus was not there. As with many ancient historians, he simply made up the speeches of famous individuals in an attempt to convey their drive and spirit. The oration is the stuff of legend. Legends will appear throughout this book, and in a way it does not matter if they are real, because a legend can take on a life of its own and so inspire a future generation.

Indeed, centuries later in 1820, Strathaven weavers carried a banner reading 'Scotland: Free or a Desert?' as they marched to what they hoped would be the rallying point for a nationwide republican insurrection on the outskirts of Glasgow. For them Calgacus was fighting for 'freedom' from oppression. Their lives in industrial Scotland were a million miles away from those of the Caledonians emerging from the Iron Age, but the Strathaven weavers faced oppression and exploitation too.

Agricola won at Mons Graupius, but the Romans, having reached the Moray Firth, decided to withdraw southwards. Agricola then briefly established a frontier running from the Clyde to the Forth before he left Britain, his term as governor having ended, and the Romans withdrew to a line running from the Solway Firth to the Tyne. Sixty years later a Roman army returned and built a turf wall between the Forth and Clyde estuaries, but after fifty or so years they gave up direct control of the Lowlands, preferring to secure the frontier marked by Hadrian's Wall through treaties and alliances with the local tribes. The emperor Septimus Severus led another campaign against the Caledonians in AD 208–11, but that ended with his death.

The Romans called their northern adversaries the Picts, the 'painted ones'. The Caledonians that Agricola encountered still painted their bodies with dye and paint, which had once been common across

Britain. The term was probably an insult but stuck. Remarkably little is known about the Picts, their exact origin or what language they spoke, which probably descended, like Welsh, from the earlier Brythonic language. They were probably matrilineal in the royal line of descent.

There is evidence that in AD 43 the King of Orkney travelled south by boat to the Roman headquarters at modern Colchester to submit to the Emperor Claudius. If true, it was some feat. Claudius stayed in Britain after his legions had conquered the south of modern England for only sixteen days, so the Orcadian visitors made a difficult journey, operating on a tight timetable.

This may sound farfetched, but excavation at Gurness, the royal capital of Orkney, has revealed Roman imports of pottery and wine. The Romans certainly knew of the Orkney Islands, and may have travelled there. Further, it was already common practice among some of the British tribes to enter into treaties with Rome rather than be conquered.[4]

In AD 211 there was an encounter between the wife of the Roman emperor, Severus, and the wife of Argentocoxus, a chieftain of the Maeatae confederation of Caledonian tribes, which might have occurred after the capture of Argentocoxus or during treaty negotiations. Severus had conducted a campaign that had taken him into northern Scotland, before, sick and dying, he returned to York. The empress mocked that Caledonian women had free sexual intercourse with whichever man they chose. The retort she got was: 'We fulfil the demands of nature in a much better way than do you Roman women; for we consort openly with the best men, whereas you let yourselves be debauched in secret by the vilest.'[5]

This was of course written by a Roman man, who seems to be indulging in some sexual fantasy, but even so, I like the sense of freedom and pride of the Pictish woman. Severus's son, who succeeded him, quickly quit Britain and gave up any plans to subjugate northern Scotland.

The Roman Empire was now on the defensive, primarily concerned with maintaining what it had. As the empire weakened, the Picts and others were drawn into raiding the south for plunder. By the beginning of the fifth century the legions were gone from Britain, caught in one of the innumerable civil wars of the late empire, never to return.

As people moved westwards into the former Roman Empire, a new people had entered Britain, the Anglo-Saxons, a Germanic people pushed out of what is now Holland and Germany by population pressure. They arrived in eastern England as raiders and traders, the two scarcely indistinguishable, but began to settle. Previous arrivals from mainland Europe had consisted of relatively small numbers who integrated into existing society, smoothly or not. This new migration represented a real invasion: the Anglo-Saxons supplanted the existing British ruling class; yet the peasants continued to farm the land as this was in the interest of whoever ruled them.

Picts, Scots and Britons

By AD 500 western Britain (Wales) was divided among a number of small-scale rulers, some using the title king. In the south-east there was a similar patchwork of Anglo-Saxon rulers whose expansion westwards would be stopped along the line of the River Severn. Three British (Welsh) kingdoms – Rheged, Strathclyde and Gododdin – fought for control of the lands south of the Forth and Clyde. They seem to have been Christian. A Welsh poetic text, 'Y Gododdin', records that around AD 600 King Mynyddog marched his army from his capital of Edinburgh to Catraeth, possibly Catterick in North Yorkshire, where they all died in battle: 'The warrior . . . would take up his spear just as if it were sparkling wine from glass vessels. His mead was contained in silver, but he deserved gold . . . The men went to Catraeth, swift was their host. Pale mead was their feast, and it was their poison.'[6]

We should not think, however, of these kings in comparison to what would follow in later times: 'They [Welsh kings] evidently fought a lot, and their military entourage is one of their best-documented features. They were generous and hospitable to their dependents, and (at least in literature) got loyalty to the death in return, although where they got the resources from is not so clear. They took tribute from subject and defeated rulers, and also tribute or rent from their own people, but the little we know of the latter implies that only fairly small quantities were owed by the peasant population to their lords; Mynyddog's gold, silver and glass were a literary image, too.'[7]

Meanwhile, in Argyll, Bute and Lochaber Irish settlers from Ulaid (Ulster) established the kingdom of Dál Riata. The new settlers ensured this area was Christian from the outset, and the Irish saint Columba (died 587) crossed over to successfully convert the Pictish king as well. Dál Riata's expansion to the south-east was checked by the Northumbrians, and it was similarly blocked from expanding eastwards by the Picts. Weakened by the wars fought between the various Irish kings, it seems the rulers of Dál Riata had to pay homage to the Pictish kings and Northumbria, and they would be unable, on their own, to resist the growing incursion by the Vikings.

In central and eastern Scotland, the kingdom of the Picts was divided from Fife to Caithness into seven provinces, with the main king being that of Fortriu. The evidence suggests that theirs was a civilisation as rich as any in northern Europe at that time. Sculpted symbol stones remain as a tribute to Pictish art. They employed a system of graphic symbols, common across Scotland: some abstract, some depicting artefacts such as mirrors and combs, or animals such as geese, horses and snakes. As Christianity spread, the Cross and scenes from the Bible were carved along with scenes of hunting and warfare.

In 2008, archaeologists revealed their finds from work at a Pictish monastery at Portmahomack on the Tarbat Peninsula in Easter Ross, which dated back to the sixth century. The monastery was made up of an enclosure centred on a church that is thought to have housed about 150 monks and workers, and was similar to St Columba's monastery at Iona, with evidence that the Pictish monks would have made gospel books similar to the Book of Kells, and religious artefacts such as chalices.

Archaeologists found more than 200 fragments of Pictish stone sculptures, including the Calf Stone, which shows a bull and cow licking their calf. The real surprise, however, was the sophistication of the building, with architectural techniques that had been thought too sophisticated for the Picts. A fragment of a sculpture with a Latin inscription was also found; unfortunately the rest has not been unearthed.

Martin Carver, Professor of Archaeology at York University, said this of the Picts:

> They were the most extraordinary artists. They could draw a wolf, a salmon, an eagle on a piece of stone with a single line and produce a beautiful naturalistic drawing. Nothing as good as this is found between Portmahomack and Rome. Even the Anglo-Saxons didn't do stone-carving as well as the Picts did. Not until the post-Renaissance were people able to get across the character of animals just like that.[8]

The Pictish monastery was burnt down, probably by Norse raiders, around 820. The complex was in use from the ninth to the eleventh centuries, possibly under the control of the Pictish Mormaers of Moray, including Macbeth.

Besides the Portmahomack artefacts, we know little about the everyday life of the ordinary people. They lived in small farming communities, breeding cattle, sheep and pigs, plus rearing small and stocky horses, which are shown on sculpted stones drawing carts and carrying members of the elite on hunting expeditions. Barley, wheat, oats and rye were grown, providing a plain diet. Fish, seals and shellfish would have been an important source of protein, as meat would have rarely been on the plates, except at festival times.

The myth might be that the land was owned by a clan, but it was administered by a chief, and long before the arrival of classical feudalism he demanded rent in the form of a share of the produce or livestock, or unpaid labour on his lands and military service. Little was to change for ordinary people for centuries, all the way to the seventeenth and eighteenth centuries in the Lowlands, and the early nineteenth in the Highlands.

The Kingdom of the Scots Emerges

It was the Celtic Church, from its base in Iona, that had brought Christianity to Northumbria and northern England. However, it was weakened by the spread of the Roman Church, which appealed to kings and nobles with its celebration of monarchy and aristocracy. The Roman Church finally won out in 664 when a synod, a meeting of bishops and senior church figures, was convened at Whitby in North Yorkshire by King Oswiu of Northumbria, who appointed himself the final judge on the issues at stake. Oswiu was hardly neutral. His son, Alchfrith, had expelled monks of the Celtic Church from the monastery of Ripon and handed it over to Wilfrid, a Northumbrian churchman recently returned from Rome.

The main issue was the practice of the Christian church in Britain and whether it should be controlled by the Pope in Rome. The Celtic Church of the late St Columba, based in Iona, had developed in isolation from Rome and was less centralised than the Catholic Church. The synod established the date for Easter and other matters in accordance with Rome, which led to the withdrawal of Celtic Church opponents from Northumbria to Iona and thence to Ireland.[9]

The Roman Church, having established itself in Northumbria, then moved to win over the Pictish and Scottish kings. The hierarchy of the Catholic Church was loyal to Rome, but generally it allied with the local royal power, and drew its senior churchmen and women from ruling circles. It provided administrators for the Crown in return for land and other rewards.

For many later opponents of the Catholic Church in Scotland, the Synod of Whitby represented a historic defeat for the Celtic Church, which had been indigenous to Scotland. It later re-emerged, however, in Presbyterian opposition to bishops and patronage of the Church by the Crown and the nobility.

The Celtic Church would be injured beyond recovery by Norse raiders and, after the union of the Pictish and Scottish realms in 844, the first king of what would be termed Scotland, Kenneth MacAlpin, began a policy of thorough-going reform, relying mainly upon Anglian and Scottish clergy who had conformed to the ways of Rome. An important step in this direction was taken in 849 with the removal of St Columba's relics, and the relocation of the headquarters of the Romanised Celtic Church from Iona to Dunkeld, which succeeded Iona as the major centre for the church in Alba.[10]

Despite the decline of the Celtic Church, the Pict kings were still in the ascendant. Southern Pictland was under attack from Northumbrian Angles who had conquered the Lothians from the British tribes and were pushing north. One king, Bridei, managed to unite the various kingdoms and tribes, and eventually in 685 the Picts achieved a victory over the Northumbrians as great as any in the history of what was now becoming Scotland. At a place called Dunnichen (also known as Dun Nechtain and Nectansmere) near Aviemore, mass ranks of Pictish spearmen drove the Northumbrians downhill and into a loch where they were butchered.[11]

Bridei established one united Pictish kingdom, but all its inhabitants now faced an even more ferocious adversary: the Vikings. In 839 the Vikings defeated a Pictish army, killing their king and many of the chiefs. That power vacuum was filled by a Gaelic warlord. Kenneth MacAlpin (Cináed mac Ailpín) who by 840 became king of Pictland and the Scottish lands. This was not the result of conquest: his grandmother was a Pictish royal, so he possibly inherited the throne, and the Norse threat probably necessitated the need for a strong military ruler.

Yet by 847 the Norwegians controlled the coast of Dál Riata, the Hebrides, Wester Ross, Sutherland, Caithness, and the Orkneys and Shetlands. In the Orkneys and Shetlands the new arrivals seem to have physically removed the Pictish inhabitants, and Norse became the language of the islands. Elsewhere they ruled over the native people, and in the case of the Scots began to adopt the Gaelic culture and language.

Around 840 McAlpin established his court in Perthshire. The language of the court was Irish (Gaelic), and this became the language of the people of the new kingdom, probably helped by the spread of the Gaelic/Irish Church. The new kingdom was strong enough to restrict the Norse to their lands in the north and west.

The death of McAlpin was followed by civil war, quite possibly because of the Pictish nobility's resentment of the new Gaelic order. It was only in 906 that King Constantine was crowned at Scone, which would become the traditional coronation site.

To the south a new threat was emerging. By 927 a united Anglo-Saxon or English kingdom had been established under King Æthelstan or Athelstan (c.893/895–939). Æthelstan established control over rival Anglo-Saxon kingdoms and Danish settlers. He had the ambition to be 'King of all Britain', and in 934 he marched north as far as Dunnottar, near Stonehaven, forcing homage from King Constantine.

Constantine, however, played for time, making a treaty with the Norse and with the British kingdom of Strathclyde. Æthelstan met with Constantine and his allies in 937 at a place called Brunnanburh, near modern-day Liverpool. It was a bloody slaughter of a battle, but Æthelstan's army controlled the field at the close of the day. In truth the losses were so great no one could claim victory, and Æthelstan was forced to cede any claims over Alba.[12]

By 1018, Malcolm II defeated the Northumbrians at Carham-on-Tweed and annexed the Lothians. His grandson Duncan had become king of Strathclyde at about the same time, and when he succeeded Malcolm II, the kingdom of Scotland's boundaries were essentially those of today. The creation of the new kingdom was largely the achievement of three kings, Constantine II (900–943), Kenneth II (971–995) and Malcolm II (1005–1034), whose relatively long reigns provided some stability. Nevertheless, the tribal lands remained contested.

The Norwegians' control of the territory on the mainland came to an end by the close of the eleventh century. Their final attempt to control England was defeated in 1066 by the Anglo-Saxons at Stamford Bridge. Nevertheless, the Hebrides joined the kingdom of Scotland only in 1266, and Orkney and Shetland remained under Norwegian control until the fifteenth century.

Feudalism Takes Control

The Norman conquest of England in 1066 may have seemed remote to the Scottish ruling class, but it heralded momentous changes that shaped Scotland as it essentially existed until 1746. But the new kingdom was not yet an effective state. Aside from those areas under Norse control (the Orkneys and Shetlands under direct Norwegian rule and the Norse-Gaelic kingdom of the Western Isles), the northern third, Moray, remained semi-independent under its own 'mormaers' (sometimes called kings). How Pictish they were we do not know, but in 1040 one Mac Bethad (Macbeth) killed King Duncan at Pitgaveny (Bothnagowan) near Elgin, and ruled as king for the next seventeen years. Duncan's son Malcolm Canmore (Bighead) fled to safety at the Saxon court of Edward the Confessor. In 1057, Malcolm, with Saxon aid, defeated and killed Macbeth and was crowned king of Scotland as Malcolm III.

Malcolm Canmore would go down in history as a 'good king', in large part because his wife, Margaret, an Anglo-Saxon princess, was made a saint by the Catholic Church for promoting its still loose hold over religious affairs. A comprehensive system of bishops and parishes was introduced. She also encouraged Malcolm to initiate new abbeys and monasteries, and to bestow them with lands and riches. These would become one of the mainstays of feudal rule because they had both a religious and an economic function. They were often more innovative than the nobility in exploiting the land, and the peasantry, amassing great wealth.

Malcolm's ambition was to obtain Northumbria for the Scottish Crown and he seized every opportunity, throwing Scotland into a series of unsuccessful wars and instigating English retribution. In response the new Norman kingdom of England began exerting its might north of the Solway–Tweed border. In 1072, William the Conqueror advanced as far as the Tay. The Scots were unable to resist the heavily armoured horsemen and disciplined infantry, and Malcolm Canmore met William at Abernethy to swear vassalage. The Norman kings to the south were content to allow the Canmore dynasty to reign, using military pressure to keep them in line. They in turn saw that the feudal state to the south gave their English counterparts greater power and wealth and began to invite Norman nobles to take over estates in Scotland, transplanting the Norman feudal system into what was still, in Scotland, a clan-based society.

It was under the Canmores that a form of English gradually became the main language of the Lowlands, encouraged by the court, the Church and the new nobility. Malcolm IV (1153–65) and William the Lion (1165–1214) were David I's grandsons and their mother was a Norman. They continued David's policy of encouraging Norman nobles to settle in Scotland. The most powerful Norman dynasty was the Comyns (Cummings), who by the mid-thirteenth century held lands in Galloway, the Borders and Moray.

The influx of Normans (many were actually Flemings) reached its peak under David I, who ruled 1124–53. He gave land in return for knight service, especially in the troublesome south-west. Robert de Brus (the Bruce) was given Annandale, Liddesdale went to Ranulf de Sules, David's constable, Hugh de Morville acquired Cunningham and Lauderdale, and Robert Avenel got Eskdale. David's steward Walter had come from Shropshire and was given the lordship of Renfrew and North Kyle. He brought his own followers who in turn were given land in return for their service. Walter and his family took over the castle at Renfrew and built another at Dundonald as well as bestowing an abbey at Paisley.[13] New settlements were created and named after their lord – Duddingston, now in Edinburgh, after Dodin, Houston, now in Renfrew, after Hugh.[14]

Initially feudalism was restricted to the royal heartlands of Lothian, but David I's successors extended these grants to Strathclyde, Angus, Perth and eventually Aberdeen and Moray at the expense of the older, Celtic nobility. Even so, by 1286 five earldoms were in the hands of newcomers but eight were in native hands, their lands now operated on the basis of a feudal relationship.

Some of these barons were appointed royal sheriffs, administering the king's law, collecting rents and maintaining order and the defence of the realm. The new royal army prevented the Norse-Celtic chief Somerled from taking control in 1164. It conquered Caithness from the Norse and defeated a Norwegian invasion at Largs in 1263. By the close of that century the kingdom of Scotland more or less corresponded to the country we know today, except for Orkney and Shetland, which remained under Norse control.

Galloway, Buchan and other areas had been brought under nominal royal control, and the new nobles such as the Bruces in Galloway, quickly asserted a degree of independence. In the north-west and the islands, royal control was weak and a Gaelic culture tied to Ireland held sway.

The new burghs were small in size. Edinburgh in the late

fourteenth century had just 400 homes, and as late as 1550, Stirling had a population of only 405 adult males. These were described by one chronicler around 1200 as 'English', meaning this was the language spoken there.[15] David I had also created a royal mint and began producing silver pennies around 1140.

One key reason for inviting Norman and Flemish knights to Scotland was to give the Scots kings heavy cavalry. The Canmore dynasty had been raiding and plundering the south, taking slaves and hostages, with their lightly armed forces that could move quickly. But by the late eleventh century the English kings began fortifying the border, building castles at Durham (1072), Newcastle (1080), Carlisle (1092) and, at the beginning of the next century, Norham on the Tweed.

In 1138, King David invaded England and reached Northallerton in Yorkshire, where an English army was waiting. The 'Scottish' army was at odds; David's Norman and English advisers wanted to put the heavy cavalry and archers in the front line, facing like with like. The Galloway contingent, which lacked armour and carried merely spears and cowhide shields, protested, reportedly telling the king: 'Why, O king, are you afraid and why do you fear those iron coats you see afar . . . we have conquered mail-clad men.'

A Scottish earl then piped up, stating: 'O king, why do you agree to the wishes of foreigners when not one of them, with their armour, will be before me in battle today, although I am without armour.'

David finally agreed to put the Galwegians in the front line. They attacked the English force but were cut down by heavily armoured knights and archers. David's army then began to disintegrate.

Thirty-seven years later, David's grandson William the Lion invaded Northumberland again, hoping to annexe it with an army of knights and Flemish mercenaries, but was defeated and captured at Alnwick. When the news reached Galloway the population rose up and destroyed the castles that had been built to guard them, killing as many incomers as they could.

But what did such wars mean for the ordinary people? The vast majority were subsistence farmers, living on the verge of starvation and frequently plagued by famine and disease. Tiny numbers lived in the royal burghs, market centres established by the Crown, where the writ of the nobility did not run and serfdom did not exist, but which were controlled by an elite of wealthy merchants, the burgesses or burghers, who were answerable to the king.

The Church was free to impose all sorts of irritating taxes for the upkeep of church buildings, for the cost of ceremonies and for simply saying mass on a Sunday. From the very start kings and nobles would vie to secure bishoprics and other lucrative positions for their sons, legitimate or not, because the Church was by now one of the biggest landlords and was no better than the nobility. Within the Church were those who opposed the lay power of the Pope, a king in central Italy in his own right, and the wealth and avarice of the Church, but it wasn't until the fourteenth century that the Church experienced a full-scale rebellion, with the Lollards in England, for instance.

The nobles maintained the myth of common kinship between themselves and their tenants because it strengthened feudal ties and also helped undercut any possible acts of revolt. One result of this was that formal, written tenantships were rare, with both sides relying on verbal agreements. Formal feudalisation was something that had to be introduced over time, because of opposition from a section of the old Scottish-Pictish nobility, as well as those in the Church who disliked Margaret's reforms, and ordinary people who clung to the remnants of the old clan system.

Though the period from Malcolm Canmore's accession to the death of Alexander III and the subsequent occupation by Edward I of England is often portrayed as some sort of golden age in Scottish history, it's worth spelling out the reality of feudal Scotland. The socialist historian Thomas Johnston wrote:

Famines and starvation ensued; none but the serfs would cultivate the land, and they only with whip over their heads . . . the process of slow robbery went on steadily and effectively. The barons were given full powers of jurisdiction over their domains . . . In their courts they tried every sort of case . . . They had the rights of *Fossa* and *Furca*, i.e. pit and gallows. By the latter they could gibbet any vassal: by the former they could immure in pit or dungeon, or, as they usually did with women, drown. Torture they specialised in.[16]

TWO

The Wars of Independence

On a stormy night on 18 March 1286, King Alexander III fell off a cliff near Kinghorn in Fife and broke his neck. Earlier that evening he had left Edinburgh Castle, where he had been wining and dining with his cronies, to spend the night with his new wife across the Firth of Forth in Fife. The next day was her birthday. All three of his children by his first marriage had died, leaving no direct heir, and Alexander was keen to rectify that and had re-married. His courtiers and the ferryman who took him across the Forth advised him not to travel, but he ignored them. En route along the coastal path he lost his guides. The next morning he was found on the seashore. One of the earliest recorded Scottish poems, collected by Andrew of Wyntoun over a century later, described the event thus:

> Quhen Alysandyr oure kyng was dede,
> Dat Scotland led in luwe and le,
> Away wes sons of ale and brede,
> Of wyne and wax, of gamyn and gle:
> Oure gold wes changyd into lede,
> Cryst, borne into Virgynyte,
> Succour Scotland and remede,
> Dat stat is in perplexyte.[1]

Alexander was a strong ruler but his death heralded the most tumultuous years in Scottish history. In the event, the nation's place in history was secured, but it was a close-run thing.

The final decade of the thirteenth century and the first three decades of the fourteenth were the years of Scotland's War of Independence against England, when resistance was kept alive by great leaders, above all William Wallace and Robert the Bruce. These men fought back against English occupation until freedom was finally won on the field of battle at Bannockburn in 1314.

The people united to rid themselves of the yoke of English oppression. At least that's the accepted view of the fight for independence. Today the National Memorial to Wallace overlooking Stirling Bridge, scene of his greatest battlefield victory, Bannockburn Heritage Centre with its statue of Bruce on horse holding his trusty axe, and the Borestone, supposedly his command post during the fight, have become places of pilgrimage.

But the story is not quite as simple as one of a nation united in common struggle against an oppressive occupier. In feudal Scotland the ruling class was comprised of the nobility and the Church hierarchy. The nobles held their lands from the king in return for providing military service. When the king was strong they generally held to that contract, but when the monarch was weak or an infant (as was often the case in Scotland, where kings could expect a short life) they did not, and looked to increase their land holdings by whatever means. The nineteenth-century Scottish historian Thomas Johnston described the Scottish nobility as '. . . a selfish, ferocious, famishing, unprincipled set of hyenas, from whom at no time, and in no way, has the country derived any benefit whatsoever'.[2]

The great families, like the Bruces and their rivals the Balliols and the Comyns, also owned lands in England for which they pledged loyalty to the English monarch; this situation undoubtedly complicated the picture still further.

The crisis of succession that followed Alexander III's death triggered a series of events that would lead to a war against English occupation, as well as a civil war between rival Scottish noble families. Their record in the fight against King Edward I of England,

Longshanks as he was nicknamed because of his height, and his son and successor Edward II was far from distinguished.

The only heir to Alexander was his granddaughter, the Maid of Norway, daughter of the king of Norway. However, the Maid died in the Orkneys en route to her new kingdom and the throne was laid claim to by a number of nobles, but the effective choice lay between two contenders, John Balliol and Robert Bruce (grandfather of the victor of Bannockburn). Both were from Norman families invited north in the twelfth century by King David I, with the Balliols granted land in Galloway and the Bruces in Annandale.

Fearing civil war, the Bishop of St Andrews invited Edward I of England to adjudicate on the matter. He was the dead king Alexander's brother-in-law and must have seemed a suitable choice to give judgement on this matter. Unfortunately, Edward I was one of the most capable and ruthless rulers of medieval England, and he planned to expand his realm by any means necessary. It was his good fortune that he was invited to judge who should succeed to the Scottish throne. One can only wonder what was expected of Longshanks when the invitation was issued; nevertheless, Bruce and Balliol agreed to abide by his decision as to which would be king.

Edward came north to Norham Castle on the English bank of the Tweed and summoned the Scottish nobility to meet with him. There he informed them that he now had sovereignty over Scotland and asked them to acknowledge this. When they did so, he then chose John Balliol as king. Balliol took the throne, but he had pledged his subservience to Edward, who subjected him to constant demands and instructions. Finally, in 1296, when he was told to send troops to assist in Edward's wars of conquest in France, he rebelled and withdrew his allegiance, seeking an alliance with France instead.

Edward hurried north in response, forded the Tweed and sacked the then Scottish town of Berwick, butchering the civilian population before advancing north to lay siege to Dunbar Castle. Balliol summoned the nobles to rally to him with their soldiers, but the Bruces and their supporters would not fight for him and joined with Edward. Balliol's army advanced on Dunbar, but Edward's, steeled in long wars in France, routed it within minutes and captured many nobles who then had to pledge loyalty to him.

After the Battle of Dunbar, the Earl of Carrick approached Edward to ask if his son, Robert the Bruce, could now be king. Both had fought for Longshanks. His reply was scathing: 'Have I nothing to do but conquer kingdoms for you?'[3]

Balliol fled north but eventually surrendered, was stripped publicly of all the robes and trappings of monarchy and dispatched into captivity in England. After that, every noble, landlord, senior clergyman and head of the religious houses was required to place his seal on a document acknowledging Edward as their liege lord. Some 1,900 did so, and it became known as the 'Ragman's Roll'. With that in his baggage, Edward returned to his wars with France. As he left Scotland, Longshanks joked: 'He does good business, who rids himself of shit.'[4]

The subsequent English occupation of Scotland was enforced by that section of the nobility who decided their fortunes would gain most by pledging loyalty to Edward of England. But the English occupation was hampered by 'financial difficulties, shortage of supply, overextended lines of communication [and] local hostility'.[5] Edward's focus was on conquering France – he claimed to be its rightful king – and the priority for his troops and funds was always there, not Scotland. That also meant the English authorities levied extra taxes and demanded conscripts for the English army in France, which created anger among the peasantry on whom the burden fell.

In May 1297, William Wallace of Elderslie, a minor noble, not even a knight, killed the English Sheriff of Lanark and began a rebellion in the name of John Balliol. Little is known about what drove Wallace into rebellion but we do know that the nobility were suspicious. Even two of the most steadfast opponents of the English occupation, Sir William Douglas and Bishop Wishart of Glasgow, were quick to assure the English general, Warenne, that they had no part in the rising.

We can guess that Wallace was able to gain support because he opposed the taxes and conscription imposed by the English but which were also often collected by the feudal overlord. The rebellion, however, could be seen to threaten the Scottish nobility. Wallace's army was made up of the ordinary people, peasant farmers who faced paying more in tax or being forced to fight in Edward's army.[6]

To the north in the Black Isle, Andrew de Moray was also taking to the field.

Some idea of what Wallace's message comes from a poem attributed to John of Fordun, in which Wallace is portrayed as saying:

> My son, I tell thee soothfastie
> No gift is like to liberty,
> Then never live in slaverie![7]

Meanwhile, the young Robert the Bruce, who until that moment had served Edward, James the Stewart, the High Steward of Scotland, and the Bishop of Glasgow also raised an army to resist Edward, but when it was confronted with an English force its noble leaders asked for terms rather than fight. The negotiations dragged on for a month, giving Wallace and Moray time to raise a stronger army.

By the late summer both men lay siege to the English garrison at Dundee. Learning that an army had been sent north to crush this rebellion, they guessed correctly that it would have to cross the River Forth at Stirling. On 11 September, Wallace and Moray gathered their men on the Abbey Craig, a hill overlooking a narrow bridge the English army had to cross, and at the foot of the hill on a causeway leading across marshy ground. The soft ground of the fields to either side were unsuitable for the English heavy cavalry, while a bit farther on the river looped around both sides of the battlefield.[8]

Wallace and Moray allowed enough of the English army to cross until they were crowded into a small area of dry ground and were thrown into confusion, unable to deploy their heavy cavalry. Then the Scots infantry attacked, downhill. They cut off the English access to the bridge and then butchered the trapped men. The English commander of the forces on the north side of the river was cornered, pulled from his horse and flayed alive.

The overall English commander, Warenne, ordered the bridge to be destroyed, sent reinforcements to Stirling Castle and then fled to Berwick. It was a stunning victory.[9]

Following this win Murray died of his wounds but Wallace was made Guardian of Scotland, charged with protecting the kingdom until John Balliol could return to resume royal rule. Wallace raided into northern England before winter forced him to retire northwards. Formally, Wallace had the support of the majority of the nobility, though not of Bruce and his supporters, and the Church leaders, but in reality they mistrusted him and his common supporters.

Edward I determined to avenge the defeat at Stirling Bridge and led his army north. In July 1298, Edward came across Wallace's army at Falkirk, where it was assembled in schiltrons: rings of spearmen protected by wooden stakes and with short-bow archers in support. However, the Scottish cavalry, made up of the nobility, quit the field before battle was joined, either as a result of treachery or as a refusal to fight such an enemy. The spear rings drove off the English cavalry but eventually Edward ordered his archers into action. They killed many Scots and broke the rings, which allowed the English cavalry to disperse the Scots. It was a bloody battle that ended in Wallace's defeat.[10]

Deserted once more by the nobility, Wallace would go to Europe in the wake of his defeat to try unsuccessfully to enlist support from the king of France, before returning to wage guerrilla warfare, raising his troops from among the ordinary people. In March 1304, Edward ordered a parliament to be held at St Andrews, at which the assembled nobles and senior churchmen once again accepted Edward as their king.

Wallace was now on the run; he had been deserted by 'all men who had property at stake'. [11] He sought shelter at the home of Sir John of Monteith at Robroyston, now part of Glasgow. His host betrayed him and handed him over to Edward. Wallace was brought to London charged with treason, though as he rightly pointed out he had never given homage or pledged loyalty to Edward. He was made to construct a crown of laurel leaves, in mockery of his supposed ambition to be king of Scotland. At his trial the verdict was never in doubt. On 23 August 1305, Wallace was found guilty and carried off to the Tower of London from where he was dragged naked through the streets to Smithfield, his place of execution. He was hung, drawn and quartered, before he was finally beheaded. His head was put on display above London Bridge while his limbs were displayed in four cities, Newcastle upon Tyne in England, and Berwick upon Tweed, Stirling and Perth in Scotland, as a warning to any who might consider opposing Edward.[12]

The film *Braveheart* portrays the brutality of his execution and gives a good account of Wallace's life. Wallace was not a commoner but he was not a noble either; later he would have been described as a laird. He is the nearest to the ordinary people of Scotland we have come.

Never mind the fiction, the success of Mel Gibson's 1995 film, with the dying hero crying 'freedom', created another legend that spoke to those fighting for liberation across the globe, and who probably could not point to Scotland on the map. But no matter, a legend was created and handed down to us. In the nineteenth century Wallace would be an inspiration to the Chartists, fighting for a radical form of democracy we are still denied today.

However, there is a gulf between the fiction and the fact. G. W. S. Barrow was probably nearer the truth when he wrote: 'Wallace was a conservative, quite as much part of the life of feudal society and breathing its air as the English king against whose might he pitted his own limited strength. Surely, the real tragedy of Wallace lay in this, that he was thwarted by the very same structure of society which he accepted without question.'[13]

In truth, war in Scotland was a distraction. The war with France was far more important to Edward and his successors. Ironically, however, having alienated many of the Scottish nobility, Edward was forced to rely on them to rule the land but found he had to return to impose order. Between 1300 and 1304, Edward waged a series of campaigns in Scotland. The two guardians of the kingdom were Robert the Bruce and John Comyn, a supporter of John Balliol. It was an unlikely alliance. Tensions between them led to Bruce's resignation and then his going over to Edward in early 1302.

In response, Edward advanced northwards, capturing stronghold after stronghold until only Stirling Castle still resisted. Before its fall in 1304, John Comyn submitted to Edward. Robert Bruce was fighting alongside Edward that year when he also became Earl of Carrick.[14]

In truth, the future 'patriot king' had already had a chequered career. In 1296, after John Balliol broke off his allegiance to Edward,

Bruce pledged fealty to Edward and served in his conquering army. A year later he raided Lanarkshire alongside an English force. The next year Bruce sided with Wallace only to surrender to Edward in return for a pardon. The year after that he fought for Edward in Galloway, although twelve months later he attacked the English garrison at Lochmaben. In 1302, Bruce attended the English Parliament (at this stage an assembly of great nobles and Church leaders) while appealing to the French king for aid in a possible rebellion against Longshanks. A year on, he was Edward's Sheriff of Lanark with his salary paid in advance. Bruce sent help to the English forces besieging Stirling Castle in 1304 and in the following year was quite possibly a witness against Wallace and was granted new lands in Carrick by the English king.

The Bruce family were out to get the kingship of Scotland by any means, and hoped Edward would confer it on them. When it was clear Edward wished to abolish any separate kingdom north of the Tweed, their thoughts turned to rebellion. This was a risky venture, as it might mean loss of their lands, certainly those the family still owned in England.

Robert the Bruce, as he would become known, had support in the west of the country where his lands lay. His opponents, the Comyns, were based in Buchan and allied to the MacDougalls of Argyll. This, the War of Independence as it became known, was also a civil war in which Bruce had to defeat the supporters of Balliol as well as those Scots nobles allied to Edward. In March 1306, Bruce was crowned king of Scotland at Scone Abbey, which, however, was missing the Stone of Destiny and much of the royal regalia which had already been looted by Edward.

In June, Bruce and his men were surprised at Methven near Perth by an English force and routed. Bruce was forced to go on the run. He may have holed up in Ireland, in Kintyre or the West Highlands, where as legend has it, despairing in a cave, he was inspired by a spider trying to spin its web from one side to the other. Six times the spider tried and failed. But on the seventh attempt it was successful. Bruce, supposedly, reckoned he had lost six battles, so why shouldn't he 'try, try again'.

The story owes much to Sir Walter Scott, writing five centuries later, but Bruce must have thought of submitting to Edward again. The king's barbaric retribution against his family must have weighed heavily with him. His brother, Neil, had been executed by Long-shanks; his wife, Elizabeth, and daughter Marjorie were captured on route to find refuge in Orkney. Both were imprisoned.

They were luckier than Bruce's sister Isabella, and the Countess of Buchan, who had crowned King Robert, in keeping with the family's traditional ceremonial role. They were placed in cages, open to the elements and suspended from the ramparts of Roxburgh and Berwick Castles for four years, before being sent to convents.

Despite these threats, Bruce had made one ally, the chiefs of a rising force in the West Highlands and Hebrides, Clan MacDonald. Descendents of the Norse-Gaelic ruler Somerled, their rivals were the MacDougalls, allies of Bruce's opponents the Comyns, and they saw alliance with Bruce as a way to win back regional hegemony.

The next year, 1307, Bruce was back on his home turf and met an English army at Loudon Hill in Ayrshire. Bruce's men held the high ground. The only approach was along a narrow track through a bog. Bruce ordered ditches to be dug on either side to ensure the advancing English were restricted to the narrow track.

The poet John Barbour would write in 'The Bruce':

> *The king's men met them at the dyke*
> *So stoutly that the most warlike*
> *And strongest of them fell to the ground.*
> *Then could be heard a dreadful sound*
> *As spears on armour rudely shattered,*
> *And cries and groans the wounded uttered.*
> *For those that first engaged in fight*
> *Battled and fought with all their might.*
> *Their shouts and cries rose loud and clear;*
> *A grievous noise it was to hear.*

The result was similar to Stirling Bridge. Hemmed in and unable to deploy their heavy cavalry, the English were defeated.

Two months later Longshanks was dead at Burgh on Sands on the English side of the Solway Firth, en route to inflict another punishment on the rebel Scots. Bruce's decisive victory over his internal enemies came in 1308 at Inverurie, where the Comyn forces were defeated. What followed was a bold and heroic conquest of one stronghold after another, with the Bruce, for instance, personally leading a night assault on Perth in January 1313 when he forded the icy moat and was first to mount the ramparts.[15]

That year Bruce's nephew Sir Thomas Randolph took Roxburgh Castle and, by clambering up the rock and over the ramparts, Edinburgh Castle. The other outstanding commander was Sir James Douglas, who also led daring attacks on English-held fortresses.

Having already convened a Scottish parliament and invaded northern England, Bruce was effectively king of Scotland. His brother Edward agreed with the English commander of one of the last castles to hold out, Stirling, that if he was not relieved within a year he would surrender. That deadline ended on 24 June 1314.

In the history books this was why Longshank's successor and son, Edward II, had to come north with his army. Just as likely was Bruce's declaration that if his noble opponents did not surrender by October 1314 they would lose their lands. Edward II had to act or his allies would be forced to surrender.

Bruce chose well as to where the Scots would make a stand at Bannockburn. It was a good defensive position, ideal for the Scottish pikemen. Before the battle he rode out on a pony to review his troops. An English knight, de Bohun, took the chance to ride out to attack him. Facing de Bohun, Bruce skilfully avoided the attack and struck the knight dead with an axe. That did no harm to the morale of the Scots army.

As the battle swung in Bruce's favour, the 'small people', his camp followers, sensing booty, charged forward. To the English this seemed to be fresh reserves, and tired and on the back foot, they broke. It was one of the few occasions in medieval history where the common people were credited with any role in a military success.

Bruce was now king of Scotland, and in 1329 the nobility and bishops gathered at Arbroath Abbey to acknowledge him as sovereign. What came out of that was the Declaration of Arbroath, which rousingly declared: 'For we fight not for glory, nor riches, nor honour, but for freedom alone, which no good man gives up except with his life.'[16]

These words reflect the fact that the War of Independence had ultimately involved a section of the common people, but it should not obscure the fact this was a nobles' document, and it was their independence that was being asserted. There was little in the way of 'freedom' for the ordinary folk over the coming centuries.

In other words, it was a warning to the king of England to stay away, but also to Robert the Bruce not to overstep the mark by attacking feudal rights.

Were those who fought at Bannockburn fighting for Scotland? The taxes imposed by the English occupiers and their press-ganging of people to serve in their army, including in France, led to ordinary people rising up. Others simply had to follow their lord if he decided to resist. The national anthem, 'Flower of Scotland', is nearer the truth when it says they were fighting for their 'wee bit hill and glen'. Most had no choice, having to fight for their feudal lord. As one historian argues: 'In Scotland it is surely unlikely that many people, at least below the class of magnates, saw their primary loyalty as being to the crown as opposed to their village, burgh or province.'[17]

It was only in 1328 that the English recognised the Bruce as king of Scotland. The new English king, Edward III, was an infant, the country was facing civil war in which the Scots might intervene and, powerless to do much else, the English authorities had to recognise independence. Nevertheless, when Edward III came of age he would renew the war to conquer Scotland. What saved the kingdom was the outbreak of the Hundred Years' War between England and France. Once more the attention of English monarchs was focused on the richer gains to be had across the Channel, and Scotland was left to itself. Yet some notion of freedom flickered in the memory. So the poet John Barbour wrote in 1375 in 'The Bruce':

> A! Fredome is a noble thing!
> Fredome mays man
> to haiff liking;
> Fredome all solace to man giffis,

He levys at ese
that frely levys!

Those words of Barbour carry greater weight because he wrote them
long after Bruce's death in order to idolise Bruce as the ideal warrior
king and his lieutenant, Sir James Douglas, as the ideal knight and
loyal vassal. The stress of the poem is loyalty to one's superior.[18]

In reality the kingdom of Scotland's independence was not guaranteed. English armies, often allied with Scottish noble allies, would
repeatedly invade over the next two centuries, not with the aim of
occupying the country but to force the Scottish kings to acquiesce to
the wishes of the king in London. Bruce's successors would find that
their power was limited by a nobility keen to maintain their control
over their territories.

The Unstable House of Stewart

For much of the fifteenth century England was gripped by civil war,
the War of the Roses, as two aristocratic factions, the houses of
Lancaster and York, fought for the throne. It was only with the
victory of Henry Tudor at the Battle of Bosworth, where Richard III
was killed and Henry took the Crown, that Scotland became the
target of English dynastic ambitions. The English kings were determined to secure their northern border from any incursion by the
Scots, who were allied by now with the French. The result was virtual
permanent war during the first half of the sixteenth century. Henry
VIII was also ambitious, and he was determined to annexe Scotland
through dynastic marriage or military means.

Elsewhere in Europe the crisis of the late Middle Ages was resolved
in two ways. In France, Spain and Austria monarchs arose who maintained the nobility in their positions of wealth but ended their right
to rule as semi-kings and domesticated them by bringing them to the
royal court, where they had to compete for favours and office.

The monarchs of these kingdoms also relied on the growing
wealth of the towns to offset that of the nobility, for example by

borrowing heavily from them. The nobility and the top churchmen retained, though, a monopoly of the top political and military positions. They were absolute monarchs, proclaiming the divine right of kings to rule, but in reality balancing different class forces, though ultimately tied to the old feudal order. As a result the monarch failed to impose control and the country effectively became governed by warring nobles.

This was especially true in Scotland. Robert the Bruce died in 1329 and was succeeded by his son David II, who suffered a series of defeats at the hands of the English, being captured and eventually ransomed. He died childless, and was succeeded by Robert II, who was effectively removed as a ruler by rebel nobles. Next up was Robert III, whose reign was marked by wars with England and between rival nobles. When his younger brother seemed set to take the Crown, the king's son James was sent to France, but was captured en route and spent eighteen years at the English court before being allowed to return to Scotland.

James I proved a capable ruler, which ensured his assassination by nobles. James II died at the siege of Roxburgh Castle when one of his cannons blew up. James III died in battle against rebel nobles. His son took the throne as James IV and was able to break the power of the Lord of the Isles, the semi-independent realm of Clan Donald, but in order to police the Highlands had to rely on magnates, the Earls of Argyll and Huntly, heads of the Campbell and Gordon clans.

James married an English princess and tried to balance England and France, but when those two states went to war he invaded England in 1514, but was defeated and killed at Flodden Field. His infant son was crowned James V, and when he assumed control, he allied Scotland with France only to be defeated and killed in battle with the English. His heir, the infant Mary, Queen of Scots, was dispatched to France for safety and then married to the French heir, the Dauphin. Her mother, the French princess Mary of Guise, ruled in Scotland with the help of a French army.

In these years Scotland was thrust into chaos. For two centuries no Scots monarch succeeded to the throne in adulthood. For much of that time the country was ruled by a regent until the infant monarch came of age. The regency was in turn fought over by the great nobles. This crisis of royal control led to the fragmentation of power throughout Scotland. This fragmentation continued longer in the Highlands, which remained free of royal control, and it was during this time that the clan system, feudal rule which used supposed kinship to reinforce its control, was created.[19]

In the course of this chaos the nobility acquired great power from the Crown, including the right to administer law as they saw fit through their own courts. The Borders, the front line with England, was relatively free of royal rule, as were the Highlands. Nobles seized hereditary control of sheriffdoms (supposedly the agents of royal control) and implemented the law through their own courts.

Such independence extended to the upper echelons of the peasantry. The churchman and historian John Major wrote in 1521 that they had a remarkable spirit of freedom and were more 'elegant' than their French counterparts, by which he meant they tried to match the dress and arms of the lesser nobility. They were quick to draw those weapons if they felt slighted and would follow their lord anywhere if he had their respect. War and feuding were a feature of their lives, along with poverty.[20]

As Stewart kings reached maturity they would try to establish control but would often meet bloody ends in battle with the English or at the hands of noble opponents. The descendants of the Norman nobles settled in the north by the Canmores adopted the customs of the Gaelic chiefs as royal control weakened, allowing them to grasp the opportunity to manage their own affairs. By the late Middle Ages these chiefs held their land under feudal charter from the Crown or another chief.

In the Highlands, clan chiefs were able to force military service from lesser landlords who had previously held their land from the Crown. They relied on 'bonding', whereby lesser men agreed to serve them in return for protection, and they claimed seniority in real or, more usually, imagined kinships.

The runrig system of agriculture is sometimes cited as a collective form of agriculture, but it was nothing of the sort. The strips of land farmed by the peasants were allocated annually not through collective decision-making but by the landlord. The system was hierarchical.

This social stratification was fixed by the belief in kinship with the chief and the legend that the clan had some collective right to the land. While the chiefs needed military service they encouraged this belief, but after 1746, when there was no need for this, the reality of who owned the land quickly hit home. Membership of a clan could cut across a feudal lordship – so MacLeans or Camerons lived on land owned by the Duke of Argyll and were subject to his baronial courts. They paid rent to Argyll and gave service and sometimes tribute to their chief. As Neil Davidson argues: 'Clans, far from being opposed to feudalism, were representative of its most extreme form.'[21] Whether in the Highlands or Lowlands, Scotland remained a militarised society where war was commonplace and life short and brutal even for the elite.

Thus far we have heard little from the ordinary people. In a feudal society they counted for little, and the records we have are those written by churchmen for the glory of God, the king and their temporal lord.

In the course of the fourteenth century, however, climate change created cooler and wetter conditions, squeezing fertile land and acting to reduce the population. Plague arrived in 1349, which further cut the number of the living. The result – as elsewhere in Western Europe – was to create a shortage of labour, and the peasantry were able to use the leverage this gave them to improve their own conditions. Rent, usually in kind, replaced labour services.[22]

Change was coming, and with it ordinary people would begin to tread the stage of history, even if hesitantly at first.

THREE

Reformation and the War of the Three Kingdoms

Reformation

In 1549, a Dumfries priest, Robert Wedderburn, anonymously published 'The Complaynt of Scotland', which gives an impression of ordinary life in sixteenth-century Scotland, living on the front line of an almost permanent conflict with England:

> I labour night and day with my hands to feed the lazy and useless men, and they repay me with hunger and the sword. I sustain their life with the toil and sweat of my body, and they persecute my body with hardship until I am become a beggar. They life through me and I die through them. Alas, oh my natural mother, you reproach me and accuse me of the faults my two brothers commit. My two brothers, nobles and clergy, who should defend me, are more cruel to me than my old enemies the English. They are my natural brethren, but they are my mortal enemies.[1]

In his disillusion with his 'betters', Wedderburn calls for unity against the invader and an end to divisions that saw some Scots nobles side with the English. Rather than wait for divine help or some turn in the wheel of fortune, he also implores ordinary Scots to rise up. This was Wedderburn's prescription to cure the affliction besetting Scotland.

At the time, the nation was in the hands of the Stewart dynasty. In 1542, after military defeat by the English, James V died in shame, uttering the final words 'it came wi a lass, it'll gang wi a lass'. The Stewarts had succeeded to the throne through marriage to Marjorie Bruce, daughter of Robert the Bruce, and now James's only legitimate heir was his infant daughter Mary. Though James V obviously had no high hopes for his daughter, Mary would not be the last of the Stewart monarchs, though not through want of trying.

Scotland had been at war because James had refused the command of England's Henry VIII, his uncle, to convert to Protestantism. Now Scotland would be ruled by his widow, the French Mary of Guise. England and France were at war and both viewed Scotland as the back door. Henry demanded that the infant Mary be married to his son, and when diplomacy failed, his troops invaded, winning the Battle of Pinkie outside Edinburgh but failing to take the city, although occupying much of southern Scotland. In response, the infant Queen of Scots was spirited off to France to marry the king's eldest son, the Dauphin. Mary of Guise brought over a French army to protect her from the English, and Scotland was now caught up in a great power conflict.

Mary of Guise, backed by the French troops, became an effective ruler, something the Scottish nobility always disliked. Because France and Mary of Guise were Catholic, the religious question became a national imperative. The Catholic Church was a feudal institution that demanded rents from its tenants and levied taxes. Throughout Scotland the Church had fallen increasingly under royal and noble control. Kings appointed their bastard sons to bishoprics and nobles ran monastic lands as their own. James V had secured five of the richest religious houses for his bastard sons while they were still infants, and none would grow up to lead a celibate life.

Consequently, the Catholic Church had few defenders. The nobility who had watched Henry VIII seize its lands south of the border were already salivating over that possibility in Scotland. Lesser gentry resented paying tithes to a church known for its wealth. Meanwhile, in the towns Protestantism had spread quickly. It already had martyrs burnt at the stake and one failed rebellion in 1546, when a gang of Protestants had murdered Cardinal Beaton then held out in St Andrews Castle for a year.

A former priest, John Knox, had been among them, and when the castle fell he was punished by being sent to work as a galley slave in the French navy. Knox stood for the purification of worship and believed that out of duty to God it was right to revolt against the Catholic religious and political establishment. But from his experiences on the Continent he was also concerned by religious radicals who had gone as far as to challenge the existing political and social order. In particular, the Peasants' War in Germany (1524–1525) had seen Thomas Munzer lead the lower orders against the nobility, preaching a form of primitive communism.

On 11 May 1559, Knox, fresh from studying in John Calvin's Geneva, preached a revolutionary sermon at St John's Church in Perth, after which the congregation rushed to attack the town's monasteries. At the time, Knox described the mob as his 'brethren' but later termed them 'the rascal multitude'.

Knox had been summoned back to Scotland by some great nobles, including the heir to the earldom of Argyll and an illegitimate son of James V, Lord James Stewart, the Earl of Moray, who had supposedly taken part in the sacking of the monasteries in Perth. Knox was prepared not just to ally himself with these nobles but, in future, to allow them substantial influence within the emerging Presbyterian Church of Scotland.

The French regent, Mary of Guise, mobilised her troops to crush these 'heretics' but similar riots followed in Dundee, Scone, Stirling, Linlithgow and Edinburgh. Knox could now call on powerful friends to raise an army for the new Protestant religion. England, fearing its northern neighbour would become a province of France, acted. In 1560, Queen Elizabeth sent her fleet to take control of the Firth of Forth, cutting off Mary's supply line to France. The subsequent peace treaty ended French involvement in Scotland's affairs and the

Scottish Parliament voted to make Calvinism the new state religion. This was a decision made up of landowners, the landed nobility and the richest men from the royal burghs.

The Reformation effectively destroyed Catholicism outside of a few pockets in the Highlands and the north-east, and brought Scotland closer into England's orbit. But it was largely brought about by a revolt of the nobility, and not by a popular movement. At the beginning the 'mob' had been useful, but very quickly it became a power struggle between rebel lords backed by Queen Elizabeth of England, and Mary of Guise and the French.

But amidst this chaos new ideas were beginning to circulate. Literacy was spreading not just in the towns, but among the peasantry. They no longer relied on priests to translate scripture, but they were free to read, interpret and dispute it amongst themselves. The original, revolutionary message of Jesus, preaching rebellion against Rome and denouncing the refusal of the great and the good to act, could still shine through and inspire.

In one sense nothing changed with the Reformation, in that noble power not only remained but was strengthened. But in other ways Scotland had changed. There was the faint glimmer of democracy within the new Kirk. More important, the idea that it was correct to rise up against tyrants, couched though it was in religious language, was set loose.[2] When Knox called on the ordinary people of Perth to rise up, he was unleashing something that could not be so easily controlled.

Yet there was one further obstacle to the ultimate success of the Reformation. In 1561, Mary, Queen of Scots, sent as a child to France and married to the French heir, returned after her husband's early death. Verbally she accepted the Reformation but was opposed by Elizabeth of England and a majority of Scotland's nobility. A tumultuous reign ended in a short civil war, Mary's flight to England and her execution there after long imprisonment.

Mary is one of those historical figures who feature on shortbread tins and other kitsch sold in souvenir shops. Knox and others attacked her morals and her love life, famously denouncing the 'monstrous regiment of women' (although this was directed at her mother, and did not endear him to Elizabeth I in England). The new queen was soon involved in the assassination of her second husband, who had previously taken part in the gruesome murder of her Italian secretary in front of her when she was pregnant. We shall not share such misogyny, but Mary was not a romantic figure swept from the throne because of ill-fated love.

She regarded herself not only as queen of Scotland but also of England, because the English queen, Elizabeth, was held, by the Catholic Church, to be illegitimate (her father, Henry VIII, had divorced his first wife to marry Elizabeth's mother) and a heretic. In order to win the English throne she was involved in all sorts of conspiracies and plots with France and, in particular, Spain and the Vatican. They wanted to topple Elizabeth as part of the campaign to destroy the Protestant Reformation in Europe and England's ally, Holland, the first capitalist state that was struggling to achieve independence from Spain. It is hard to shrug off the anti-Catholic sectarianism that has blighted modern Scotland, but if one can, this can be seen as an attempt by the old feudal order to strangle a new society, struggling into life, and Mary was quite conscious of what she was involved in.

Mary's infant son, James VI, took the throne and was fought over by rival sections of the nobility, who abducted and tried to murder him. On reaching adulthood he used conciliation and coercion to exert a degree of control through a strong Privy Council and overcame the strict Calvinists to create bishops in the Church of Scotland, as agents of royal power.[3]

In the meantime, parts of Scotland remained relatively free of royal rule. In the north-east the earls of Huntly remained Catholic, and in 1594 defied James's order to renounce their religion or quit Scotland. The Earl of Argyll was ordered to raise an army to assert royal power, and mobilised 8,000 of his clansmen and their allies. In Glenlivet they met with Huntly and Errol's smaller force of 2,000, but their cavalry and artillery were able to rout Argyll's clansmen.[4]

James's continued attempts to disarm and demilitarise the Highland clans had limited success, but he still had to rely on powerful magnates such as the Campbells to maintain some kind of order. Nevertheless, a number of clans became Calvinist at the diktat of their chief: the Campbells, Frasers, Grants, Munros and Rosses would generally support the government over the next century and a half. Not only were the Highlands physically divorced from the Lowlands, but now they were also divided along religious lines.

The dispossession of Church lands following the Reformation benefitted the nobility, not the peasantry. Nevertheless, Calvinism had its attractions for the lower orders, being based on regional presbyteries, made up of delegates, and with the election of local ministers. In response, nobles used their power to attempt to dominate much of these proceedings. The Kirk held itself as being above the power of a king and thus represented a challenge, never far from the surface, to royal rule.

The absence of peasant rebellions is something that contrasts Scotland with other Western European countries during the period. It can be explained by the very struggle to survive, the dominance of the nobility and the lairds, and the frequency of war and feuding. The historian Victor Kiernan argues, regarding the power of Calvinism, that 'It may not be surprising if some strata of the peasantry learned to hold fast to a dogmatic creed as a substitute for the inherited patch of soil that peasants in other countries clung to.'[5]

Scotland differed from the development of feudal society in Western Europe during the fifteenth, sixteenth and seventeenth centuries. Unlike in France, Spain and Austria it had no royal standing army nor a numerous and capable state bureaucracy. Here the chaos characterising this period meant royal control remained limited while the nobility retained and increased its power.

By the seventeenth century the peasantry seldom owned the land they worked. Crops were sparse and rents could be as high as a third of what was grown, with payments in kind or service on top. At some point leases, it seems, grew longer, offering the peasantry more security. Smallholdings and small estates were, however, more numerous in the south-west, which was farther from royal control and in close contact with Ireland. This was the one area that would produce a rural rebellion later on.

During the Thirty Years' War, Protestantism was pitted against the old, Catholic order. In Scotland, identification with the Kirk and anti-Catholicism meant a popular national consciousness emerged. But it also meant that because Scotland was too weak, and faced an internal, non-Calvinist 'enemy within', it needed English protection. The overthrow of Mary, Queen of Scots, meant Scotland was firmly allied to England.

Scotland was weak in other respects, as Thomas Johnston noted nearly a century ago: 'Scotland was not a nation: it was a loose aggregation of small but practically self-supporting communities, and scanty supplies and high prices at Aberdeen may quite well have been coincident with plenty and comparatively low prices in Dundee and Glasgow.'[6]

But fortunes would change for the Scottish king. In 1603, Elizabeth of England on her deathbed named James VI as her heir. When news reached Edinburgh he took off to London with alacrity, not surprising given his experience of being abducted, threatened and bullied. As he travelled south, James VI was impressed at the wealth of the English lords who joined him on his journey to be crowned. They no longer lived in fortified castles; in Scotland they still did.

Once he had settled in London, he wanted more than the Union of the Crowns, thinking of the possibility of direct rule from London, but sensed that the Scottish nobility would resist any attempt to bring that country under one rule. Despite the best efforts of his Calvinist teachers, James believed in the divine right of kings, but he had a poor hand to play. The English Parliament, which he did not control, held the purse strings and was reluctant to finance any royal army. Nevertheless, James played this hand well, extending royal power in Scotland where he could. But this good governance would not last long.

The War of the Three Kingdoms

In 1639, the Moderator of the General Assembly of the Church of Scotland, Alexander Henderson, wrote: 'The people make the magistrate (king) but the magistrate maketh not the people. The people may be without the magistrate but the magistrate cannot be without the people. The body of the magistrate is mortal but the people as a society is immortal.'[7] The Union of the Crowns in 1603 created a British state but there were, as yet, few cross-border institutions. The two kingdoms ran their own affairs. Yet it would be a rebellion in Scotland against James's son Charles that triggered the English Revolution of the 1640s and war throughout Britain and Ireland.

For more than a century a battle would be fought by those who wished to retain a church hierarchy, bishops appointed by the Crown, and more radical Calvinists who held that there was no justification in scripture for this. A year later in 1638, Henderson was the principle author of the National Covenant, a dour, religiously orthodox document, but which rallied the majority of Scots against the king.

In 1581, a radical Calvinist blueprint for the Kirk, drafted by the theologian and scholar Andrew Melville, had been agreed by the General Assembly, which did not permit bishops, with church government based on the General Assembly, Kirk sessions and presbyteries, and superior to royal rule. In 1640, the issue returned. Previously, James VI had succeeded in getting the General Assembly to pass five articles requiring observance of holy days, confirmation of ministers by bishops, private baptism, communion for the infirm and kneeling at communion. Radical Presbyterians had consequently refused to accept these measures and formed private conventicles boycotting Kirk services on holy days and communion where they were required to kneel. In Edinburgh, 'They provocatively opened their shops at the time of services, and tried to persuade others not to attend . . . Every communion was a dramatic event, as people watched to see who would kneel when the sacrament was given.'[8]

James did not push matters further, sensing that to do so would prompt resistance. In particular, he allowed local presbyteries considerable control of their parishes, which appeased the nobility who generally controlled them through patronage. Nevertheless, it raised fundamental issues for theologians such as Henderson: 'The king's insistence on a state-dominated Church rather than a Church-dominated state as the Presbyterians would have desired, prompted the latter to band together locally in covenants.'[9]

When James's son took the throne, he showed none of his father's tact. Father and son believed in the divine right of kings to rule as they pleased, but James had understood that in England he was beholden to Parliament for his budget, and that in Scotland he needed to keep the nobility on his side. Charles looked to the absolute monarchies of France, Spain and Austria with longing but lacked his father's guile.

Between 1629 and 1640, Charles attempted to rule England without Parliament, finding ways to raise money through extra taxes that created widespread opposition, and he also tried to move the Church of England towards more ornate forms of worship, which many believed heralded a return to Catholicism. His attempt in Scotland to recover royal lands lost to the Scots nobility made them hostile towards him. When he did finally retreat more than a decade later, it was only to introduce another, more provocative measure.

When Charles visited Scotland in 1633, it became clear that he wanted to change the form of worship and introduce a book of prayer, regarded as 'Papist' by most Presbyterians. Three years later the Scottish Privy Council, a body appointed by Charles, announced the introduction of the new prayer book which emphasised that ministers were subordinate to bishops, who in turn were subordinate to the king. Charles insisted on his right to decide when the Kirk's General Assembly would meet. The role of the Scottish bishops in drawing up that prayer book and the appointment of the Bishop of St Andrews as Charles's Chancellor for Scotland meant their very existence now became a matter of controversy.

A radical minority of Kirk ministers understood that this was their chance and began orchestrating opposition to Charles. They formed an alliance with discontented nobles who did not trust Charles because of his threat to their lands, and the burghers in the towns and cities who opposed changes to their religion. On 23 July 1637, the new prayer book was due to be read in the High Church of St Giles in Edinburgh, where Scotland's great and good were in attendance. Jenny Geddes pushed her way to the front of the congregation and sat upon her three-legged stool, because she could not afford to pay to sit in a pew. We know little more about Jenny; she was clearly of a humble background, but she was about to enter history.

As the Dean of Edinburgh mounted the pulpit in his new white surplice instead of the old black one and began to read, Jenny rose to her feet and shouted, 'Villain, dost thou say mass in my lug!' and launched her stool at the man's ear. Bedlam broke out. The Bishop of Edinburgh took over at the pulpit, appealing for calm to no avail, so the congregation was cleared from the Kirk, but kept up such a noise that the service could not continue. As they left, the dean and bishop were greeted with cries of 'Pull them down – pull them down! A Pope – a pope! Antichrist – Antichrist.'[10]

Some have asserted that there is no mention of Jenny Geddes in contemporary accounts, but there is a plaque in her honour in the High Kirk of St Giles.[11] Jenny was celebrated in this nineteenth-century song:

'Twas the twenty-third of July, in the sixteen thirty-seven,
On the Sabbath morn from high St. Giles the solemn peal was
   given;
King Charles had sworn that Scottish men should pray by
   printed rule;
He sent a book, but never dreamt of danger from a stool.
. . .
And thus a mighty deed was done by Jenny's valiant hand,
Black Prelacy and Popery she drove from Scottish land;
King Charles he was a shuffling knave, priest Laud a meddling
   fool,
But Jenny was a woman wise, who beat them with a stool![12]

In response to Charles's policies, the nobility, clergy, gentry and representatives of the burghs formed what was a counter-government, the Tables – effectively a parliament – which commissioned a National Covenant for the population to sign. This stated that if the king did not uphold the true faith, the people had the right to resist him.

In February 1638, the nobility gathered in Edinburgh's Greyfriars Kirk to sign the National Covenant against popery and laws that broke acts of God. They were in favour of church matters being decided by the General Assembly and pledging resistance to any attempts to challenge the Kirk. Later that year a General Assembly meeting in Glasgow Cathedral did away with bishops and re-asserted itself as the dominant body in the Kirk, agreeing to meet annually. The signing of the Covenant could be regarded, as Victor Kiernan argues, as '. . . a stepping stone from old feudal and clan feeling towards a new national consciousness'.[13]

It ensured that for the next three centuries a Scottish sense of identity was tied to Calvinism and excluded all others who did not share the faith. The reasons behind this growing conflict were economic as well as religious. The nobility wanted a Scotland that was relatively free of royal control. This was a time of inflation, which was reducing the value of rents and their income, so standing up to Charles might offer a way to improve their fortunes.

In 1639, the conflict boiled over into the short Bishops' War. The Scots commander Alexander Leslie introduced the latest military techniques, learned during the European conflict, in which large numbers of Scots mercenaries served. In contrast, Charles, desperately short of money, could rely only on raw recruits raised under the old feudal muster. Morale was poor, and after his troops reached Berwick on Tweed they made just one advance into Scotland, retreating hastily when Leslie approached.

Grasping military reality, Charles backed down and agreed to the convening of the first General Assembly in two decades. This voted to abolish bishops and, out of Presbyterian zeal and hatred of the king's placemen, to implement a radical Calvinist programme. Parliament then endorsed this, voted out the king's powers to decide when it met and created a Committee of Estates, made up of the four groups that constituted the Tables. It was a body blow to royal power.

In a desperate response, Charles declared all this void the following year, gathered another army and prepared to march north. The Covenanters, as his opponents were now called, were one jump ahead and marched south, taking Newcastle, cutting off London's coal supplies. Charles had to sue for peace and pay money he barely had to the Scots.

This time Charles had to agree to the Scottish terms and pay compensation for the expense of the war. To raise this he had to re-convene Parliament in London, which had the power to raise taxes, but it refused to give him the money he wanted until he met its demands. The Scots had effectively reduced the king to a figure-head, giving effective control to the parliament in Edinburgh. That set an example to the parliament in London, leading to a clash that would result in civil war.[14]

In 1642, Charles raised an army, intending to march on London, the centre of opposition to his rule. The Covenanters, whose main leader was the Duke of Argyll, stood aside until the autumn of 1643. Once the English Parliament had agreed to ratify the National Covenant and adopt Presbyterianism, the Scots sent their army south to fight Charles's Royalist army. At this point the bulk of the Scottish nobility must have thought they held all the aces because they had the most experienced army in this war of Three Kingdoms. They were about to get a rude shock. The Scottish army fought at the parliamentary victory of Marston Moor in 1644 and there saw for the first time Oliver Cromwell's 'Ironsides' in action. This was a new kind of army, not made up of conscripts, its officers chosen for their military skill, not their noble origins. These would become the nucleus of the New Model Army that defeated Charles, who surrendered to the Scottish army in Notting-hamshire in 1646. The Scots, however, later sold him to the English parliamentarians.

What followed was a series of complex events that shattered the unity of the Covenanters. By the summer of 1644, the Marquis of Montrose, formerly one of the military leaders of the Covenant forces, raised an army from among the MacDonalds and other West Highland clans who, like him, resented the Duke of Argyll's growing power. They were joined by 2,000 Irish troops under a formidable warrior, Alasdair Mac Colla. In a series of stunning victories, Montrose and Mac Colla took control of northern and western Scot-land, sacking the Campbell capital, Inverary, and forcing Argyll to flee in a boat.

Like the Thirty Years' War, the conflict was quickly marked, on both sides, by the killing of civilians and prisoners for religious reasons, reflecting the religious zeal of the conflict. Montrose and

Mac Colla had different aims, with the former wanting to take control of the Lowlands and then link up with Charles, while Mac Colla wanted to secure control of the West Highlands in order to link with the rebel forces who'd taken control of virtually all of Ireland (they professed loyalty to Charles but were effectively a Catholic force). The two men went their separate ways and both were thus defeated by the Covenanter army.

But after Charles's surrender in 1646, the English Parliament was progressively pushed aside by Cromwell and the New Model Army, who wanted a far more radical church than the Kirk north of the Tweed, and broke the agreement with the Scots.

As a result, a section of the Scottish nobles, the Engagers, reached an agreement in 1647 with the imprisoned Charles, in which he promised to support the imposition of Presbyterianism in England for a period of three years. Another faction of the Covenanters around Argyll, the Kirk Party, did not sign up to this. Nevertheless, when a second round of civil war, initiated by the royalists, broke out in 1647, the Engagers sent an army south, which reached Preston in Lancashire, where Cromwell routed it. Within weeks, Cromwell's forces had recaptured the king and destroyed all opposition.

On 31 January 1649, Charles Stuart stepped out from a window on the first floor of the Banqueting House onto a scaffold jutting out into London's Whitehall. A few minutes later the executioner held up his head to the crowd. The decapitation of the king stunned the Scottish nobility. They had rebelled against the bad policies of the king, usually blaming his advisers, but not against the monarchy. Cromwell's declaration of a republic in England and Wales alienated them further. This was a threat to all who claimed blue blood in their veins.

A year after Charles's execution the Scottish nobles entered into an alliance with his son, later Charles II, who promised support for the Covenant and arrived in Scotland to be crowned king of Britain. After he heard the news, Cromwell broke off his conquest of Ireland and marched into Scotland, inflicting a stunning defeat on the Scottish army at Dunbar. At the start of the battle the Scots commander occupied high ground and had greater numbers, so victory seemed assured, but his political commissars, the ministers, demanded he descend to smite the enemy. He followed orders with disastrous results.

Afterwards, as Cromwell advanced on Perth, the pretender prince took the desperate gamble of marching south, hoping to inspire a royalist rebellion in England, whereupon he suffered another humiliating defeat, at Worcester. Thousands of Scottish prisoners were sent as forced labour to English colonies in North America and the West Indies.

Meanwhile, war was accompanied, as was usually the case, by plague or typhus, which brought mass death as armies and refugees spread disease through the country. Aberdeen lost about a fifth of its population, with 1,600 deaths, and Leith nearly half, with 2,421 deaths.[15] The burden of fighting fell heaviest on the peasantry, who faced conscription as part of their feudal service, with ministers rallying them.

After his victories at Dunbar and Worcester, Cromwell created the first all-British state, with Scotland under military occupation and allowed thirty seats in an all-British parliament. Cromwell abolished the General Assembly but allowed religious freedom to all apart from Catholics. After fresh rebellions in the Highlands his troops took control there.

Cromwellian rule showed that a British state could control Ireland and the Highlands, the two back doors for invasion of England, and created a formidable navy that laid the foundations of empire (Jamaica was conquered under the Commonwealth). The first Navigation Act was passed in 1651, effectively excluding the Dutch, Britain's main commercial rivals, from the domestic market and that of the British colonies.

Cromwellian rule in Scotland contrasted with its violent suppression of Ireland. The country was under military occupation but benefitted from free trade with England, taxes were unified across the country, serfdom and baronial courts were abolished and justices of the peace put in place to administer the law. There was toleration for the dissident Calvinist sects that had emerged.

Colonel John James set forward the Cromwellian policy for Scotland: 'It is the interests of the Commonwealth of England to break the interest of the great men in Scotland, and to settle the interests of the common people upon a different foot from the interests of their lords and masters . . . The great men will never be faithful to you so long as you propound freedom to the people and relief against their tyranny.'[16]

The Cromwellian republic looked to the 'middling sort' for support, and deliberately taxed the towns lightly to gain popularity. But Scottish commercial interests were too small to form a stable base of support. The Lowland peasantry were sullen towards the occupiers, while in the Highlands throughout the period there were Royalist rebellions.

Amidst all this a more radical force emerged in the south-west of Scotland. In 1648, a radical Covenanting force came out of Dumfries and Galloway, seizing control of Edinburgh in the 'Whiggamore Raid', declaring the 'Rule of the Saints', which has been described as:

> A strange combination of social revolution and fanatical repression; they purged church and state of all 'malignants' and moderates, made parishes responsible for the relief of the poor and sick, established schools in every parish, made church attendance compulsory and encouraged a return to witch-hunting. But their rule was brief, ended by Cromwell's conquest less than two years later.[17]

The Covenanters

The death of Cromwell in 1658 was followed by two years of confusion with no one strong enough to maintain republican rule. In 1660, the commander of the army in Scotland, General Monck, marched south in support of the restoration of Charles II to the throne. No one was prepared to withstand him. The return of Charles II to the throne led to the return of baronial courts and the Scottish Parliament – in other words, noble rule. In addition, the new king also brought with him the spectre of popery because he was widely seen as a crypto-Catholic.

Throughout Britain, Charles re-imposed bishops, though he allowed the Kirk sessions to continue. This was his grandfather's system, but this time more than 300 ministers quit the Kirk. Across parts of the Lowlands, particularly in the south-west, they began to gather large congregations at services, Conventicles, outside the established church. The government ordered troops to break them up, but the Covenanters, as they termed themselves, resisted.

On 13 November 1666, near Dalry in Kirkcudbrightshire, government troops stopped and held an old man charged with refusing to acknowledge the new episcopacy. They threatened to strip him bare and roast him alive in his own home, but four fellow Covenanters intervened, shooting the corporal and taking the other three prisoner.

News of this took twenty-four hours to reach the garrison in Dumfries. Meanwhile, the Covenanters had overrun the sixteen-strong government garrison at Balmaclellan and, on 15 November, with their numbers put at between 150 and 500, captured Dumfries, taking the government commander in his nightgown. For the next week, they moved around the south-west, threatening to march on Glasgow, before deciding on Edinburgh, where they believed their friends were set to rise. Meanwhile, the government commander, General 'Black Tam' Dalyell, had been ordered to bring them to battle.

The Covenanters were ahead of Dalyell as they marched towards the capital, but discovered the city had been made secure by the Crown. Dalyell caught up with them on 24 November at Rullion Green, seven miles south, where it took three charges for the regular troops to break the Covenanters, and when they did, 'darkness afforded escape.'[18] Nevertheless, 120 were captured and 50 killed. Of those captured, 36 were executed in Edinburgh, their heads and body parts put on display around Scotland. On the scaffold, a captain in the rebel army, Andrew Arnot, prayed for his fellow accused, threw out a proclamation in support of the Covenant and then '. . . pluckt out a pocket butt of sack and with a roaring voice uttered . . . that he would drink no more of the wyne till hee had it new in his father's kingdome'.[19]

In 1679, a group of Covenanters dragged Archbishop Sharp of St Andrews from his carriage at Magus Muir in Fife and slashed him to death. Once more royal troops were sent to root out illegal conventicles. That June a force of dragoons under John Graham, the Laird of Claverhouse, a Royalist who had been in exile and had served in the French and Dutch armies, came across one at Drumclog near Kilmarnock. Warned by lookouts, the minister told the women and children to depart and ended his sermon thus: 'Ye have got the theory; now for the practice.'[20] In the battle that followed, Claverhouse was defeated, losing thirty-six men.

The Covenanters now advanced on Glasgow, but internal divisions and the authorities' capacity to hold the city meant they did not press the attack. Eventually, they faced the royal army at Bothwell Bridge. For over an hour, Galloway men held the south side of the bridge but, on running out of ammunition, were told to rejoin the main force, allowing the government forces to bring across the artillery. The Covenanters broke under cannon fire. Four hundred were killed and 1,500 captured. Seven of their leaders were executed and 250 who refused to submit to the Crown were sent as forced labour to the West Indies. En route their ship sunk off the Orkneys and 200 drowned.[21]

What followed became known as the 'Killing Time'. Royal commanders went around the south-west demanding that individuals swear loyalty to the king's Church. If they refused, they were summarily executed.

In the following years low-level guerrilla war took place across the region until the Glorious Revolution in 1688 brought an end to the repression. Some ninety Covenanters were executed. During this period the Covenanter Alexander Shields came to the conclusion that the terms *king* and *tyrant* were interchangeable. Radical Covenanters began to advocate a Republic of Jesus Christ.[22] One of the radicals, James Renwick, aged just twenty-six, returned from exile and ventured to Edinburgh, despite there being a price on his head. He exchanged shots with government troops before being captured. He mounted the scaffold, ready to meet the martyr's death he craved, and quoted Revelation 19 to the crowd: 'Come and gather yourselves together unto the supper of the great God; that ye may eat the flesh of kings.' He then called out, 'Lord, I die in the faith that you will not leave Scotland. But that you will make the blood of your witnesses the seed of your Church, and return again and be glorious in our land. And now, Lord, I am ready.'[23]

Later, in the nineteenth and twentieth centuries, radicals and socialists would hold up the Covenanters as fighters for equality and freedom of speech, and opponents of royalty and aristocracy. In *Grey Granite*, the final volume of the trilogy *A Scots Quair*, Lewis Grassic Gibbon, one of Scotland's finest novelists, has Ewan Tavendale talk of those 'funny chaps the Covenanters', how 'he had always liked them – the advance guard of the common folk in those days, their God and their Covenant just formulae they hid the social rebellion in'.[24] But for all their heroism and sacrifice they were fighting for a land ruled by the Presbyterian elect.

The social upheaval of the age meant new forms of disorder involving the lower orders were also appearing. Noble control was beginning to weaken in Lowland Scotland. In 1682, a group of young men were press-ganged in Edinburgh for military service and marched to the port of Leith. A chronicler of the city wrote: '. . . some women called out to them: "pressed or not pressed?" They answered "Pressed" and so caused an excitement in the multitude. A woman who sat on the street selling pottery threw a few shards at the guard, and some other people, finding a supply of missiles at a house that was building, followed her example.'[25] The soldiers fired on the rioters, killing nine and arresting three, but the local assize refused to find them guilty.

In 1685, Charles II died and was succeeded by his brother James, a Catholic, who was also seen as an opponent of parliamentary rule. In 1688, the English parliamentary leaders invited the Dutch king, William of Orange, a Protestant married to James's daughter Mary, to take the throne. As a Dutch army marched on London, James lost his nerve and fled to France.

The 'Glorious Revolution' of 1688 heralded parliamentary rule in which the new commercial class was dominant, but across the border in Scotland noble rule and feudalism was still in place. The existence of two different systems within one island under the same Crown was not going to last for long. Among a section of the Scottish nobility and clan chiefs there was support for the return of James and his successors.

Scotland was in for a tumultuous six decades.

FOUR

Union, Jacobites and Popular Unrest

I n May 1999, on the opening day of the Scottish Parliament, the
veteran SNP member Winnie Ewing declared that the Scottish
parliament 'adjourned' in 1707 was 'hereby reconvened'.[1] It was
a nice rhetorical flourish, but whatever the faults of the current
parliamentary body in Holyrood, it's better than what existed prior
to 1707, an elite body elected by the nobility and the burgh notables.
In that year four in every thousand had a vote in parliamentary elections in England; in Scotland it was one in every thousand.[2] The only
form of pressure the lower orders could apply was extra-parliamentary. Before the first decade of the eighteenth century, there had been
little or no tradition of that, but now things were to change.

'A parcel of rogues' is how the poet Robert Burns described
members of the Scottish Parliament who voted for union with
their London counterparts. 'Bought and sold for English gold.'[3]
Many were in fact bribed, but that is not the main reason the Scottish Parliament voted for its own extinction. To understand why,
it's important to understand what the Scottish Parliament was like
in 1707.

Despite the fact that he had been deposed as king of England in
1688, for a year James VII remained king north of the border, until
a Convention of the Estates (nobility, clergy, gentry and

representatives of the burghs) met in Edinburgh in early 1689 to decide who was monarch on the basis of two letters – one from the exiled James VII and one from King William and Queen Mary, the new joint monarchs of England and Wales.

James's letter was haughty and threatening, while William and Mary's was conciliatory, stressing their determination to uphold the Protestant religion. James got only four votes. As a result, his staunchest supporter, Claverhouse (now Viscount Dundee), left with fifty horsemen to raise his banner of revolt on Dundee Law, hoping to amass a substantial army for James in the north-east and the Highlands.[4]

He was able to raise just 2,000 men, and on 26 July 1689 he lay in wait at the Pass of Killiecrankie in Perthshire for a stronger government army of 4,500, made up of Scots led by General Hugh Mackay. Mackay's force passed through the narrow pass, with just one shot fired at them, to find Claverhouse's troops lined up and their charge scattered the government army handing the Jacobites (supporters of James) victory. But Claverhouse was killed and lost 40 percent of his soldiers, dead or wounded.[5]

The Jacobites' attempt to march south was blocked by Cameronian volunteers (one of the Covenanting sects) in a street fight in Dunkeld, and on 1 May 1690 the remaining Jacobite force was scattered by cavalry at Cromdale on the Spey. Meanwhile, James was losing control of Ireland, which, with the exception of the Protestants of Ulster, had rallied to him. By the end of 1690 the Stewarts seemed a spent force. But events were to intervene to give them a new lease of life.

As part of the new reign, the rebel clans in the Highlands were forced to take an oath of loyalty to the monarchs, but one small clan, the MacDonalds of Glencoe, missed the deadline. The king's Secretary of State for Scotland, Sir John Dalrymple, Master of Stair, decided to make an example of them and sent troops to massacre them all, men, women and children. Thirty-eight MacDonalds were murdered and another forty women and children died of exposure in the Highland winter.[6] The massacre was carried out by men from the Earl of Argyll's Regiment of Foot, and deepened the divide between the Campbells and other clans in the West Highlands; it also fed Jacobite propaganda.

Another source of support for the Stewarts came from developments in the Church of Scotland. The Glorious Revolution had ended bishoprics – the bishops had all been avid supporters of James – and restored the General Assembly. The Episcopalian ministers who would not accept this broke away to form the Episcopalian Church (roughly equivalent to the Church of England), which became strong in parts of the Highlands and in the Lowlands north of the Tay. This would become the social base for those seeking the restoration of the Stewarts, the Jacobites.

South of the Tay, the Kirk emerged stronger than ever. The local Kirk Session spied on those breaking the Sabbath and not attending church, sexual encounters and much else. Wrongdoers might sit on the 'stool of repentance' in the Kirk or, in the case of gay men, be burnt alive on Edinburgh's Castle Hill. Single women suffered even more persecution, with up to 4,500 executed because they were supposedly witches. The figure for England in the same period is around 1,000.[7]

In the Lowlands there existed parish schools, providing a degree of education and creating, above all, a largely literate peasantry by the seventeenth century. Yet Scotland had not witnessed any of the peasant rebellions of the late Middle Ages that shook France or England, probably because the ties to the nobility remained stronger due to constant war, feuding and poverty. This was still a country where feudal relations dominated; it was still a rural society. Nobles had their own baronial courts where they could try misdemeanours, and while serfdom had been effectively abolished in Western Europe, Scotland saw its introduction to the coal mines and salt pans in 1606 by act of the Scottish Parliament.

Despite this, all the signs seemed to promise better times once James VII was ousted, but disaster followed. In 1690, Scotland had a population of one million – with nine out of ten living off the land. The following decade was marked by a famine on such a scale it burned itself into popular memory, the worst deprivations coming in 1695, 1696 and 1698. Food prices rose steadily across the decade. In Torryburn in

Fife, the minister noted that the number of deaths rose from some 21 a year in 1696 to 114 in 1697, and 81 in 1699. On the streets of Leith men died of hunger. The population fell by between 5 and 15 percent. From the parish of Monquhitter the minister would record:

> Of sixteen families that resided on the farm at Littertie, thirteen were extinguished. On the estate of Greens, which presently accommodates 169 individuals, three families (the proprietors included) only survived. The extensive farms of Toucher, Greeness, Overside and Burnshide of Idoch, now containing more than 100 souls, together with some farms on the parish of Turiff, being entirely deserted. The inhabitants of the parish were diminished by death to one half, or as some affirm, to one fourth of the preceding number . . . Until the year 1709, many farms were waste.[8]

Scotland tottered on the verge of catastrophe, with those in power able to do little in response. But they did look south and see that England was accruing a colonial empire that brought in significant riches but from which Scots were excluded by law. The idea took seed that Scotland might create its own empire.

The Scottish Parliament was described by the historian T. C. Smout as 'little more than a solemn rubber' for the monarchy.[9] But the Glorious Revolution had abolished the Privy Council, which had controlled parliamentary affairs. From then until the Act of Union the Scottish Parliament did exert a degree of independence, most notably in authorising the Darien Scheme.

In 1695, the Scottish Parliament passed the Act for a Company Trading to Africa and the Indies. Two forces conspired in the company's foundation – desire in Scotland to find new markets overseas, and the wish of certain London merchants to circumvent the monopoly of the East India Company.

As official disapproval became clear, however, London's interest in the new scheme melted away, and Scottish investors went ahead alone. The enthusiasm for such a risky venture, in so poor a country, was astonishing. The nation's hopes were committed to the idea of establishing a colony in Panama as an entrepot for world trade. The first expedition of would-be colonists sailed in July 1698. The Scots colonists found themselves in a swampy, disease-ridden land with the Spanish determined to remove them. The king in London refused to do anything to protect them. By March 1700, after 2,000 lives had been squandered, the remaining colonists submitted to the Spanish, whose monarch had long claimed the territory on which 'Darien' stood.

Spanish hostility was one factor in the experiment's failure, diplomatic opposition by King William was another. But the Scottish historian Neil Davidson argues that both these problems 'could have been coped with had either the Scottish state or civil society been resilient enough to sustain the venture'.[10] Scotland had neither the wealth not the military and naval clout to take on Spain, unless England backed it up, which was not going to happen because of the close alliance between the grandees who ran the rival East India Company and the Crown.

Following their recent experience of famine, this destruction of a Scottish attempt at economic breakout created uncertainty and a sense that 'something must be done'. Meanwhile, another crisis was developing 400 miles to the south.

Queen Anne, who succeeded William III to the throne in 1702, had no heir, and the Whig ruling class in England were determined that, on her death, the Crown would pass to the Protestant candidate, George, the Elector of Hanover. England was a contending world power, but it was also an emerging capitalist economy. As such it was pitted against feudal-absolutist France, which wanted to expand its empire but also to exert hegemony over Europe. War inevitably followed throughout the century following the Glorious Revolution, and the French saw that a Jacobite rebellion could undermine their opponents.

The English ruling class needed the Scottish Parliament to accept the Hanoverian succession, and was determined to stop it backing the return of the Stewarts. In the wake of Darien, the Scottish Parliament voted in 1703 that it should get to decide on Anne's successor and also that if Britain was at war, it could vote for peace. Within the nobility and elite burghers who made up the parliament, a Jacobite minority of government loyalists and others understood that this was an opportunity to negotiate, but when push came to shove they could not stomach a return to Catholicism, because that was what a return of the Stewarts would entail.

The Scottish Parliament's assertion of its authority was nevertheless unacceptable to London. In 1705, the English Parliament passed the Alien Act, which recommended to Anne that commissioners be sent to Edinburgh to negotiate a parliamentary union. If the Scots did not comply from Christmas Day onwards, Scots visiting England would be treated as aliens and Scottish imports would be stopped. It was economic blackmail at its most aggressive.

As this legislation was going through Parliament, a ship of the East India Company, the *Worcester*, anchored in the Firth of Forth on 12 August 1704. It was a bad time to dock. The East India Company had just had the Company of Scotland's last remaining vessel seized, as part of its relentless campaign to destroy its erstwhile rival. Now the English ship was seized and its crew put in jail. Feelings were running high. The secretary of the Company of Scotland had the sailors charged with piracy and murder, claiming they were responsible for the disappearance of a company ship a year earlier, lost at the hands of English pirates. The *Worcester*'s captain and two others of the crew were sentenced to be hanged. Queen Anne appealed for clemency but the Scottish Privy Council voted to uphold the verdict. On 11 April 1705, the three men were marched from Edinburgh Castle to the gallows on Leith Sands. It was claimed a crowd of 80,000 (far in excess of Edinburgh's population) lined the route and the shore, hurling abuse at the doomed men. This was mob rule in a real sense and it was not pretty, because the convicted men were clearly innocent.

The Edinburgh mob was fiercely anti-union but it was the elite who would decide the future of the nation. The supposed leader of the opposition was the Duke of Hamilton, feted on the streets of Edinburgh but a landowner in England who was secretly in league with the government in London. In 1706, this rhyme was overheard on the streets of Edinburgh:

> Come to the union lett us ryde
> Wee shall do great matters there

Scotland shall be England's bride
Or else be fuckyt by Earl of Stair[11]

There was popular opposition to the Union, including from the country's small merchant and commercial class, and from the lower classes of town and country. For several months the Edinburgh mob was almost permanently on the streets, demonstrating and rioting. Their fear was that union would be followed by Anglicisation of the Kirk, the one institution with any element of democracy, and that it would bring higher taxes. The riots and demonstrations did not stop the treaty going ahead but they did manage to get several of the most offensive clauses changed or deleted. In the end, the lords pushed the treaty through Parliament because the English regime was prepared to guarantee the preservation of their feudal jurisdictions and legal system – their class position.[12]

A majority of the nobility sensed that union would open up new opportunities to them: in London, in the army and through being able to sell their cattle and other produce in England. The Earl of Roxburgh explained in 1705: 'The motives will be, Trade with most, Hanover with some, ease and security with others.'[13]

Why did the English ruling class want a united British state? Apart from closing the back door to invasion and securing the Hanoverian succession, they were at war with France and the army was a British one. Its commander, the Duke of Marlborough, wanted a centralised state and his argument carried sway.

The English negotiators conceded that the Church of Scotland would be left untouched and the privileges of the royal burghs and their elites left alone. The nobles could keep their private courts and, most important of all, free trade with England and the colonies was granted, something denied to Ireland. This would create the biggest trading area in the world, no small part of the subsequent rise of what was, in effect, the new British state.

By 1705, a joint Anglo-Scottish parliamentary commission had drawn up a draft treaty of union. The Scottish representatives were selected from supporters of the Hanoverian succession, followers of the Dukes of Queensberry and Argyll. Nonetheless, anger was mounting as it became clear that this was an elite stitch-up. In both Dumfries and Stirling the treaty was burned in public, and rioting broke out in Glasgow and Edinburgh. The writer Daniel Defoe reported a 'Terrible Multitude' on Edinburgh's High Street led by a drummer, shouting and swearing and crying 'No Union, No Union, English Dogs and the like'.[14]

Defoe, there as an agent for the London government, added that the Scots were a 'hardened, refractory and terrible people' and the Scottish 'rabble' the worst he had experienced. As the vote was to be taken, troops surrounded the parliament building and the royal palace of Holyrood while two more regiments were stationed in Leith and Musselburgh.[15] It was sufficient to allow the vote to ratify the treaty to be held.

What drove the crowd that rioted outside Parliament as it ratified the Union in 1707? The Kirk was the one institution that defended their interests and provided them any say, in addition to poor relief, and it appeared under threat. Another reason is that they knew higher taxes on salt, ale and other basics would follow; also, tighter custom controls based on the English model would crack down on smuggling, which was widespread.

Although there was a growing sense of nationhood, this could not overcome the distinction between Lowlands and Highlands, and the exclusion of Catholics and Episcopalians. The Union, in the end, maintained the independence of the Kirk and both the educational and legal systems. It did so, as the historian Neil Davidson points out, 'to preserve the function of the Scottish *state*'.[16]

By the time, in 1707, that the Scottish Parliament approved the Act of Union, the key political figure, the Duke of Argyll, was back fighting the French, but he had received an English peerage and been made a lieutenant general for helping to ensure the outcome. Twenty thousand pounds had been sent north from London, some used for bribes, the rest as the usual reward for loyalty.[17]

Scotland had became an integral part of what was effectively a new state. Few people in 1707 or for years after would describe themselves as British, but that had changed by the end of the century. More important, Scotland was not Ireland and was free to prosper in the United Kingdom. Nevertheless, dislike of the Union opened up possibilities for the Jacobites, the one force that seemed to oppose it. Popular discontent in Scotland, and to a lesser extent south of the border, could often find expression in Jacobite slogans, symbols and songs, but it generally foundered on the Catholicism of the Stewarts.

The chances of the Stewarts regaining the throne depended on France providing military support, without which their supporters in England, and many in Scotland, would not move. In 1708, a French invasion fleet, with the 'Old Pretender', the supposed James VII and III, on board, reached the Firth of Forth. Several local lairds took up arms in support, but the French commander refused to land and fled when the Royal Navy arrived.

The accession of George I to the British throne in 1714 was not popular, and in response the Jacobites planned a rising: a French invasion force to land in south-west England. This was to be the main thrust, followed by a rebellion in Scotland. With the collapse of the English rising before it ever started, however, all efforts were concentrated on Scotland.

Good news came when the Earl of Mar, an architect of the Union, was sacked by George as Secretary for Scotland and he now switched allegiance to James. In September 1715, he gathered a force of 600 men at Braemar and proceeded to take control of Scotland north of the Tay. By October, Mar was sitting in Perth but failed to move, giving the Duke of Argyll time to raise a smaller force. Both armies were made up of tenants pressed into service by their lords, and the majority of the Jacobite force came from the north-east.

When, in November, Mar finally advanced from Perth he was met by Argyll at Sheriffmuir. The battle was famously indecisive but in the end, despite having overwhelming superiority in numbers, the Jacobite commander withdrew. James's arrival did not boost the rebels' fortunes, and when Argyll advanced, Mar evacuated Perth. James returned to France and Mar ordered his army to stand down.

On the same day as Sheriffmuir, a Jacobite force made up of rebels from Northumberland and the Borders, reinforced by troops sent by Mar, which had advanced into Lancashire, surrendered at Preston. Thus ended the Jacobites' best chance of seizing back the throne.

In the wake of 1715 it was clear more was needed than relying on the power of Clan Campbell to hold down the Highlands. The Duke of Argyll was introducing commercial methods onto his estates and his new tenants were not required to give military service, replacing feudal obligation with modern contracts and capitalist relations. The London government built a network of military roads and garrison forts, but the most effective work was done by the Kirk via the Society for Promoting Christian Knowledge, which converted Highlanders to the Church of Scotland and worked effectively to eradicate Gaelic in its schools and churches.

Meanwhile, economic change was sewing rthe seeds of popular unrest. In the south-west the economy was improving, with Galloway sending black cattle to meet London's demand for meat and by 1720, landowners were enclosing arable land with stone dykes, behind which cattle grazed.[18] The economy of Galloway was centred on cattle-rearing and was in that way similar to the Western Highlands. The peasantry of the Lowlands had gone through much, but this was the first time they suffered being cleared off the land.[19]

The beneficiaries of enclosure included Jacobite landlords such as Sir David Dunbar of Baldoon and Sir Robert Maxwell of Orchardton. Dunbar used the money he earned from the cattle trade to buy more land.[20] In 1715, Dunbar's great-grandson Sir Basil Hamilton joined the Jacobite forces raised in the Borders and Northumberland but was taken prisoner at the Battle of Preston. His family secured his release, and to stop any loss of his estates his mother took ownership of them, with Hamilton running them on her behalf. 'In 1723, Hamilton built a cattle park near Kirkcudbright on land originally owned by the McLellans.'[21] The Earl of Galloway, Sir William Maxwell, Sir Godfrey McCulloch, Sir James Dalrymple and the Laird of Logan were landowners who followed Dunbar's example and built cattle parks. These landlords were Episcopalians or Jacobites, or both.

Fears of a Stewart return were revived, in the early summer of 1719, by a small-scale invasion of Kintail in the north-west Highlands by a few hundred Spanish troops, which succeeded in rallying some local Jacobite clansmen, although it was swiftly defeated by

Hanoverian troops.[22] Hatred of enclosure and of supporters of the Stewarts helped create a rural uprising in the south-west. For four months in 1724 a popular movement swept Galloway, with crowds 'levelling' the dykes used to enclose the cattle parks. The first dyke-breaking occurred on 17 March at Netherlaw near Kirkcudbright, and in early April a call to a meeting against cattle parks was fixed to church doors in Borgue, Twynholm and Tongland parishes.

The *Caledonian Mercury* reported that this meeting was addressed by a 'mountain preacher' and 'big with that ancient levelling Tenet', several hundred armed persons subsequently demolished dykes in the neighbourhood.[23] The landlords demanded troops be sent, and in May, four troops of Stair's Dragoons arrived in Kirkcudbright. Just prior to their arrival, a call for people to gather at Sir Basil Hamilton's new cattle park at Bomby Muir was put up on eight church doors. In answer, nearly two miles of dykes were levelled by 1,000 people.

Despite the fact that the ordinary people of Galloway were staunchly Presbyterian and the south-west had been a stronghold of the Covenanters, the General Assembly of the Church of Scotland voted through a denunciation of the dyke-breaking. Many of the Calvinist groups that had operated in Covenanting times were still outside the Kirk, however, and they helped provide an ideological and organisational framework for the rebellion.[24]

All through the summer the levelling continued, and the concern was such in both Edinburgh and London that a government inquiry was promised. The Levellers sent a letter to the officer commanding the Dragoons in Kirkcudbright, explaining,

> We unanimously agreed to throw down Mr. Murdoch's dykes which enclosed the Barony of Airds out of which two or three years ago great multitudes of good and sufficient tenants were driven away and also the same Mr. Murdoch's dykes which were a building about the lands of Kilwhannadie and Macartney, like wise great tracts of land which tenants were immediately to be turned out.[25]

In October, troops arrested some 200 Levellers but allowed almost all to escape en route back to Kirkcudbright. The dyke-breaking continued into the next year and the Levellers' actions halted the pace and extent of enclosure in the south-west.[26] Indeed, the Galloway Levellers had so 'frightened the authorities' that the process of agricultural improvement and clearances in the Lowlands proceeded more cautiously and slowly.[27]

Levelling was not confined to Galloway. As early as 1718, enclosure walls on the estate of Sir James Carmichael of Bonnington near Lanark were torn down, and this continued after the Galloway events. In Cromarty in 1732, a 500-strong crowd pulled down a dyke and put up trees to block access to the local peat bog.

Another form of protest also became a feature of Scottish life in this period. Riots are almost always an expression of popular anger when no other channel exists and in Inverurie in 1724 townspeople rioted when they were taxed to fund a road- and bridge-building programme. In the same year farther south, the Baillie of Duns, John Grey, had his house attacked and his life threatened after he tried to stop the town's annual football game on 'Fasting Even'. And in Irvine, Ayrshire, there was a series of riots in the 1740s and '50s over the enclosure of the town's moor.[28]

High food prices also led to riots. In 1720, food riots broke out in the coastal burghs of Angus, Perthshire, Fife and West Lothian, with crowds ranging from 50 to 2,000 breaking open barns and warehouses belonging to farmers and merchants believed to be hoarding oatmeal and grain. Men and women wielding axes and hammers boarded ships taking grain for export, tearing down sails, removing rudders and driving holes through their hulls. In Methil, Fife, colliers and sailors were to the fore in the crowd.[29]

The town of Dysart in east Fife was in the hands of the crowd for three days. Led by a bayonet-wielding woman, they drove off one party of soldiers before the army retook control. A ballad praising the 'Valiant Wives of Dysart' describes this woman: '. . . shipped through the Gate / And pass'd throw the Kirk yard. / Calling where is that stinking Beast, / The Ugly Swine the Laird'.[30]

Riots broke out over aristocrats' control of town councils or their imposition of ministers on congregations.[31] Women played a prominent role in the riots and popular disturbances. A nineteenth-century local historian of Renfrewshire noted that in the customs and excise riots in Greenock and Port Glasgow of the previous century, 'women . . . of a class above the lowest – were active participants in the riots that generally accompanied seizures of contraband articles'.[32]

Christopher Whatley points out that in Dumfries and Galloway, '. . . between 1711 and 1718 there were at least four major incidents involving virtually all-female crowds of one hundred and up to two hundred people . . . It was attacks by armed females on the queen's warehouses and their fellow officers that terrified the customs service in Dumfries in the first post-Union years.'[33] In 1725, a tax on malt led to riots in Stirling, Dundee, Ayr, Elgin, Paisley and, most seriously, Glasgow. There, rioters burned down the house of the local MP, fought the local garrison, losing eight lives, and driving them out of the city, before the arrival of General Wade with 400 dragoons and accompanying infantry to restore order. Christopher Whatley, who has charted much of these disturbances, notes the high involvement of women among Covenanters of the south-west, and in the Galloway Levellers' Revolt of 1724 against evictions and enclosure.[34]

The Porteous Riot became the centrepiece of Sir Walter Scott's novel *The Heart of Midlothian*. In March 1737, a convicted smuggler, Andrew Wilson, was hanged in Edinburgh's Grassmarket. He was a popular man, and the evasion of duty on spirits, something imposed after the Act of Union, was equally popular. After the gruesome deed had been carried out, a section of the crowd pelted the City Guard with stones and rubbish. In response, its commander, Captain James Porteous, gave the order to open fire. Nine people were killed.

The resulting anger was so great that the city magistrates had Porteous charged with murder; he was found guilty and sentenced to be hanged on 7 September. At the last minute a royal pardon arrived from London, prompted, it was said, by the same magistrates who had been in the habit of playing golf with Porteous. A crowd broke into the Tolbooth, where Porteous was still in custody, dragged him out and hanged him.

In 1740, an Edinburgh magistrate who talked his way out of a food riot 'had to be protected from the women and most dangerous party of ye Mob . . . who called out to knock him down'.[35]

Meanwhile, the old order in the shape of the Stewarts was about to make its last appearance. In 1744, with France and Britain at war, the French gathered an invasion fleet at Dunkirk, where it was joined by the Old Pretender's son, Charles – 'Bonnie Prince Charlie', or Prince Charles Edward Louis John Casimir Sylvester Severino Maria Stewart, to give him his full name. A storm devastated the fleet and the expedition was called off.

Charles decided to press ahead nevertheless, and in July 1745 set off with three ships, only the one carrying him reaching the Hebrides, from where he crossed to Knoydart. The absence of a French army meant little support was forthcoming, but after promising Cameron of Lochiel that he would be guaranteed financial security in France if a rebellion failed (it was one of the few promises Charles kept), he was able to gather a small army of 1,300 at Glenfinnan.

The government ordered General Cope to march north to crush this rebellion, but he diverted to Inverness and then Aberdeen, allowing the Jacobites to march south and take Edinburgh, meeting no opposition. When Cope sailed south with his troops, the Jacobites under their capable military commander, Lord George Murray, routed them at Prestonpans.

Charles had only a few thousand troops, but if he had decided to hold Scotland he might have brought George II and his government to the negotiating table; instead, he wanted to take England, and swung his council by just one vote to march south with promises of French help and support from English Jacobites.

The Jacobite army is usually portrayed as a Highland force, but West Highland clans supplied only around 44 percent, with a similar percentage from the north-east, Angus and Perthshire.[36] As they marched into England few joined, with the greatest support coming from Manchester, where some 400 men, many Catholics, enlisted. Charles had made no attempt to contact Jacobite sympathisers, but there was no indication from them that they were ready to take up arms.

The invasion reached Derby, attracting little support. Three armies were now in the field against them. One, led by General Wade, was still in Yorkshire, too far away to affect things; a second, led by the king's son the Duke of Cumberland, was trailing behind him; and another was gathering at Finchley, north of London, to defend the capital, where there was panic in ruling circles.

Charles wanted to go on, but his council refused and the army turned back, despite defeating a government army at Falkirk, a victory Charles did not exploit. The retreat continued to Inverness, with Cumberland following. Murray was now sidelined, and Charles and his courtiers decided military strategy. When Cumberland's army forded the River Spey, 2,000 Jacobite troops were on high ground overlooking them but were ordered to withdraw.

On 16 April 1746, the Jacobite army, outnumbered, tired, hungry and with an easterly wind blowing rain into their faces, made their last stand at Culloden. During the night, they had been made to march on Cumberland's camp in an abortive attempt to carry out a surprise attack. Retreating towards Inverness, many fell asleep when they halted.

Charles had chosen the battlefield, despite Lord George Murray pointing out that a flat moor benefitted Cumberland's artillery and cavalry. As the Jacobite army waited for an order to attack, Cumberland's artillery blew great gaps in their ranks. Eventually the men charged but few reached the government's lines. Those that did found that their opponents had been trained to withstand the Highland broadsword. As the Jacobite forces broke and fled, the commander of the Hanoverian cavalry, Lieutenant General Henry Hawley, ordered his men to charge. He would report that they 'cleared all the country for three miles before them and . . . made great slaughter every way'.[37]

The few French regular troops, mostly Irish exiles, fighting with the Jacobites were allowed to surrender and treated according to the rules of war. When Cumberland arrived at Inverness, he discovered that Major General Bland had 'taken about a hundred of the Irish officers and men prisoner but not one Scotchman'.[38] Hawley's aide James Wolfe (the future conqueror of Quebec), wrote to his uncle: '. . . as few prisoners were taken of the Highlanders as possible'.[39]

This was not a case of troops escaping control, this was a vicious reprisal sanctioned at the very top. Innocent civilians who had tried to observe the battle, or who were found on the road or in the fields, were cut down or shot. After the battle, Cumberland's troops went on to ravage the Highlands, burning crops and crofts, driving off cattle, looting and murdering.

In the aftermath of Culloden, the Abolition of Heritable Jurisdictions Act ended the right of Scottish nobles to dictate justice on their own estates through baronial courts. The only rights accorded to them were those of landownership. Lords who were loyal to George II were compensated for the loss of such powers, with the Duke of Argyll receiving £21,000. This legislation effectively destroyed feudalism in Scotland.[40]

The estates of Jacobite lords such as Cameron of Lochiel, Fraser of Lovat and MacDonnell of Keppoch were confiscated. These remained annexed to the Crown until 1784, when by Act of Parliament the king could grant them to the heirs of the original owners. This is largely what happened, because by then they had raised regiments to fight for the House of Hanover in its wars with France.

Highlanders were banned from wearing the kilt (a recent introduction to the Highlands by an English industrialist), playing the bagpipes and carrying arms. The region was effectively demilitarised.

The 1745 rebellion was not just the last throw of the Stewarts but also of the Scottish nobles who had clung to their feudal rights. Many of their counterparts, such as the Duke of Argyll, had already begun producing crops and cattle for the market, improved their estates and introduced tenants who took out commercial leases. Among the Jacobites, Lord George Murray was one such. But most of the clan chiefs, Lowland gentry and nobles who rallied to Charles, were facing bankruptcy, and were saved only because privilege prevented their prosecution. As Lord Kilmarnock explained before his execution: 'For the two kings and their rights, I cared not a farthing which prevailed; but I was starving, and, by god, if Mahommeds had set up his standard in the Highlands I had been a good Mussulman for bread, and stuck close to the party, for I must eat.'[41]

Many have seen Culloden portrayed as a clash between Scotland and England; it was not. The majority of Scots opposed any return of the Stewarts. In Perth the population celebrated King George II's birthday in November 1745, despite the town having a Jacobite governor, and laid siege to him and his supporters in the council house. The Jacobites were saved only by the arrival of some Highland troops. In Glasgow they met with open hostility, and as they retreated north, Stirling resisted the Jacobites and agreed to open the gates only after they were promised there would be no reprisals.[42] It is also important to mention that a majority of the clans did not rally to Charles Edward Stewart. Some, as we have seen, were pro-Hanoverian. Most did not want to join a risky adventure.

Despite the truth, the myth would grow of Charles Edward Stewart as a hero to grace the shortbread tins. His evasion of the Hanoverian troops during the summer of 1746, the help he received from Flora MacDonald and his eventual escape back to France facilitated that. In reality, he was a desperate gambler who failed. He was little interested in Scotland except as a stepping stone to the throne in London. The army he took south was a feudal one marching into an emerging capitalist society, and was regarded as alien. At Culloden it came up against regular troops bloodied in wars with France. He chose the field with disastrous results. He would die in Rome, a hopeless alcoholic, secretly playing on the bagpipes.

Peter Watkins's documentary *Culloden*, shown by the BBC in 1964, left no doubts that Cumberland earned the title 'The Butcher'. But it also showed Lowland Scots ready to butcher prisoners and Jacobite soldiers pressed into military service by the threat of having their home burned and their cattle driven off. Culloden cleared the way for the launch of capitalist Scotland. It was a bloody birth, but that's the norm for capitalism.

FIVE

Enlightenment and Capitalism

I n 1814, Walter Scott wrote in his first novel, *Waverley*, 'There is no European nation which, within the course of half a century, or little more, has undergone so complete a change as this kingdom of Scotland.'[1] Most Scots would have been aware of changes taking place around them. In 1700, just 5.3 percent of Scots lived in towns of more than 10,000 inhabitants, but by 1800 the figure was 17.3 percent, one of the fastest rates of urbanisation in Europe. Scotland transformed itself from a society more akin to Ireland or Poland to one on a level with England and Holland, an economic powerhouse with an economy centred on profit.

Industrialisation also took place at breakneck speed, comparable to what happened in late twentieth-century China. Between the early 1770s and the late 1790s, exports from Scottish ports increased from £0.5 to £1.35 million. By 1814, they were worth more than £5 million. The rise of cotton was the most spectacular case of growth; at the beginning of the 1770s, 0.15 million pounds of raw cotton arrived on the Clyde; by 1801 the amount stood at 7.5 million tons. The agricultural revolution the country experienced enabled the population to grow by 50 percent between 1770 and 1820.

Between 1740 and 1790 there was a spectacular growth in the cattle trade with England, driven, in part, by the demand from

Britain's armies and navy, with prices increasing by 300 percent in those years. Wool exports also increased and prices rose too. To meet demand, sheep farming spread across the Southern Uplands and from there north into the Highlands. Farming rather than rents became the best source of revenue, and landowners competed as to who was the best 'improver', introducing the latest techniques.[2] One French observer noted in 1800: 'If Scotland were not prospering, Glasgow would not be growing as fast as it is, the size of Edinburgh would not have doubled in thirty years, and they would not now be building a New Town whose construction is employing close on ten thousand immigrant workers.'[3] Walter Scott, a conservative, was disturbed by all this:

> The state of society now leads so much to great accumulations of humanity that we cannot wonder if it ferment and reek like a compost dunghill. Nature intended that population should be diffused over the soil in proportion to its extent. We have accumulated in huge cities and smothering manufactures the numbers which should be spread over the face of a country and what wonder that they should be corrupted? We have turned healthful and pleasant brooks into morasses and pestiferous lakes.[4]

This rapid transformation of Scottish society was driven by the creation of an all-British economy, a growing empire and the demands of constant war. Capitalist farming reduced the numbers living off the land, first in the Lowlands and later in the Highlands. Some emigrated, and many found employment in the growing industries of the central belt. In the subsequent centuries we have seen how such rapid industrialisation and creation of a working class creates an explosive mix.

Scotland After the Union

In the immediate aftermath of the Union of 1707 few Scots identified themselves as British. Yet within a century that was to change. The Scottish upper classes had to rely on the British state to defeat the Jacobite threat (always backed up with the threat of foreign invasion). The destruction of feudalism in the wake of Culloden in 1746 opened the way to the development of full-scale capitalism dependent on the British market. In addition, the creation of the Empire was a common enterprise in which eager Scots played no small part. By 1772 one in nine of the East India Company's civil servants was a Scot, as well as one in eleven of its common soldiers and one in three officers. By 1803 the most important six agencies that controlled Calcutta's trade were controlled by Scots, and in Bombay, they ran three out of five.[5]

Because the Union was not the simple incorporation of Scotland into the English state, but the eventual construction of a new British state, Scots could share their sense of nationhood within that common British identity. The historian Linda Colley points out that the Empire was always the British Empire, never the English one.[6] This, together with eight decades of war against the French, created a British nationalism that Scots shared, in large part because Scots, Highlanders and Lowlanders made up a significant percentage of the British army.

Industrialisation meant that Scotland (Central Scotland at least) was not on the periphery of the British economy, and Scots were at the fore of the British ruling class.[7] The emerging Scottish capitalist class were not even junior partners, they were a major component of the British ruling class, and their nationality was no obstacle to their becoming prime minister, running the colonies or simply amassing a fortune.

Yet the romanticism of the great novelist and poet Sir Walter Scott created a Scottish national identity that for the ruling and middle classes could sit easily with their role within this imperium. As a unionist and a Tory he was a fervent defender of Scotland's rights, including its right to issue its own bank notes, but was happy to champion the British state. In four great novels, *Rob Roy*, *The Heart of Midlothian*, *Waverley* and *Redgauntlet*, Scott brought to life recent Scottish history and created the modern novel. These deserve to be read by anyone interested in history.

It was Scott who orchestrated the first royal visit to Scotland in over a century and a half. In 1822, King George IV, unpopular in London, visited Edinburgh for a fortnight of pageants, balls and celebrations, orchestrated by Scott, and all with a Celtic and High-land flavour. He summoned the remaining Highland chiefs to Edinburgh with their retainers, and told them to choose a clan tartan (there were no specific tartans as yet apart from for the Highland regiments of the British Army). This was just seven decades after Highland dress had been banned and held up as the garb of savages. Now it was being worn in the salons of Edinburgh and would become adopted by Lowland Scots who had once despised it.

Nonetheless, elite control of Scotland was unchallenged in the eighteenth century. The Campbells (the Dukes of Argyll) dominated Scottish political affairs for the first half of the century. The second Duke of Argyll became Commander in Chief of the British Army in 1742. His brother who succeeded him as the third Duke served as Lord Justice General of Scotland from 1710 to 1761. En route to the family seat at Inverarary Castle, which he had rebuilt, the earl, if passing through Edinburgh or Glasgow, expected to be 'waited upon' by the Lord Provost.[8] The seventh Viscount Stormont, who would be made Earl of Mansfield, was Lord Chief Justice of England and Wales from 1756 until 1788. He rebuilt the family seat of Scone Palace near Perth, fitting it out with French furniture. In addition, his London home was Kenwood House on Hampstead Heath.[9]

But the greatest political figure of the age, eclipsing even the Dukes of Argyll, was Henry Dundas, Viscount Melville, who became Scot-land's Solicitor General in 1766 at the age of twenty-four, and was elected an MP for Midlothian in 1774. He held the position of naval treasurer from 1782 to 1800 and was a cabinet minister from 1796 until his impeachment in 1806. Dundas effectively ran Scotland during the government of William Pitt the Younger.[10]

Scottish MPs at Westminster were 'managed' to ensure they supported government measures, and in return were given a say over matters Scottish, and rewarded with patronage. Their 'manager' would decide on Scottish legislation in Edinburgh, in consultation with Scottish law officers, the Faculty of Advocates, the Convention of Royal Burghs, county freeholders and the Kirk.

The system worked smoothly enough, first under the House of Argyll, for the Whigs, and then under Henry Dundas, for the Tories.

Scottish politicians such as the Earl of Bute – a favourite of King George III and briefly prime minister – were hated in the 1760s because they represented the right wing of British politics, and Scotland was the least democratic part of the United Kingdom. That's why that hero of the London mob, John Wilkes, was so effective in his campaign against Scottish influence.

Meanwhile, the Scottish aristocracy transformed itself with the cash it received from its improved estates and from the Empire. Aristocratic landowners in the fertile coastal plains of East Lothian and Berwickshire did well from the 'Age of Improvement'. In the final decades of the eighteenth century, the Earl of Haddington built Mellerstain House, the Earl of Lauderdale built Thirlestane House and the Duke of Buccleuch, the biggest Lowland landowner, Dalkeith Palace.[11] Then, in 1803, the Irish Second Earl of Moira married the heiress Flora, Countess of Loudon. The new couple ran through their fortune rebuilding Loudon Castle as the 'Scottish Windsor'. To restore his wealth, Moira became Governor General of India, in turn being made Marquess of Hastings.[12]

Their lives contrasted with that of those working the land. Alexander Somerville was born in 1811. His father had been a small independent farmer in the Ochils but lost his land to 'improvement' when the local landowner amalgamated, so that after working as a carter in nearby Alloa, then as a docker in Limekilns after his horse died, he eventually became a farm labourer on a new, improved farm in Berwickshire. Alexander described his house there, home also to his mother and father and seven siblings:

> About twelve feet by fourteen, and not so high in the walls as will allow a man to get in without stooping. That place without ceiling or anything beneath the bare tiles of roof; with no floor save the common clay, without a cupboard or recess; with no grate but the iron bars which the tenants carried to it, built up and took away when they left it; with no partition of any kind save what the beds made; with no window save four small panes at one side – it was this house, still a hind's house at Springfield, for which, to obtain leave to live in, my mother sheared the harvest and carried the stacks.[13]

This was a largely literate society. According to some estimates, the male literacy rate in 1750 stood as high as 75 percent, compared with only 53 percent in England. Scotland had become 'Europe's first modern literate society', which meant 'there was an audience not only for the Bible but for other books as well'.[14] Despite his poor upbringing, Alexander Somerville went to school and became one of the first in a long line of working-class intellectuals.

Scotland was still a Calvinist country. This is what marked it off from England in the eighteenth century, but the Kirk always faced opposition to its strict disciplinary code. When a man from Fetteresso in Kincardineshire was threatened with excommunication in 1748, he replied: 'What care I? The Pope of Rome excommunicates you every year, and what the waur are ye o' that?'[15] Even the poet Robert Burns would be forced to sit on the 'Stool of Repentance' in the Kirk, and it continued to exercise close social control. But new thinkers were emerging who did not accept its writ.

Until the eighteenth century the myth that the land was communally owned still endured. In the Lowlands, leases were often for as little as a year, but no one complained because they were always renewed. Communal grazing lands existed by custom, but there was no legal guarantee of access.

After the Union, Scottish landowners began to notice the improvements in crop yields and livestock that their English counterparts were making, and the increased rents they were pocketing. What they saw around them were cotters relying on methods of agriculture rooted in feudal times. In order to generate greater profits, drastic change was needed.[16]

A new system of agriculture was developed, producing wonders like Aberdeen Angus beef and hugely increasing the amount of food available. But this agricultural revolution was based on mass eviction. As the year-long leases came to an end, landlords, having secured legal recognition of 'their' land, including the common grazing land, started drafting new leases with vastly increased rents. Evictions followed. Unlike the nineteenth-century Highlanders, the fate of the Lowland peasantry is not remembered today. That is because the Lowlanders simply slipped away to the cities, where new industries demanded labour, or took ship to North America.

Meanwhile, the Highlands were also undergoing a great deal of change. The most obvious was that no longer did peasant farmers have to partake in military service. Baronial courts were abolished. Commercial rents were now being introduced by chiefs who were moving away to enjoy life in Edinburgh or London. For most tenants, subsistence farming remained the rule but they could enhance their income by migrating south to work in the new industries for part of the year, through service in the army, by working in the kelp industry (turning seaweed into fertiliser) and by fishing for herring.

The Committee of Forfeited Estates, which administered the lands of the rebel chiefs and nobles, was run not by English politicians but by Edinburgh lawyers. In 1784, it was considered wise to return these estates to their original owners, who repaid their debt by acting as recruitment agents for the British Army.

In many ways, the years after Culloden saw changes that benefitted the Highlands. The price of cattle, the region's main export, rose by 300 percent between then and the 1790s. The introduction of the potato gave the peasantry a cheap and easily grown food. Demand for wood increased. On the coast, demand for kelp was fuelled by the glass and soap works of the south, while fisheries expanded. The price of wool rose as well, and the new Blackface and Cheviot sheep, with their high yields, started to appear. But sheep runs demanded the removal of peasant farms.

Despite this, emigration was on the rise. Between 1768 and 1775, 20,000 people left Scotland for North America, two-thirds of them Highlanders.[17]

Enlightenment

The second half of the eighteenth century saw Scotland shift from being on the intellectual periphery of European and North American intellectual life to become the leading centre of a new rational and scientific school of thought, with major contributions in the fields of philosophy,

political economy, engineering, architecture, medicine, geology, archaeology, law, agriculture, chemistry and sociology. Among the towering
thinkers and scientists of the period were Francis Hutcheson, Alexander
Campbell, David Hume, Adam Smith, Dugald Stewart, Thomas Reid,
Adam Ferguson, Joseph Black and James Hutton. The philosopher
David Hume was in correspondence with the great French thinkers
Voltaire and Rousseau, and was visited by Benjamin Franklin, the
outstanding American thinker and scientist of his day, and subsequently one of the Founding Fathers of the United States.

In the wake of Culloden, a new Scottish ruling class also emerged.
Landowners, however great their title, had to improve their lands to
generate income, and some of the greatest, such as the Duke of
Argyll, led the way. Beside them were the tobacco and sugar merchants
of Glasgow and those involved in an emerging textile industry.

Their ideological outriders were Kirk ministers, university lecturers and lawyers. These new professionals preached a gospel of rapid
capitalist development, and the fact that they were making history
shines through in the writings of Smith, Hume, Ferguson and,
slightly later, Walter Scott. At the centre of the emerging Enlightenment was Scotland's capital. The future US president Thomas
Jefferson stated there was '. . . no place in the World can pretend to a
competition with Edinburgh'.[18]

What the Scottish Enlightenment did was theorise about how
human beings could act to change the world. That was because the
world in which they lived had gone in the space of a few decades
from a backward, feudal society to one at the centre of the new
emerging global system, capitalism. Hume joined the nobility and
the bourgeoisie in fleeing Edinburgh's medieval Old Town for the
Georgian splendour of the New Town. Smith was teaching in Glasgow, where the skyline was becoming dominated by the chimneys of
the new cotton plants and where his dinner companions boasted of
their wealth accrued from the tobacco trade. English liberals were
drawn to Edinburgh University, and the *Edinburgh Review* pioneered
the views of what would become nineteenth-century liberalism.

Today the most celebrated of these men (women could not go to
university and were effectively barred from higher education) was

Adam Smith, considered to be the founder of modern economics, whose most famous book, *On the Wealth of Nations*, was first published in 1776. It provides an analysis of the beginning of the industrial revolution, and attempts to explain where wealth comes from and how markets work. Smith is today portrayed too often as a precursor of Margaret Thatcher, the first neo-liberal, but this is a caricature. He did believe that left to themselves markets would produce outcomes beneficial to all, but he went beyond that.

His key work begins not with the centrality of the market, but with labour, which Smith saw as the source of wealth. New techniques leading to a division of labour were capable of creating levels of previously unseen wealth: 'The annual labour of every nation is the fund which originally supplies it with all the necessaries and conveniences of life.'[19] One famous example – illustrated alongside Adam Smith on the back of the new £20 note – involves the manufacture of pins: 'One man draws out the wire, another straights it, a third cuts it, a fourth points it, a fifth grinds it at the top for receiving the head . . . The important business of making a pin is, in this manner, divided into about 18 distinct operations which, in some factories, are all performed by distinct hands.'[20]

The free marketers who claim Smith today pass over this 'labour theory of value'; yet it is central to his analysis. Adam Smith was very un-Thatcherite when, regarding working-class protests and strikes, he observed: 'Whenever the legislature attempts to regulate the differences between masters and their workmen, its counsellers are always the master.' Earlier, another great Enlightenment thinker, Adam Ferguson, warned in *An Essay on the History of Civil Society* (1765): 'we make a nation of helots, and have no free citizens . . . In every commercial state, nothwithstanding any pretensions to equal rights, the exaltation of a few must depress the many.'[21]

The values of the Scottish Enlightenment did not extend to all parts of the globe or even to all its people. David Hume was a great historian and a very important philosopher who established materialism, but he never gained a top post at Edinburgh University because of his vocal atheism. He also attempted to provide a rationale for the slave trade based on 'scientific' racism.

Glasgow's fortune in the eighteenth century owed much to its tobacco trade with the slave states of North America, and that legacy is kept alive in street names: Glassford Street and Buchanan Street are named after tobacco merchants; Jamaica Street and Virginia Street are named after colonies.

Richard Oswald was the majority shareholder in Grant, Oswald and Co., the owners of Bance Island, a major slavery shipping point on the Sierra Leone River in West Africa. Within a short time of the company taking over, it was shipping 1,000 slaves a year across the Atlantic. The island had a golf course with caddies, recruited from nearby villages, wearing tartan loincloths woven in Scotland. Oswald traded slaves for tobacco and sugar, which he sold in Britain, making himself rich. Based in London, he was well favoured in ruling circles but fell from grace because he was seen as pro-American during the American War of Independence. No matter, he could retire to his 100,000-acre estate at Auchincruive, where he entertained the likes of Benjamin Franklin, James Boswell and Laurence Sterne.[22]

His wife, Mary Ramsey, was the daughter of one of the biggest Scottish slave owners in Jamaica. On her death Robert Burns wrote this:

Ode, Sacred to the Memory of Mrs Oswald of Auchencruive

> Dweller in yon dungeon dark,
> Hangman of creation, mark!
> Who in widow-weeds appears,
> Laden with unhonoured years,
> Noosing with care a bursting purse,
> Baited with many a deadly curse?
> View the wither'd beldam's face
> Can thy keen inspection trace
> Aught of Humanity's sweet, melting grace?
> Note that eye, 'tis rheum o'erflows,
> Pity's flood there never rose.
> See those hands, ne'er stretched to save,

Hands that took – but never gave.
Keeper of Mammon's iron chest,
Lo, there she goes, unpitied and unblest
She goes, but not to realms of everlasting rest!

During the American War of Independence immigrant Highlanders rallied to George III, including former Jacobites. Among them was Allan MacDonald, whose wife, Flora, is celebrated on many a short-bread tin for her role in helping Charles Edward Stewart escape arrest. They owned a plantation in North Carolina and, in 1776, mobilised 13,000 Highlanders to fight for the House of Hanover. Four years later this Highland army was defeated at the Battle of King's Mountain by an army largely made up of Ulster Scot Presbyterians – refugees from persecution at home.

In this conflict Lowland settlers generally sided with the revolution. The Enlightenment thinkers back home were critical of George III's treatment of the American colonists, and the success of the American revolution would make an impact in Scotland.

Scotland was also part of the movement to abolish the slave trade. In 1789, the freed slave Olaudah Equiano visited Edinburgh, Paisley, Glasgow, Perth, Dundee and Aberdeen, addressing public meetings and promoting his autobiography, detailing his capture and enslavement in present-day Nigeria. A year later, another ex-slave, Thomas Peters, addressed a public dinner in Glasgow's Tontine Tavern.[23]

In 1792, the London-based Society for Effecting the Abolition of the Slave Trade, having launched a new national petition to parliament, sent a young clergyman to Scotland to see how the anti-slavery movement was proceeding. He reported on a huge public meeting in Edinburgh thus: '. . . so orderly it was and so silent . . . not a whisper but when plaudits made the place resound – No less than 3685 signed on the spot . . . all with the most admirable decorum – the magistrates had ordered the castle troop of the town guard to be in readiness – and a troop of horse were brought in from the country – this was their duty.'[24]

The reaction of the 'City Fathers' was a reflection of the growing nervousness of the effects of the French Revolution in Scotland.

Thirteen thousand people signed the same petition in Glasgow, a city that owed much to the slave economy in North America.

REBEL LIVES: ROBERT BURNS

There are two Robert Burns. The first is the one found on shortbread tins and whisky bottles, the romantic poet who portrayed Scottish life. This is the Burns celebrated at Burns Suppers every 25 January, clothed in tartan that Burns could hardly have ever come across in his short life, and certainly never wore. The other is the radical, indeed Jacobin, supporter of the American and French revolutions whose poems and songs were sung by those fighting for democracy and social justice.

In his recent biography of Burns, *The Bard*, Robert Crawford produces evidence that Burns was a member of a republican circle in Dumfries and remained a 'staunch republican' until his death. He adds that 'it takes a tin ear and narrow mind' to ignore the radical message in so many of Burns's poems.[25]

Burns lived at the close of the eighteenth century, when Scotland was undergoing a sudden, rapid transformation. The agricultural revolution was driving the peasantry from the land – this was the class Burns was born into. The Industrial Revolution was changing the lives of Scots, for better and for worse. Burns was born in Alloway, just outside Ayr, the eldest of seven children, in a single-room thatched cottage with a barn and cowshed. His father worked as a gardener, but in order to support his family became a tenant farmer. By the age of fifteen, Robert was the principal labourer on the farm, interrupting his school days to help his father.

Burns tried his hand as a tenant farmer, but with rising rents it was hard to make a living. Despite his poetry and songs being widely acclaimed, Burns also failed to find a wealthy patron. Eventually, in 1789, he moved to Dumfries and took a job as an excise man (a customs officer), which he held until his death in 1796.

The greatest event in Burns's life was undoubtedly the French Revolution of 1789. The new ideas of the Enlightenment had challenged the hold of the Kirk and the oligarchic political system. Now the French revolutionary slogan of 'Liberty, Equality, Fraternity' spoke to Burns as it did other Scots, and he read Tom Paine's revolutionary text *The Rights of Man*. This fervour is reflected, directly and indirectly, in his poetry.

He knew poverty and injustice too, and lived a life that was shocking to the Calvinist faithful. As one of Scotland's foremost folk singers, Alastair Hullet, explains, 'Cam Ye Ower Frae France' is a scathing attack on the new Hanoverian King George that possesses an astonishing level of vitriol. These authentic period pieces gave rise to the use of faux-Jacobite verse as a veil for promoting egalitarian ideas in support of a universal franchise and social equality. This was at a time when Britain was a virtual police state and many of the 'Jacobite' songs form part of this legacy.

In 1793, in Dumfries, Burns was effectively on trial because a government spy had told his employer, Her Majesty's Custom and Excise, that he was the head of a group of Jacobin sympathisers. Burns responded by denying all, writing a letter to his employer stating, 'I know of no party in this place, either Republican or Reform, with which I never had anything to do . . .'[26] However, privately and anonymously he continued to write poetry for the movement. 'A Man's a Man for a' That' was written two years after he took his vow of silence. He described it as the ideas of Tom Paine's *Rights of Man* worked up into verse. One stanza says:

> Ye see yon birkie, ca'd a lord,
> Wha struts, an' stares, an' a' that;
> Tho' hundreds worship at his word,
> He's but a coof for a' that:
> For a' that, an' a' that,
> His ribband, star, an' a' that:
> The man o' independent mind
> He looks an' laughs at a' that.

It ends:

> Then let us pray that come it may,
> (As come it will for a' that,)
> That Sense and Worth, o'er a' the earth,

> Shall bear the gree, an' a' that.
> For a' that, an' a' that,
> It's coming yet for a' that,
> That Man to Man, the world o'er,
> Shall brothers be for a' that.

Burns took his display of loyalty further. In 1795 he signed a petition to set up the Dumfries Volunteers to resist a French invasion, and then wrote them an anti-French anthem. He was not the first to run for cover when times were hard, but his allegiances remained true.

He also wrote songs and poems for the movement he supported. One of his most famous songs was a contender for modern Scotland's national anthem, 'Scots Wha Hae'. It was published anonymously in 1793, coinciding with the trial of the most prominent Scottish champion of the French Revolution, Thomas Muir. Bruce's army marched to its tune on the way to Bannockburn, or so Burns believed. Its words are an attack on tyrants and despots, and a call for liberty.

> Scots, wha hae wi' Wallace bled,
> Scots, wham Bruce has aften led;
> Welcome tae your gory bed
> Or tae victorie.
>
> Now's the day and now's the hour;
> See the front o' battle lour;
> See approach proud Edward's power –
> Chains and slaverie.
>
> Wha will be a traitor knave?
> Wha can fill a coward's grave?
> Wha sae base as be a slave?
> Let him turn and flee.

When news of Burns's death, in 1796, reached Belfast, the *Northern Star*, newspaper of the republican United Irishmen, published 'Scots Wha Hae'. Their rebellion would follow two years later. Unfortunately,

French help arrived too little and too late, and the British administration in Ireland had sufficient time to prepare. Although initially successful, the United Irishmen were eventually defeated and subject to merciless persecution.

'Scots Wha Hae' would be sung by radical reformers and Chartists in the 1820s, '30s and '40s, not simply in Scotland but south of the border too, in tribute to the idea of freedom. In 1839, the Chartist leader Feargus O'Connor, touring Scortland, reported back from Kilmarnock that the 'whole population' could sing the song in perfect harmony.[27] Few of those who recite 'Scots Wha Hae' at school or at a Burns Supper will be aware they are inciting revolution.

SIX

Radicals and Chartists

At the close of the eighteenth century, class warfare erupted into life in central Scotland. In 1787, Calton was a village on the outskirts of Glasgow and home to a burgeoning community of weavers, most of whom were members of the Clyde Valley General Weavers Association – a risky thing when unions were proscribed. In June of that year the weavers learned that the manufacturers planned to reduce their payments for weaving muslin. This came on top of other cuts, which in total would now mean a reduction in wages by a quarter.[1]

The weavers refused to work for the new rates and gathered on Glasgow Green for a mass meeting where they elected committees 'to meet with the master, receive their ultimatums and report'. When negotiation failed, they seized the webs from the looms of three weavers who refused to stop work, and carried them in procession through the town.[2]

Throughout that summer, Glasgow was gripped by tensions, with the authorities itching for a showdown. On 3 September the Lord Provost, along with the magistrates and city sheriff, tried to address a crowd of several hundred weavers, demanding they return to work. The authorities were met by a hail of missiles and retreated quickly, but that afternoon they returned with soldiers. When missiles were again thrown the order was given to open fire. Three weavers were shot dead immediately and three others later died of their wounds. Some six thousand people attended the funeral of the first three.

The next day the city council issued a proclamation describing the shootings as a 'disagreeable necessity', but warning they would 'continue their utmost exertions to suppress these daring combinations, by every legal means within their power, whatever the consequences may be to the unfortunate individuals, who may suffer by these exertions'.[3]

Despite their regrets, the council had rewarded the soldiers and bought their officers a dinner at the Tontine Tavern. They also pressed ahead with the prosecution of James Granger, charged with organising a union ('combination') and assaulting two scabs. At his trial in Edinburgh he was found guilty, despite his vehement denials that he was involved in any violence, and sentenced to be whipped through the capital's streets by the common executioners before being transported to Australia for seven years.

Faced with all this, the strikers returned to work. After his exile Granger returned to Glasgow, where he died aged seventy-five and was buried alongside the three weavers who had been shot. Fifty years after the killings a monument was erected at the Abercromby Street Burial Ground in Bridgeton. The inscription on one stone read: 'They are unworthy of freedom who expect it from other hands than their own.'[4]

Two years after the weavers' strike, the French Revolution of 1789 impacted directly on a society where democracy was in short supply, with the country ruled by a landed oligarchy centred on the figure of Henry Dundas. It was calculated that in the 1796 general election Dundas controlled or influenced thirty-six out of Scotland's forty-five parliamentary seats. Dundas was also treasurer of the navy, and his secretary, Alexander Trotter of Dreghorn, was in the habit of walking across the road from the naval secretary's office, depositing a cheque for £100,000 in his personal account at his cousin's bank, Coutts, and sometime later paying back the amount but keeping the interest – a slice of which went to Dundas and some to improving the family home, Dreghorn Castle, outside Edinburgh.

In the aftermath of the eruption in Paris, May 1789 saw the government ban 'seditious' meetings and pamphlets. On 4 June, King George III's birthday, rioting occurred in Edinburgh, lasting for three nights, with an effigy of 'King Henry IX' (Dundas) being burned in the streets and the windows of his brother Robert, the lord advocate, being smashed. Troops were rushed in and gunfire used to quell the riot, killing one man and wounding six others. Three men were brought to trial for this, with two being found not guilty while another, Alexander Lochie, was sentenced to be transported for fourteen years. He was subsequently set free on remission. His lawyer was a young radical, Thomas Muir of Huntershill.

Across Scotland, effigies of Dundas were burned in towns and villages, in the Borders, toll-bars were attacked and in Portsoy in Banffshire, a cannon was fired by 'the mob' on the anniversary of the French Revolution as the discontent manifested itself in varied forms.[5] From Edinburgh a government spy, informing London regarding the success of Tom Paine's defence of the French Revolution, *The Rights of Man*, reported: 'Paine's book, it is known, has been industriously circulated among the lower classes of our people, and its damnable doctrines eagerly embraced by them. Of liberty and equality they are constantly talking, and making laws, fixing prices on every necessity of life.'[6]

In Edinburgh, on 4 June 1792, the celebrations of King George III's birthday took a novel turn. The city authorities knew pro-democracy handbills calling for protest had been circulating and stationed city constables and soldiers accordingly, but they were surprised by the thousands who took to the streets in protest. The city elite gathered in Parliament House to toast the king and to watch the customary fireworks. The mob outside tore down a sentry box on the High Street and carried it off to the Netherbow to be burned. The Sheriff Depute then read the Riot Act but was stoned by the crowd. Dragoons were then called from the castle and Musselburgh to clear the streets. Two nights of rioting followed. On the night of 5 June a crowd numbering 2,000 gathered in George Square to burn an effigy of Henry Dundas and afterwards to attack the house of his mother, Lady Arniston. After the Riot Act was read again, the military fired on the crowd, killing one and wounding six.[7]

The Scottish Friends of the People, formed in 1792, brought together eighty or so different clubs and societies, from Wigtown in the south to Thurso in the north. The societies charged members threepence a quarter, allowing skilled workers to join. Each society was in regular correspondence with revolutionaries in France, the Corresponding Societies in England and the United Irishmen.[8]

Perth was one of the new grouping's strongholds, with the Friends of the People being formed on 14 August 1792 during a meeting at the Guildhall. The purpose of that society was to achieve 'A free and Equal Representation of the People (and) A Short Duration of Parliaments'. Among its members were weavers, hatters and other workers and tradesmen. By October 1792 it could claim 1,200 members and send nine delegates to the first Scottish Convention in Edinburgh.[9]

The Scottish Friends of the People was able to bring together 150 delegates at its first convention that December. Its leaders were solidly middle class, including Thomas Muir and a Fife farmer, William Skirving, but membership was open to all. During the convention Muir read out greetings from the United Irishmen, Ireland's first republican organisation centred on Presbyterian radicals in Belfast, which said: 'We rejoice that you do not consider yourselves as merged or melted down into another country and that in the great national question you are still Scotland.' At the end the delegates rose from their seats, held up their right arms and swore the French oath, to 'live free or die'.[10]

News that the French Republic had defeated the invading army of Austria and Prussia at Valmy that August electrified the supporters of the revolution. When in November the French took Brussels, celebrations turned into virtual uprisings. In Perth it was reported that 'several hundred of the lower class' burned Dundas in effigy, shouting 'liberty, equality and no king!' The capture of Brussels by the revolutionary army was celebrated by the erection of a Tree of Liberty at Perth Cross, while church bells were rung from eight in the morning till six at night, and townspeople put lit candles in their windows.

Farther down the Tay, in Dundee, a few people assembled in the High Street, to erect a Tree of Liberty, which was pulled down by some young gentlemen. In response, hundreds took to the streets in response, shouting 'Liberty and Equality'. After smashing the town hall windows they returned to the High Street to re-erect the Tree of Liberty, bearing the scroll 'Liberty, Equality and no Sinecures'. Only the arrival of troops on the following Monday ended the disturbances.[11]

The government tried to organise assemblies in support of Pitt and Dundas, but this tactic backfired because the radicals used them to initiate a debate, and at a second one in Perth, attended by 2,000 people in St John's Church, got a pro-reform resolution passed. Within the Perth Friends of the People the moderate, pro-Whig element denounced the demonstrations and riots, but the more radical wing corresponded with France and began collecting arms, though government spies kept the authorities informed of this.

Protests spread across the county, with an effigy of Dundas being put on trial in Crieff and being burned at the conclusion; in Scone his effigy was hanged on a gibbet; not to be outdone, Perth protesters blew his effigy up with gunpowder. In November 1792 there was a demonstration outside the Perth Hunt Ball, where the Duke of Atholl was greeted with calls for him to be guillotined.

Prussia and Austria, financed by the government of William Pitt the Younger in London, had invaded revolutionary France in July 1793. Pitt, Dundas and company decided to crack down on supporters of the revolution and, on 2 January 1793, James Tytler, editor of the *Historical Register*, was summonsed for advocating non-payment of taxes without universal suffrage, but took flight to America. The lawyer Thomas Muir was arrested on his way to defend Tytler but was released on bail. Three Edinburgh printers, John Morton, James Anderson and Malcolm Craig, were sentenced to nine months' hard labour for making a toast 'to George the Third and last, and damnation to all other crowned heads'.[12]

Muir knew time was running out, and in January 1793 decided to make a 'flying trip' to Paris to argue against the execution of the king on the grounds that it would provoke war. Dundas had declared that he was 'resolved to lay him by the heels on a charge of high treason.' The Lord Justice Clerk, Lord Braxfield, declared Muir an outlaw.[13]

The execution in Paris of Louis XVI, on 21 January 1793, led to the outbreak of war between Britain and revolutionary France on 1 February. It was opposed by the Perth Friends of the People, who three days earlier had held a protest meeting in the Guildhall and published a pamphlet, *A Solemn Protestation Against War*. But war brought a government-orchestrated witch-hunt against the radicals and increased state repression. In October only one delegate went from Perth to the All-British Convention in Edinburgh.

Louis's execution and the subsequent outbreak of war meant Muir faced difficulties returning, eventually doing so via Ireland. On his landing at Portpatrick he was arrested and sent for trial before Braxfield, accused, amongst other charges, of making 'a most inflammatory and seditious [speech] falsely and insidiously representing the Irish and Scottish nations as in a state of oppression and exciting the people to rise up and oppose the government'.[14]

The jury was specially picked, consisting of nine landlords, one bookseller, two bankers and three Edinburgh merchants; when one of these merchants, John Horner, was passing the bench, Lord Braxfield addressed him thus: 'Come awa, Maister Horner, come awa, and help us to hang ane o' thae damned scoundrels.'[15] The verdict was never in doubt. When there was a challenge to a member of the jury who said he would condemn any member of the British Convention, Braxfield dismissed it, saying: 'I hope there is not a gentleman of the jury, or any man in this court, who has not expressed the same sentiment.'[16]

Before sentencing, Muir told the court:

As for me, I am careless and indifferent to my fate. I can look danger, and I can look death in the face; for I am shielded by the consciousness of my own rectitude. I may be condemned to languish in the recesses of a dungeon. I may be doomed to ascend the scaffold. Nothing can deprive me of the recollection of the past; nothing can destroy my inward peace of mind, arising from the remembrance of having discharged my duty.[17]

Braxfield's concluding remarks had no such dignity. They bristled with hatred: 'A government of every country should be just like a corporation, and in this country, it is made up of the landed interest, which alone has a right to be represented'.[18] Muir was sentenced to be transported to the penal colony of Botany Bay in Australia for fourteen years.[19]

He eventually managed to secure his escape from Australia on board an American ship, switched to a Spanish ship to avoid the Royal Navy and landed in Mexico only to be arrested because Spain was now at war with Britain. Transferred to Cuba, he was then sent in a convoy to Spain. The convoy was intercepted by the Royal Navy and Muir took part in the fighting, having his cheek blown off. When his ship was captured a crewman revealed his presence but the captain said he had been killed and so badly disfigured that his corpse could not be recognised. Muir himself was sent ashore with the wounded to Cadiz, and after much wrangling, the French secured his release. Back in Paris, Thomas Muir worked with other Irish, Scottish and English exiles until his sudden death on 26 January 1799.[20]

Back in Scotland, despite Muir's conviction, Skirving pressed on with plans for a further Convention of the Friends of the People in Edinburgh, in November 1793, inviting the United Irishmen and radical democrats from England. Dundas was determined to stop this, and warrants were issued for three of the six English delegates, Maurice Margarot, Joseph Gerrald and Charles Sinclair, as well as Skirving and Alexander Scott, the editor of the radical *Edinburgh Gazetteer.*

On 5 December, the opening session of the convention was broken up by the police, led by Edinburgh's Lord Provost. The next evening, Skirving convened a further session in a joiner's shop. Gerrald was in the chair, and when police arrived carrying lighted torches, he rose and cried, 'Behold the funeral torches of Liberty!' The next evening Skirving tried to hold a street meeting in protest at the dispersal of the convention.[21] The arrest warrants were now carried out and the five men brought before Lord Braxfield. Margarot, Gerrald and Skirving were each sentenced to fourteen years transportation whilst Scott fled the country and Sinclair's case was dropped when he turned informer.

At the trial, Gerrald told the court that the English had deprived the Scottish people of their rights from the time of the Union of 1707, 'But if that Union has operated to rob us of our rights, it is our objective to regain them!' Margarot likewise wrote from his cell that the Scots must form 'armed associations' and 'get arms and learn the use of them'.[22]

Unrest expressed itself in other ways. In 1795, grain exports at a time of hunger and following a poor harvest led a crowd of several hundred to march on the harbour of Annan in Dumfriesshire in an attempt to stop ships sailing.[23] In 1797, the need for extra conscripts to fight the French led Pitt's government to introduce a Militia Bill that forced young men to be conscripted via a ballot, except those who could afford to buy their way out or gain an exemption. This meant the majority facing conscription came from the labouring classes. It was greeted by a wave of rioting. The house of the Duke of Montrose in Dumbarton, the Duke of Atholl's Blair Castle and William Forbes's house in Falkirk came under attack. In Dalry, protesters planted a Tree of Liberty, and in Lanarkshire, they demanded an end to taxation on horses.[24]

At Carstairs a mob burned the schoolhouse and carted off the parish registers. In the mining villages of Prestonpans and Tranent, miners' wives and children, led by Joan Crookston, sacked the village schools and forced the schoolmasters, who were tasked with drawing up the ballots, into hiding. The 'mob' passed a resolution to be sent to the ballot officers, saying: 'Although we may be overpowered . . . and dragged from our parents, friends and employment, to be made soldiers of, you can infer from this what trust can be reposed in us, if ever we are called upon to disperse our fellow-countrymen or to oppose a foreign foe.'[25]

In response, the authorities sent in the Cinque Ports Cavalry from southern England on 28 August, and after the Riot Act was read they charged. The rioters had stones, the cavalry pistols and sabers. After dispersing the crowd, the horsemen attacked innocent travelers and farmers. The official death toll was eleven.[26]

In the Perthshire Highlands, it was reported that 16,000 people mobilised at a call from Angus Cameron, a wright from Weem, forcing the Duke of Atholl to pledge that the ballot would not be held there. The crowd then marched on Taymouth Castle in search of arms, but when government troops arrived they melted away. Cameron was caught and tried but, on being bailed, fled.

In the spring of 1797 a new secret body, the United Scotsmen, was growing in support. It was organised into cells modelled on the United Irishmen, who were planning an insurrection to take place the next year.

In Perth the radicals set up such an organisation. Reports circulated of one group of twenty men drilling with arms in Auchterarder and other towns. Nevertheless, government agents succeeded in infiltrating the group, and Walter Miller and Robert Sands were amongst many radicals arrested in what was called the 'Pike Plot'. They were charged with trying to obtain 4,000 pikes. Sands spent seven months in Edinburgh awaiting trial.[27]

An uprising was planned, with the first target being the houses of the very rich, but it was betrayed by government informers. In Dundee, George Mealmaker, a weaver, was tried on the charge of delivering illegal oaths and distributing seditious literature, and transported for fourteen years by a jury made up of men who believed their homes were targeted for burning. Other arrests took place and the United Scotsmen were broken by repression. Robert Watt's end was a gruesome business, for he was hanged at the Tolbooth on Edinburgh's High Street, after which his body was cut down and laid on a table. The head was cut off, with the executioner holding it up and crying, 'This is the head of a traitor.'[28]

Radicals were silenced and driven underground for a decade and a half as Britain pursued its war with Napoleon. The reign of Dundas did, however, come to an end. He had been pocketing money from naval funds for years, but by 1805 (the year of the Battle of Trafalgar) money was scarce and sailors had to do without pay. Dundas was impeached, and while he escaped a guilty verdict, he had to resign in shame and died shortly afterwards.[29]

The Radical Legacy

Today the Thomas Muir memorial that stands outside his home in Huntershill carries his statement "I have devoted myself to the cause of the people. It is a good cause. It shall ultimately prevail. It shall finally triumph.'[30]

In this manner Scottish radicals could combine appeals to Anglo-Saxon (English) liberty with the reaffirmation of a native Scottish radical tradition. At the first convention in Edinburgh, a young Scottish medical student, Alexander Aitchison, told delegates: 'But in faith we had nothing more to ask, than to be restored to our original rights – That he was certain that by the English Constitution so long ago as the days of King Arthur every free man had a vote in choosing his representative and that in those days Parliaments were annual.'[31]

At his trial Thomas Muir fought on the grounds of free speech; meanwhile, his fellow defendant William Skirving drew on the gains of the 1688–89 revolution and made comparison with the repression of radicals and the religious persecution in the sixteenth century, adding that the High Court of Judiciary might be compared to the Star Chamber and saying his trial represented 'a revival of the conventicler persecutions with a vengeance.'[32]

After his escape to revolutionary France, Thomas Muir took up this theme, writing a brief history of Scotland for its government that defended the Calvinist republicans of the sixteenth century and strongly denied the accusation that these were simply religious fanatics.[33]

Identification with past struggles for freedom was something evident in radical politics: in 1810, for example, the colliers of Falkirk laid the Wallacestone, a monumental stone, on the site where Wallace's army camped before the Battle of Falkirk. The radicals focused more on Falkirk, because of the betrayal of the people by the nobility which resulted in defeat, whereas the upper classes concentrated on the victory at Stirling Bridge.[34] In 1844, the Scottish Political Martyrs Monument was erected in Edinburgh's Old Calton Cemetery, by the Friends of Parliamentary Reform in England and Scotland. The funds had been raised by public collection. It commemorates Muir, Thomas Fyshe Palmer, William Skirving, Maurice Margarot and Joseph Gerrald – the Scottish Martyrs.

In the twentieth century, Adam MacHaughton would write this song, 'Thomas Muir of Huntershill':

> My name is Thomas Muir, as a lawyer I was trained,
> Remember Thomas Muir of Huntershill.

But you've branded me an outlaw, for sedition I'm arraigned,
Remember Thomas Muir of Huntershill . . . Gerrard, Palmer,
Skirving, Thomas Muir and Margarot,

These are names that every Scottish man and woman ought to
know . . .[35]

The Radical Wars

As Scotland entered the nineteenth century, class warfare was never
far beneath the surface, whatever repressive measures were employed.
Despite the suppression of radical groups, the first decade of the
nineteenth century saw a Scotland-wide strike by paper workers, a
series of strikes by calico printers in defence of working conditions
and, in 1808, the founding of the General Association of Operative
Weavers in Scotland. They demanded minimum payments for their
work, and to win for their members '. . . fair hours and proper appli-
cation, to feed, clothe and accommodate himself and his family'.[36]

When their demands were rejected, they struck, with some 30,000
looms lying idle. They also went to court, using legislation that
allowed Justices of the Peace to regulate wages, and won. The employers ignored the verdict and the courts did not enforce their
adjudication. The sheriffs of Lanarkshire and Renfrewshire instead
had the strike organisers arrested, and as the strike crumbled the law
regulating wages was scrapped.

Between 1780 and 1820 the number of weavers increased from
25,000 to 78,000, but that increase served to cut wages. In addition,
the years immediately after the end of the Napoleonic Wars in 1815
saw an economic depression and rising food prices. The English
reformer William Cobbett, touring Scotland and blaming bad
government for people's ills, advocated a complete change of government. In October 1816, an estimated 40,000 people came to hear
him talk at Thrushgrove outside Glasgow. This was the biggest political gathering in the country's history and heralded a new age of mass
political involvement.

On 18 August 1812, Edinburgh's new police force, together with soldiers from the castle, were sent to deal with 'a riotous crowd in the Grassmarket who had seized meal carts and attacked the homes of meal-sellers after an extraordinary rise in the price of oatmeal'.[37] A further riot broke out in December 1818 after the bungled execution of one Robert Johnson outside the main post office in the High Street. The rope was too long and the crowd rescued Johnson before magistrates and police took him back, revived him and hanged him to death. In the rioting that followed, 'nearly 200 panes of glass were smashed in the vicinity'.[38]

In September 1819, the *Edinburgh Magazine* reported on events from the 11th of that month, when a crowd of 12,000–18,000 had gathered for a reform rally at which sheriffs had banned flags and banners, sending in constables to seize them: 'The crowd resisted and commenced throwing stones and other missiles, by which the council chamber windows were broken.'

The magistrates called in troops from Glasgow, and by three a.m. they had dispersed the crowd, but rioting broke out again the next day, Sunday, when the magistrates went to church: 'They were insulted by the populace and rioting again commenced, and many enormities committed. The riot act was read thrice before nine o'clock; and the military in clearing the streets were at one time seriously opposed by numbers who had armed themselves with bars of iron from the railings in front of a church.'

The next day, crowds gathered but soldiers cleared the streets after the Riot Act was again read. But that night trouble broke out in Glasgow: '. . . a mob collected to the amount of 3000, apparently for the sole purpose of mischief and plunder. They accordingly proceeded to break the lamps in different streets, to plunder provision shops, and to attack some private homes.' At 9 p.m. the Riot Act was read and soldiers sent in to retake the streets.[39] In the wake of the cutting down of scores of demonstrators demanding parliamentary reform at Peterloo in Manchester, a protest rally in September 1819 drew 15,000 to 18,000 to Meikleriggs Moor outside Paisley. As the rally ended, a crowd marched down Paisley High Street carrying flags in defiance of orders from the authorities banning such protest. Special constables, the magistrates and the town provost blocked their route, and the provost ordered the flags to be seized. In the fighting that followed, the forces of law and order fled, leaving the rioters in control of the town. For five days the people had control, with running battles taking place whenever the authorities tried to inter-fere. Eventually troops were brought in to restore order.[40] Radicals also demonstrated in Johnstone, with banners proclaiming, 'Sir William Wallace like our ancestors we'll defend our liberty and our laws' and 'We are the descendants of Wallace and Bruce'.[41]

The fire of rebellion continued to smoulder, and across the West of Scotland there was talk of an uprising, but when it came it was abortive. On 1 April 1820, posters appeared in Ayr, Dumbarton, Glasgow and Renfrew proclaiming the creation of a Scottish provi-sional government. The 'Address to the Inhabitants of Great Britain and Ireland' called on soldiers to transfer their loyalties from despotism to freedom, and on workers to strike until their rights as free men had been recovered. The address also proclaimed an immi-nent armed uprising in Scotland and England. Sixty thousand workers – mainly weavers and cotton spinners, but also coal miners, machine-makers and foundry workers – struck in and around Glas-gow in the first general strike in history. 'Almost the whole population of the working classes have obeyed the orders contained in the treasonable proclamation by striking work', wrote the Lord Provost of Glasgow to the Home Office.[42] One historian notes: 'For several days, an estimated 50,000 in the industrial west stopped work and some groups openly carried weapons and took part in military drill.'[43]

The posters had also said there would be an uprising in Glasgow with two bands of radicals assembling, one on Cathkin Braes to the south of the city and one to the north in the Campsie Hills. The authorities moved quickly to mobilise every possible soldier and yeoman, ensuring that the population of the city felt quelled. But a dozen miles south, a band of a dozen or so weavers set off for Cathkin Braes from Strathaven, led by a long-time activist, James Wilson, and carrying a banner with the words 'Scotland free or a desert' (Tacitus's words being used for an altogether different purpose). At East

Kilbride they were told there was no uprising, but pressed on to Cathkin Braes with hopes that would be dashed.

Meanwhile, in Glasgow a band led by Andrew Harvie assembled in Anderston, aiming at seizing the Carron Iron Works, with its stock of cannon and ammunition. They marched along the Forth and Clyde Canal and at Condorrat were joined by another group, led by John Baird. Passing through Castlecary, the band was spotted by a soldier who warned the garrison at Kilsyth, which moved to intercept the radicals, catching them at Bonnymuir outside Bonnybridge. In the ensuing engagement, four of the radicals were wounded before all forty-seven were captured. They were armed with just five muskets, two pistols and pikes.

The government in London demanded a special commission be set up to try the rebels under English law, so they could face the charge of high treason. Eighty-eight people were found guilty, most being sentenced to transportation and three, Hardie, Baird and James Wilson, to execution. There was little or no evidence against the latter, but he was a thorn in the side of the authorities, who were glad to see him removed. When the public executioner who cut off the dead man's head held it up, shouting 'the head of a traitor', from the crowd came cries of murder. The body was then deposited in a common grave, but his family rescued it and returned it to Strathaven. Elsewhere, the call for a strike and national uprising found strong support that April. On 2 April a general strike took place in Paisley and a mass meeting was held at Maxwelltown to decide how to respond to any attempt by the authorities to intervene. Groups were sent to acquire arms from the homes of landowners, and in the process one striker was shot dead. The next day, Paisley was placed under military occupation, and troops went from house to house searching for arms and to arrest whichever strike leaders they could find.[44] The defeat that followed was due to 'poor planning, the failure of English radicals to respond and the loyalty of the Scottish propertied classes and the military'.[45]

For a long time it was believed the authors of the posters proclaiming the uprising were agents provocateurs, but in 1999 T. M. Devine argued that the evidence indicated that they were written by three weavers from Parkhead in Glasgow, rather than spies.[46]

The impact of such unrest was felt even in rural Scotland. In 1820, Alexander Somerville, a schoolboy in Berwickshire, and his schoolmates played a game of militia versus radicals, with the better-off being the militia. Somerville, a radical, was sentenced to be hanged. Perhaps because of that he wrote sympathetically about the radicals: 'They were people who complained that the country was not governed as it should be, that the laws were not made by those that should have made the laws. They were grieved to be excluded from voting for members of parliament, and they felt at the same time that food was dear, wages low and taxation very high . . . the great body of the radicals was composed of honest working men.'[47]

The Radical War of 1820, as it became known, and the preceding social unrest marked the emergence of the working class as an organised social force in Scotland, and one that, in however a rudimentary form, had already employed the highest forms of class struggle: a general strike and an attempt at armed insurrection. Yet this was also the last gasp of the insurrectionary tradition, which had existed from 1789 onward. In the immediate aftermath, attention switched to securing parliamentary reform and the passing of the 1832 Reform Act, which was blocked by the Tories with their majority in the House of Lords – despite it being a very modest step extending the vote to £10 tenants in the burghs, and £10 owners (only males, of course) in the counties.

The debate that preceded the first Reform Bill brought rioting to Edinburgh's New Town. Fearing that the legislation might be blocked, a crowd of 10,000 gathered in the High Street. Supporters of reform had 'illuminated' their windows by lighting candles. Noting the lack of light in the windows of the New Town, the crowd moved down there, smashing the windows of the Lord Provost and touring the streets, breaking unlit windows and chanting, 'Up with the Reform light, down with Tory darkness'.[48] In Glasgow, 100,000 people marched in support of this Whig measure.

When the House of Lords kicked out the bill in 1831, things took a more serious turn. In Lanark, the Tories were attacked at the hustings and, after the Riot Act was read, soldiers charged the crowd. In Hawick, a hundred weavers gave Walter Scott a rough welcome;

and in Rothesay, Lady Bute was stoned as she drove in her carriage. (Thomas Johnston points out the instigator as a Whig mill owner who was happy to employ children under five.) In May 1832, workers across Glasgow struck and 120,000 marched with banners saying 'Liberty or Death' and 'Better to die in a good cause than live in slavery'.[49]

In Perth, 7,000 people, described in contemporary accounts as being overwhelmingly working class, marched through the town. There was no violence but it was also a show of strength that frightened the local aristocracy and bourgeoisie.[50]

When the reforms were passed and finally received royal assent from a reluctant William IV, it was discovered that property qualifications effectively barred the working class from having the vote. This reality led to further radicalisation and Chartism. Neither did the passing of the Reform Act change the daily reality of the relationship between employers and workers, even though many of the employers had supported the bill, and had even joined demonstrations in its support. When it came to dealing with their own workers, they remained ruthless. Consequently, by 1833 the West of Scotland Female Powerloom Weavers Association could boast 6,000 members.[51]

The confidence of the women and the solidarity between the male mechanics (tenters) and the power-loom weavers is illustrated by the following incident in Glasgow. A male handloom weaver, James Hewit, took a job at Mr Broughton's factory. The majority of the power-loom weavers were women and they were angered that Hewit had accepted wages two shillings less than the union rate. On a late, dark December afternoon the gas lights suddenly went out on the factory floor. A crowd of women weavers emerged from the dark to jeer at Hewit and by force of numbers ushered him into a dark corridor where the waiting Mary Morrie struck him with her 'loom semple'. A manager rushed in and immediately sacked two women he regarded as ringleaders, Janet Cain and Sarah Quin, but Cain just 'shook her fist in [Hewit's] face and called him all the old buggers she could think of – said it was he who was the cause of this and if God spared her she would be revenged on him'.[52]

Cain was as good as her word. When Hewit left work that night he was surrounded by a crowd of women, and Cain and Quin set about him, with the former stabbing him in the eye with her power-loom hook.

In 1833, employers launched a full-scale assault on the unions. The masters of calico printing introduced women and children together with impoverished hand-loom weavers to replace higher-paid male workers. They underestimated the solidarity of the local communities and the determination of the existing workforce, which went on strike. When scabs tried to start work at Kelvindock (in Maryhill, Glasgow), women power-loom weavers from a neighbouring factory joined the strikers, all of whom lived in nearby Botany Row (also known as Reform Row), and stoned them. Eventually the dispute was resolved and the male workers accepted their female counterparts.[53]

The cotton spinners were also well organised in the city, but by 1837 demand was falling and employers cut wages. The Glasgow Cotton Spinners Union called a strike and the employers began a lockout. The dispute was a violent one, and the spinners' leaders were arrested and stood trial for murder and conspiracy. Five of them were sentenced to transportation after being found guilty of lesser charges. After three weeks, funds were exhausted and the union said they would accept the wage cuts and return to work. But the employers said wages would now be cut by 40 percent. The strike continued, sustained by regular collections and donations from Manchester and the Lancashire cotton industry.[54]

The employers then recruited large numbers of scabs, or 'nobs', housed inside the factories to avoid pickets. One did leave to go shopping with his wife in the city centre in July 1837, and was waylaid by strike supporters and shot from behind, dying shortly afterwards from his wounds. A reward of £600 was offered for the arrest of the guilty men, and consequently two former spinners went to the notoriously anti-strike Sheriff of Lanarkshire, who, acting on their claims, issued arrest warrants for the entire strike committee. A few days later the man reputed to be the killer was arrested. He and four members of the union executive were brought to trial in

Edinburgh in January 1838. The prosecution was carried out by Sheriff Archibald Alison, a Tory who regarded unions as a 'moral pestilence' and believed Glasgow was in the grip of 'insurrectionary fever.' He could provide no evidence associating the men with the killing, but that did not stop the Whig judge, Lord Cockburn, from sentencing them to seven years' transportation.[55]

Their trial and the campaign to secure their return to Scotland coincided with the launch in London and Birmingham that year of the People's Charter and its six demands – universal suffrage, and end to property qualifications, a secret ballot, equal electoral constituencies, payment of MPs and annual parliaments. The case of the Glasgow cotton spinners became a major factor in the Chartists developing a national profile across Britain. The defeat of the strike encouraged Scottish workers to look to political change, through Chartism. The effect of its defeat, rising unemployment, attacks on the unions and the abundance of cheap labour, as a consequence of the Highland Clearances and Irish Famine, not only undercut industrial militancy, but also helped ensure the timidity of Scottish Chartism.

Chartism in Scotland

As the cotton spinners were being deported to Australia, the first of the more famous Tolpuddle Martyrs were returning from their sojourn abroad. They addressed meetings in support of the Glasgow spinners along with the Chartist leaders Feargus O'Connor, Augustus Beaumont and Bronterre O'Brien. The Irish champion of Catholic emancipation, Daniel O'Connell, formerly regarded with favour by British radicals, chose the Glasgow case as a way of attacking trade unions, causing great bitterness.[56] In Glasgow itself, it was claimed that 200,000 people attended a Chartist rally in support of the strikers in May 1838, which helped the Chartists establish themselves in Scotland.

A Newcastle Chartist broadsheet published the following:

Ye working men of Britain come listen awhile,
Concerning the cotton spinners who lately stood their trial,

Transported for seven years far, far awa'
Because they were united men in Caledonia.

Success to our friends in Ireland, who boldly stood our cause,
In spite of O'Connell and his support of whiggish laws,
Away with his politics, they are not worth a straw,
He's no friend of the poor in Ireland or Caledonia.

Success to O'Connor who did nobly plead our cause,
Likewise to Mr Beaumont, who abhors oppressive laws,
But all their efforts, justice and law,
We are banished from our country, sweet Caledonia.

Whigs and Tories are united, we see it very plain,
To crush the poor labourer, it is their daily aim,
The proverb now is verified, and that you can all knaw,
In the case of those poor cotton spinners in Caledonia.[57]

The historian W. Hamish Fraser stresses the significance of the cotton spinners' strike in 1837:

> . . . the full weight of the united capitalism, plus the state, was brought to bear to smash the hand mulespinners' union. It was the end of an era . . . Like the miners' strike of 1984–85, the implications of the defeat of the spinners went far beyond their own union. It had great symbolic importance, marking the defeat and break up of an organisation that, for two decades, had been the most tightly knit and dynamic in Scottish society. It was a deterrent to vigorous action.[58]

In his history of Chartism in Britain, John Charlton contrasts Chartism in Scotland, 'marked, largely, by its moderation' and Chartism in Wales, which had an insurrectionary character.[59] This was by no means because of lack of support. The cotton weavers of Glasgow, the shawl weavers of Paisley and the linen and jute weavers of Dundee gave great support to Chartism. One report from Dunfermline said: 'Among the weavers there are 1800 who pay for newspapers – those go into the workshops and are read by all the men and boys in them so that a man who does not read newspapers is rarely met with . . .'[60] In Aberdeen, 10,000 people attended a Chartist rally in August 1838 and the city provided more than 8,500 signatures for the first national petition, which was presented to Parliament, and rejected, that year.[61]

Summer 1842 saw the first general strike in world history. Its storm centre was north-west England but it spread to Scotland, and Dundee in particular, where local Chartists provided leadership. In August, a public meeting demanded that wages, which had been cut due to an economic downturn, be returned to their 1839 level. Shortly afterwards a hundred delegates from forty-six of the town's fifty-one textile mills agreed to strike for the People's Charter. The vote was put to a mass meeting of up to 14,000 on Magdalene Green the next day, and agreed.

In response, at Baxter's in Maxwelltown, twenty-four weavers were told by the owner he would give them a rise when the other owners did, and that they should leave their looms under his lock and key. They struck immediately. At Ferguson's, the owner expressed sympathy but refused any rise. The sixty-one weavers there declared they were 'ready to strike for the Charter, but not for wages'. At Blaikie's, the seventy-five men similarly said they would 'not identify themselves with the movement for wages but turn out for political privileges'. At Walker's Mill the twenty-nine workers were striking for the Charter, the same at Johnson's Lower Factory, while the seventy workers at Steel and Hutton wanted 'to go full hog, but not for wages'.[62]

The strike began on 22 August but many of the city's mills and factories kept running, so the next day, a procession of strikers tried to march on the mills on Perth Road. A local magistrate and mill owner read the Riot Act and police dispersed the demonstrators. Nevertheless, 400 marched to Forfar to join their brothers and sisters there. After a march through the town they returned to Dundee. That town's magistrates then enrolled special constables to bolster the police and banned all assemblies, effectively breaking the strike. Several Chartist leaders were tried and jailed for their role in the affair.[63]

In the coalfields that August, 12,000 miners in the Monklands and Glasgow districts were out on strike, with a network of strike committees. The strike spread into Ayrshire, Midlothian and East Lothian. The issue was wages and conditions, but there was considerable support for the Charter. In Monklands, Chartist branches were active in Coatbridge, Airdrie and Holytown, leading the sheriff there to believe he was facing a Chartist-led uprising.

For the first three days of the strike, across North Lanarkshire, miners patrolled the roads, picketing and holding marches and rallies. There was no strike fund, and with some 70,000 mouths to feed the miners took food from farms and gardens, seized it from carts and looted company stores. Large groups of women from Dundyvan attacked strikebreakers. Police and troops were drafted in from Glasgow and Edinburgh to face the unrest, and the local sheriff-led cavalry went on night-time patrols. Anyone caught taking food faced sixty days in jail.

In short order, a number of companies conceded and as the number of strikers fell the authorities cracked down hard on the remainder, with three Ayrshire miners sentenced to be transported for ten years, as were six Airdrie miners who had besieged the local prison, freeing miners held there. By October, the miners had returned to work, the majority having lost the fight.[64]

Nevertheless, the 'moral force' of Chartism remains true. Scotland led the way in establishing formal Chartist churches – the first being set up in May 1839 in Hamilton, Paisley and Bridgeton. Two years later, a convention of Chartist churches boasted they existed from Ayr to Aberdeen.[65] Temperance also marked Scottish Chartism, and this created a tradition where working-class meetings did not take place in pubs.

The authorities in London, fearing revolution, faced down Chartist attempts to force acceptance of their demands between 1839 and 1842. They were not hampered by any debate about whether to use moral or physical force, and were quick to unleash repression.

Hunger, not the Charter, was the root cause of rioting in 1846, as the potato crop failed across Scotland and Ireland, threatening starvation in the Highlands and causing deadly famine in Ireland. In Macduff, crowds barricaded the quay to stop food exports and looted shops. In Aberdeen, flour mills and carts were seized. The sheriff was forced to release rioters when the crowd intervened, and in Avoch, when the sheriff read the Riot Act, the people replied that they might as well be shot as starved. Warships were moved into the Moray Firth and soldiers sent to Caithness before the government initiated a relief fund that ensured people were fed.[66]

Scotland marked 1848, a year of revolution across Europe, by economic downturn and unemployment. On 6 March a crowd of several hundred unemployed rallied on Glasgow Green to protest the City Council's failure to deliver on the promise of soup kitchens. All seemed to have passed peacefully, and police had returned to the Central Police Station when crowds began attacking food shops and a gun shop in the Trongate and London Road. During the Glasgow riots, Chartist slogans were shouted along with cries of 'Vive la Republique', stoking fears among the upper classes.[66] For two hours the crowd controlled the city centre until troops were brought in. The next day, rioting broke out in Bridgeton, where special constables opened fire, shooting six people.[67] The *Sunday Post* complained that the police had left the city in the hands of rioters for two hours.

The wave of revolutions that swept Europe in 1848 encouraged a revival of the Chartists and a new sense of militancy. The economy was in recession with between 30,000 and 40,000 receiving relief (food handouts) in Paisley alone. The lack of genuine relief and the excitement caused by news of revolution in France, which had overthrown the monarchy, encouraged unrest.[67] In both Paisley and Airdrie railway lines were torn up.

April saw major demonstrations, with Ernest Jones, an English friend of Karl Marx, addressing a rally of 25,000–30,000 in Edinburgh and 30,000 in Paisley. In Glasgow the organisers claimed 100,000 were present, the *Scotsman* reported 25,000 and the *Glasgow Herald* 40,000.[68] In Aberdeen, 5,000 Chartists defied the police, and in Holytown in Lanarkshire the yeomanry reported a 'slight brush' with miners. There were meetings in Dundee, Dunfermline and other towns across Scotland.[69]

There was further unrest in Edinburgh in July when a rally on Calton Hill was followed by a crowd demonstrating outside Calton Jail, which was prevented from proceeding to County Hall only by a specially mobilised police force.

The question of using physical force came to the fore once more. Could the workers succeed without their own force? From France came the example of the National Guard, based on the popular militia that emerged in revolutionary Paris. An Edinburgh Chartist told an audience in Dundee that it was absolutely necessary to overthrow the government, or in a short time they would all be starved. He asked the hall: 'Was William Wallace a moral force man?'[70]

One Irish nationalist, John Daly, told a Glasgow Chartist rally: 'Prayers and petitions are the weapons of cowards, arms are the weapons used by the free and the brave.' They could best help Ireland by keeping the army in Scotland.[71]

Just the discussion of physical force was enough to get the authorities nervous, leading to a number of prosecutions. Among those put on trial was an elderly shoemaker, James Cumming, charged, on the basis of an intercepted letter, with forming a National Guard. At his trial details of this National Guard and the clubs affiliated to it were made known:

[Thomas] 'Muir Club,' 200 [members]; [John] 'Mitchell [Irish nationalist leader] Club,' 56; [John and Andrew] 'Baird and Hardie [executed in Stirling in 1820] Club,' 20; [Joseph] 'Gerald [the London Corresponding Delegate to the 1793 People's Convention in Edinburgh, who was deported with Hardie] Club,' 26; [Robert] 'Burns Club,' 25; [George] 'Washington Club,' 25; [Feargus] 'O'Connor [Irish Chartist leader] Club,' 12; Besides these there were 500 enrolled in the National Guard and an unascertained number in the [Robert] 'Emmet [Irish nationalist executed after the 1803 rising] Club.' The National Guard had given an order for 40 muskets with bayonets, 'but a great many have provided themselves with arms.'[72]

Things came to a head later that year when, in the wake of the Chartists' disastrous attempt to deliver the last monster petition to Parliament, which was called off by the leaders, faced with the might of the state forces guarding London's Whitehall. After this failure the movement declined in Scotland, as elsewhere.

One legacy of Chartism was that Karl Marx and Friedrich Engels's *Communist Manifesto* first appeared in English in the radical Chartist paper the *Red Republican*, translated by a Scotswoman, Helen McFarlane. Louise Yeoman of BBC Scotland took up McFarlane's story in November 2012. She was born in Crosshill near Barrhead in 1818 to a wealthy family prepared to bring in troops to break strikes. But her father went bankrupt and she had to become a governess. Finding work in Vienna, she experienced the tumults there in 1848 and was, in turn, won to revolution. Back in London, she threw herself into the left wing of the Chartist movement.

McFarlane was the first translator of the *Communist Manifesto*, using the male pen name Howard Morton. She was a feminist, fighting for a world without slaves. 'A republic without poor; without classes . . . a society, such indeed as the world has never yet seen, not only of free men, but of free women', she wrote. No wonder Karl Marx called her a 'rara avis', a rare bird, and praised her original ideas.[73]

McFarlane fell out with the editor of the *Red Republican* and married a French revolutionary exile, Francis Proust, but when the family attempted to emigrate to South Africa her husband became ill and had to be taken off the ship before it sailed. Subsequently her baby daughter died in South Africa. She returned to find her husband was dead. She then re-married a Church of England minister but died at the age of forty-one in 1860.

Chartism failed in its immediate goal of securing the demands of the People's Charter, but in Scotland and elsewhere it laid the groundwork for the emergence of a strong trades union organisation and for the political representation of the labour movement in the British Parliament.

SEVEN

The Highland Clearances and Resistance

I n 1750, a third of Scotland's population still lived north of the Highland Line; today it is just 5 percent. In 1811, there were 250,000 sheep there; by the 1840s there were almost a million. Within that period sheep replaced people driven from their homes by direct eviction or through hunger and destitution. After the sheep and overgrazing came deer and the creation of hunting grounds for the elite. By 1884, a tenth of Scotland's land was given over to deer forests, an area greater than the size of Wales, and taking up the great majority of the land in the crofting counties.[1] These bald facts are the result of the darkest chapter in Scottish history – the Highland Clearances.

At the time of Culloden, townships existed across the Highlands and Islands, even in what are now remote glens. Their ruins can still be found among the bracken and the heather. These were made up of clachans, a collection of stone-and-turf houses and their outbuildings. Close to them lay the best land on which the people grew crops. Outside the settlements was a mix of arable, grazing and fallow land, and beyond that common grazing land. Cattle were sold or traded, alongside horses and butter. This was a feudal society and hunger was never far away. The land was allocated by the tacksman, who was the main leaseholder from the landowner, and rent was paid to him.

Culloden was not followed immediately by the Clearances, but it did bring fundamental changes. Already the Duke of Argyll leased his lands to those who'd pay best, rather than to his supposed Campbell kin. Mass evictions had already taken place. After the battle, the feudal rights of the Highland nobility were destroyed and the Highlanders disarmed, and the clan chiefs now sought to maximise revenues either to improve their estates or to pay for a lavish lifestyle far away in Edinburgh or London. 'Improvement', another term for profitability, was carried out by landowners with no respect for the wishes of their tenants.

In Perthshire and Argyll, land was sold or leased to small or middle-sized farmers who could make a living off it, but that was not the case farther north. Here, tenants were evicted from the good arable land and moved onto what was once regarded as common land, and here new townships were created.

These new townships were based on the assumption that crofting was not sufficient to support a family and therefore the workers would need to seek employment from the landlord in order to feed their families. There was little incentive to improve the land, because too often that would mean a rent increase. In coastal areas crofters were encouraged to work in fishing and in making kelp – the burning of seaweed to make soda ash, which was sold to the southern manufacturers of glass and soap. Both industries boomed during the Napoleonic Wars when imports were cut off by the French occupation of much of Europe. Wartime demand for fish and beef also ensured a degree of prosperity.

The communities of the south and east experienced modest population growth, but that of the western seaboard and islands was more pronounced, growing by 55 percent between 1801 and 1841.[2] Ullapool was established in the 1780s by the British Fishing Society on land bought from the Cromartie Estate, in order to provide employment in the fishing fleets. But from 1815 the decline in demand for kelp and beef coincided with a sudden fall in the herring catch, and the return of young men from the armed forces pitched a fragile economy into crisis. The potato, which until now had never been central to Highland life, now became the main form of sustenance for many and an easy crop to grow.

Meanwhile, the landlords continued to develop large sheep-grazing farms, with Cheviot and Blackface sheep – bigger sheep that needed more grazing land – that were imported from the Lowlands along with shepherds, factors and estate managers. These new sheep needed to be brought down from the hills, onto what had once been arable land, and they took over pasture where Highlanders had raised their cattle and their smaller breed of sheep.

There had already been opposition to this. More than two decades before Waterloo, in 1792, Bliadhna nan Caorach (Year of the Sheep), there was a virtual uprising in Ross against the new sheep walks, it being reported: '. . . a Mob of about four hundred strong are now actually employed in collecting the sheep over all this and the neighbouring county of Sutherland.' By early August some 6,000 sheep were being driven south. When troops intervened, the men simply melted away. A few were captured, some banished from Scotland and one transported to Botany Bay. The commander of the troops wrote to London, however, that '. . . no disloyalty or spirit of rebellion, or dislike to His Majesty's Person or His Majesty's Government is in the least degree concerned in these tumults.'[3]

The collapse of the Highland economy after the end of the Napoleonic Wars meant landlords now looked to turn over all their lands to sheep grazing, removing the crofters all together. The most infamous Clearances were on the huge estate of the Countess of Sutherland. Her husband, Lord Stafford, removed between 6,000 and 10,000 tenants between 1807 and 1821. The Strath of Kildonan was cleared of its people between 1813 and 1819, with such savagery that it provoked a reaction.

In December 1812, an agent for Lowland sheep farmers visited the Strath, asking questions of the tenants, who proceeded to run him off their land. He immediately claimed he had been threatened with his life, and the Marquess of Stafford grabbed at his claims to mobilise his male estate workers as special constables and to summon a detachment of soldiers. Faced with this resistance, the locals desisted and the Upper Strath was cleared within three months. The crofters were offered re-settlement in the town of Helmsdale or emigration. Many of the young chose to leave for Canada.[4]

However, Stafford's agent, a Lowland Scot named Patrick Sellar, believed this response had been too soft. And so worse was to follow in the parishes of Farr and Kildonan. Later in the century the Highland historian Alexander Mackenzie wrote a *History of the Highland Clearances*, published in 1883, which described Sellar's ill-treatment:

> As the lands were now in the hands of the factor himself, and were to be occupied as sheep farms, and as the people made no resistance, they expected, at least, some indulgence in the way of permission to occupy their houses and other buildings till they could gradually remove, and meanwhile look after their growing crops. Their consternation was therefore greater, when immediately after the May term day, a commencement was made to pull down and set fire to the houses over their heads. The old people, women and others, then began to preserve the timber which was their own but the devastators proceeded with the greatest celerity, demolishing all before them, and when they had overthrown all the houses in a large tract of country they set fire to the wreck. Timber, furniture, and every other article that could not be instantly removed was consumed by fire or otherwise utterly destroyed. The proceedings were carried on with the greatest rapidity and the most reckless cruelty. The cries of the victims, the confusion, the despair and horror painted on the countenances of the one party, and the exulting ferocity of the other, beggar all description. At these scenes Mr. Sellar was present, and apparently, as sworn by several witnesses at his subsequent trial, ordering and directing the whole. Many deaths ensued from alarm, from fatigue, and cold, the people having been instantly deprived of shelter, and left to the mercies of the elements. Some old men took to the woods and to the rocks, wandering about in a state approaching to, or of absolute, insanity and several of them in this situation lived only a few days. Pregnant women were taken in premature labour, and several children did not long survive their sufferings.[5]

In total, 2,000 people were removed from Kildonan. When Sellar was charged with murder, for burning down an old woman's house, a hand-picked jury of landowners found him not guilty, but he had brought bad publicity to the Sutherland Estate and lost his job.

James Loch was an Edinburgh lawyer who, from 1812, for forty years was commissioner for the Marquess of Stafford. He would write an apology for his employers but his loathing for their tenants was never far from the surface, with him complaining: '. . . [their] habits and ideas, quite incompatible with the customs of regular society, and civilised life, adding greatly to those defects which characterise persons living in a loose and unformed state of society.'[6] His concern was to provide wool for the 'staple manufactory of England' and to convert the people to 'the habits of regular and continued industry'.

A young journalist sent by the *Scotsman* to the Highlands exhibited the same antipathy, writing in 1847 that the Highlanders were 'an inferior race to the Lowland Saxon'.[7] Robert Knox, the Edinburgh surgeon who bought the bodies stolen by the grave snatchers Burke and Hare, believed in the superiority of the 'Anglo-Saxon race' and wrote that the Highlanders 'must be forced from the soil'.[8] Sellar would have concurred with this because he regarded the Highlanders as racial degenerates. In his view they were 'the aborigines of Britain shut out from any general stream of knowledge . . .'[9]

In the preface to his *History of the Highland Clearances*, Mackenzie raised this question, and answered it: 'Some people ask "Why rake up all this inquiry just now?" We answer that the same laws which permitted the cruelties, the inhuman atrocities described in this book, are still the laws of this land.'[10]

It might be argued that the Clearances on the Sutherland Estate were the most excessive, and most people were removed with less savagery and on a smaller scale, but they were coerced off their land. At the height of the Clearances there was resistance but it was never organised or effective. Obedience to the clan chief still counted, even when it was he who was ordering you onto the emigrant boat, while ministers stressed obedience to the law, even when they sympathised with their flock.

In 1846, matters became desperate as the potato blight brought the likelihood of famine to the Highlands. In response, Charles Trevelyan, Under-Secretary at the Treasury, wrote: 'The people cannot, under any circumstances, be allowed to starve.' Two years later he did the opposite in Ireland, letting hundreds of thousands die, arguing that the famine there was 'a mechanism for reducing surplus population'.[11]

As the Highlands tottered on the verge of famine, the Clearances continued, but resistance was growing. In 1852, the Cromartie Estate attempted to remove tenants from Badenscallie in Coigach (Wester Ross) to Badentarbat, about three miles to the west, in order to create a new sheep farm. Eighteen tenants ordered to quit refused to co-operate despite police accompanying the estate's agent and sheriff officer to serve judicial papers on them. Men and women had lain in wait all night, and in the morning ambushed the party, burning the eviction papers. A second attempt to enforce the evictions ended with the police being driven off, and a further attempt ended with the summonses being seized and burned, and the boat that had brought them dragged onto the shore. When the sheriff officer tried again the following year, his legal papers were seized and he was stripped naked. Reports noted that women were at the forefront of the resistance, despite official claims that they were men dressed as women. The evictions were never carried out.[12]

There were further instances of resistance in the 1870s after Sir James Matheson purchased the Isle of Lewis and a smaller island adjoining it, Bernera. He appointed a solicitor, Donald Munro, to be his factor, and Munro began clearing the estate in the usual heavy-handed way. In 1874, he sent a sheriff officer to Bernera to serve fifty-eight eviction notices, but when the bailiffs arrived at Tobson they were pelted with a shower of clods of earth. The sheriff officer had his coat torn and he issued a threat that 'if he had a gun . . . Bernera mothers would be mourning the loss of their sons'.[13] Three crofters were arrested but hundreds of people marched on Matheson's home, Lews Castle in Stornoway. Matheson claimed Munro was acting without his instruction, and dismissed him the following year. Meanwhile, in a celebrated court case the three arrested men were acquitted.

By the 1880s the battle for the land in Ireland helped inspire resistance in the Highlands and Islands, and soon links were being established. In 1881, Michael Davitt, of the radical Irish Land League, spoke in Glasgow in favour of nationalisation of the land and a taxation of land values. Davitt was leading the fight against absentee landlordism in Ireland, the 'Land War'.[14]

The leader of the Irish Home Rule Party, Charles Stewart Parnell, entered the fray too, speaking at a meeting organised by Highland societies in Glasgow's City Halls in 1881. At that time there were evictions taking place in Skye, and the Irish Land League sent £1,000 to help fund the fight to stop them.[15] A Land League was formed in the Highlands, and its leader in Lochcarron, John MacRae, wrote:

> Ah then we would know exactly what to do –
> We'd drive out the keepers, and the English who come here,
> To ruin us and our land for their sport on the hill.
> We'd drive the deer that have taken over our ploughing land
> Up, high on top of the mountains – And down would come
> Nimrod.[16]

The Braes on Skye was home to a crofting community that eked out a living along the Sound of Raasay. In the summer months the men followed the herring shoals, leaving the women to tend the croft: '. . . a few acres of land, with a few sheep, perhaps a cow or a pig or a horse, and a potato patch'.[17] In early 1882 the landlord revoked the longstanding right of these crofters to graze their sheep on Ben Lee. After offering to rent the pasture and being refused, the crofters simply turned their sheep out onto the hillside.

The Sheriff of Invernesshire responded by ordering sixty police from Glasgow to the island. At dawn on an April morning they moved into the Braes, arresting six crofters. But as news spread hundreds gathered to pursue them back to the town of Portree: 'At one point they rained boulders from the top of a cliff onto the police on the road below. There was hand-to-hand fights, baton charges, split heads. Amazingly no one was killed, but when the police finally reached Portree there were many injuries to be attended to.'[18]

Disturbances spread to Glendale and the Isle of Lewis, with fences being pulled down and hay ricks set on fire. The authorities, as ever, were desperate to blame 'outside agitators', but one report was clear who was to blame for 'inciting' the crowd. 'The women, with the most violent gestures and imprecations, declared that the police should be attacked.'[19] The 'Battle of the Braes', as it became known, received considerable press coverage, most of it sympathetic, and forced the government in London to appoint a commission to investigate conditions in the crofting areas that would slate the poverty it found.

Despite the efforts of Highland landlords to prevent any legislation coming into effect, the Crofters' Holding Act of 1886 gave security of tenure to crofters and a system for arbitration of rents, together with compensation for improvements carried out by tenants. The legislation put through by the Gladstone government failed to include one of the commission's key recommendations, that the crofters had a right to more land. That was a fight for the future.

Gaelic Voices Against the Clearances

Màiri Nighean Iain Bhàin (Mary Macdonald), or Big Mary as she became known, was born on 10 March 1821 at Skeabost in Skye.[20] She left for Inverness in 1847 to marry Isaac Macpherson. When he died in 1871, she was left with four children to care for alone, suffering a short imprisonment for theft. While in prison she turned to writing poetry in her native language to voice her innocence and to express her anger.

During her time in Inverness, Mary supported Charles Fraser Mackintosh (Teàrlach Friseal Mac An Toisich), who stood for Inverness Burgh in the Westminster general election of 1874, on a programme in support of land rights for the crofters. Mary campaigned for him using song to win support among Gaelic-speakers at a time when newspapers were published only in English. Her fellow poet Sorley MacLean writes: 'Her personal sense of injustice and empathy with the sufferings of her people gave a unique force to her poetry.'[21]

After her release she worked in Glasgow as a nurse before returning to Skye in 1882, a year when the island was at the centre of the land agitation. Her Gaelic songs were used in the election campaign of the Highland League (also entitled the Highland Land Law Reform Association). Five of its members were elected to Westminster in the 1885 UK election, including an old associate of Karl Marx, Gavin Clark, in Caithness. Another of the MPs was D. H. MacFarlane, a Scottish Roman Catholic who had previously sat for an Irish constituency.[22]

They helped secure the Crofter's Holding Act of the following year, which gave the crofters security of tenure and appointed a commission that reduced rents. The Land League's best known slogan was 'Is treasa tuath na tighearna'. This Gaelic saying or proverb is usually translated as 'The people are mightier than a lord'. As well as parliamentary politics, they encouraged direct action.[23]

Mary Macdonald's last poem is 'Prophecy and Blessing to the Gaels':

> And when I am in the boards
> my words will be a prophecy.
>
> They will return, the stock of the crofters
> Who were driven over the sea.
>
> And the aristocratic 'beggars'
> will be routed as they [the crofters] were.
>
> Deer and sheep will be carted away
> and the glens will be tilled;
>
> A time of sowing and a time of reaping,
> and a time to reward the robbers.
>
> And the cold ruined houses
> will be built up by our kin.

Today across much of the Highlands and Islands you can still see the remains of the clachans where Gaelic-speaking communities lived.

Their destruction was one of the final chapters in the emergence of capitalism in Britain. That began with the enclosure of the common lands in England, which would spread north to Lowland Scotland, and included the wealth accrued by the slave trade and the creation of Empire, accompanied as it was by war and famine. The dry-stone walls of those crofts still visible today are one more memorial to the victims of that bloody chapter, whose end we still have not reached.

EIGHT

Scotland in the Nineteenth Century

Empire and the Scottish Identity

From 1848 until the end of her long reign in 1901, Queen Victoria spent each autumn at Balmoral Castle in the Cairngorms, setting a pattern followed by British monarchs ever since. A piper played beneath her windows each morning and the royal family donned tartan and the kilt, at play in the Highlands.

Nothing underlines more the difference between the position of Scotland in the United Kingdom and that of Ireland. Victoria visited Ireland just four times during her reign. Repression was a constant feature of Irish society and Irish risings against British rule occurred in 1848 and 1867, the latter followed by a Fenian bombing campaign. During the 1870s and '80s the Land League agitation led to landless labourers and small farmers going on rent strike and taking direct action to win ownership of the land. The latter years of Victoria's reign were dominated by the Irish question and the issue of whether Britain should grant the island Home Rule. The introduction of two Home Rule bills, in 1886 and 1893, by the government of William Ewart Gladstone divided the Liberals, the dominant party of the

British ruling class in the mid-nineteenth century. Despite Gladstone's time in Downing Street being so much occupied by the Irish Question, the Liberal prime minister visited Ireland only once in his long life. Gladstone was of Scottish descent and represented Midlothian in Parliament.

Ireland was a colony of Britain and was treated as such – during the Great Famine people were left to die, as was the case later in Victorian India. During those same years famine stalked the Highlands, but the British government and landlords acted to prevent deaths there, regarding it as part of Britain.

The Scottish middle and upper classes took to Empire with gusto. The East India Company utilised them in creating its privatised Indian Empire, and when Henry Dundas secured control of its Board of Control, he doled out offices to men whose rapaciousness became legendary. The Hong Kong–based corporation Jardine Matheson and Co. was founded by two Scots, and built its fortune peddling opium to the Chinese.

The two Calvinist churches took over the work of the Scottish missionary David Livingstone in 1873, and for eighty years effectively ran Nyasaland, today's Malawi. Dundee controlled the global trade in jute and did not just rely on raw material from Bengal but ran the industry that developed there.

As late as 1937, Evgenia Fraser from Broughty Ferry would travel to join her husband on the banks of the Hoogly in Bengal. He was the *kerani*, the man in charge of a jute mill. Evgania wrote: 'The keranis of the mills, up and down the river, were young men recruited from Dundee and its district. Most of them had a grammar school background and had served their apprenticeship in the offices of the jute mills and brokers . . .' Life was far removed even from the middle-class homes they had left behind in Dundee and Broughty Ferry: 'The whole compound, including gardens, tennis courts and the swimming pool was looked after by an army of gardeners and workers . . . It was pleasant to get up in the morning, secure in the knowledge that breakfast was prepared, the beds would be made, the house cleaned, lunch and dinner cooked and served.' She added: 'As for the Indians, I don't ever think we got to know them.'[1]

The Scottish upper classes were not 'junior partners' in Empire, they were at the centre of it. This imperial role shaped the Scotland of the nineteenth century, as did the existence of a Scottish capitalism – something that did not long outlast the turn of the century. Christopher Harvie points out that economic downturns and recession were regular in the nineteenth century but Scottish capitalism was resilient enough to overcome them: '. . . at each crisis it was the Scots who seized on new options and took the initiative: cotton in the 1780s, iron in the 1820s, ships in the 1860s, steel in the 1880s.'[2]

The nineteenth century shaped Scottish identity and culture in a very specific way. Ray Burnett argues: '. . . much of our shared "British" ideology as it manifests itself in Scotland draws its vigour and strength from a specifically Scottish heritage of myths, prejudices and illusions.'[3] The historian Michael Lynch takes up a similar theme: 'Bourgeois respectability linked arms with the new British state, which had emerged after the Reform Act of 1832 . . . The concentric loyalties of Victorian Scotland – a new Scottishness, a new Britishness and a revised sense of local pride – were held together by a phenomenon bigger than all of them – a Greater Britain whose stability rested on the Empire.'[4]

The death of Walter Scott in 1832 is a convenient point to mark the passing of the Enlightenment in Scotland (it remains a work as yet uncompleted). The legacy Scott bequeathed was of a romantic Scotland that would translate into kailyard and kitsch, as Tom Nairn argues: 'While the Enlightenment was only an episode, Romanticism entered her soul.'[5] Elsewhere, Nairn has added that romanticism created a national identity in a distinctive way: 'But the way in which it did so was markedly different from that of other European nations. Whereas, in Italy or Germany, Romanticism was part of the formation of national identity, in Scotland, particularly in the work of Sir Walter Scott, it acted as another substitute for it.'[6]

Nevertheless, even this romanticised identity could not quell protest. In 1853, the National Association for the Vindication of Scottish Rights could attract 5,000 people to a public meeting in Glasgow to hear complaints that Ireland received more from government funds than Scotland, it did not have its fair share of MPs and that the Scottish Privy Council should be restored.[7] Public subscription in the late 1850s enabled the building of the Wallace Monument overlooking the site of his victory at Stirling Bridge, with the aforementioned National Association for the Vindication of Scottish Rights being an enthusiastic backer.

Nationalism led to demands for some form of autonomy within the United Kingdom. In the 1880s, the Earl of Roseberry and the Duke of Argyll spearheaded a successful campaign to create the post of Secretary of State for Scotland, and in 1886 the cross-party Scottish Home Rule Association was formed, existing until 1914.[8] Yet these, like Walter Scott's earlier defence of the right of Scottish banks to issue separate notes, were the concern of the middle and upper classes, and remained comfortably within a wider British, imperial identity.

The dominance of the Liberal Party following the 1832 Reform Bill strengthened its hold. There were few outstanding Scottish Liberal MPs, but prominent English ones, including two prime ministers, Gladstone and Asquith, held Scottish seats. All of this was reinforced by the glorification of Scottish militarism in service of Empire, appropriating the dress and pipes of the Highlanders, so recently branded rebels.

Thus, until recently, national identity was still found in the celebration of Ensign Ewart at Waterloo, and the 'Thin Red Line' at Balaclava in the Crimea, just as we would be invited to celebrate 'Mad Mitch', Lieutenant Colonel Colin Mitchell, for the brutal repression of Yemeni nationalists in Aden.

Following a pitch invasion in 1886 during an FA Cup tie between Queens Park and Preston North End, there was one declaration of independence, with the Scottish Football Association ordering its members to withdraw from that competition, fastening the national identity of the SFA and the game north of the border. Following this, the most obvious celebration of Scottish identity was on the terraces of Hampden Park or, as a similar Scottish Rugby Union emerged, at Murrayfield.

By the close of the nineteenth century, Scottish capital was being invested not in native industry but in overseas development – helping to create a massive problem within a few short years as Scotland's staple industries failed to modernise. In 1914, UK overseas investment was £4,000 million, an average of £90 per person. Scotland's share was £500 million, £110 per person.[9] Dundee was dependent on Bengal and the jute industry, Glasgow on a narrow base of heavy industry. As industry grew in Bengal, and American and German competitors out-priced Clydeside shipbuilders, the economy suddenly faced trouble.

Industrialisation

In 1842, when Queen Victoria became only the second head of the United Kingdom to visit Scotland since the Act of Union in 1707, she encountered a divided nation. There was a yawning gap growing between the Highlands and Lowlands. With a population of 2.6 million, the country's population had doubled since the first accurate count in 1775. The most dramatic change was in the cities. Glasgow was twelve times bigger than it had been sixty-five years before; Dundee had grown by 35 percent. The 1851 census recorded a fall in the Highland population, a product of land clearances and hunger following the failure of the potato crop, and every census for the next century recorded a decrease. The rise of the cities continued through-out the century. Glasgow's population grew to 784,000, nearly tripling in size from 1841 to 1911. In the same period Edinburgh grew to 401,000, Aberdeen to 164,000 and Dundee to 165,000.[10]

Glasgow had an economy that bound together shipbuilding, engi-neering, steel and coal mining. In the 1890s and 1900s there was growth in engineering, tool-making and metalwork, linked to the shipyards. Shipbuilding was the symbol of Scottish industry. Between 1851 and 1870 the Clyde built two-thirds of British shipping.[11] Closely connected was the steel industry, which 'in Scotland in 1873 was capable of produc-ing 1,119 tons of steel . . . output reached 485,000 tons by 1890'.[12]

In addition, though in decline, the textile industry still employed 18,000 male workers in 1911, and there were 12,000 male clerks. But seven out of ten male and female workers were skilled, an unusu-ally high proportion. Unskilled workers were 27 percent of the workforce, but of those 44 percent of them were Irish-born males (an even greater percent could claim Irish heritage if the second and third generations of Irish migrant families were included).[13]

Industrialisation had brought even more spectacular change:

> . . . the iron industry of Lanarkshire doubled the population of Old and New Monkland parishes between 1831 and 1842, and created Airdrie, population 12,400, but attracting another 10,000 on pay nights from the surrounding mining towns to fight and drink. It had the ramshackle and dangerous character of a frontier town, where rival bands of Orange and Green beat one another up outside the pubs (it had one for every twenty males), the truck shops and the towering furnaces.[14]

The numbers of coal miners increased from 46,900 in 1870 to 147,500 in 1913, with just over half concentrated in the west. Output grew almost threefold in these decades, from 14.9 million to 42.4 million tons.

Scotland Divided

Rapid industrial growth brought huge contrasts between those at the top of Scottish society and those who created their wealth. The concentration of wealth in Edinburgh, ensuring that the Lothians had the highest living standards in the country, was unmatched in any British city except London. Censuses show that those employed in professional work in Edinburgh represented 20.8 percent of its population in 1830 – more than three and a half times the proportion in Glasgow (5.9 percent), and throughout the nineteenth century approximately one male in eight was employed in professional work, far in excess of any other British city.[15] Edinburgh was the UK's third-richest city in 1879, with Glasgow in fifth place.[16]

Scottish capitalism was in the hands of magnates who held sway during the high tide of the Victorian era. Calculations for the years between 1809 and 1914 show six Scots among the forty richest Britons. One, the third Marquess of Bute, made his money in South Wales;

two were Lanarkshire ironmasters, William Baird (died 1864) and William Weir (died 1913); two were Paisley sewing thread manufacturers, Peter and James Couts (both died 1913); and the other was the Glasgow chemical manufacturer Charles Tennant (died 1906). All were worth more than £2 million and all were based on Clydeside.

The grandfather of that Charles Tennant, also named Charles, had established the family fortune through the manufacture of bleaching powder at the St Rollox works in Glasgow. Bleaching powder soon replaced urine, sunlight and other inferior bleaches in the textile industry, and from this base the firm diversified into sulphuric acid, caustic soda and soap manufacture. By the time of his death in 1838, Charles Tennant employed 500 men in his factory, described by the New Statistical Account of the 1840s as 'the most extensive of any of the kind in Europe. In the furnaces are upwards of 100 furnaces, retorts and fire-places. In this great concern upwards of 600 tons of coal are consumed weekly.'[17]

Dependent on coal and reliant on the canal owners to supply him with chemicals, Tennant jumped at the chance to build Scotland's first railway, in 1831, from Glasgow to Garnkirk, connecting the coalfields of Lanarkshire to the St Rollox works. Tennant was a Whig who, when the new industrial capitalist class was excluded from political power, campaigned for political reform and abolition of the Corn Laws, although he showed his disapproval of working-class reformers. He remained radical enough to refuse a peerage when it was offered to him shortly before his death.[18]

Charles was followed by his son, John, who expanded the firm's operations to Tyneside, where he established an even bigger factory than the one in St Rollox, and bought the Tharsis mines in Spain, where a Scottish colony of several hundred oversaw mining operations employing 2,000, producing iron ore, copper and sulphur. Like his father, he was a stalwart of the Liberal Party in Glasgow.

The Tyneside plant paid higher wages, John Tennant claimed this was because coal was cheaper there, but the real reason was that in Glasgow there was an abundant supply of cheap labour, with migrants from Ireland and rural areas crowding into slums in Garngad, beside the St Rollox works.

John's son, Charles Tennant II, took the business to new, giddy heights. His policy was to keep wages at rock bottom, and in Garngad there was a stready supply of cheap unskilled labour to be found. But his Tyneside works were unionised, and so too was Hallside Steel Works in Lanarkshire, and at both he was not always able to pay wages as low as he would have liked. A visitor to the Tennant household in 1897 noted, 'my host is possessed by an almost maniacal hatred of trades unions and all their works.'[19]

Despite this, Tennant continued the family's commitment to the Liberal Party, serving as a Glasgow MP from 1877 to 1880 and then representing Peebles and Selkirk. By the start of the twentieth century, however, he was a Tory in all but name, supporting Joseph Chamberlain's unsuccessful campaign to end free trade and to impose import controls. This was despite one of his daughters marrying Herbert Asquith, a future Liberal prime minister. His biography mirrored those of much of the British bourgeoisie, worried by the fact Britain had been overtaken industrially by the USA and Germany, and fearful of working-class discontent. He died in 1906 with a fortune of more than £3 million, a half-billionaire in today's terms.[20]

Scottish cities were small enough to ensure constant tension. The upper classes, with their servants, inhabited a world of country estates for the very wealthy and seaside homes for the middle classes, a million miles away from the world of the workers, despite living together cheek by jowl in town. Hyndland in the west of Glasgow peered down on Partick and across the river on Govan. In Edinburgh it was a short walk from Morningside or Newington across the Meadows to slum housing, the worst of which was in the Cowgate.

Just how different their lives were was spelled out by a Royal Commission in 1840 that investigated the appalling conditions in Scotland's pits. Among the places its members visited was Liberton, then a mining village south of Edinburgh, where the commission reported children were working down the mine: Janet Cumming, aged eleven, told how she works 'with father, have done for two years. Father gangs at two in the morning. I gang with the women at five and come up at five at night, work all night Friday and come away at five in the day.'

For Agnes Reid, aged fourteen, things were still worse: 'I bear coal on my back. I do not know the exact weight, but it is something more than a hundredweight. It is very sore work and makes me cry and few lassies like it . . . but I suppose father needs me . . .'

William Woods at fourteen was probably already falling victim to silicosis: 'I have been three years below. I gang at three in the morning and return at about six. It is no very good work, and the sore labour makes me feel very ill and fatigued. It injures my breath.'[21]

Two years later the Children's Employment Commission produced a report with interviews it had carried out. At a pit outside Edinburgh a twelve-year-old boy told them:

I have worked two years at Sheriffhall, and go below at two or three in the morning, and hew til six at night; after that I fill and put the carts on the rails to the pit bottom . . . The pit I work in is very wet; we used to fall asleep; am kept awake now. It is most terrible work; and I am wrought in a thirty inch seam, and am obliged to twist myself up to work on my side; this is every day work except Friday, when I go down at twelve at night, and come up at twelve to noon.[22]

The Mines Act of 1845, which followed the commission's work, banned women and girls from underground labour and set an age limit of ten years for boys.

From the 1830s on, Coatbridge in the Monklands was at the centre of the new, hot-blast iron industry, with six ironworks and fifty blast furnaces, reliant on mining coal and ironstone. This 'black country' was seen as Scotland's Wild West. Between 1831 and 1841 the working class in the area doubled to 40,000. The next year, when Lanarkshire coal and ironstone owners tried to impose wage cuts, there were strikes at 140 pits in the Airdrie and Coatbridge area alone, with 8,000 out of 10,000 miners taking part across the county.

The self-taught poet Janet Hamilton wrote this verse, 'Oor Location', describing her home town, Coatbridge, in the 1850s:

A hunner funnels bleezin', reekin',
Coal an' ironstone, charrin', smeekin',
Navvies, miners, keepers, fillers,

> Puddlers, rollers, iron millers,
> Reestit, reekit, raggit ladies,
> Firemen, enginemen, an' Paddies;
> Boatmen, banksmen, righ and rattlin',
> 'Bout the wescht wi' colliers battlin',
> Sweatin', swearin', fectin,' drinkin,'
> Change-house, bells an' gill stoups clinkin'

In 1858, the newly formed Glasgow Trades Council was addressed by Alexander McDonald, who six years before had founded the Scottish Miners' Association: 'He said that 1600 miners were killed every year, leaving 700 widows. He added that 10,000 men were unfit for employment because of accidents in the mines. Mr McDonald mentioned cases of boys working in the mines from two am to seven pm.'[23]

The worst mining accident in Scotland was on 22 October 1877, when an explosion rocked the Blantyre mine in Lanarkshire, killing 209 men. Ninety-two families, with a total of 250 children, were left without a father.[24] Showing no pity the pit owners, Dixon's, took out eviction notices on thirty-four widows still living in company-owned cottages six months after the disaster. Two weeks later, on 28 May 1878, they were evicted.[25]

This traditional song, 'Blantyre Explosion', gained international fame in 1985 when the Irish singer and writer Christy Moore recorded it (although earlier still, Ewan MacColl had done the same):

Sobbing and sighing, at last she did answer,
'Johnny Murphy, kind sir, was my true lover's name.

Twenty-one years of age, full of youth and good-looking,
to work down the mine of High Blantyre he came.
The wedding was fixed, all the guests were invited
that calm summer's evening my Johnny was slain.

The explosion was heard, all the women and children,
with pale anxious faces made haste to the mine.
When the truth was made known the hills rang with their mourning.

Two hundred and ten young miners were slain.
Now children and wives and sweethearts and brothers,
that Blantyre explosion they'll never forget.
And all you young miners who hear my sad story,
shed a tear for the victims who were laid to their rest.'

Housing was awful for the majority of the people of Glasgow. The first real census to record details, in 1861, found 34 percent of the population lived in a single room, 37 percent in just two rooms. Two-thirds of the population lived in a single end or a 'but-and-ben', a two-room cottage.[26] Twenty years later, a quarter of Glasgow's citizens still lived in such cramped conditions, and 50 percent in a room and kitchen.[27]

In 1892, the Royal Commission on Labour was told of the houses provided by William Dixon's mining company at Auchenraith. Forty-two single-room and forty-one twin-room houses provided accommodation for 492 people: 'There were no wash houses or coal cellars (coals were kept under the bed): there was an open sewer behind, with twelve doorless "hen roost privies" (so called because you could not sit down): there were two drinking fountains.'[28]

By 1911, half of all Scots still lived in one- or two-bedroom homes. In England and Wales the figure was 7 percent.[29] Among those who paid the price were the newborn. Scottish infant mortality was 118 per 1,000 births in 1855–59, rose to 130 in 1895–99 and still stood at 122 in 1900–04. In 1908, the Glasgow socialist John Wheatley published an index of infant mortality across the city and argued: 'You may see at a glance that the infant death-rate in working-class wards is three, four and almost five times higher than in Kelvinside [in the affluent West End].'[30]

All of this explains why at the height of Scottish capitalism the country was haemorrhaging people. Between 1830 and 1914 nearly two million emigrated overseas, with another 600,000 moving south of the border.[31]

A Bastion of Liberalism

The 1832 Reform Bill increased the Scots electorate from around 4,500 to 65,000. Landlords were able to exploit loopholes and to use their control to sway the vote. Reform led to the dominance of the Liberals (as the Whigs were now known). Between 1831 and 1919, Edinburgh was a Liberal stronghold, not returning a single Tory MP in all that time. It remained so during the crisis over Irish Home Rule in 1886, which led to a party split in Glasgow, and it even bestowed the freedom of the city on the Irish nationalist Home Rule leader Charles Stewart Parnell.[32] Between 1832 and 1886 the voters of Glasgow only once returned a Tory MP.[33]

By 1843, the Church of Scotland had gone through a ten-year conflict that led to a third of its ministers marching out of the General Assembly to form the Free Church of Scotland. At issue was the right of patrons, landowners or, as in 30 percent of parishes, the government, to select the parish minister. The leader of the breakaway sect, Thomas Chambers, was politically conservative but objected to such interference, championing the right of presbyteries to elect their own ministers, and kirk control of education and poor relief.

In rural areas, especially the Highlands, the aristocracy blocked the new church from building places of worship, and the Liberal press made hay of this. In the burghs, middle-class Free Church members rallied to the Liberal Party, strengthening its hold there. In reality, however, the split weakened the hold of the churches, and allowed the state to take control of schools.

Trade unions were weak, largely confined to male skilled workers, and clung to the Liberal Party. So, for example, the miners' unions always urged its members to vote Liberal. In Edinburgh, from 1870 until they lost the fight in 1885, the Trades Council allied with sections of the city's lower middle class to oppose attempts by the rich and powerful to convert George Heriot's Hospital, which had been endowed by James VI's watchmaker in order to educate the poor, into the select, fee-paying school it remains to this day.[34]

The crisis over Gladstone's Irish Home Rule Bill of 1886, however, saw the Liberals shed the support of those who wanted no concessions to Irish nationalism and allowed the breakaway Liberal Unionists to win a majority of Scottish parliamentary seats, including every seat in Glasgow.[35] After a further Home Rule crisis in the

1890s, the Liberal Unionists and the Tories would eventually unite, with the Conservatives using the name Unionist on the ballot and election material until long after World War II.

Sectarianism: A Blight on Scottish Society

Religious sectarianism has blighted Scottish society for more than two centuries. Today its main expression is in the rivalry between the two main Glasgow football teams, Celtic, identified with the Catholic population, and Rangers, seen as the Protestant team. In the nineteenth century and in the first half of the twentieth century sectarianism was expressed in violence on the streets and in the close links developed between the Protestant Orange Order and the Tories in the west of Scotland.

Sectarianism was rooted in the arrival of Irish Catholic immigrants in the nineteenth century; before that the two countries had had a rich history of exchange, with Scotland benefitting most. However, the Great Famine of the 1840s increased immigration into the west of Scotland, West Lothian, Fife and Dundee, where industrialisation was already under way. By 1852, the Irish in Edinburgh reached a peak, numbering 12,514 in 1851, 4.5 percent of the city's population. They were concentrated in the Grassmarket, the Cowgate, St Mary's Wynd and Leith Wynd in the Old Town, and their main jobs were labouring, dealing in old clothes, scavenging and street lighting.[36] By 1851, 7.2 percent of Scotland's population was Irish, compared with 2.9 percent in England and Wales.[37]

The main Irish concentration was in the west and Dundee. There was antagonism towards the immigrants, particularly in the Lanarkshire coalfields, where they were believed to drive down wages by working for less pay. Yet even before the Famine, sectarian violence was in evidence. The organisation that personified anti-Catholic bigotry was the Orange Order. Its first Orange Lodge in Scotland seems to have been formed in Maybole in 1799 by returning members of the Ayrshire and Wigtownshire Militia, who had served in Ireland suppressing the United Irishmen's rebellion of the previous year.

Serious rioting broke out in 1831 in Girvan when armed Orange-men broke up a reform march in the town. The *Glasgow Herald* reported an anti-Catholic riot in Airdrie in July 1835 and pointed out the sympathetic attitude of the police: 'The crowd seemed to have the tacit support of the local authorities. When the crowd attacked the home of a Protestant by mistake, the head of the Airdrie police merely pointed out the error to them, but made no effort to dissuade them. One of the burgh magistrates was also reported to be in the midst of the mob.'[38]

Immigration preceded the 1846–51 Irish famine as a result of the collapse of native industry. However, the arrival of a significant Irish immigrant population was the driving force behind Orangeism. Since the Reformation, this had been a Protestant and indeed Calvin-ist state, with pockets of Catholicism only in the Highlands and Islands. The 1841 census showed 126,321 people of Irish birth in Scotland, some 5 percent of the population (16 percent in Glasgow). Ten years later the number of children born in Scotland to Irish immigrants totalled 207,367, including 18 percent of Glasgow's population.[39]

Sectarianism did not take root everywhere. By 1851 Dundee had a higher proportion of Irish-born residents, 18.9 percent, than Glas-gow. The bulk of these were women, attracted to work in the jute mills, and few were from Ulster. The Irish population there was quicker to join the labour movement, helping elect two Labour MPs in 1906, and in unionising the jute mills prior to World War I.[40]

Reinforced by Protestant immigrants from the north of Ireland, more Orange Lodges were set up in Ayrshire, Lanarkshire and Inverclyde, and were involved in brawls and riots with immigrant Catholic Irish, but were seen as 'a "party" or fighting society and certainly not as a credible organisational mechanism for propagating militant Protestantism'.[41] In 1852, when anti-Irish mobs took over the streets of Greenock, attacking Irish homes, a man charged with trying to kill a Catholic policeman with a knife and pistol received a sixty-day sentence, but the central government intervened to suspend the local magistrates and town clerk.[42] In 1854, miners in Airdrie struck, demanding the removal of the Irish.[43]

A quarter of the Irish in Glasgow by the 1860s were Protestants from Ulster. Until 1860, Glasgow had no Orange Lodge, but by 1878 there were more than a hundred in the city.[44] The Ulster-born Robert Gault, superintendent of the Free Church Anti-Popish Mission, was the first clergymen to promote the Orange Order, being a regular speaker at its events.

What transformed the fortunes of the Orange Lodge were the Home Rule crises of 1886 and 1893, when the Liberal government was defeated in introducing devolution for Ireland, in the first case losing a vote in the House of Commons, in the second having it blocked by the House of Lords. The Liberal Party split, and as a result, in Scotland the Tories moved into an alliance with the Orange Lodge. This alliance worked well in opposing Gladstone and less well when the Tories gained office after his defeats.[45]

The President of the Glasgow Conservative Association, Colonel Archibald Campbell, later Lord Blythswood, hosted Orange social evenings as early as the 1870s, and likely joined the order, though he did not stoop to join processions.[46] In 1875, there was rioting in Partick when an Irish nationalist procession was attacked. The Orange Lodge attempted to disassociate itself, claiming its members maintained discipline and had been asked by the police to assist them.[47]

Across Britain from the 1870s on, power was shifting with capitalists moving from the Liberal to the Tory Party. It was not simply because of Irish Home Rule, but because the Tories were recasting themselves as being aggressively pro-business. The reality of having been overtaken industrially by the USA, and with Germany coming up fast behind, sharpened the need to cut labour costs and to boost productivity. On Clydeside, the shipyard owner William Pearce and the ironmaster Sir James Bain stood for Parliament in 1880 as Tories, and enlisted the Orange Lodge in their support. By the 1892 Westminster general election, the Tory candidate in Bridgeton was an Orangeman, the candidate in the College constituency addressed a meeting of the Cowcaddens lodge and, in the election's aftermath, the West Renfrewshire candidate sent his sincere apologies that he could not attend the 12th of July celebrations. Sectarianism remained never far beneath the surface.

Scotland also offered a home to migrants fleeing the repression, anti-Semitism and poverty of the Tsar's Russian Empire. By 1901, Jews made up 24.7 percent of Scotland's foreign-born population. The main centre of the Jewish population was the Gorbals in Glasgow, with an estimated 6,500 living there in 1901, rising to 9,000 within eighteen years. As families began to prosper they started to leave the slums of the Gorbals behind, moving south towards Pollokshields.[48] Dundee had a small Jewish community, beginning with German textile merchants who settled there in the 1840s. Four decades later it saw the arrival of Yiddish-speaking East European Jews, who were much poorer than the earlier arrivals. Most lived in the Hilltown area and made a living selling goods in the Green Market or the city arcade, running tearooms, lodgings, pawnbrokers and small shops selling groceries or clothes.[49]

Scotland was not free of anti-Semitism but it never took the organised form that it did in early twentieth-century Germany, nor did it experience anything like the Dreyfus Affair, which split France at that time. There is little or no record of specifically anti-Semitic organisations operating in Scotland in the nineteenth century.

From the 1880s, coal mine and iron work owners in Lanarkshire and Ayrshire began recruiting Lithuanian workers, promising them work and homes. Some 8,000 came, with 2,600 working in the mines by 1911. At first the 'Poles', as they were known, were treated with hostility by their fellow workers, who feared, sometimes rightly, that they were being hired to cut wages. This happened in 1902–1903 at Thankerton, Tannochside and Neilsland in Lanarkshire. But many of the newcomers had fled political persecution, and the Lithuanians established their credentials as union members, playing a central role as as pickets in Lanarkshire and West Lothian during the 1912 national strike.

The Kailyard and the Reaction

The late nineteenth century was dominated by the rise of the 'kailyard' – sugary, sentimental tales of rural Scotland – which appeared in journals such as *British Weekly* (subtitled 'A Journal of Social and

Christian Progress') and the *Christian Leader*. J. M. Barrie, today best remembered as the author of *Peter Pan*, had success with three novels, *Auld Licht Idylls* (1888), *A Window in Thrums* (1890) and *The Little Minister* (1891), set in his mother's hometown, Kirriemuir (renamed Thrums in the books) and centring on the lives of family members belonging to the 'Auld Lichts', a strict Calvinist sect to which Barrie's own grandfather had belonged.

Ian MacLaren's *Beside the Bonnie Brier Bush* was published in 1894, and Queen Victoria and William Gladstone were among its readers. A year after publication it was the best-selling novel in the USA.[50] Its opening line, 'There grows a bonnie brier bush in our kail-yard', gave the name to this school of literature with its idealised view of Scottish rural life, so far from the reality of the slums of Clydeside or the miners' rows of the coalfields. By 1908 it had sold 256,000 copies and 485,000 in the USA. Maclaren was the pen name of the Rev. John Watson, a minister of the Free Church of Scotland, and his stress on family values won praise from Christian evangelicals on both sides of the Atlantic.

Others were keen to emulate such success, and a flood of kailyard novels and short stories followed, often written with the North American emigrant market in mind. For six years between 1891 and 1897, kailyard authors appeared in the American top-ten best-seller lists. S. R. Crockett's *The Lilac Sunbonnet* sold 10,000 copies on its first day of publication in 1894. Like Watson, Crockett was a Free Kirk minister.[51]

While Scotland was a success story, the working class was still not a force in Scottish society, and there was little need for the middle class to dwell on its social problems. It could instead comfort itself in this idyllic view of Scotland. This was also the image developed by the music hall artist Harry Lauder, who always appeared on stage in his kilt with a crooked walking stick, and who gained huge success in Britain and America, becoming the first artist to sell a million records. It would live on with sanitised versions of Burns poetry and songs in the *Sunday Post* and on the *White Heather Club*, a variety show which appeared on BBC TV between 1958 and 1968.

But this image was challenged at the time of its high point in popularity. In 1901, George Douglas Brown published *The House with the Green Shutters*, focusing on the dark side of Calvinist Scotland, drink and all. Its representation of rural life is a million miles from that of Maclaren, Barrie and Crockett – 'a brutal and bloody work' was its author's description. He added: 'Every clachan in Scotland is a hot-bed of scandal and malevolence.'[52] His Barbie has, on the surface, similarities to Drumtochty, where Maclaren set his stories, and indeed Brown starts by portraying Barbie in a kailyard way, but spiteful gossip and petty hatreds are never far from view. Barbie's population are the 'Bodies', a group of malicious gossips who rub their hands in glee when things go wrong for their neighbours. The novel stands the test of time.

Class Warfare in Victorian Scotland

In the 1880s, wages in Scotland were lower than in England, with those in shipbuilding, iron and steel, cotton and brewing averaging £70 per annum compared with a UK average of £76. A report to the US Congress in 1872 described wages in Scotland as a 'mere pittance'. Trade union membership was lower than south of the border. These were all factors in encouraging the American Singer Sewing Machine Company to build a plant in Clydebank in 1900.[53]

Employers were determined to try to keep trade unions cowed. One way of doing this was by employing women in the belief that they were immune to unionisation. Between 1871 and 1911, Dundee's jute works employed between two-thirds and three-quarters of Dundee's working women.[54] The 1901 census showed that 31 percent of the female population of Dundee was employed in the city's mills and factories and, in the same year, 'the proportion of married women who had remunerative occupations was exceptionally high' – at least 24.1 percent compared with 6.1 percent in Glasgow and 5.6 percent in Edinburgh.[55]

Nevertheless, women mill workers went on strike in Dundee in 1871, with one newspaper reporting: 'Those on strike today paraded the streets in grotesque processions, bearing emblems of their trade suspended from poles, such as mats, jugs etc. . . . They also indulged in shouting and singing . . . Besides this they held threatening demonstrations in front of the works where nobody had turned out.'[56]

In 1893 a general strike occurred across Dundee against a 5 percent reduction in wages. The strike had originated at the city's Tay Works, and according to the *Dundee Advertiser*, 'it was here that the most violent scenes were witnessed':

> On Monday at 6 o'clock . . . the employees who had agreed to stand by the resolution assembled outside the gates, and amused themselves by hooting at their fellow workers who felt it their duty to continue at their work. Before breakfast the strikers numbered 500, after breakfast 2,000 . . . It was observed that many of the younger workers, both male and female, had come provided with wooden laths. The 10 o'clock whistle began to sound and as the shrill notes were heard a few antistrikers made their way towards the entrance. They were immediately set upon by those armed with sticks, and ran the gauntlet under a shower of hearty blows. At the same time they were loudly hooted and subjected to remarks of a far from complimentary kind. In this way, about 100 workers, chiefly men found their way in.[57]

Elsewhere, Scottish coal was still hacked out of the ground by hand, and pit owners wanted to squeeze everything they could from their workforce. In 1870, the Fife miners won an eight-hour day after a stay-down strike (an occupation) at a time when demand for coal was high. But four years later the price of coal fell and with it came the usual wage cuts. The Scottish miners' union, led by Alexander McDonald, decided to target the pits of one company, Merry and Cunningham, having sufficient funds for strike pay to the men there and in the hope that a victorious strike would force other employers to reverse the cuts. But in response the employers enforced a lockout across the Motherwell and Wishaw district and began evictions in Logan Rows in Motherwell and Merry Square in Craigneuk. Miners at the Braidhurst pit near Logan Rows were warned by the owners not to take the evicted families in. For several weeks, a hundred families had to camp in Craigneuk. Hunger and cold beat them back to work.[58]

In 1879 and 1880 the miners fought back against wage cuts and for a reduction in working hours, and the strike lasted sixteen weeks. Once again the company used evictions and the law to impress its power on the workers. Two miners were sentenced to fourteen days' hard labour for intimidation, and three wives from Berryhill Rows, Wishaw, were jailed for two days for throwing stones and coal slag at scabs. A group of women from Camp Rows, Motherwell, were tried for harassment, but got off with fines and a warning. Eventually the union exhausted its funds and the strike folded.[59]

In Lanarkshire during the Caledonian Company rail strike of 1891, miners came to the aid of railworkers facing eviction from company houses. Fifty hussars were sent from Glasgow's Maryhill Barracks to maintain order, but failed to stop a crowd of 20,000 smashing a signal box and the glass roof of Motherwell Station.[60] Scottish workers could fight hard, but politically they were undeveloped. Already, however, there were those determined to change that.

The Liberal Party dominated Scottish parliamentary politics in the second half of the nineteenth century, and unlike its counterpart south of the border, was not under any great pressure from the trade unions and working-class supporters that it had to select 'Lib-Lab' candidates. In England and Wales the Liberals were prepared to select working-class candidates, usually trade union officials, often from mining areas where they could appeal to working-class voters concentrated in tight communities. But in Scotland, such was their dominance, the Liberals did not feel this to be necessary, which fed demands for independent working-class representation.

Instead, a radical wing developed inside the Scottish Liberal Party, represented by John Ferguson, a Glasgow-based Irish Home Rule activist; the traveller and adventurer Cunninghame Graham, who was won over to socialism in the 1880s and helped form the Scottish Home Rule Association in 1886 when he was a Lancashire MP; and the socialist novelist 'John Law' (Margaret Harkness), as well as Christian socialists.[61]

One of this group was Kier Hardie, who had been involved in two failed strikes, in 1880 and 1881. In the second he had turned his home into a soup kitchen for strikers, but to no avail. In April

1888, Hardie contested the Mid-Lanark Westminster by-election. His vote was not impressive, polling 617 against his Liberal opponent, a Welsh barrister, who took 3,847. The intransigence of the mine owners, the anti-working-class views of the Scottish Liberal leadership and the failure of Gladstone's governments to bring any significant reform led Hardie and Graham to form the Scottish Labour Party four months later, following the government's use of troops to break a miners' strike in the previous year despite 20,000 people marching through Glasgow in its support.[62] As the labour historian James J. Smyth argues, this move flowed from the weakness of the trade unions in Scotland: 'It was the inability of Scottish trade unionists to make local Liberal Associations accept trade union or working class candidates that forced miners' leaders such as Keir Hardie into a reappraisal of the organisational link with Liberalism.'[63]

Five years later, the Scottish Labour Party had 150 delegates from twenty-four branches at its conference. Nonetheless, a year earlier it had played a central part in the formation in Bradford of the Independent Labour Party into which it would fold and from which today's Labour Party would emerge.[64]

Marxist ideas grew small roots too, with the likes of William Morris touring the country. Aberdeen developed a strong radical tradition, initially tied to the Liberals but moving left as that party was seen to ignore working-class issues. James Leatham, a compositor, helped set up a branch of the Scottish Land and Labour League in 1886, holding open-air meetings on a Sunday in Castlegate. At the first he told his audience: 'Ye sing of your bonnie Scotland and your heather hills. It's not your bonnie Scotland. It's not your heather hills. It's the landlord's heather hills. And if you want enough earth to set a geranium in you've got to pinch it.'[65]

On his second outing Leatham was arrested, charged with preaching socialism on the Sabbath. A lively free-speech campaign helped ensure his acquittal.

In 1896 the national chair of the ILP, Tom Mann, stood in the parliamentary seat of Aberdeen North, securing 2,476 votes against his Liberal opponent's 2,909.[66] David Howell observes: 'Aberdeen had been . . . a stronghold of New Unionism [the upsurge in the early 1890s among unskilled, formerly non-unionised workers] and much of Mann's keenest support seems to have come from the dock areas.'[67]

These albeit small political advances were all signs that something profound was about to change in the Scottish working class.

REBEL LIVES: JAMES CONNOLLY

On 12 May 1916, James Connolly was driven into the prison yard of Dublin's Kilmainham Prison strapped to a chair; set down, he was shot dead by a British firing squad, despite the fact that he was already dying from his infected wounds. Beforehand he had smuggled out a statement through his daughter Nora, which said, 'We went out to break the connection between this country and the British Empire, and to establish an Irish Republic.'[68]

Connolly was a socialist who took part in the 1916 Easter Rising in Dublin at the head of the Irish Citizens Army because he wanted to strike a blow against World War I and imperialism. He regarded himself, rightly, as being Irish, but he was born in Edinburgh on 5 June 1868, at 107 Cowgate, in the heart of the capital's Irish ghetto. Both his father and mother were immigrants. He worked as a manure carter for Edinburgh Corporation; his mother had been a domestic servant. Leaving school, he could not find regular work and enlisted in the British Army, from which he probably deserted.

The politics of the Cowgate were those of the Irish National League, connected to the Home Rule Party in Ireland, and run by the local clergy. But James's elder brother, John, had joined the Marxist Social Democratic Federation (SDF). It seems that James joined too, after visiting his brother in Dundee, where he was living, in 1889.

The city magistrates had attempted to ban the SDF from holding outdoor meetings in the city, but 20,000 people came to a rally in Albert Square from where they marched to High Street, into the area covered by the ban. Two leading SDFers were arrested. Undeterred, the left in the city refused to back down and instead the magistrates had to make a U-turn.[69]

The Edinburgh SDF contained some talented people: Andreas Scheu was an Austrian journalist, Leo Meillet had been mayor of a Paris commune, Rev. W. Glasse would translate the 'Internationale'. The Irish-born John Lincoln MacMahon joined after forming a Republican Club in the city, and John Leslie, another Irish-Scot from the Cowgate, would help shape Connolly's view of the Irish situation.

The SDF's leadership in London was very dogmatic and sectarian, arguing that strikes were futile and that workers had to overthrow capitalism. The development of the New Unionism of the 1890s, the strikes that organised unskilled workers for the first time on any scale, met with their scorn, but in Edinburgh the SDF branch supported a strike by printers, backed the call for an eight-hour day and helped organise the 1890 May Day march.[70]

Three years later, Connolly had become the party secretary in the city. In a report to the SDF national paper, *Justice*, in August 1893, he described the population of Edinburgh as being 'snobs, flunkeys, mashers, lawyers, students, middle class pensioners and dividend-hunters, even the working class portion of the population seemed to have imbibed the snobbish would-be-respectable spirit of their "betters" . . .' He reported that the SDF wanted to build membership in Leith because it was 'pre-eminently an industrial centre'.[71]

The eventual defeat of the New Unionism led many socialists to look to standing working-class candidates for Parliament as a means to advance. Connolly attempted, unsuccessfully, to get the Irish National League to switch from backing the Liberals to supporting Labour candidates, but he disliked the ILP leadership's attempts to seek alliances with the Liberals and to court the Irish Home Rule Party, and in 1894 resigned all his positions in the party to devote himself to the SDF.

In this he was influenced by the publication in 1894 of John Leslie's pamphlet 'The Irish Question', in which he argued that the creation of an Irish parliament would not solve the country's ills. Even though he backed independence he argued that the economic grip of the landlords had to be broken, quoting the radical national-ist Fintan Lalor to good effect. Leslie was attacking the politics of the

Irish National League, which held that the workers of the Cowgate should unite with the publicans, priests and slum landlords who made up their own, small middle class. He argued that 'despite their patriotism [they] were from a working class point of view, not much better, if any, than those they rebelled against . . .' Irish workers, he continued, had to understand that 'The emancipation of their class from economic bondage means emancipation from all bondage; that the interests of the working class are paramount . . .'[72] Leslie was joined by Connolly in attacking any attempts by the left to curry the favour of the Home Rule Party.

Connolly would stand as a socialist candidate in St Giles Ward at the centre of 'Little Ireland' in 1894. His election manifesto expressed his hopes for his brothers and sisters: 'Perhaps they will realise that the Irish worker who starves in an Irish cabin and the Scottish worker who is prisoned in an Edinburgh garret are brothers with one hope and destiny. The landlord who grinds Irish peasants on a Connemara estate and the landlord who rack-rents them in a Cowgate slum are brethren in fact and deed.'[73]

Five hundred attended his first election rally, and he also held an open-air meeting for carters in Kingstables Road. But many of those listening were denied a vote (nearly half the male working class had no vote, and no women, of course).

The Irish National League attacked Connolly as an 'atheist' and said he was betraying his faith and country. In the end he came third – the Liberal won with 1,056 votes, the Tory took 467 and Connolly 263. Connolly understood the limitations of electoral politics, writing: 'The election of a Socialist to any public body is only valuable in so far as it is the return of a disturber of the political peace.'[74] He became a national figure on the Scottish and British left but could not obtain full-time employment as a political organiser. In 1896, he answered an advert for the post of organiser for the Irish Socialist Republican Party in Dublin and emigrated, leaving Edinburgh behind.

Connolly remained a regular visitor to Scotland, however, and an opponent of a growing reformism in the SDF. In the end his supporters walked out to form the Socialist Labour Party. The new party was hard on the 'Labour Fakers' but was too doctrinaire. In the build-up to 1916 it printed Connolly's newspaper and smuggled it into Ireland after the British authorities suppressed it.

In the wake of his execution, few on the Scottish left defended him. Tom Johnston responded to Connolly's involvement in the Easter Rising by saying, 'the psychology of it is a mystery to me.' *Forward* stated that 'in no way do we approve of armed rebellion.'[75]

There was one exception. John Maclean knew Connolly well and defended the Easter Rising and Connolly's role in it from the outset, just as he would side with the subsequent Republican struggle for independence.

NINE

The Clyde Runs Red

Scotland at War

In August 1914, Scotland went to war. Official propaganda told the people that war was necessary to save 'poor little Belgium', which had been occupied by crazed Huns, the racist term used for Germans who were busy raping nuns and butchering civilians. In reality, Britain was fighting to ensure Germany did not dominate Europe and to protect its position as the world superpower.

Scotland paid a high price for this imperial conflict. Of 557,000 Scots who enlisted, 26.4 percent were killed, compared to the UK average of 11.8 percent. Only Serbia and Turkey had a higher mortality rate.[1] T. C. Smout says of the war dead, 'One well-argued estimate put the figure at 110,000, equivalent to about 10 percent of the Scottish male population, and probably about 15 percent of British war dead . . . Thirteen out of fourteen were privates and non-commissioned officers from the working classes.'[2]

The outbreak of the Great War divided Labour, a majority of whose MPs were pro-war. Keir Hardie, ill and about to die, was openly anti-war. The Labour leader, Ramsay MacDonald, was a pacifist and privately against the war, but he kept quiet in case the party might split over the issue. Nevertheless, by December 1914, 25 percent of Scotland's male workforce had volunteered. In the Lothian coalfield 36 percent of the miners enlisted after its Eastern European export market collapsed. In the Lanarkshire coalfield the figure was just 20 percent. Christopher Harvie explains this high rate of enlistment as being down to the 'herd instinct – "following one's pals" – and the expectation of a short war'.[3]

A pamphlet produced by the National Service League entitled 'The Briton's First Duty' admitted, 'Want and hunger are, unfortunately for us, the invisible recruiting sergeants of a great portion of our army.'[4] Economic hardship had a pronounced effect on enlistment rates.[5]

My paternal grandfather volunteered in 1915, lying about his age, alongside his two brothers; one lies still outside Ypres. As shale miners anything might have seemed better than what they were doing, and anyone who's been to Tarbrax in Midlothian, where they lived, would understand the wish to escape. He would regret his youthful enthusiasm and was bitter about what he experienced. (My other grandfather objected to the war on religious grounds but when conscripted agreed to be a stretcher-bearer – he never talked about what he saw.) In the main, the workers' organisation in Glasgow was anti-war but many felt the pressure of the jingoist agitation. *Forward*, despite its anti-war stance, was compelled to print a pro-war column.[6] Yet it would not take long for social and economic issues to resurface.

Glasgow was notorious for its housing conditions, but a fresh influx of workers to fuel its armament factories added to the pressure. Rents were higher than elsewhere in the UK and, with accommodation in demand, landlords raised rents. Existing tenants, who could not afford the increase, faced eviction – even the families of those away fighting in the trenches.

The government found in October 1915 that a third of rents had increased by 5 percent, while in 'Govan and Fairfield, the centre of the storm, all the houses . . . suffered rent increases ranging from 11.67% to 23.08%'.[7] Across Glasgow and the west of Scotland a network of Independent Labour Party branches, tenants groups,

Co-operative Society branches, the Govan and Glasgow Trades Councils, trade union activists and socialists were able to organise a rising groundswell of discontent.[8] The *Partick and Maryhill Press* reported the 1915 May Day rally in Glasgow thus: 'Over 165 labour and socialist organisations took part . . . and Glasgow Green was crowded with thousands of spectators. There were twelve platforms. Among those represented were those of the Socialist and Labour Party, Internationalism, Glasgow Housing Committee, the Anarchist Group, Socialist Children's School and Women Trade Unionists.'[9]

Women took the lead in winning the single greatest victory notched up on Red Clydeside. One of the organisers of the rent strike, Helen Crawfurd, had been a radical suffragette jailed three times before the war for actions that included smashing the windows of the Ministry of Education in London and an army recruitment office in Glasgow. Seán Damer notes: 'The Glasgow suffragettes had a tradition of militancy which included blowing up all the telegraph and telephone cables, cutting the wires around the city.'[10]

Mary Barbour arrived in Govan in 1896, a newly married engineer's wife, and became active in the Independent Labour Party. She began organising over rents by holding meetings, large and small, in kitchens, in closes and in backcourts, attracting her audience with a football rattle.[11]

In April 1915 the eviction in Govan of the family of a soldier serving in France was met with angry protests, as Willie Gallacher, a leader of the shops stewards' movement on the Clyde, describes:

In Govan, Mrs. Barbour, a typical working class housewife, became the leader of a movement such has never been seen before, or since for that matter, street meetings, back-court meetings, drums, bells, trumpets – every method was used to bring the women out and organise them for struggle. Notices were printed by the thousand and put up in the windows: wherever you went you could see them. In street after street, scarcely a window without one: WE ARE NOT PAYING INCREASED RENT.[12]

One landlord had applied for an eviction order against a mother and family for non-payment of rent at a time when the man of the house was fighting in France and a son was recovering from war wounds. The court supplied the necessary authorisation despite an offer from the local miners' union to pay the rent debt within a week. However, the attempt at eviction was successfully resisted by a large crowd that had to be restrained from physically attacking the land-lord.[13] Similar scenes were repeated across the city, for instance in Partick: '. . . a seventy year-old-pensioner living alone was due to be evicted on a warrant issued by Sheriff Thomson for refusing to pay a rent increase. The old man barricaded himself in his tiny tenement flat and a large crowd gathered outside in his support, making his "castle" impregnable. Again no official showed face.'[14]

Gallacher records that 'the factors [agents for the property owners] could not collect the rents'.[15] When a factor turned up in Partick in late October, the *Glasgow Herald* reported, 'he was pelted with bags of peasemeal and chased from one of the streets by a number of women, who upbraided him vociferously'.[16] The landlords then applied to a judge for an eviction warrant, and executing it fell to the city's sheriff, who asked the police to carry out the task:

> But Mrs. Barbour had a team of women who were wonderful. They could smell a sheriff's officer a mile away. At their summons women left their cooking, washing or whatever they were doing. Before they were anywhere near their destination, the officer and his men would be met by an army of furious women who drove them back in a hurried scramble for safety.[17]

In every window of every house there were notices that read, 'We are not removing'. Within weeks, thousands of notices were displayed in street after street. Soon all of Glasgow was involved: from Park-head to Govan, Pollokshaws to Calton.[18]

Throughout 1915, John Maclean, the leading revolutionary on Clydeside, spoke at meeting after meeting outside the shipyards and other workplaces, demanding action on rents. On Sunday nights he addressed huge open-air meetings in Bath Street while his Marxist night class had an average attendance of 493, mainly shop stewards. In October he was brought to court under the Defence of the Realm Act for opposing the war and was bound over on agreement that he would not speak publicly on the war, though he made it clear he would still speak out over rents.[19] Because of this conviction, Maclean faced the sack from his teaching position.

By October 1915, 15,000 refused to pay rent increases, and a month later it was 20,000. That month a factor took eighteen tenants to court, providing a focus for the movement, as Mrs Barbour's women marched on the City Chambers. Tom Bell would write that en route: 'The women marched in a body to the shipyard and got the men to leave work and join them in a demonstration to the Court.'[20] *Forward* estimated the crowd outside the City Chambers as being 4,000 strong.[21] John Maclean was among those who spoke, denouncing the evils of capitalism.[22] His arrival was unusual: 'On their way from Govan one contingent marched to the school where John Maclean, already under notice of dismissal from Govan School Board, was teaching. He was taken out and carried shoulder high through the streets to the court.'[23]

Helen Crawfurd would remember: 'I will never forget the sight and sound of those marching men [from the shipyards]. Thousands of them marched through the principal streets to the Sheriff Court and the surrounding streets were packed. John Maclean . . . was one of the speakers, who from barrels and up-turned boxes, addressed the crowds.'[24]

The government in London was worried by the scale of the protests and that the eviction of rent strikers might be the spark for a walkout in the Clyde yards.[25] It responded quickly, hurrying through the Rent Restriction Act of 1915, which returned rents to pre-war levels. This was a major victory for working-class people of Britain, won by the working women and men of Glasgow.

A Revolutionary Storm-Centre Second to None

The rent strike coincided with the beginning of grass-roots trade union organisation, which would challenge the employers, the government and the union leaders who were determined to police their promises that there would be no strikes during wartime.

The factory owners took the initiative when the hawkish, anti-union William Weir brought American engineers to his Cathcart plant, paying them a bonus of six shillings a week, in order to bring in US working practices and to undermine the union. In response, the engineering workers walked out on an unofficial strike in defiance of their union leaders. The strike at Weir's quickly spread to twenty other factories, with an official ballot of engineering union members over-whelmingly rejecting the employers' offer. Shop stewards from all the striking plants met to co-ordinate the action, forming what was to be the Clyde Workers' Committee, made up of 200–300 shop stewards who met each Sunday. Its attitude was summed up thus:

> We will support the officials just as long as they rightly represent the workers, but we will act independently immediately they misrepresent them. Being composed of Delegates from every shop and untrammeled by obsolete rule or law, we claim to represent the true feeling of the workers. We can act immediately according to the merits of the case and the desire of the rank and file.[26]

Without strike pay and under a media attack orchestrated by the munitions minister, Lloyd George, the strike began to crumble. A ballot agreed to a deal hammered out by government arbitration, which gave a penny-an-hour raise and 10 percent on piece rates.

In February 1915, the Clyde Workers' Committee (CWC) led a campaign demanding a twopenny pay increase, promised before the war, but denied by a wartime pay freeze, despite rocketing prices. Ten thousand workers responded, two-thirds of Clyde's engineering workforce. They faced not just the government but the hostility of their own engineering union, which called on them to return to work.[27] The employers were forced to concede, but they negotiated a raise of one penny, not with the CWC but with the engineering union. The engineering unions had agreed a no-strike deal with the government in March 1915, 'with a view to accelerating the output of war munitions or equipments'.[28]

The next industrial flashpoint was at Fairfield's shipyard in July 1915, with a call for two strikes to protest the necessity for anyone switching jobs to be given a leaving certificate by management to indicate good time-keeping and service. This was seen as a means of discriminating against 'troublemakers'. The two walkouts that summer led to seventeen strikers being convicted, with three refusing to pay their fines. The issue was resolved only when the national union paid their fines after talks with the government.

The Clyde Workers' Committee restricted itself to shop-floor issues – pay, conditions and protecting job status – and refused to address wider issues like the war, the one issue that defined everything else. Their attitude was summed up in that of Gallacher, who was a member of the British Socialist Party and spoke against the war at weekends, but kept this separate from his trade union work.[29]

The CWC has often been dismissed as an association of skilled workers, labour aristocrats, concerned with protecting their status as unskilled men and women were introduced into engineering. However, the radicalisation of skilled engineers and metalworkers was a feature of the period across Europe. Traditionally, the response of these skilled workers was to try to maintain their standing above their unskilled fellows. But now they saw the attacks on them as part of a more general war on all trade unionists.

The CWC's concentration on dilution, the replacement of skilled workers by semi- or non-skilled workers, meant it did not take up the issue of conscription, which would be introduced by the government in January 1916, but had been much debated beforehand. Opposing conscription would have allowed the CWC to broaden out to other sections of the working class on the Clyde.[30] While it did become involved in solidarity with the rent strike, no attempt was made to bring that together with the growing industrial unrest. If the housing agitation, labour unrest and opposition to war came together on Clydeside, Maclean argued, that could create a revolutionary situation.

Meanwhile, the government toughened up the Munitions Act and Dilution of Labour Act, making it nigh impossible for a worker to leave one job for another – any who did were subject to military law

– and enforcing the replacement of skilled labour by unskilled. In the interim, the government had also noted the existence of the CWC, and a paper dated 24 November 1915 states: 'To obtain a reasonably smooth working of the Munition Act, this committee should be smashed.'[31] That month, the government tightened wartime laws against strikers and decided to send Lloyd George to address Clydeside munitions workers, hoping to trade on his pre-war reputation as a radical for his opposition to the earlier Boer War in South Africa and his attacks on Tory aristocrats.

However, when Lloyd George visited Weir's and Albion Motors, shop stewards refused to meet him, as agreed with the CWC. At Parkhead Forge the union convenor David Kirkwood broke ranks and did receive him, causing splits in the committee that were papered over for a time. On Christmas Day (not a holiday in Calvinist Scotland), Lloyd George was to address a mass meeting of munitions workers in an attempt to directly appeal to them to rally behind the war effort. The meeting was packed. David Kirkwood took the chair, and introduced the future prime minister: 'This, fellow workers, is Mr Lloyd George. He has come specially to speak to you and I have no doubt that you will give him a patient hearing. I can assure him that every word he says will be carefully weighed. We regard him with suspicion because every act associated with his name has the taint of slavery about it.'[32]

Defying government orders that there should be no publicity, *Forward* published a comprehensive report of the meeting, with Kirkwood demanding to know whether Lloyd George was prepared to give the workers responsibility for managing the plants, but the minister replied that the workers were not capable of managing factories. Kirkwood responded that the shop stewards had the confidence of the workers, 'Who runs the workshops now?' Lloyd George replied that giving workers any say in management was a revolutionary proposal and pointed out that Labour leaders now in government, such as Arthur Henderson, who was present, shared responsibility for the Munitions Act. Kirkwood responded, 'We repudiate that man, he is no leader of ours. If you, Mister Lloyd George, wish to know the mind of the workers, don't go to such men. If you wish to do away with the discontent in the workshops, then do away with the cause.' At this point, Lloyd George left the meeting, to the accompaniment of 'The Red Flag' sung by a chorus of shop stewards.[33]

After the debacle of the Christmas Day meeting, the government determined to get revenge. After *Forward* published its account, the paper's offices were raided and new issues were prevented from appearing for a month. As the demand for munitions rose and rose, the government announced in January 1916 that it would enforce 'dilution'; the engineering shop stewards of the Clyde Workers' Committee pledged to resist this. Nonetheless, within three days, 'three Dilution Commissioners arrived on the Clyde'.[34]

The Munitions Ministry official in charge of labour wanted the CWC leaders and John Maclean deported from the city, but planned to do so if and when a strike against the dilution of labour broke out.[35] The Scottish Director of Munitions was the Glasgow industrialist William Weir, who determined to ram through the scheme in a select number of Clydeside workplaces in a matter of days in order to break the unity of the CWC. The police and army were on hand to deal with trouble, and Weir could call on the powers of the draconian Defence of the Realm Act. But none of this was needed, because David Kirkwood agreed to accept the scheme in return for assurances he would have a say in the running of Parkhead Forge.[36] A member of the ILP, Kirkwood took the view that the interests of the workers he represented were paramount over those of the working class as a whole.

Meanwhile, an article in the CWC paper, *The Worker*, headlined 'Should the Workers Arm?' provided the authorities with an opportunity to act – even though the author answered his own question 'No'. Willie Gallacher, John Muir and the paper's publisher, Walter Bell, were arrested and charged with sedition. In response, workers at Weir's, Coventry Ordnance Works, Beardmore's in Dalmuir, John Brown Engineering, Albion Motors, and Barr and Stroud walked out on strike. But Parkhead Forge, where Kirkwood was corresponding with Lloyd George about his ideas for running production, did not. The strike ended when the three men arrested were released on bail.

News that Kirkwood had broken ranks once more in negotiating a dilution scheme at Parkhead Forge led to bitter recriminations among members of the CWC, whose goal had been a Clydeside-wide strike against dilution. Despite Kirkwood's initial actions, the next flashpoint would be at Parkhead Forge when the first women workers arrived on 29 February. Kirkwood wanted them to join the National Federation of Women Workers and he addressed them soon after they started. The next day, management banned him from the women's section, and he later was again banned from entering another department where a dispute had arisen. When the owner, Beardmore, would not back down, the shop stewards voted to strike on 17 March.

The Parkhead strike was joined by strikes at the North British Diesel Engine Works, at Weirs, and another by the gunmakers at Beardmore's in Dalmuir. But resentment at Kirkwood's previous behaviour meant stewards elsewhere did not argue to join the strike. Sensing a victory, the government deported Kirkwood and eight other shop stewards from the striking plants under wartime emergency laws.

On 29 March, at a special tribunal, thirty strikers were fined £5 each, and two days later a big rally was organised on Glasgow Green against the deportations, but the strike had lost momentum and workers were beginning to drift back to work. The CWC had failed to respond to this attack, with leading figures like Gallacher allowing their anger at Kirkwood to get in the way of providing solidarity.

For a year the Clyde was quiet. The biggest strike of the war, which began in Sheffield in May 1917, after the protection against conscription previously provided to skilled workers was lifted, did not cross the border.[37] Scottish historian Christopher Harvie has noted that 'the government was fortunate' to have broken the CWC before 'really huge casualty lists came in from the Somme.'[38] But during the demonstrations that took place in 1916, protesters took up the ditty 'Henry Dubb' penned by James Maxton, who was in jail for refusing to serve:

> Oh, I'm Henry Dubb
> And I won't go to war
> Because I don't know
> What they're all fighting for.

To Hell with the Kaiser
To Hell with the Tsar
To Hell with Lord Derby
To Hell with GR.
I work at munitions
I'm a slave down at Weir's
If I leave my job
They'll give me two years.

To Hell with the sheriff
To Hell with his crew
To Hell with Lloyd George
And Henderson too.

I don't like the factor
His rent I won't pay
Three cheers for John Wheatley
I'm striking today.

To Hell with the landlord
I'm not one to grouse
But to Hell both with him
And his bloody old house.

The movement was not fully broken. In the autumn of 1916, John Maclean's economics classes drew 200 shop stewards each week. They increased over that winter: his Central Halls class had 'recruited 500 members by November 1917; while the Govan class had 100 members. MacLean conducted three Marxist classes in Fife, and three in the West; while James MacDougall also taught eight classes in Paisley and in Lanarkshire, mainly in the mining communities where he and rank-and-file miners were leading the reform movement within the union, demanding workers control in a socialized industry.'[39] Some 2,000 students attended such classes across Scotland, with 854 signing up in Glasgow.

But opposition to the slaughter in the trenches was growing, and the outbreak of the Russian Revolution and the overthrow of the Tsar in February 1917 found ready support. For the May Day march that year in Glasgow, the *Glasgow Herald* gave a figure of 70,000 participants. A year later it quoted the same number, despite the march taking place on a weekday during work hours. On his release from jail for sedition, Gallacher re-formed the CWC in September 1917, and it made its presence felt in disrupting the government minister Sir Auckland Geddes when he addressed munitions workers, demanding greater output.[40]

That September, the CWC was also able to call a strike over wages, and while it had to be called off after a few days, they retreated in good order. Subsequently, the government awarded a 12.5 percent pay increase. In November, four women workers at Beardmore's East Hope Street shell factory were victimised for taking part in a go-slow, and the factory stopped, demanding their reinstatement. Their union disowned the strike but the CWC called a solidarity rally on Glasgow Green. The women won reinstatement.

In January 1918, 10,000 shipyard workers struck over pay, and the action spread to engineering plants. James Hinton, a historian of the shop stewards' movement, argues: 'By January 1918 the Clyde was back in the vanguard of the national movement.'[41]

That same month the Lloyd George government passed the Manpower Bill to increase conscription both into the armed forces and the war industries. A government minister was sent to Glasgow to sell it to workers. He was first shouted down then allowed to speak before a resolution was passed, saying Glasgow and Clydeside would 'do nothing at all in support of carrying on the war but . . . everything we can to bring the war to a conclusion'.[42] The resolution was seconded by Jimmy Maxton, and after it was passed, the crowd marched to George Square.

The May Day demonstration of 1918 saw up to 110,000 on the streets, and the rally passed motions in solidarity with revolutionary Russia and the working class of Germany, with whom Britain was still at war.[43]

The Red Flag in George Square

As the war came to a close, demobilisation meant that unemployment now rose to 11 percent by February 1919. The Scottish Trades Union Congress had already backed a motion for a thirty-hour week in April 1918. That August, its Parliamentary Committee joined Glasgow Trades Council and the Scottish Advisory Committee of the Labour Party to lobby the Westminster government for a forty-hour week.

The engineering union, the ASE, agreed to a forty-seven-hour week with the engineering employers in January 1919, and this was narrowly approved in a ballot by 36,000 votes to 28,000. But now breakfast had to be eaten before work started because there was no longer a break at 9 a.m. as before, so workers had to get up early to go to work and did not get back any sooner.[44]

Clydeside shop stewards met and rejected the forty-seven-hour week, electing an eight-man committee to fight for a forty-hour week and to call for industrial action if necessary. Factory gate meetings were held prior to votes being taken at shop-floor meetings in support of a strike call. A further shop stewards' conference took place in Glasgow on 16 January with delegates from all over Scotland. It was reported that well over half the workshops where a vote had been taken were in favour of thirty hours a week, less for a forty-hour week and few for forty-seven hours.[45]

The ASE responded by attacking the shop stewards for defying a ballot decision, but a strike date was set nonetheless for 27 January. That morning some 40,000 workers responded to the strike call and by the close of the week there were 1,000,000 on strike in Clydeside, where engineering plants and shipyards in Glasgow, Paisley and Dumbarton were solid; and 14,000 on the Firth of Forth, with 8,000 shipyard workers in Leith on strike alongside engineering and printing workers in Edinburgh, Rosyth naval dockyard workers; and another 1,000 in Grangemouth.[46]

In west Fife a strike that began in Cowdenbeath on 23 January, to demand that demobilised tradesmen be taken back on, quickly spread to Bowhill, Lochgelly and Glencraig pits, with the Fife Miners

Reform Committee co-coordinating the action and raising the demand for a six-hour day and a five-day week. On 30 January, 10,000 miners marched on the official union HQ in Dunfermline, demanding the stoppage be made official, something the union leaders opposed. They called a ballot across the Fife coalfield and secured a narrow majority against the strike.[47]

In Lanarkshire it was a similar story. On 27 January many miners stopped work despite an appeal from the Scottish Executive of the miners' union not to do so. Pickets spread the strike to Hamilton and Holytown. On the Wednesday afternoon, 1,500 strikers met in Hamilton's public park and rejected appeals from their officials to return to work. Instead, they agreed to stay out and to send a delegation to the union's Lanarkshire executive committee. That evening they rallied outside its offices in Hamilton, occupying them as the crowd sang 'The Red Flag'. The union was forced to call a strike across the coalfield, and the next day 15,000 miners and supporters marched through Hamilton. On the Saturday, however, the executive took off to Edinburgh, where it met to vote for an end to the action. By the following Tuesday the strike was over. The local Hamilton paper condemned the mass picketing that had been central to the action.[48]

Mass picketing was a key feature of the Forty-Hour Strike. On the first day of the stoppage, 2,000 workers from the Albion car plant in west Glasgow marched on Barr and Stroud and brought it out. In Dalmuir, Beardmore's was similarly brought out, and the next day John Brown's. On the Tuesday, 5,000 strikers marched through Dumbarton and formed mass pickets at Dennystoun Forge and Babcock and Wilcox, stopping work there. On the Thursday, strikers marched up through the Vale of Leven to bring out the munitions plant in Alexandria.

In Dumbarton, mass meetings were held each morning to decide where to picket, and unemployed workers helped in spreading the strike. Both there and in Paisley were elected strike committees that sent a delegate each to the strike centre in Glasgow mid-morning to report in, to return to the strike committee in the early afternoon and then back to Glasgow by 4 p.m. In this way secure lines of communication were kept open.[49] The trams ran in Dumbarton only if they carried the strikers' new bulletin in their windows. The daily strike bulletins, sold for a penny, had a readership of 20,000.

The Scottish section of the Federation of Women Workers backed the strike, and in Clydebank a special mass meeting of women from across the town voted in support. Afterwards some successfully picketed and stopped apprentices attending an official trade union meeting called in opposition to the strike.[50] The *Paisley Express* reported from the picket lines: 'It was noted that the women were not silent onlookers but in some cases showed more zeal and demonstrated more in speech than the men.'[51] The central strike committee reported, 'we have had as many as five thousand females forming one of our massed pickets.'[52]

On Wednesday 29 January, there was a demonstration at Glasgow City Chambers to demand the Lord Provost request that the government intervene and to back the strike's demands. He told them to come back on Friday at 2.30 p.m. to get the government's reply.

Thus, 30,000 strikers gathered in George Square on the Friday. The most famous image of the demonstration shows the Red Flag raised from the middle of the crowd outside the City Chambers. The police were there in large numbers and used the pretext that the trams had to run through the square to begin baton charges. A young seventeen-year-old apprentice in the shipyards, Finlay Hart, was there:

> I marched with the Clydebank contingent eight miles to George Square on 'Bloody Friday'. We walked on the tram lines and never let a tram-car pass us. When we reached George Square, the baton charge had taken place, and we marched through the Square on to Glasgow Green. The tram-cars were halted in the centre of the city, because the marchers pulled down the electric cable and bent them. The police would charge, the crowd would scatter, then reform and the police would charge again.[54]

The *Daily News* reporter on the scene wrote on 3 February: 'I have no hesitation in saying that the baton charge made with the object of clearing a way for a tram car was the beginning of the trouble.' And political historian Iain McLean points out: 'But no tramlines ran along the east side of the square, in front of the City Chambers, in 1919. Nor where there any in North Frederick Street . . .'[54] Under attack the crowd fought back. The strikers commandeered a lemonade lorry and used its bottles to pelt police lines. Willie Gallacher ran to remonstrate with the chief constable and was knocked to the ground by a police baton. Eventually, the crowd left the square when their leaders asked them to march to Glasgow Green for a rally. Three of those leaders, Gallacher, Davie Kirkwood and Emmanuel Shinwell, were arrested.

The Secretary of State for Scotland told the War Cabinet, which met on the afternoon of 'Bloody Friday', that this was not a strike but 'a Bolshevist rising'.[55]

The next day, the city awoke to find itself under military occupation. Troops from English and Highland regiments had been ordered in because Whitehall was worried the local garrison might be unreliable. The strike continued into its second week but there was no more mass picketing. The press then went on the attack. At the same time, lack of money began to bite (there was no strike pay because the stoppage was unofficial) and to cap it all the union officials grew louder in attacking their members' action in stopping work.

The Clyde shop stewards had hoped that the strike would spread, and Belfast engineering and shipyard workers had been out since 25 January for a forty-four-hour week. In England there were stoppages on Tyneside, Merseyside and on the Humber, but union officials held the line in preventing an all-out strike. On 6 February, the engineering union suspended its Glasgow, Belfast and London district committees. The following Wednesday, the joint strike committee in Glasgow ordered a return to work.

In the meantime, the Glasgow District Committee of the engineering union had shifted towards a more militant stance, advocating, alongside the CWC, a five-day, thirty-hour week. Nationally, the engineering and shipbuilding workers had voted to accept a forty-seven-hour week, as agreed with management.

The strike was defeated. One cause was the failure of the Glasgow strikers to try to co-ordinate with other centres south of the border. Shop stewards' organisations existed in Sheffield, Coventry and elsewhere but there was no national co-ordination. Delegations went south after Bloody Friday but that was too late. The Sheffield shop stewards' leader J. T. Murphy argued that the Clyde Workers' Committee's 'greatest mistake' was that '. . . it had done nothing to prepare the movement beyond the Clyde. Although it was represented on the National Council of the Shop Stewards, it had not even acquainted the committee of its plans.'[56]

Later, in his book *Revolt on the Clyde*, William Gallacher claimed, 'We were leading a strike when we should have been leading a revolution. A rising was expected – a rising should have taken place.'[57] Gallagher was wrong. Glasgow was not Petrograd in October 1917. A rising was not on the agenda. But a victory for the strike could have opened up a revolutionary crisis. Britain was facing a strike wave and the British state was faced with a developing liberation struggle in Ireland. Its troops were spread over the globe – occupying Germany, Istanbul, Iraq, Palestine and in Revolutionary Russia fighting the 'Reds'.

The strike leaders called off mass pickets and made no plans to try to win over the troops sent into the city. Only John Maclean made attempts to link up with unrest in the coalfields. Above all, the CWC did not link, as we've argued, with shop stewards who were similarly organised in Sheffield, Manchester, Coventry, London and Belfast.

Everything had been possible in January 1919. The Lloyd George government understood that, and it played to win. Nevertheless, despite the failure of the Forty-Hour Strike, something fundamental had shifted in Scotland. Prior to Red Clydeside, Scottish workers were not renowned for their militancy. Now they had gained a reputation as determined fighters, and had produced a generation of leaders who gained international repute. Glasgow and the west of Scotland were seen as a bastion of the left.

There are those who want to undermine that legacy or even suggest that Red Clydeside was simply a legend. The ruling class had suffered a great fright and wanted to eradicate any collective memory of such working-class insurgency. If it became a legend, it was because it was the stuff of legends.

REBEL LIVES: JOHN MACLEAN

Of the Clydeside socialist John Maclean, in 'Krassivy, Krassivy' the great poet Hugh MacDiarmid said this:

> Scotland has had few men whose names
> Matter – or should matter – to intelligent people.
> But of these Maclean, next to Burns, was the greatest.

Maclean's parents were Highlanders, his father from the Isle of Mull and his mother from Corpach, beneath Ben Nevis. In 1903, in his early twenties, Maclean joined the Social Democratic Federation (SDF). This was Britain's main Marxist organisation but it was a dogmatic one that saw its role as the teacher of the working class, saw socialism as inevitable and denounced strikes for dealing with the effects of exploitation, not its causes. Its stress was on propaganda, outdoor meetings in summer and indoor in winter, and elections. Its leader, H. M. Hyndman, was a wealthy businessman, an autocrat and inclined to nationalism.

A year before Maclean joined, the SDF had disaffiliated from the Labour Representation Committee (the precursor of the Labour Party) because of its refusal to openly proclaim socialism. The Scot believed this was a mistake because the SDF could have helped shape the new party and because it would have widened its audience. He believed revolutionaries should not be a sect apart from the working class. Later, a majority of its Scottish branches broke away because they believed in a general strike as the means to achieve socialism, and wanted to create 'one big union'.

It was his experience of the 1907 Belfast dockers and carters strike, which had united Catholic and Protestant in that divided city, that convinced Maclean of the importance of strike action, and the potential for it to politicise workers. He was active around the strike wave of 1910–11, the Great Unrest, which made him a popular figure among the Clydeside working class. He was also to the fore in opposing, from 1910 on as the war danger grew, the patriotic stand of the leadership of the British Socialist Party (as the SDF had come to be known).

Opposition to war and militarism became a central theme for Maclean in the years and months before the outbreak of war in August 1914, and may help explain why he could maintain his open-air meetings, which elsewhere were broken up by pro-war crowds.

'Jingoism', argued Maclean's comrade James D. MacDougall, 'was at a discount in Glasgow from the very beginning of the war; it was the sole place in the British empire where there was perfect freedom of speech for international socialists and opponents of the war.'[58]

Less than a month into the war, Maclean stated:

It is our business as socialists to develop 'class patriotism', refusing to murder one another for a sordid world capitalism. The absurdity of the present situation is surely apparent when we see British socialists going out to murder German socialists with the object of crushing Kaiserism and Prussian militarism. The only real enemy to Kaiserism and Prussian militarism . . . was, and is German social democracy. Let the propertied class, old and new, go out and defend their blessed property.[59]

By the autumn of 1915, Maclean's Bath Street meetings were drawing large crowds and his Marxist economic classes were attended by 400 workers. But that October he was charged after saying in Bath Street, 'I have been enlisted in the Socialist army for fifteen years. God damn all other armies!'[60] When he was fined £5 he refused to pay and was jailed for five days. Meanwhile, Govan School Board dismissed him from his teaching post.

The following year, Maclean was unequivocal in his defence of the Easter Rising in Ireland and of James Connolly's leading role in the rebellion, on the basis that it was a major blow against British imperialism. The war continued to radicalise him, and after 1917 he was appointed as the consul for the Soviet Union in Scotland. This last straw seemed to spur the authorities to action. The General Officer commanding the army in Scotland was, in February 1918, fearful of the mood on Clydeside, warning that 'indications of unrest continually prevail'. He wanted further legal action taken against Maclean.[61]

In April 1918, Maclean was arrested once more on the grounds of sedition. When he set off to face trial in Edinburgh, some 100,000 workers took time off work to march behind him through Glasgow. He famously told the court: 'I am not here, then, as the accused; I am here as the accuser of capitalism dripping with blood from head to foot.'[62] He was jailed for a second time, sentenced to three years' hard labour for his anti-war activities.

Prisoners in Scotland then were denied books, writing materials and much else. The regime in Peterhead Prison, where Maclean was sent, was particularly harsh. The campaign for his release extended across Britain, with 10,000 gathering in North London's Finsbury Park and the Labour Party national conference voting in support of his release, which came in December 1918 – a month after the war ended.[63]

On his release he was thrown into a general election campaign in which he stood in the Gorbals against George Barnes, who had been elected on the Labour ticket but had refused to follow the party when it quit the coalition government led by Lloyd George at the war's end. Maclean polled 7,436 votes against Barnes's 14,247.

His immediate hope at the end of the war was that a general strike could be achieved, and even the defeat of the Forty Hours strike on Clydeside did not dim his hopes; in particular he looked to the miners carrying out propaganda work in the coalfields.

The years 1919 and 1920 saw unprecedented class struggle across Europe, with Britain experiencing a strike wave. On May Day in 1919, 150,000 marched in Glasgow, with the Irish anthem 'The Soldier's Song' being sung along with 'The Red Flag', and that evening Maclean shared a platform with John Wheatley and the Irish republican, and comrade of James Connolly, Constance Markievicz.[64] But the revolutions in Germany, Italy, Hungary and elsewhere were defeated and the economy went into recession, undermining working-class insurgency. Maclean had to adapt his strategic vision.

After a visit to Dublin he launched a 'Hands Off Ireland Campaign' and wrote a pamphlet, 'Ireland's Tragedy: Scotland's Disgrace', demanding Scottish troops not be used to suppress the republicans. Some 20,000 copies were sold in just a few weeks.[65]

Despite political differences he supported the struggle of the Irish

Republicans, explaining: 'The Irish Sinn Feiners, who make no profession of socialism or communism and who are at best non-socialists, are doing more to help Russia and the revolution than all we professed Marxian Bolsheviks in Britain . . .'[66]

As a result of his meetings he faced prosecution again, being sentenced to three months. Incredibly, Maclean was given the status of a political prisoner, something unprecedented in Scotland, with books, writing materials, food, two visitors and one letter per week. Released in August, he was again charged that autumn, accused of telling the unemployed to take food rather than starve. At his October 1921 trial he told the court: 'I argued that the workers should not confine themselves to industrial action, but should take political action as well. Neither political nor industrial action would do separately . . .'[67]

For Maclean revolution was necessary to stop a new world war between Britain and America – the old global hegemon and the new one – to aid revolutionary Russia and to help destroy the British Empire. Conditions, he held, were more favourable in Scotland: 'Scotland is firmer for Marxism than any other part of the British Empire. Clyde speakers get bigger and better audiences in Scotland . . .'[68]

His decision to organise a Scottish Workers Republican Party was also justified by his opposition to those leading the British Communist Party, among them Willie Gallacher, who he regarded as opportunists.

In his final years his key concern was organising the unemployed. The jobless total had been mounting since the end of 1920 and, unlike, in England, there was no parish relief, it being illegal under Scots Law to give relief to the unemployed. Up until April 1921, when the law was changed, allowing poor law authorities to give relief, the unemployed were destitute. Maclean fought to win them food and shelter. After initial gains in 1921, the focus shifted to winning relief at the same rate as south of the border.

Maclean never visited Russia, despite being appointed Soviet consul in Scotland immediately after the revolution, and being pinpointed by Lenin as one of the key opponents of the war. He demanded a passport from the British government and refused to go until one was issued.

Just a week before his death, Maclean stated in his election address to the voters of the Gorbals: 'The social revolution is possible sooner in Scotland than in England . . . Scottish separation is part of the process of England's imperial disintegration and is as help towards the ultimate triumph of the workers of the world.'[69]

Earlier, in November 1922, while standing for Parliament for the Gorbals in support of a Scottish Workers Republic, his election address had begun with these words: 'I stand in the Gorbals and before the world as a Bolshevik, alias a Communist, alias a Revolutionist, alias a Marxian. My symbol is the Red Flag, and I shall always keep it flying high.'[70]

A month before his death he told an old friend he was getting 3,000 people to his open-air meetings in West Regent Street, 'the biggest crowds ever held Sunday after Sunday in Glasgow'.[71]

John Maclean went to an early grave, an internationalist and a revolutionary, along with James Connolly the finest this country has produced.

TEN

The 1920s: Economic Decline and General Strike

The End of Scottish Capitalism

Before the war, the Scottish economy was largely owned and managed by a native elite. Within a few short years of the armistice, this state of affairs came to a sudden and startling end. For example, in 1917, Lord Pirrie, head of Harland & Wolff shipyard in Govan, believed that he would have full order books after the war and so purchased Caird's yard at Greenock and embarked on rapid expansion. When he died in 1924, his ever-expanding empire expired with him. Caird's was closed and stood empty for years.[1] The profound economic difficulties of the inter-war years pushed Scottish society to the verge of catastrophe.

The post-war period showed that the UK was overreliant on the old staple industries such as steel, coal, textiles and shipbuilding, but this was particularly true of Scotland. Lack of investment, poor management and no strategy for diversification would only add to the problem. The car industry was a success story in England between the wars, but whereas before World War I there had been seven companies making cars in Scotland, by 1930 there was only one, Albion in Glasgow, which concentrated on making commercial vehicles.[2]

In addition, employment in Scottish shipbuilding declined from 100,000 in 1920 to 50,000 in 1925 and just 10,000 in 1929, a 90 percent decline. In the face of foreign competition more than half of Scotland's iron furnaces were dismantled in 1927, while the coal industry contracted by one-third in the 1920s and the fishing industry also saw a drop of 30 percent in tonnage.[3]

In December 1925, the *Scotsman* reported from Tarbrax, a shale-mining village then in South Lanarkshire, under the headline 'Situation at Tarbrax: Faced with Starvation', which reported: 'Workers from Tarbrax, to the number of nearly 400, marched in procession to Carnwath, nearly ten miles distant, on Thursday night last for the purpose of asking poor relief. Relief under the emergency clause of the Poor Law Act, which enables people in a state of absolute destitution to get relief, has been given to a number of people in Tarbrax on the recommendation of the doctor there. A meeting of Carnwath Parish Council has been called for today to consider the whole situation.'[4]

The old industries hung on if they could, waiting for better times. But these did not come until the close of the 1930s and re-armament in the build up to World War II. Survival meant a strong emphasis on cutting labour costs by holding down wages. For working people these were desperate times. In the 1920s, 400,000 Scots emigrated, most moving south of the border.[5]

The inter-war years were disastrous, too, for the Highlands and Islands. Between 1921 and 1931 Shetland lost 17 percent of its people, Ross and Cromarty 12 percent and Caithness 11.5 percent. The crofting communities had, thus far, relied on being able to find work locally in the fishing industry or in domestic service and the shipyards farther south, returning for the harvest, but this tradition collapsed. Herring had been a major export to Eastern Europe but demand dried up, mechanisation meant farming required less labour and there were fewer domestic servants hired in the Lowland cities. The fall in the population of the Hebrides was greater than at any time in the previous century, with the Islands losing 28 percent between 1911 and 1951.[6]

The soap magnate Lord Leverhulme bought the Isle of Lewis in 1918. He wanted to turn Stornoway into a modern fishing port and fish-processing centre. Farms near the island's capital were switched from crofting to dairy production. But the young men who had returned from the war had been promised land and responded to Leverhulme's schemes by taking it.[7]

At the first meeting where Leverhulme outlined his plans he was shouted down by a crofter, Alan Martin, who challenged him: 'What we want is land – and the question I put to you is: Will you give us the land?'[8] By the summer of 1920, sixteen out of the twenty-two largest farms on Lewis had been taken over by the raiders.[9] By the late 1920s, the Lewis crofters had won back nearly half a million acres from the landlords.[10] One of the raiders, Alec Graham, recalled: 'We didn't care at that time whether there was legal action or not, no. We just wanted the land – and if we didn't get it, well, we had just come out of the war and we were right for anything as you might say.'[11]

But this was not enough, unfortunately, to stop the loss of people. In April 1923, two Canadian Pacific liners took 600 Hebrideans from Lewis, Barra, North Uist, South Uist, Benbecula and Harris from Lochboisdale and Stornoway to new homes in Alberta and Ontario in Canada. They were taking advantage of the year-old Empire Settlement Act, which granted subsidised passages to Canada, following a lecture tour of the Hebrides by a Canadian emigration agent that year.[12]

Such a mass exodus was remarkable given the popular resistance to emigration. It can only be explained by the harsh economic conditions that led the British government to fear a return to the famine years of the 1840s, and by the dashed hopes that finally the crofters would be given the land.

The Rise of Labour

World War I also broke the hegemony held by the Liberal Party over Scottish politics. The party had split in two after Lloyd George ousted Herbert Asquith as prime minister in 1916, with the former munitions minister then heading a coalition government with the Tories. Asquith himself served as MP for East Fife from 1886 until his defeat in 1918, and then from 1920 was shoehorned into what had once been the safe seat of Paisley. The winners in the short term during the inter-war years were the Tories, or Unionists as they called themselves north of the border, who took the lion's share of Scottish votes in UK elections in those early post-war years. But these victories concealed the growth of Labour in Scotland. By the time the war ended in November 1918, the Independent Labour Party in Scotland had seen its number of branches double, and its membership triple compared with 1914.[13] By September 1918, it had grown to more than 9,000 members in 192 branches, a third of the total British membership. Elsewhere in Britain, Labour Party membership in World War I went down.[14]

The December 1918 Westminster general election was run on the basis of whether or not you approved of Lloyd George's wartime coalition uniting the Liberals and Tories, and with thousands of soldiers taking part far from any campaigning and with no chance to hear opposition voices. Nevertheless, Labour in Scotland ran thirty-nine candidates, with its vote going up tenfold compared to the last election in 1910 and achieving an average of 22.9 percent across Scotland. Labour held Dundee and West Fife and took Central Edinburgh, South Ayrshire, Glasgow Govan and Hamilton with a Liberal MP elected in North Aberdeen also crossing over. More important, they had come second within a greater number of seats than the divided Liberals. The stage was set for a breakthrough.[15]

In November 1920, Labour took a third of the seats in Glasgow's municipal elections. The Irish vote, around 15 percent, swung behind Labour as Lloyd George's policy of repression in Ireland broke the back of its traditional support for the Liberals. Labour ensured it kept this vote by supporting state-funded Catholic schooling and dropping its support for the prohibition of alcohol.[16]

The headline-grabbing breakthrough came in the 1922 Westminster general election, when Labour increased its vote to 32.2 percent of the vote and took twenty-nine seats, half in Glasgow and the surrounding area.[17] It was met with an explosion of joy and expectation: across Glasgow the newly elected MPs addressed mass meetings, and on Sunday 20 November a service of dedication was held at St Andrews Hall, where the audience sang the 124th Psalm: 'Had not the Lord been on our side'. The climax came with the departure of the victorious MPs from St Enoch Station to London, with 250,000 people packing the surrounding streets. The crowd sang 'Jerusalem' and finished off with 'The Red Flag' and 'The Internationale'.[18]

Facing defeat in local politics, the Glasgow Tories and Liberals joined together in an alliance in which they divided up the seats and stood as moderates in order to keep Labour out. As a result, though Labour received just over 50 percent of the vote in the elections in late 1923, the party did not win control of Glasgow City Council.[19] Despite this, Labour held ten out of fifteen seats in the city in the December 1923 Westminster general election. In Scotland as a whole, Labour won thirty-four of the forty-eight seats it fought, sixteen in seats where either the Tories or Liberals stood aside in an effort to block Labour. The *Scotsman* commented: '. . . the advance of socialism in our midst is the most unpleasant feature of the situation. Formerly its strength lay mainly in Glasgow and the Clyde and the industrial parts of Lanarkshire but it has now spread its tentacles considerably in Eastern Scotland, particularly in the mining areas bordering on the farms.'[20]

Across Britain, Labour won fifty extra seats with a total of 192 MPs to the Tories' 258 and Liberals' 151. The two ruling-class parties were split, however, over the issue of free trade and economic protectionism, with the Liberals championing the former, therefore unable to back a Tory-led government. Nonetheless, Scottish Labour MPs such as John Wheatley and James Maxton were not willing to see a Labour–Liberal coalition. The Labour leader, Ramsay MacDonald, was prepared to form a minority government, arguing that to refuse would be a missed opportunity and that in office Labour could prove it was fit to govern, to demonstrate that 'working men could hold the highest offices of state with dignity and authority'.[21]

The likes of Maxton and Wheatley argued that Labour should push ahead with a bold programme of socialist measures and if it was voted down, fight an election on that basis. But MacDonald was having none of that; he was determined to show Labour could govern on behalf of the nation as a whole rather than the working class.[22] J. H. Thomas, who would become the new Secretary of State for the colonies, reassured his betters that 'the Labour Party were proud and jealous of, and were prepared to maintain, the Empire'.[23] As a result, in the words of later party leader Gordon Brown: 'In all economic matters the new Government did little . . . Labour's measures were completely inadequate.'[24]

MacDonald seemed more concerned with what to wear when he visited Buckingham Palace and the views of his aristocratic friends than with securing change on behalf of his supporters. The government lasted less than a year, and the ruling class was prepared to tolerate it if only as a necessary means of house-training a new litter. The sole victory for the workers was won by John Wheatley, who succeeded in steering a relatively bold housing programme through Parliament.

During the general election of 1922 a majority of Labour candidates signed an open letter from the Scottish Home Rule Association in favour of creating a Scottish parliament. The ILP-sponsored MP George Buchanan presented a Home Rule Bill in May 1924, supported by MacDonald. At a rally in Glasgow in support of the bill, Maxton said there was 'no greater job in life than to make English-ridden, capitalist-ridden, landowner-ridden Scotland into the Scottish Socialist Commonwealth'. Later he was to regret the use of 'English-ridden' explaining he had no quarrel with the English people.[25] However, Tory MPs talked the bill out and MacDonald refused to take any measure to carry devolution forward.

The year 1927 saw the local party in the west of Scotland split over more local matters. At a time when birth control advocates began campaigning in mining communities, Labour councillors and the ILP in Glasgow were rocked by controversy over whether or not the city's libraries should stock *Birth Control News*. When the issue came to a vote in November, all the Moderate councillors voted against while twenty Labour councillors voted for it, but around a dozen failed to vote because of the opposition of the

Catholic Church to the measure. *Forward* refused to run adverts from birth-control advocates.[26]

In defiance of the party leadership, ILP members such as Mary Barbour and Mrs Auld in Glasgow helped set up birth-control clinics in working-class areas like Govan. Barbour campaigned to raise the funds needed to maintain the staff of women doctors and nurses.[27] As a councillor she also fought for the introduction of municipal banks, wash-houses, laundries and baths; a pure milk supply free to schoolchildren, child welfare centres and play areas; home helps and pensions for mothers.

When Labour was returned to government in 1929, MacDonald refused to appoint Wheatley once again as housing minister. The Glasgow MPs in the ILP, who represented the left of the party, understood they had now been frozen out. They did not stand around in the cold for long.

Scotland and Irish Independence

The 1919 Glasgow May Day march drew 150,000 people. Joining John Wheatley on the platform was Constance Markievicz of Sinn Fein,[28] while the Irish tricolour was carried on the march and the anthem of the new, illegal Irish Republic, 'The Soldier's Song', was sung along with 'The Red Flag'. At the Scottish conference of the ILP the following year, recognition of the Irish Republic was passed, though by a narrow margin of 268 votes to 207.[29]

Sinn Fein and the Irish Republican Army organised in Scotland. By September 1919, the IRA in Glasgow had a battalion made up of eight companies. The Falkirk company was 100 strong at its foundation that year, while the Motherwell and Wishaw companies comprised some 300 men. In addition, there were eighty Sinn Fein clubs and fourteen branches of Cumann na mBan, the Republican women's organisation. In September 1920, the Procurator Fiscal reported that the IRA had 3,000 volunteers in the city: 'They have no rifles but the police have now obtained information . . . that they are in possession of numerous revolvers which have been picked up here and elsewhere.'[30] By 1922 the number of Sinn Fein clubs had risen to eighty-eight, with an annual income that had increased to £22,000 from £700 in 1917. The Dumbarton club boasted 600 members and that in Greenock 1,000.[31]

A high point for Scottish republicans was the visit in 1920 of the Archbishop of Melbourne, Daniel Mannix. An outspoken critic of British policy in Ireland, Mannix had attempted to travel to Ireland but his ship had been intercepted by the Royal Navy and he was brought to Penzance in Cornwall, where he was informed that he could not visit Ireland or any British city with a substantial Irish population. Despite this he was allowed to come to Scotland, addressing enthusiastic crowds in Edinburgh, Greenock, Dalmuir, Kilmarnock, Dumbarton, Cowdenbeath and Dundee. A planned meeting in Glasgow was banned; however, in defiance the archbishop addressed a rally of more than 50,000 people in Whifflet, outside Coatbridge.

The organisation was of real significance by 1921, when the guerrilla war in Ireland was at its height; so much so that Tom Gallagher has claimed that almost every town in Scotland 'with a sizeable Irish presence' was home to an IRA company. Each had to forward revolvers, ammunition and rifles to headquarters in Glasgow from where they were smuggled to Ireland. Gelignite and gunpowder was stolen from quarries, coal pits and shale mines, and eight raids were successfully carried out on Glasgow munitions works. On one occasion a Royal Navy gunboat undergoing a refit at the Finnieston dockyard was raided and arms taken with the crew held at gunpoint. As one IRA volunteer would later describe their role, 'Our job was to raise money and obtain guns which were then smuggled to Ireland.'[32] The commander of the Scottish IRA, Seamus Reader, gained access to the Chemistry Department at Glasgow University to produce explosive devices which were sent to Dublin.[33]

Women such as Julia Foy, who ran a second-hand clothes shop in Glasgow, acted as couriers and provided safe houses. Ex-servicemen helped train volunteers for service in Ireland, and on two occasions high-ranking IRA officers travelled from Ireland to review the volunteers on remote moorland.[34]

Frank Carty, an IRA commander from Sligo, had escaped to Glasgow after breaking out of Derry Jail, but was arrested by police in the city. On 4 May 1921, he was being ferried in a police wagon from the Central Police Court in St Andrews Square to Duke Street Prison. Three armed police were in the front of the van. As the police van turned off the High Street into Duke Street, bullets started to fly as IRA volunteers stormed the van from three directions. One police escort fell from the van wounded and lay in the street, while his two colleagues returned fire. The IRA rescue party surrounded the van and tried to force the doors, one shooting at the lock twice, but it would not open. The volunteers then dispersed. A police inspector lay dead and a detective sergeant was seriously wounded.

That night the police carried out a wave of arrests in the Calton area. One of those taken away was a young priest from St Mary's Church in Abercromby Street, Fr Patrick McRory. The arrests provoked riots in the Calton. On 22 July the charges against him, ten other men and seven women were dropped and they were welcomed back to the Calton by large crowds waving the Irish tricolour. Subsequently, the case against twelve IRA members of conspiracy and murder was found 'not proven' at Edinburgh High Court.[35]

In July 1921, the Lloyd George government agreed a truce with the leadership of the IRA and Sinn Fein, and in December a treaty was agreed between the two sides in London. The exclusion of six Ulster counties from the new Irish Free State (three Ulster counties that had a nationalist majority were ceded to the new state) provoked a split in the republican movement, which led to civil war from June 1922 to May 1923. A majority of republicans in Scotland opposed the treaty and Glasgow became the centre for arms supplies to the anti-treaty IRA and was their propaganda centre for a period after they were driven from Dublin.

On 11 March 1923, detectives carried out a series of raids across central Scotland, arresting twenty-eight republicans in Glasgow, five in Lanarkshire, two in West Lothian and one each in Dundee and Dumbarton. The information about these men and women came from the government in Dublin, keen to stop arms supplies to their opponents, and all were shipped to Ireland to be interned by the Free State authorities. The eventual defeat of the anti-treaty forces led to an end of IRA activity in Scotland.[36] Eamon de Valera, the president of the Irish Republic from 1919 to 1922, said of Scotland's assistance: 'The financial contribution to the Irish struggle from among the Scottish communities was in excess of funds from any other country, including Ireland.'[37]

In the aftermath, the Scottish-Irish vote largely transferred to Labour. But in difficult times sectarianism towards Scotland's Catholic minority was never far away. It was not just confined to the terraces of Rangers' Ibrox Stadium or to working-class areas. Anti-Irish and anti-Catholic sentiment was evident at the highest levels of Scottish society throughout the 1920s and '30s.

The Orange Order was represented on the Western Divisional Council of the Conservative Party from 1893 onwards.[38] Sir John Gilmour, Conservative MP for East Renfrewshire, 1910–18, and for Glasgow Pollok, 1918–40, and the first Secretary of State for Scotland in 1924, was a Deputy Grand Master of the Orange Lodge.[39] Within the Church of Scotland there was an elite campaign to outlaw Irish immigration. In 1922, the Rev. Duncan Cameron of Kilsyth, a member of the Church of Scotland's sub-committee on Irish immigration, stated that Scots could not be expected to live alongside 'weeds'. He blamed Irish immigrants for the upsurge on the Clyde two years earlier: 'Nearly all the leaders were Irish. In the course of time instead of a Scottish proletariat there would be a body of people who had no regard for the United Kingdom and who were prone to revolutionary ideas.'[40]

This reflected a strong anti-Irish sentiment within the Kirk during the inter-war years, with constant warnings at General Assemblies about the danger of Irish immigration. Four years later, a former Moderator of the General Assembly and co-convenor of the Kirk's Church and Nation, the Rev. John White, argued that the Scottish 'race' had to be protected from being 'corrupted by the introduction of a horde of Irish immigrants'.[41]

A Presbyterian Joint Committee visited London in 1928 to meet the Home Secretary and Scottish Secretary to demand Irish immigration be halted and anyone of Irish birth on benefits should be deported.[42] In response, government officials were able to produce figures refuting their claim that there was a flood of Irish immigrants to Scotland.

Despite this, in 1930 the Rev. White, now first Moderator of the now re-united Church of Scotland, stated that the Kirk's priority would be combatting Catholicism and the 'menace' of Irish immigration.[43] In 1933, the newly formed Church Interests Committee urged the Church of Scotland to join the International League for the Defence and Furtherance of Protestantism (ILDFP). Based in Berlin, this organisation was Nazi-dominated, anti-Semitic and anti-Catholic.

This flirtation with Nazism was soon considered a step too far, and the Church swiftly rowed back on its anti-Catholic, anti-Irish crusade.

Rent Strikes – Second Round

The condition of Scotland's housing remained a national scandal. The Lloyd George government had promised returning servicemen 'homes fit for heroes', but in reality they returned to the same housing they had left, and discovered no repairs had been carried out during the war.

As a consequence of the 1915 Glasgow rent strike, rents had been frozen at their 1914 level. In 1920, the government produced a Rents Bill, which proposed increases of 10 percent, and 25 percent if significant repairs were carried out. Clydebank Town Council immediately passed a resolution expressing 'grave concerns [at] the indignation and discontent of the tenants in this vicinity caused by the Government's proposed Increase of Rent Bill.'[44]

In August 1920, the Scottish Labour Housing Association, connected to the ILP, organised a conference in Glasgow, chaired by John Wheatley. They called for a rent strike and a twenty-four-hour general strike, which went ahead later that month in Glasgow and Clydebank, with demonstrations against the rent rises in which notice of the increases were burned.

But by the end of the month, the *Glasgow Herald* reported that in the city the new rents were being collected with little sign of opposition. In Clydebank it was a different story. There, tenants refused to pay en masse. Among the organisers of the rent strike was Jane Rae, who had been one of the workers sacked by Singer in 1911 for striking; she had chaired a suffragette rally with Emily Pankhurst in Clydebank's town hall, had opposed the war and was a councillor from 1922 until 1928.[45] Another organiser, Janet Kerr Reid was active in physically resisting evictions and would go on to sit as a Communist councillor for the town's 5th Ward.[46]

By April 1924, £1 million was owed in rent arrears as a result of the strike which involved 12,000 tenants. The Clydebank Housing Association, which organised the strike, was described by the *Times* as 'a kind of local Jacobin Club'.[47] The battle reached its peak later that year when landlords evicted tenants in arrears with the help of police. Cyclists toured the town ringing hand bells to alert supporters of the rent strike, who gathered to resist the evictions, clashing with police. When the police departed, however, the crowd simply picked up the belongings and furniture of the tenants from where it had been dumped in the street outside, and moved it back into the house.

As the strike continued, mass meetings and protests were regular occurrences in Clydebank. The *Times*, searching to explain the longevity of the strike, put it down to 'Communist influence working on a population which is largely of Irish origin'.[48] In July, the *Glasgow Herald* reported that landlords had decided on a 'systematic campaign of ejectment', noting that the rent strike was supported by 75 percent of Clydebank's population, 700 families, and that £10,000 of rent was being withheld each month.[49]

By the close of 1924 evictions began with new fervour. From faraway Australia, the *Barrier Miner*, published in the trade union stronghold Broken Hill, reported from Clydebank on 31 December: 'Four evictions were carried out at Clydebank this morning . . . The eviction officers were compelled to shatter the barricaded doors amidst the screams of the occupants. Scouts warned the neighborhood. Hundreds of women and children were crying piteously. The crowds jeered and hooted the officers, especially at the fourth house, whence agonising screams proceeded while the door was pounded in. The eviction officers found the kitchen barricaded with a sewing-machine, tables, and beds. The inmates rushed an officer when he penetrated into the interior. Police came to the rescue and restored order.'[50] The decision to carry out the evictions on Hogmanay was seen as deliberately vindictive.

The landlords used new tactics to defeat the strike, with the same paper reporting two months later: 'A firm of Clydebank agents to-day carried out a surprise move against two of four tenants. Joiners and plumbers cut off the gas and water supplies and removed windows and doors, whereupon the tenants departed and new tenants occupied the houses.'[51] The town council, the local MP, the Scottish Labour MPs and others attempted to broker a settlement but the residents held out for a 'fair rent' – frozen at 1914 levels.

The decision of a Tory government in 1925 to initiate an official report into private rentals meant some of the momentum behind the rent strike was lost. The issue was finally resolved in individual court actions that generally ruled tenants should pay only 50 percent of the arrears; while it was no victory, the rent strike saved them money.

Miners, Resistance and 'Little Moscows'

Crawlin' aboot like a snail in the mud,
Covered wi' clammie blae,
Me, made up after the image of God –
Jings! But it's laughable tae.

Howkin' awa' 'neath a mountain o' stane,
Gaspin' for want o' air.
The sweat makin' streams upon my bare back-bone,
And my knees a' hauckit and sair.

Strainin' and cursin' the hale shift through.
Half-starved, half-blin', half-mad,
And the gaffer he says, 'Less dirt in that coal
Or you up the pit, my lad!'
So I gi'e my life to the Nimmo squad,

> For eicht and fower a day,
> Me! Made up in the image o' God –
> Jings! But it's laughable tae.

'The Image o' God', written in the 1920s by Joe Corrie, a miner from Bowhill, Fife, who was a socialist, a poet and playwright, offers a glimpse into the miners' working conditions.

Mary Docherty, the daughter of a miner, described conditions in the 1920s in west Fife. 'They always talk about how red Clydeside was, but Fife was just as radical,' she said. 'It seemed revolution here was just round the corner. Middle-class people were terrified. You had to lie to your employer about attending marches and hope they did not see you. The London headquarters of the Communist Party even got in touch with Fife to say slow down. We were so far ahead.'[52]

Jock Kane was brought up in the mining village of Stoneyburn in West Lothian. The youngest of six, he was the only one born in Scotland after the family emigrated from Connemara: 'At the full, there would be 500 or 600 men working at the pit, all from the village. It was small by present-day standards, 300 or 400 houses maybe. There were plenty of Irish – God, aye – one thing we were never short of in the pits was Irishmen. Anywhere there's bloody hard work and slavish labour you'll find Irishmen, won't you? They used to crack on about my father, Mick, that the boys from back home, when they came across and got off at Glasgow, they'd ask "Where's Mick Kane's pit?" and find their way to us.'

In 1924, Jock joined the Communist Party; his brothers had already joined on its formation in 1920. 'At that time there was a Communist Party branch in the village. They called them "locals" in those days. We called ours "the local" – and it absolutely ran the village.'[53] The miners were thus thrust into the front line of the class struggle in Britain in the 1920s when wartime state subsidies for miners' wages came to an end, and with the price of coal dropping as a result of the economic downturn, coal owners and the government were determined to cut their pay in order to boost profits and reduce the price of coal for industry.

The Miners Federation of Great Britain refused to accept this, and on 1 April owners locked mineworkers out of the pits. Immediately on the heels of this provocation, the government put into force its Emergency Powers Act, drafting soldiers into the coalfield.

In the face of such aggression, the union formed a Triple Alliance with the rail and transport workers, who had pledged to strike with them. But on what became known as 'Black Friday', 15 April 1921, the other two unions issued no such strike call. The miners were forced to fight alone.

The Scottish and South Wales coalfields saw the greatest number of mineworker strikes in the inter-war years, with the Welsh taking part in the most strikes in the 1920s, and the Scots in the 1930s. In both coalfields the fight for union recognition had been a long and bitter one, and in both there was a strong tradition of rank-and-file organisation. The Lanarkshire Miners' Reform Committee began in the summer of 1917 (inspired by John Maclean and his comrade James MacDougall, who was working in the Blantyre pit), and the Fife Reform Union was set up in 1923 to combat the right-wing local leadership of the union.[54]

The 1921 coal strike saw bitter clashes between strikers and police across Britain. A miner's daughter, Mary Docherty, writes about Cowdenbeath in Fife:

> there were lots of riots between the miners' pickets and the police. The army was brought in and some were billetted at the Church Hall in Church Street. The soldiers were also guarding the Gordon and Dora pits. They had to pass our house to go to the pit, so my father got talking to them. They said they would not use their arms against miners as many of them were themselves from mining families.[55]

She went on to describe events after pickets tried to stop managers pumping water out of the Dalbeath pit: 'The police assembled in the middle of the High Street and nobody was allowed to go past them. Shop windows were broken with police batoning the men and pushing them against the windows. In all three baton charges that took place miners and police were badly hurt.'[56]

Docherty's obituary in the *Independent* included this recollection of the strike:

> The 1921 miners' strike, which led to a state of emergency being declared, is stamped on Miss Docherty's memory. She was 13 when the Army was drafted into Cowdenbeath to back police against pickets. The situation grew ugly after her father and other pickets and their families tried to throw a pit manager in a pond. Later there were pitched battles between police and pickets. Some miners spent more than a year in prison. The charges only stopped when all the streetlights went out and the place was in darkness. 'I had seen my father earlier that morning make a baton with a part of the shaft of a pickaxe.'[57]

After three months the miners were forced back to work, resulting in a dramatic fall in union membership. In the two-year period following the strike, membership of the Federation dropped by more than 200,000. But from March 1923, a groundswell of energy and purpose began building again in the coalfields, a groundswell that within another three years would lead to a conflict that would dwarf the great lockout of 1921.

In December 1923, the miners voted to fight again – to get rid of the terrible agreement that had been forced on them in 1921. In the spring of 1924, following the report of a government Committee of Inquiry, the coal owners and the MFGB executives agreed a deal that removed the worst of the pay cuts imposed three years earlier.

In March 1926, the Samuel Commission published its report recommending a reduction by 13.5 percent of miners' wages along with the withdrawal of government subsidy to the industry. Two weeks later, the prime minister, Stanley Baldwin, announced that the government would accept the report. Mine owners declared that from 1 May, miners would have to accept new terms of employment that included a longer working day and pay cuts of between 10 and 25 percent, or else be locked out. The Miners' Federation refused to accept this blackmail and appealed to the Trades Union Congress (TUC), which promised to call a general strike in support of the miners if the coal owners did not back off. The coal owners did not.

The 1926 General Strike, which began on 3 May and lasted ten days before the TUC called it off with nothing gained, is often portrayed as a very 'British' affair – workers playing football with police or parading to church services, all so very different from their hot-headed counterparts across the English Channel. The reality was very different. In Scotland there were bitter clashes with police and scabs. In the coalfield of west Fife, workers began to take control of their communities, forming Councils of Action to co-ordinate picketing and solidarity.

The striker John Wheatley summed up what was at stake: 'The miners occupy the front trenches of the position singled out for attack and if their wages are reduced it will be the beginning of a general wage reduction.'[58] Winston Churchill understood too, writing: 'It is a conflict which, if it is fought out to a conclusion can only end in the overthrow of parliamentary government or its decisive victory.'[59]

The ruling class understood this was a critical clash and was prepared. Neither the TUC nor the Miners' Federation had been so prescient. Only in Fife had the miners and other workers prepared for battle. At the beginning of April, Lochgelly Trades Council convened a conference that set up a Central Committee of Action for Fife, Kinross and Clackmannan, and on 22 April, Methil Trades and Labour Council met to discuss initiating a workers' defence corps.[60]

Such organisation was necessary because they were up against not just the employers and the state but the local right-wing leadership of the Miners' Federation of Great Britain, led by the local Labour MP, Willie Adamson. The Methil Council of Action was the most militant in the country. Formed by the town's trades council, it issued a daily bulletin from its headquarters in the Co-operative Hall. A leading Communist miner, David Proudfoot, reported after the strike:

The organisation worked like clockwork. Everything was stopped – even the railway lines were picketed. The Council had a courier service second to none in Britain with three motor cars (and a maximum of six available), 100 motor cycles and as many push bikes as were necessary. They covered the whole of Fife taking out information and bringing in reports, sending out speakers everywhere, as far north as Perth.'[61]

Its chair, John MacArthur, recalled: 'Our slogans locally were: "All power to the councils of action." We said each organisation had to give up power to the Council of Action. There was no disagreement.'[62]

A notable feature of the Methil Council was its formation of a Workers Defence Corps, which was formed following police attacks on pickets. At the start, 150 joined, and that number soon rose to 700. Marching in military formation through the town, the Corps joined the picket line. David Proudfoot recalled, 'The police did not interfere again.'[63]

Elsewhere in Scotland, similar Workers Defence Corps were formed in Denny and Dunipace in Stirlingshire.[64] Abe Moffat, later leader of the Scottish miners, described the situation in Cowdenbeath in Fife:

All motor vehicles had to get permission from the trades council before travelling up the Great North Road. We had pickets in various parts of the road to ensure than no one passed without the permission of the trades council. To ensure than no one would pass, miners had a rope across the road. If a motor vehicle had a pass it got through, if it had no pass it had to turn back.[65]

'All solid' is how the historian of the National Union of Railwaymen described the response of its members in Aberdeen.[66] From Dundee it was reported: 'Here as elsewhere our greatest difficulty in the first week was in preventing men ceasing work before being called on to do so.'[67] It was a similar story in North Lanarkshire: 'by the end of the first week even second-line men came out on strike before they were officially called out.'[68]

The level of organisation in Methil contrasts with Glasgow, where the strike committee was chaired by a Communist, Peter Kerrigan, but was dominated by trade union officials who toed the TUC line. When Kerrigan proposed mass picketing, this was rejected and he went along with the decision. Later he admitted that at no time was the authority of the TUC questioned by the strike committee. Kerrigan admitted he was taken completely by surprise by the decision of the same General Council to call off the strike.[69]

Outside of Glasgow, the main industrial centre at the time was North Lanarkshire, a centre for coal mining, steel, engineering and rail. Twenty-three Councils of Action were set up across the county with a Joint Committee that brought them together, meeting in the Lanarkshire Mineworkers' Union head office in Hamilton. Mass pickets up to 4,000 strong brought everything to a halt by the third day of the stoppage. The local Motherwell paper reported after the strike: 'Motherwell, red and revolutionary Motherwell has been a perfect model of peace and quietness . . . it was also one of the towns where solidarity was the keynote all during the conflict.'[70]

In Cambuslang, Lanarkshire, the strike was so solid that pickets were sent into Glasgow at the request of the city's tram car workers, who asked them to target the Ruby Street depot where students and other scabs were being billeted before taking the cars out in the morning. Five hundred Cambuslang pickets marched on the depot, and violent clashes followed as police used baton charges. Twelve pickets were arrested, and later were sentenced to three months' hard labour.[71]

Some 7,000 'volunteers', including 300 university students, had been recruited to break the strike, and there were soon clashes between them and the strikers.[72] The fighting at Ruby Street was the first major clash in Glasgow but others quickly followed, as even the next day police baton-charged strikers in Bridgeton who were attempting to persuade two students operating a tram car to stop scabbing. Later that day, a mass picket at the Dennistoun depot was also attacked by baton-wielding police.

As pickets of the tram depots continued, there were more arrests in Bridgeton later that week. At a tram depot near the university, police dispersed strikers protesting the use of student volunteers. On 8 May, the Saturday following the initiation of the strike, women organised pickets at tram stops in Govan to stop people using them, and police baton charges of protesters were followed by rioting and looting in Dennistoun, Bridgeton and Anderston.[73]

Rioting continued for four nights. The *Evening Times* reported: 'The struggle was of the wildest description; pots and pans, iron bars, pickheads and hammers were used as missiles, but fortunately no police were injured. Over sixty arrests were made.'[74] The government stationed warships on the Clyde and naval ratings joined the scabs in shifting strike-bound goods.

In Condorrat, East Dunbartonshire, on the main Glasgow–Edinburgh road, several hundred miners armed with long poles and stones blocked traffic despite police baton charges and arrests.[75] Farther west in Renfrewshire, the Johnstone and District strike committee reported: 'Never before has such solidarity been shown in an industrial dispute, Orangemen being active pickets and taking part generally in the struggle.'[76]

On the east coast, the high number of student, public schoolboy and middle-class 'volunteers' in Edinburgh added to the tension. On Thursday evening, 6 May, a serious riot broke out in the High Street and Canongate. The local newspaper reported that thousands of women and children had joined a huge crowd around the Tron Church, which refused to disperse despite police charges. At 9.15 p.m. police retreated to the central police station in the High Street. For half an hour the crowd waited in silence, and then down the High Street came mounted police followed by hundreds of police wielding batons.[77]

In the East Lothian pit town of Tranent that same night, strikers blocked roads and a crowd of 1,000 laid siege to the police station, smashing all its windows. Police reinforcements had to be brought in to break the deadlock. Attacks on trains running on the main East Coast Line to London were so numerous that police were stationed on it.[78] Farther north there were baton charges in Aberdeen after a crowd of 6,000 attacked scab buses and trams, smashing windows.[79]

In Govan, the 'Emergency Press Special Edition' reported on 12 May that women wearing red rosettes were 'standing at the stopping places on the [tram] car routes endeavouring to persuade members of the public not to use the cars'. In Dundee a spinner, Jessie Latto, was arrested and fined £3 for throwing a missile at the driver of a scab lorry. The number of women in the dock was, the *Scotsman* reported, 'a remarkable feature of the cases arising out of the strike disturbances heard at Glasgow Sheriff Court.' Among them were twenty-six women prosecuted for attacking a blackleg bus driver in Govan, and a group of women charged with throwing bags of flour in the faces of scab transport workers, and then resisting police when they tried to intervene.[80]

Far from the strike weakening prior to the TUC decision to abandon it on 12 May, a Ministry of Labour report on Glasgow that was written just before the strike was called off, noted: 'There is not the slightest sign of any break whatever in the strike. In fact many of those now working wish to join in.'[81] One Scottish ILP activist in Perth expressed the hopes of those taking part: 'There's never been anything like it. If the blighters o' leaders here . . . dinna let us down we'll hae the capitalists crawlin' on their bellies in a week. Oh boy, it's the revolution at last.'[82] In contrast, J. R. Clynes, head of the General and Municipal Workers, said: 'I am not in fear of the capitalist class. The only class I fear is my own.'[83]

On 12 May 1926, the TUC General Council visited Downing Street to announce its decision to call off the strike, provided that the government offered a guarantee that there would be no victim-isations. The government responded that it had 'no power to compel employers to take back every man who had been on strike'. The TUC agreed to end the dispute without such an agreement.

When news came through that the TUC General Council in London had called off the strike there was shock. John McArthur in Methil recalls:

> When the strike was called off after nine days of growing power and organisation, we couldn't believe it. We were stunned. Each day it went on we had gained in confidence. We had new and marvellous experiences in struggle. We had mass meetings every night, wonderful meetings, five and six thousand strong. We were full of vim and go. We were spreading out, too, sending speakers to Perth and other places.[84]

The capitulation would cost workers dear. In Glasgow, Outram Press, which published the *Glasgow Herald* and *Evening Times*, went non-union, even banning its journalists from having dinner with union members. From Edinburgh an engineering union official bewailed that 'immediately after the very precipitate and badly arranged calling off of the strike, we are in a sea of trouble in connection with the complaints of members who had failed to secure reinstatement'.[85] Across the UK, some 3,000 strikers were brought to court for actions undertaken during the General Strike; about half for incitement. Victimisation of union activists was common and many never worked in their industry again.

The capitulation by the TUC was the green light for employers to go on the offensive for the next decade and more. Meanwhile, the miners were left to fight on alone throughout that summer.

In west Fife, the Council of Action set up soup kitchens. John McArthur recalled:

> In each area we would organise a kitchen committee elected by popu-
> lar vote. Each committee had to have a kitchen convenor and assistant
> convenor . . . We had an organisation to go round the gardens getting
> whatever produce there was there. We had people out round the farm-
> ers begging, borrowing or stealing tatties and the rest. Some responded
> very well. Fish merchants gave us box after box of kippers. From
> bakers we had rolls for the morning. We were able to provide three
> meals daily, more than people got in 'normal times'.[86]

It was a good summer, but as the lockout went on the strikers faced further problems. The shoes of strikers and their families were falling apart. The Council of Action organised shoe repairs and hair-cuts, and distributed the penny coins needed to feed gas meters.

The poem 'The General Strike', probably written by Bob Young of Bothwellhaugh, catches the spirit of that summer:

> As lads we ran aboot the braes
> In wee bare feet an' ragged claes;
> Nae such thing as 'Dinna Like',
> For then oor faithers were on strike.
>
> Yet in these times they still could sing
> While haulin' hoose coal frae the bing;
> Nothing then tae waste or spare,
> Still everyone would get their share.

> They'd share their last with those in need,
> There wisnae such a thing as greed,
> A piece on jam was something rare,
> An' no so much o' that to spare.

To maintain morale, miners' gala days were held and bands played at concert parties. As a participant, one young melodeon player and striking miner laid the basis for a long career as a musician and band leader, Jimmy Shand from East Wemyss.

John McArthur, a Communist from Buckhaven, was elected to the parish council. Single men and the women who worked at the pit head were refused any assistance, so it was decided to protest to the council at Thornton. Three thousand women and men demanded access to the poorhouse, but there being no room, assistance was paid.[87] Hugh Reynolds, from Plean in Stirlingshire, recalled: 'Thursdays were special days. We had mince and tatties on Thursdays. All the other days, it was bone soup. The church in Plean gave us the use of the mission hall, and we used the boiler at the back to make soup. You would go up with a can and, according to the numbers of your children, you would have a plateful; it was fair to everybody. Some of the farmers were very good and gave us tatties. But others weren't so good and wouldn't give us any.'[88]

Jock Kane recounted the solidarity shown for the striking miners:

> We used to get all sorts of prizes from chocolate firms, and McVities would send us a box of biscuits here and there. We'd groups which went out to Edinburgh and surrounding towns selling raffle tickets.
>
> I spent six weeks in Dundee and I went to Edinburgh. When you knocked on the door regular on Friday night or Monday or Tuesday morning, eventually they'd come to accept you just like the insurance man or debt collector. They'd have their tuppence there, or their four pence if they were taking two tickets, and you'd sell them a raffle ticket and they were there, they were waiting on you coming, very poor people.

I'll never forget it. I went one Saturday night to deliver a prize – a box of McVities biscuits – at one of these tenements in Edinburgh. We always had to fetch the tin back because that was one of the conditions – McVities gave us a tin and took away an empty tin, so we always had to fetch the tin back. I went to this house to tell the woman: 'You have won this prize.' I went in and there were rags in the corner and another woman stretched out and two or three kids running about, just little ragged vests on them, and there was a table and a chair and nothing else in that bloody room, you know. But they would still find that tuppence.[89]

The Glasgow ILP ran ten of its own communal kitchens and assisted another two, and raised in total almost £3,500 for the miners.[90] In West Calder at the end of August, a Labour councillor, Sarah Moore, known as 'Ma Moore', led a sit-down protest lasting several days over the council stopping relief payments to locked-out miners and their families. One evening police intervened, insisting that the good-natured crowd clear the road. When one man was pushed to the pavement and suffered a bleeding head wound, anger at police heavy-handedness boiled over. Police drew batons and in response the protesters overturned two vehicles. Frightened by such scenes, the council immediately met with Moore and promised to restore relief payments the next day.[91]

Special constables were recruited and by September parts of Lanarkshire and Fife were under virtual martial law. One night in Glencraig in Fife, police ran amok, batonning anyone they caught, including women and children. The mining companies evicted strikers from company-owned homes and brought in blacklegs instead.[92]

In the end hunger won, and in November the mining union ordered a return to work on company terms.

Towards the Abyss

As the decade drew to a close, Scotland was in a weak position economically even before the onset of the global recession that resulted from the Wall Street Crash of 1929. The 1926 defeat brought with it the Tory government of Stanley Baldwin, which was thoroughly anti-working-class. The trade unions were on the back foot and retreated from confrontation in the wake of the General Strike. The Labour Party under Ramsay MacDonald was elected to office in 1929, desperate to stress its moderation and its commitment to standard, free-market economics. In 1929, MacDonald would make it into 10 Downing Street just as the country and the world toppled into an abyss.

REBEL LIVES: HELEN CRAWFURD

Helen Crawfurd (1877–1954) was born Helen Jack on 9 September 1877 in the Gorbals. Her family moved to Ipswich when she was quite young and she was educated in England before the family returned to Glasgow when she was seventeen.

Her family was intensely religious and at home she took part in discussions about justice and equality. In her early twenties she married a Church of Scotland minister, the Rev. Alexander Montgomerie Crawfurd of the Brownfield Church in Anderston. The marriage was a happy one, despite a significant age difference between them, with the Rev. Crawfurd holding strong temperance and anti-militarist views. He died in 1914, leaving Helen to concentrate on her political work.

In 1910, Helen Crawfurd had joined the Women's Social and Political Union (WSPU) and two years later she travelled to London for a mass window-smashing operation, in which she targeted the Ministry of Education, receiving a one-month prison sentence. Of this she said: 'Participation in the raid was right. If Christ could be a Militant so could I.'[93]

Under the terms of what was called the 'Cat and Mouse Act', Crawfurd was barred from further suffragette activity but, undeterred, she was one of the stewards trying to stop Emmeline Pankhurst being arrested when she spoke in Glasgow in March 1914. The next day, she took part in a protest outside the army recruiting office, smashing two windows and being arrested and sent to Duke Street Prison for a month. Crawfurd along with other suffragettes went on hunger strike and the WPSU organised protests outside the jail. After just eight days, she was released.

Crawfurd continued to take part in the fight for women's votes. The royal family was due to visit Perth in 1914, and as they paraded through the streets Crawfurd was arrested when she tried to approach their carriages. After five days on hunger strike she was again released, but she returned to Perth that summer to address a rally protesting the incarceration of two fellow suffragettes. She was arrested again for making 'inflammatory remarks', and returned to the prison for three days, during which she refused food.

She was sent to prison for a fourth time following a bomb attack in Glasgow's Botanic Gardens, and went on hunger strike once more, securing her release after just three days.

Crawfurd joined the Independent Labour Party after hearing George Lansbury speak at a public meeting: 'Though never formally associated with the WSF [Sylvia Pankhurst's Workers Socialist Federation], Crawfurd seemed to revive its language of "social soviets" and housewives' as well as workers' and soldiers' councils. Claiming that "a housewife" had not the fear of getting the sack, as the men did', and that 'far better rebels would be made out of the women than out of some of the men.'[94] On her decision to join the ILP, Crawfurd explained, 'Skilled creators of the city's wealth were living in squalor, in hovels unfit for human beings. I began to think that there must be something wrong with a system that could allow this.'[95] The fact that her husband's parish covered the docks clearly influenced her: 'coming into contact with Dockland life, and human misery indescribable . . . the living conditions appalled me, a lover of beauty. It struck me as ugly, inhuman and cruel.'[96]

Alongside Mary Barbour, Agnes Dollan, Jessie Stephens and other women, Helen Crawfurd was key in organising the 1915 Glasgow rent strike against profiteering landlords. She wrote later: 'The housing conditions in Glasgow in 1914 were appalling, the Labour Party before the war initiated a Glasgow Women's Housing Association . . . [it] took up this issue [rent increases] and in the working class districts, committees were formed to resist these increases in rent. Cards, oblong in shape, were printed with the words: RENT STRIKE. WE ARE NOT REMOVING, and placed in the windows of the houses where rent increases were demanded.'[97]

When World War I broke out in August 1914, Emmeline and Christabel Pankhurst, Helen Crawfurd's former comrades in the struggle for women's suffrage, suspended the fight for the vote and became vehemently pro-war. However, Crawfurd would have no part of that. The ILP was active against the war, holding a 'No Conscription' demonstration in Glasgow in December 1915, drawing 7,000 people. Crawfurd spoke alongside Emmanuel Shinwell, Willie Gallacher and John Maclean.[98] Earlier in 1915, alongside another leading ILP member, Agnes Dollan, Helen helped form a branch of the Women's International League in Glasgow, and the following year helped to organise a Women's Peace Conference in the city. The conference took the decision to launch the Women's Peace Crusade (WPC), which began its activity in 1917 with Helen Crawfurd as its Honorary Secretary. The WPC held pickets, protests and meetings across Scotland against war and conscription. Crawfurd was twice arrested for her anti-war work.[99] That year she also rallied in support of the October Revolution in Russia.

Two years later, she was part of the British delegation to the Conference of the Women's International League for Peace at Zurich in 1919, which included Ethel Snowden (a prominent Labour Party member), Charlotte Despard (suffragette and Irish republican), Ellen Wilkinson (a future left-wing Labour MP), Emmeline Pethick-Lawrence (a central WPSU leader before her expulsion by Christabel Pankhurst in 1912) and others. The delegation chose Helen to deliver the report from Britain to the conference.

By 1918, Crawfurd had become Vice-President of the ILP, and travelled across Scotland and Britain addressing meetings. Nonetheless, she was moving towards revolutionary ideas, forming in 1920 an unofficial grouping within the ILP known as the Left Wing Committee, with a journal, the *International*. This group would join the Communist Party on its formation in 1920, with Crawford put in charge of the new organisation's work among women. That year she also travelled to Moscow to attend the Second Congress of the Communist International, arriving after proceedings had ended.[100] However, Crawfurd did find the opportunity to meet Lenin, already seriously ill, and other revolutionary leaders.[101]

Looking back shortly before her death, Crawfurd wrote: 'What a job the Bolshevik leaders undertook. What a magnificent job they have done. Anyone who refuses to see the significance of what the Russians have done can only be either dishonest or dead mentally!'[102]

Back in Britain, Crawfurd was involved in organising a Communist Women's Day with Sylvia Pankhurst.[103] A year after her visit to Moscow, Crawfurd became Secretary (in 1921) of the Workers' International Relief Organisation (WIR), which raised money for the famine-stricken people of the Volga region. In 1926, she organised food and money collections for the miners left to fight alone after the TUC called off the General Strike. She also organised support for those facing hunger in the west of Scotland and in the Highlands. She recalled: 'Jim Larkin lent us a car to visit far parts of Ireland and carry food to the hunger stricken people of Donegal.' The relief in Donegal was particularly acute because of extensive flooding. Helen worked with Constance Markievicz, Charlotte Despard, Peadar O'Donnell, Father Flanagan and the Dundee Communist Bob Stewart, who stated, 'These three women (Crawfurd, Markievicz and Despard) formed a wonderful trio. With entirely different backgrounds they had worked miracles in the struggle for women's rights, yet it took the flood relief in Ireland to bring them together'.[104]

Helen Crawfurd stood as the Communist candidate for Govan Ward in the 1921 Glasgow council elections, her manifesto stressing the fight for women's equality. She remained a party member to the end, loyal to Stalin's Russia. After 'retiring' to Dunoon at the end of World War II she was elected the town's first woman councillor at the age of 68 and served for two years.

On her death in 1954, one woman member of the Glasgow Communist Party, Margaret Hunter of Polmadie, wrote this:

Her distinguished appearance, her warm personal charm, her lively wit, her single-minded devotion to the cause of the workers, and clarity of purpose, her fearlessness and courage, her nobility of mind and sterling character, made her loved, admired and respected by all the friends who knew her, and from her foes, who may not have loved her, she compelled admiration and respect.[105]

ELEVEN

The Great Depression:
Suffering and Resistance

Another day thus upon the mountain
And great Scotland under the doom of beasts
Her thousands of poor exploited
Beguiled to a laughing stock,
Flattered, deceived and anointed
By the nobles and the godly bourgeois
Who make a bourgeois of Christ

– Sorley MacLean
'The Cuillin'[1]

The 1930s were a decade of unemployment, sub-standard housing and poor levels of health in Scotland. Glasgow acquired many of the negative stereotypes still attached to it: a centre for drink, razor gangs and religious sectarianism, as portrayed in Alexander MacArthur and Herbert Kingsley Long's 1935 novel *No Mean City*. One contemporary report described the unemployed in these words: 'With drooping shoulders and slouching feet they moved as a defeated and dispirited army. They gave their names, signed the necessary forms and shuffled out of the Exchange. This, twice a week, was the only disciplined routine with which they had to comply.'[1]

After the Wall Street Crash of 1929, unemployment in Scotland reached a quarter of the workforce in 1931–33. The UK average was a fifth, although until 1933 unemployment levels in north-east England were worse than in Scotland. Despite rearmament bringing jobs in the late 1930s, Scotland's jobless total was a third higher than the UK average.[2]

Throughout the 1920s, unemployment never dropped below 10 percent of Scotland's workforce, but in the '30s it averaged over 20 percent. Motherwell and Wishaw had unemployment rates of 49 percent and 53 percent respectively during late 1932 and early 1933.[3] The demoralisation caused by long-term unemployment left deep scars, and came as a shock to skilled workers who had never been out of work for any length of time before.[4]

The Orcadian poet and socialist Edwin Muir toured Scotland in 1933 and wrote of the idle shipyards:

> The weather had been good for several weeks, and all the men I saw were tanned and brown as if they had just come back from their summer holidays. They were standing in their usual groups, or walking by twos and threes, slowly, for one felt as one looked at them that the world had not a single message to send them on, and that for them to hasten their steps would have meant a sort of madness. Perhaps at some time the mirage of work glimmered at the extreme horizon of their minds but one could see by looking at them that they were no longer deceived by such false pictures.[5]

The dole was means tested so that the unemployed were forced to sell possessions before they could qualify. An Inspector of Poor in Airdrie in the '30s recalled: 'The means test was iniquitous and a shatterer of homes. It broke up families, it penalised the tryers, it starved children, it drove people to suicide and insanity.'

For the children of unemployed parents in the 1930s, there would be long memories of food scarcity, homes with little or no heating, overcrowding and parents struggling to provide life's treasures. A 1935 report by the biologist and doctor John Boyd Orr 'showed that the diet of the Scottish poor was insufficient to maintain health.'[6] Diphtheria was rife among children, and as late as 1940, 15,069 cases were reported. Of Glasgow children evacuated during the war, 31 percent were found to be infested with fleas and lice, and scabies was common.[7]

The suffering of the 1930s was real but working people, in and out of work, also fought back and Scotland was to the fore in joining the great issue of that decade, resisting fascism both at home and abroad. Any hope in the Labour government elected in 1929 was dashed by its insistence that it had to balance the books. In 1931, the Labour prime minister, Ramsay MacDonald, quit his party to form a coalition with the Tories and Liberals. He did so because he accepted the economic orthodoxy that held austerity as the answer to the economic crisis, and because of opposition to his proposed cuts in the dole.

In the aftermath of his departure, the Labour Party seemed to suffer a reverse in its forward march. From 1932 until the formation, in 1940, of a new wartime coalition including Labour, Britain was effectively ruled by a Tory government. In the 1931 Westminster general election, coalition candidates won sixty-four Scottish seats to Labour's seven. In 1935, there were forty-three Unionist MPs returned, just three Liberals, twenty Labour and five Independent Labour Party.

The ILP had broken with Labour in 1931 because of its refusal to adopt a clear socialist programme. But while the ILP's leader, Jimmy Maxton, was joined by four other Glasgow MPs, they did not win over the party in the city itself. Rather, that was dominated by the machine led by Patrick Dollan. In 1933, Labour took control of Glasgow City Council, the Scottish Protestant League taking votes and seats off the moderates. Working-class politics was being shaped in a way that would hold true until the end of the millennium.

The Hunger Marches

The situation facing those out of work north of the border was grimmer even than that facing the unemployed in England and Wales. Under the Poor Act of 1845, parish councils in Scotland were responsible for the destitute, but they were not required to build workhouses or to levy a poor rate. Consequently, they could provide little for the unemployed, who were left to appeal to the parish guardians or to rely on family or charity.

After World War I, Westminster did expand the National Insurance scheme but this was only to supplement parish relief and was always under pressure from governments keen to cut public spending. To claim the dole you had to sign on at least twice a week, but the labour exchange brought together the unemployed and became places where they could organise.[8]

Scotland had a strong history of organisation among the unemployed. In the early 1920s that work was led by John Maclean and his comrades in the Tramps Trust Unlimited, who dominated the Glasgow Unemployed Committee, resisting efforts to incorporate it into the Communist Party. This initiated the National Unemployed Workers Movement, which organised on an all-British basis, because Maclean claimed the Party was too concerned with committees rather than agitation. But in July 1922, Maclean's key ally in the work, Harry McShane, decided to join the Communist Party, and became the right-hand man of the NUWM's leader, Wal Hannington.[9]

The NUWM had already organised hunger marches in the 1920s, but with the onset of mass unemployment it organised such protests on an even greater scale. In 1930 there was a Scotland-to-London hunger march and in November of that year, the NUWM in the Vale of Leven organised a march on the labour exchange, 2,000 women and men in protest at a change of day for signing on. They won a day's money that they had lost because of the change, 'a small but significant victory'.[10]

On 24 September 1931, the NUWM in Glasgow called what the *Daily Record* described as the biggest unemployed demonstration seen in Britain since the war, in protest at the National Government, led by Ramsay MacDonald, and its 10 percent cut in unemployment benefit. Contingents from across the city converged on Jail Street and together the crowd of 30,000 made their way to St Enoch Square, where an effigy of Baillie Fletcher was burned. Fletcher had angered the crowd by saying the unemployed were not 'citizens they could be proud of'.[11]

The next day, Harry McShane led a delegation of some 30,000 to Glasgow City Corporation, demanding they petition Parliament in London against the cuts. The council refused to do anything. That evening, the protesters gathered to hear a report from McShane. The *Daily Record* described events outside Glasgow Green:

> Before the crowd realized what was happening, fifteen mounted [police] men, who had come down Saltmarket in sections of four, spread across the wide thoroughfare in one rank and headed for the mass of humanity jammed in the semi-circular space around the gates of the green. Behind the mounted men came the foot police who tackled what the mounted police had left. The crowd scattered in every direction and as they scattered the crash of shattered windows could be heard along Saltmarket.[12]

The 1932 Hunger March from Glasgow to Westminster began with the departure of the Scottish contingent, led by McShane. One woman explained why she was there:

> The reason why I am marching is because of the Means Test. For instance, a friend of mine in Glasgow is working in a steel works and earns 10s a week, and because of this his son, who has the misfortune to be idle, gets nothing from the labour exchange. In addition the housing conditions in Glasgow are so bad they are difficult to describe. Four-storey tenement buildings, with seven or eight single apartments on each floor, which are bug infested and not fit for human beings to live in. I am the mother of two girls, and, although not as hard hit as many of my class, I felt it my duty to come on this hunger march in order to help those less fortunate than myself.[13]

On arrival, having joined with other marchers from all across the UK, they would have to physically fight the police in order to access Hyde Park for a rally and, three days later, to battle past the Met's finest in order to present a petition to Parliament.

In 1933, the NUWM organised a hunger march from Glasgow to Edinburgh. When it arrived, it occupied the centre of the capital for three days and nights. They paraded through the royal palace of Holyrood with their band playing 'The Internationale' and other socialist tunes, and when the city council refused to provide accommodation, their leader, Harry McShane, said they'd sleep on the pavement of Princes Street, the city's most prestigious thoroughfare.

On the first morning, women marchers blocked the tramway while men shaved using the windows of the big department stores to see their reflections. Tom Ferns remembers: 'And they couldnae ha' picked a better spot than Princes Street. Under the Conservative Party headquarters, the Liberal Party headquarters and the big luxury hotels, here was hundreds and hundreds o' angry unemployed. Obviously a sight like that is not seen every day, particularly in the capital city of Edinburgh.'[14] Another marcher, James Allison, said, 'the police were going mad'.[15] Yet the Edinburgh police were not keen on inciting a pitched battle, as Hugh Sloan recalled: 'At dinner time our field-kitchen came along and the police chief told Harry McShane, "This is Princes Street, you can't feed here." Harry told them, "It was good enough for us to sleep here, it's good enough for us to feed here."'[16]

The marchers then demanded free transport home. Eventually, the city's chief constable and deputy town clerk told them they would provide transport if McShane guaranteed there would be no more marches to Edinburgh. He refused, and the chief constable, worried about disturbances on the capital's streets, backed down.[17]

The NUWM provided other forms of support. In 1934, it raised over £100 for a children's outing to Battery Park in Greenock that 4,700 children attended, each getting half a pint of milk and a bag of buns on arrival, and an orange and a bag of toffee on departure.[18] Nor was its work confined to the west of Scotland. In 1935, 3,500 unemployed from Aberdeen travelled to Glasgow for a Scottish hunger march. In 1938, an NUWM branch was set up in Inverness and grew to fifty paying members, who organised a children's Christmas party and representation for those appearing before the Public Assistance Committee. That winter, it organised a hunger march from Inverness to Edinburgh. Tom McKay, then a clerk on the railways, recalled that about a dozen people marched the whole way with others joining for shorter distances or as it passed through a town.[19]

The autumn of 1936 saw a hunger march to London, with the first contingent setting off from Aberdeen. That leg continued south through Dundee and Edinburgh before crossing the border. The second group started from Glasgow. Eventually 700 unemployed marchers reached London, with 100,000 people joining them to demonstrate in the city. A number of the marchers would fight in Spain, including the leader of the Aberdeen contingent, Bob Cooney.

Sectarianism

The 1930s is the decade most associated with sectarianism in Scotland. By 1931 the Catholic population of Scotland had reached 662,000, up from half a million in 1911. Discrimination was already rife, but in the 1930s the Catholic population was the target for worse.[20]

Anti-Catholic bigotry is usually associated with the west of Scotland, but in this decade its worst expression occurred in genteel Edinburgh. A former serviceman, John Cormack, formed Protestant Action, and was elected to the city council for South Leith in 1934. At the peak, in 1937, it had nearly 8,000 members in the city.[21] That might have been its high point in terms of membership but in terms of the street that was undoubtedly in the summer of 1935.

In April that year, the city council hosted a civic reception for the Catholic Young Men's Society. Prior to it, Cormack told a 3,000-strong protest rally in the Usher Hall: 'On the 27th day of April, this peaceful, cultured, enlightened city of Edinburgh, that has never known in my lifetime what a real smash-up means, is going to know it that day if this civic reception comes off.'[22] On the night of the reception, some 10,000 people joined the protest in the High Street. One man jumped on the Catholic archbishop's car and councillors were heckled. The Lord Provost refused to address the reception and shook hands with Cormack, who hailed the raucous rally as a victory and was carried through the crowd. Later they tried to march on the Cowgate, where young Catholic men were ready to defend St Patrick's Church, but police barred their way.

The next morning, a Sunday, some thousand people gathered outside the city's Catholic cathedral to abuse those attending mass. They shouted 'No Popery' and sang 'God Save the King', and a favourite chant was 'One, two, three a-leerie, / Kick the Pope and De Valeerie', the last being in reference to the Irish prime minister, Eamon de Valera.

Worse was to follow that June. Edinburgh was the venue for a Roman Catholic Eucharistic Congress. Cormack promised a demonstration outside, and on the evening before the Congress he drew 3,500 to a protest rally in the Usher Hall. The next day, the Congress centred on a meeting for Catholic women in Waverley Market in the city centre. Cormack led a protest that the *Scottish Daily Express* numbered at 7,000. When the Cardinal's car arrived they rushed to attack it but were driven back by police batons. Four priests were beaten up.

That night, the crowd marched on St Patrick's in the Cowgate. The church bell was rung to rally defenders, and missiles and buckets of water were thrown at the mob from tenement windows before police ended the fighting.

The next day, Sunday, was the culmination of the Congress, a religious service in a priory in sedate Morningside. Once again Cormack's supporters heckled those attending and at its close tried to bar the exit, being thwarted when police took worshippers out of the rear entrance to waiting coaches.[23]

Throughout that summer, Cormack kept up nightly anti-Catholic street meetings across the city. It also saw the launch of Kormack's Kaledonian Klan, modelled on the Ku Klux Klan, a group supposedly formed to defend his meetings from attack. That autumn in the city's council elections Protestant Action (PA) took 23.37 percent of the vote (the Moderates polled 41.99 percent and Labour 34.86 percent). In the working-class port of Leith, PA beat Labour into third place.[24]

But Cormack's victory was short-lived: two years later, fresh elections saw Labour come top, taking 36.93 percent over the Moderates' 36.66 percent, with PA taking 25.28 percent. Cormack stood in both North Leith and Gorgie, but failed to win either.[25] He would soldier on nevertheless as a councillor in South Leith until his retirement in 1962, having been elected a bailie by Progressive (Tory) councillors in 1952.

Sectarianism was on display in Glasgow, too, in the 1930s, but took an electoral form under the leadership of a preacher, Alexander Ratcliffe, who formed the Scottish Protestant League, winning two council seats in 1931: Dennistoun, where Ratcliffe was elected, and Dalmarnock. When challenged by an ILP councillor that the SPL's programme was simply 'Kick the pope', Ratcliffe responded: 'Yes, we *do* kick the Pope! That *is* our job! It *is* our programme!'[26]

In 1932, the SPL took another council seat and won nearly 12 percent of the total vote across Glasgow. A year later it stood in twenty-three wards, won four seats and polled 71,000 votes, 23 percent. All four seats were taken from the Moderates (the Tory-Liberal alliance).[27]

The SPL vote that year had lasting significance; by cutting the Moderate vote it allowed Labour to take control of the city council for the first time. Nevertheless, the organisation fell apart as Ratcliffe's dictatorial style alienated his supporters and a dispute over funds ended up in court. The other SPL councillors defected to the Moderates, and when Ratcliffe had to defend his Dennistoun seat he lost, despite the Moderates standing down to give him a clear run. After a visit to Germany in April 1939 he became pro-Nazi and switched his attacks to the Jews, but he was a peripheral figure and died in relative obscurity in 1947.

Fighting Fascism

Other social divisions were making themselves apparent during the 1930s. In 1934, *The Blackshirt* described the British Union of Fascists branch in Dalbeattie as being 'several hundred strong' and 'the largest and most active branch in Scotland'. Its leader was James Little, who combined the post of town clerk with being a local bank manager.[28] Special Branch described its membership as 'business men, mostly in a small way'.[29]

Sir Oswald Mosley's British Union of Fascists (BUF) attempted repeatedly to build in Scotland, but with limited success. There was, however, support for fascism within Scotland's upper class. The Lord High Constable, Lord Erroll, joined the BUF in 1934. The Earl of Mar was a Mosleyite and the Duke of Buccleuch was pro-Hitler.[30] The Tory MP for Peebles and South Midlothian, Captain Archibald Henry Maule Ramsay, was a member of the anti-Semitic Nordic League and would be detained in 1940 for his pro-Nazi stance.[31]

The BUF's Scottish membership, which probably totalled around 1,000, had 'a clear professional, military and middle class bias'.[32] This composition was confirmed by other accounts. In Motherwell the BUF had an active branch, holding open-air and indoor meetings, and for a time had their own hall in the town centre. In May 1934, they were given the lease of the tennis courts in Calder Park. After Lady Mosley, the mother of the party's leader, spoke there in June 1934, she reported that she 'didn't know of any branch of the movement that had started on such strong lines as the one at Motherwell'.[33]

The BUF had its Scottish headquarters in Glasgow, and in June 1934 the *Glasgow Herald* reported that several thousand anti-fascists had 'trapped' the fascists in their headquarters and that only police intervention got them out.[34] One Glaswegian anti-fascist recalled protesting a gathering in which William Joyce, a BUF leader better known during the war as 'Lord Haw-Haw', attempted to speak: 'Joyce came to speak at Queen's Park recreation ground and we organised a counter demonstration. We organised, a number of us from the working class, the Labour League of Youth, Young Communist League and other youth organisations, who all agreed to disrupt this meeting. I had the privilege of taking one of the platform legs and throwing the platform up in the air.'[35]

Another Communist, and later an International Brigader, Garry McCartney, stated that anti-fascism became integral to left-wing activity and identity in the city: 'The working class movement was very much informed and very much involved in the anti-fascist struggle. Glasgow at the weekend was a forum of meetings, all over the city, at street corners, and in the centre of the city. We had tramp preachers, we had the YCL [Young Communist League], ILP . . . it was a whole seabed of discussions.'[36]

Despite the opposition, Mosley organised two rallies in Edinburgh. On the first occasion, in 1934, hundreds of uniformed Blackshirts – many of them bussed in from the north of England – clashed with anti-fascist opponents after the close of the meeting. As the Blackshirts' busses drove away, 'stones and bricks were thrown', smashing many of the bus windows and causing several of their passengers to require hospital treatment. One Blackshirt was partially blinded. The meeting itself, attended by 2,500 people, was less eventful, with just a few minor interruptions, giving Mosley the opportunity to outline his party's policy in relation to Scotland to an audience of 'ministers of religion, prominent lawyers, city councillors, farmers, clerks, shop assistants and artisans' – at least according to the BUF's own propaganda.[37]

In 1936, Mosley organised a second rally, of which one Communist Party member who would later serve in the International Brigades, George Watters, recalled: 'I remember gaun to a meeting in the Usher Hall, having been supplied wi' a ticket by some of the students at Edinburgh University. I landed right down in the second front seat in the Usher Hall . . . My job was to get up and create a disturbance right away by challenging Sir Oswald Mosley, which I did. At that time I had a pretty loud voice. And Sir Oswald Mosley wasn't being heard . . . There was a rush and in the rush I got a bit of a knocking about, and taken up to High Street [police station].'[38] Later he was fined £5 for breaching the Public Meetings Act.[39]

October 1936 also saw anti-fascists protest outside and inside Ibrox Park, home of Rangers FC, when Scotland played Germany at football. They were further angered when the swastika flag was flown above the grandstand.[40]

In his book *The Fascists in Britain*, Colin Cross argued that for the BUF, 'the most difficult area was Scotland where throughout its existence the BUF found it impossible to make headway'. He does point to one exception, stating Aberdeen was 'the real centre of Scottish Fascism where W.K.A.J. Chambers-Hunter, a former planter from Ceylon, who had lost an arm in the war, ran a keen, lively group'.[41]

John Londragan was a railworker who went from fighting fascists in Aberdeen to fighting fascism in Spain with the International Brigades, because for him '. . . the fight, whether it be here in Aberdeen against the British Union of Fascists or against Hitler and Mussolini in Spain, was exactly the same fight to me, no difference at all'.[42] Things came to a head on Sunday, 16 July 1937. The BUF was determined to hold a rally at the prime spot in the city, the Market Stance, a traditional meeting spot for the left.

The BUF leader Chambers-Hunter hoped that a Sunday evening during the city's summer holidays would catch the anti-fascists wrong-footed; he was proved wrong. That morning, Bob Cooney, a local Communist, addressed a crowd of 2,000 anti-fascists at the Links. They promised to return that evening to prevent the Fascist rally. The Fascists arrived with an armour-plated van, a public-address system, and their own stewards together with a police escort. But when Chambers-Hunter clambered onto the roof of the van to start the meeting, the crowd surged forward, cut the electricity cables and drove the Mosleyites away so that by 8 p.m. there were none left. Bob Cooney was one of many arrested, serving four days in jail.[43]

On occasion, the Communists received word of BUF gatherings in advance, including in September 1938 when 'a hostile mob of over 6000 people' attacked Chambers-Hunter as his van rolled into Torry, greeting him with 'a shower of burning fireworks, sticks, stones and pieces of coal'.[44] In a new turn of events, the police on this occasion stood by, more concerned with directing traffic than throwing themselves in the way of the anti-fascist onslaught. The three fascists – including Botha and Chambers-Hunter – eventually managed to flee, later requiring hospital treatment.

Anti-semitism was key to Mosley's propaganda but it does not seem to have attracted much support in Scotland. Not that it was absent. In Glasgow, there was a strong Jewish community in the Gorbals estimated by 1939 to be approximately 10,000. The neighbourhood was attractive because of its cheap accommodation, but once roots had been established and individuals began to prosper there was a movement towards Pollokshields and later farther south. The community was relatively well integrated into Gorbals life and young Jews in the 1930s often gravitated leftwards into the unions and associations.

In Glasgow, the Workers' Circle, composed of left-wing Jews, took part in directly opposing the BUF, organising demonstrations and actions when the Fascists tried to hold an event. Jewish anti-fascists were particularly active in opposing the BUF's attempts to gain a foothold in Govanhill, just south of the Gorbals, where the mass of Glasgow's Jews lived. Morris Smith, its secretary, has said that the BUF were 'howled down. They never got a turnout. That was the line then, we had to stop them appearing on the streets.'[45]

The determination of anti-fascists to prevent the Mosleyites organising in Scotland was, in large part, central to ensuring that the BUF did not gain significant support. Many of those who had fought the Fascists on the streets of Aberdeen, Glasgow and Edinburgh would carry that fight farther afield.

Aid for Spain

In the summer of 1936, the call came out for volunteers from across the world to rally to the side of the Spanish Republic. The Spanish military, under General Francisco Franco, had risen up to overthrow an elected left-wing government and was receiving help from Hitler and Mussolini. Democratic governments like those of Britain and France did not aid the threatened government in Madrid, but nonetheless thousands made their way to Spain to help stop fascism. Among them were many Scots. The numbers of those from Britain who volunteered to fight fascism in Spain is estimated at 2,400; 23 percent came from Scotland. Of the 540 British volunteers who died in Spain, 134 were Scots.[46]

They were predominantly working class – miners, railworkers, engineers, printers and other skilled workers, as well as labourers. Some were unemployed and a few were students or white-collar workers.[47] The vast majority of those who fought in Spain did so with the International Brigades, organised by the Communists, and the majority of them were Communist Party members and supporters. Others were members of the Independent Labour Party or anarchists. The ILP contingent fought with the militias of the Spanish Partido Obrero de Unificación Marxista (POUM), labelled Trotskyists by the Communists. In May 1937, the POUM was suppressed by the Republican government, its leader Andreu Nin arrested and killed by the Soviet secret police, the NKVD.

Those who volunteered to fight were driven by a hatred of fascism and the stark reality of inter-war Scotland. They made their way to London and then moved on to Paris, travelling on a weekend ticket that did not require a passport. From the French capital they went south by train and then crossed the Pyrenees into Spain on foot.

Tommy Bloomfield from Fife had been navvying before getting a job with a contractor in Kirkcaldy prior to going to Spain: 'The gaffer was a pig. He shouted from one end of King Street in Kirkcaldy to another. "Hurry up, come up here." When I got up there I said, "Here you don't want me to run?" He says, "Hurry up, hurry up!" I says, "Look, gie's the books. I'd rather go to Spain to shoot bastards like you."'[48]

Annie Murray served as a nurse for most of the Spanish war. Born in Aberdeenshire to a political family, she had led protests over working conditions while at Edinburgh Royal Infirmary, and joined two of her brothers who volunteered for the International Brigades. She would recall: 'It was the most important thing of my life. It was a terrific experience I would have never liked to have missed. I have certainly no regrets at having gone there at all.'[49]

From the first battles at Brunete and Jarama in 1937 to the final Republican offensive, the Battle of the Ebro in 1938, they were fighting against the odds, against a professional army backed up by the air power, tanks, munitions and men of Fascist Italy and Nazi Germany. At Jarama the International Brigades blunted Franco's advance to the east of Madrid. Forty-five Scots died there, one of whom was Bob Mason of Edinburgh. His family wrote this tribute to him, which was published in the *Daily Worker* in March 1937: 'When Bob volunteered to go to Spain, it was not with the object of personal gain or with the spirit of adventure. He had every reason to hate fascism by his knowledge of the brutal and murderous suppression of the working class movement under Hitler and Mussolini.'[50]

A volunteer from Glasgow's Possilpark, Alex McDade, wrote 'There's a Valley in Spain Called Jarama', which became the anthem of the British Brigade and continues to be sung today. Its first verse goes:

> There's a valley in Spain called Jarama,
> That's a place that we all know so well,
> for 'tis there that we wasted our manhood,
> And most of our old age as well.[51]

Eventually, the International Brigades were withdrawn from the fight, after the Republic agreed that all foreign fighters would leave the country. The defeat of the Republic in March 1939 left a bitter taste but did not dampen the determination of the volunteers to continue to fight fascism when Britain went to war with Germany six months later.

But the fight for Spain was also fought at home in Scotland. In August 1936, news that a businessman in Ayr was re-fitting aeroplanes to sell to Franco led 400 townspeople to demand the delivery be stopped. In Kirkcaldy, anti-fascist pilots dropped leaflets defending the Spanish Republic over the crowd attending a British Empire air display. In Glasgow's Argyll Street on a Saturday evening, Communists could sell 2,000 copies of a *Daily Worker* special edition on Spain.[52]

This took place against the background of 30,000 marching against the means test in Lanarkshire, and in September, a stay-down strike by miners over pay and conditions at the Dickson pit in Blantyre. When management refused to allow them food and water, thousands of Lanarkshire miners walked out in solidarity.[53]

Committees to raise aid for Spain spread across towns and villages in late 1936. There were fifteen in Glasgow alone. The city's 1937 May Day march was the biggest since the General Strike, with 15,000 demonstrating under the slogan 'Solidarity with Spain'.[54]

The *Daily Worker* reported from Edinburgh on 7 December 1938 that 'Over £20 and two wedding rings were collected at a meeting in the Oddfellows Hall.' Four days later it further added, 'Eight members of Granton Young Communist League borrowed a barrow from the manager of the local Co-operative and collected 1 cwt. of food.' [55]

In Lochgelly in the Fife coalfield, local pipe bands were used to help with street collections of money and tinned food. Despite poverty and unemployment, the response was generous. Mary Docherty writes of the response in Fife to the Aid for Spain campaign: 'Teams were formed for the different areas of Cowdenbeath. Bob Selkirk [a Communist councillor] and my father and members of the NUWM went round every Friday in the fourth ward with a two wheeled barrow, even though there was mass unemployment in Cowdenbeath at that time, there was a great response to our appeal.' [56]

NUWM activists in Hawick took over a disused woollen mill, running it as a co-op, producing clothing for Spanish Republican troops. The town council had earlier voted down support for such a scheme when it was proposed by the town's only Communist councillor. [57]

Naomi Mitchison, Catherine Carswell, Edwin Muir, Hugh MacDiarmid and William Soutar were among the literary figures who signed an appeal for the 'ancient peoples of Catalonia and the Basque Country' following Franco's final victory in the Spanish Civil War. Meanwhile, in the aftermath of Britain's appeasement of Hitler in September 1938, Edwin and Wilda Muir together with Eric Linklater issued an open letter expressing their sense of shame. [58]

Nevertheless, among the upper echelons of Scottish society there was support for Franco. After visiting rebel territory, Major General Sir Walter Maxwell-Scott (a great-great-grandson of Sir Walter Scott) launched the Scottish Friends of Nationalist Spain (FNS), with Cameron of Lochiel among the vice-presidents. In March 1938, it attempted to hold a rally in Glasgow's St Andrew's Hall. Some five hundred anti-fascists tried to storm the hall, being met with police batons. More were inside, heckling Maxwell-Scott and other speakers and hanging the Red Flag from the balcony.

June saw 500 people attend a FNS public meeting in Edinburgh's Usher Hall, fewer than the 800 who'd protested against it on the previous evening at the Mound. The meeting seemed to have passed off peacefully, but as the audience filed out to their waiting buses, 800 anti-fascists ambushed them, blocking their departure.[59]

In the end fascism was victorious in Spain, with the Spanish Republic deserted by those who claimed to uphold democracy. Its defeat ensured that Hitler felt confident to go to war in the summer of 1939.

The sacrifice of these volunteers was appreciated at the time and ever since. When in December 1938 eight volunteers arrived back at Edinburgh's Waverley Station, the *Scotsman* reported on their reception: 'When the train arrived there were scenes touched with great emotion on the platform when the men were welcomed by their relatives. The welcome they were given on the station roadways was loud and prolonged, the station rang with the cheers of the crowd. "The Internationale" and "The Red Flag" were sung and accompanied by a band.'[60]

Looking back, Tommy Bloomfield from Kirkcaldy wrote this: 'Today as a pensioner, I live on social security but I'm the richest man in this world having known my comrades of the International Brigades and the leaders of the National Unemployed Workers Movement along with the outstanding men and women of my era. If I had to live over again I would do the same as there is no other way.'

Striking Once More

The defeat of the General Strike had sapped the morale of workers to strike and win. The unemployment of the early 1930s was another blow. But in the mid-1930s there was a brief upturn in the economy, which meant a revival of confidence on the shop floor. The experience of fighting unemployment and fascism fed into that newfound mood of resistance. One of the first major strikes occurred in March 1935 at the Richmond Park Laundry Company in Cambuslang, the largest single laundry in Britain at this time, employing 1,000 workers.

The action began when the laundry management refused to recognise the trade union National Union of Distributive and Allied

Workers (NUDAW). As the NUDAW journal *New Dawn* reported following the strike, 'The intimation of non-recognition coupled with one or two other irritating incidents roused our members to the pitch which demanded immediate action.'[61] The workforce had also recommended a general increase in wages and two weeks holiday with pay. When the management refused these demands the workers went on strike. At least 500 workers were involved in this one-week strike, the vast majority young women. In the course of this strike the women attended outdoor and indoor meetings, picketed the laundry with large numbers of their supporters and marched through Ruther-glen and Cambuslang.

In order to prevent other laundries carrying out the work of Rich-mond Park Laundry, deputations of girl pickets were dispatched to laundries across the west of Scotland with national organisers from NUDAW to distribute leaflets to fellow laundry workers. According to *New Dawn*, they won the support of these workers, who, 'although unorganised, they immediately responded and . . . let their respec-tive employers know that any attempt to get this work done would lead to trouble and consequently working class solidarity triumphed.'[62]

It seems that the laundry management made a number of attempts to intimidate the young women into returning to work, going as far as to write to their parents, presumably to urge them to exert pressure on their daughters to return to work, as the management also threat-ened to dismiss all of the strikers. Despite management intimidation the strike continued and, as *New Dawn* reported, the threats of dismissal only resulted in greater support from the local community for the strikers.

The strike then became tumultuous and the police intervened as strikers and their supporters gathered on the second day and a tram-car was smashed by the crowd. On the following night the crowd stopped trams and buses, attacked the police, threw stones and 'howled' at blacklegs, which resulted in the police charging the crowd. Later, 600 strikers and supporters gathered at Cambuslang where house windows were smashed.[63]

A number of altercations took place between the management, the strikers and their supporters and the police. As *New Dawn* reported: 'In addition to fighting the employers our members also had to fight the police who showed in no unmistakable fashion "upon which side their bread is buttered", our pickets were batoned by the police on two successive days and for cowardly brutality we haven't seen the like of it. Heads were smashed by the "keepers of the law and order" and of course it goes without saying that the casualties were not all on one side.'[64]

An important feature of this strike was the support the strikers received from large sections of the local community and the unemployed who joined with the strikers in their demonstrations. As a result, the strike ended with the company ceding union recognition and some improvements in wages and conditions.

Elsewhere, troubles continued. Conditions on the Clyde shipyards can be summed up in the story told by a retired worker to the historian Richard Croucher about a riveter who had fallen to his death in the shipyard. The foreman simply ordered that his body be put in a cart, covered, and taken home to his wife.[65]

Beardmore's at Parkhead Forge had, exceptionally, retained strong shop steward organisation from the early 1920s, and in March 1937 the members brought 1,300 members of the engineering union out on strike over pay, demanding a penny an hour more. The national union refused to recognise the strike but it quickly won solidarity across Glasgow. The strike went on until May, holding up vital parts for the luxury liner *Queen Mary* being built on the Clyde. The workers returned when management agreed to sit down to negotiations.

In 1937, as the economy went through a brief recovery and re-armament meant orders, apprentices across Scotland began to organise, sharing grievances with those in Aberdeen by issuing a leaflet headed 'We Are Nobody's Baby' in complaint at the way they were treated by management.[66] Engineering and shipyard apprentices had not been paid two wage increases given to older workers. The demand for an 'evening up' of their wages now caught an echo. A committee elected from across Clydeside was sent to meet the employers, who refused to see them.

The Beardmore's strike now acted as an example, and three days after it began 500 apprentices stopped work at Fairfield's shipyard and used mass pickets to bring out their fellows across the Upper Clyde shipyards. On 5 April, the *Daily Worker* reported that 3,700 apprentices were out and the strike was spreading across the engineering industry to 130 factories. The spread of the strike to John Brown's shipyard, where the *Queen Mary* was being built, added pressure on the employers.[67]

The Govan apprentices took over a disused shop as their headquarters and organised an 'apprentices' Olympics' and a football competition involving forty-eight teams.[68] The central strike committee elected by 160 shop stewards and yard delegates and chaired by Stuart Watson of the Young Communists, met daily and from it circulated a strike bulletin distributed by 150 cyclists.

By the second week of April, more than 11,000 apprentices were out and the strike spread to Edinburgh, Teesside and Belfast. Five hundred women 'trainers' had come out at Barr and Stroud in Glasgow for an extra penny an hour and asked to join the strike but were told they were not apprentices and could not. Feeling 'rather hurt', they would have to wait until November, when a women's strike got under way.[69]

The engineering union recognised the strike two weeks later, and on 16 April adult workers stopped work for the day in solidarity. That morning, chalked up on the walls outside workplaces across Clydeside were messages such as 'Don't Let Us Down', 'Don't Scab Today' and 'Don't Work Today Daddy!'. Some 150,000 workers answered the call and downed tools.[70]

The union leaders and the Conciliation Officer of the Ministry of Labour secured talks with the employers, and on 5 May the apprentices agreed to return to work, having won substantial pay increases but not recognition for the union to represent them. Nevertheless, they retained their strong rank-and-file organisation.[71]

The Clydeside apprentices launched their own paper and had a green, red and blue badge, green for one side of the religious divide, blue for the other and red for socialism.[72] The Clyde set an example that was quickly followed by apprentices in Manchester, Lancashire and Coventry.[73]

The Birth of the SNP

Today's Scottish National Party was formed in the 1930s – a decade of misery for working-class Scots but also one of deep uncertainty bordering on fear for the middle and upper classes. Economic power had shifted southwards, with the takeover of so many Scottish concerns by London-based corporations.

As the Great Depression began in 1929, the industrial giant Beardmore's was brought near to bankruptcy. Its shipyard on the Clyde was closed the following year and its engineering company sold off.

In 1932, the president of Edinburgh's Chamber of Commerce warned that the blood was being drained out of Scotland's economy: 'Business after business was being bought up by English money and factories, one after another, closed down . . . if the process of English absorption is not stopped, Scotland will drop to a position of industrial insignificance.'[74]

There was a move away, too, from a political commitment to Home Rule. The once-powerful Liberal Party had fractured and was marginalised. The Labour Party shifted from its intent to create a Scottish parliament. In 1922, on the departure of the 'Red Clydesider' MPs for London, John Wheatley had championed Home Rule but changed his mind after the defeat of the 1926 General Strike, arguing that only the power of the whole British state could protect the working classes from the predatory nature of international capitalism. Another MP, Tom Johnston, agreed: 'What purpose would there be in our getting a Scottish Parliament in Edinburgh if it has to administer an emigration system, a glorified poor law and a desert?'[75]

That chimed with the direction of the Labour Party, its identification with the British state, and within the ruling class the acceptance of the economic theories of John Maynard Keynes, which proposed that an element of state direction was needed to revive the economy. Supporters of Home Rule saw Labour's support for it ebbing away.

The National Party was launched in June 1928 by intellectuals, most notably the poet Hugh MacDiarmid, nationalists, students and former ILP members, such as its dynamic organiser John

MacCormick. A year earlier, a Home Rule bill had been defeated at Westminster and the new party took up the demand for a Scottish parliament.

In the 1931 Westminster general election, the National Party stood five candidates, winning 21,000 votes – gaining 9.4 percent in Edinburgh East, 14.9 percent in Inverness, 10.9 percent in Renfrew West and 13.3 percent in St Rollox in Glasgow. The Communists stood eight candidates, winning 35,000 votes.[76]

In 1931, the Unionist constituency party in Glasgow Cathcart broke away in support of Scottish Home Rule within a wider federation of British dominions, forming the Scottish Party. The disgruntled Tories, led by a Glasgow solicitor, Kevin MacDowell, were joined by the Duke of Montrose and Alexander Dewar Gibb, Professor of Scots Law at Glasgow University. He warned that 'inferior' people of Irish stock were 'usurpin'' the land of a 'dwindling, though virile and intelligent, race'.[77] MacDowell was an enthusiast for the British Empire and wanted to modernise it.

John MacCormick quickly opened discussions with the new grouping, arguing that the National Party of Scotland 'could not allow the Scottish Party to continue in its separate existence. It was led by men whose names were far better known to the public than were many of ours and who command the respect which is always given, whether due or not, to rank and position.' The pursuit of such men involved MacCormick engineering the expulsion of Hugh MacDiarmid, regarded as too radical for such men.[78]

The emphasis of both organisations became one of addressing middle-class concerns about the loss of Scottish identity, with its leaders supporting either devolution or independence within the Empire. At a House of Commons special debate in November 1932, George Buchanan, MP for the Gorbals, reported that the surge of nationalist sentiment was now coming from the professional and middle classes: 'I meet lawyers and sheriffs, and nearly every one of them is in sympathy with the movement . . . same with the doctors and the higher-paid civil servants.'[79]

The nationalists polled well enough in the 1933 UK general election, garnering 16 percent of the vote across the eight seats they contested, but rather than that being a bridgehead for advance, it was its pre-war high mark. In 1934, the two groups finally joined together in the Scottish National Party, which claimed 10,000 members but by 1939 was down to 2,000.

The party began to polarise between those who saw the creation of a Scottish parliament as the immediate goal and those who advocated nothing less than independence. By the close of the decade it seemed to be a waning and fractious force. Time was to prove that impression wrong.

What was true was that the 1930s had left a deep imprint on Scotland. The working class was determined that it would never have to repeat what it had suffered in those years. The confidence of the upper classes had been badly knocked. As war approached, re-armament would bring orders to the shipyards and engineering plants, but that alone could not shake off an awareness of decline.

REBEL LIVES: HUGH MACDIARMID

Scotland has produced two of the world's finest poets. The first, and most obvious, is Robert Burns. The second is Hugh MacDiarmid, the pen name adopted by Christopher Murray Grieve. MacDiarmid's reputation is greater after his death than in his lifetime, in large part because his poetry has become more widely available than it was when he died of cancer in 1978. But interest in him has also grown as interest in Scotland's culture and the debate on her place in the world have grown.

MacDiarmid was a difficult man, who loved an argument and never suffered fools gladly. For most of his adult life he had two passions – Scottish nationalism and communism. In *Who's Who* he listed Anglophobia as one of his hobbies.[80] MacDiarmid was not just cantankerous; he verged on misogyny, as is evident from this quote: 'Scottish women of any historical interest are curiously rare . . . our leading Scotswomen have been . . . almost entirely destitute of exceptional endowments of any sort.' Despite such statements, his two wives, Margaret 'Peggy' Skinner and Valda Trevlyn, were fiercely independent women.[81]

Born in Langholm in the Borders in 1892 to a father who was a postal worker and a mother who was the caretaker of the town's library, he was proud of his solidly working-class roots. He wrote in his autobiography: 'My development owed a very great deal to my growing up in a working class family and being fed on out-and-out Radicalism and Republicanism when still a child.'[82]

During World War I he served in the Royal Medical Corps. He recalled his reaction to news of the 1916 Easter Rising in Dublin: 'I was in Barracks, in Sheffield of all places . . . If it had been possible at all I would have deserted at that time from the British army and joined the Irish.'[83] After the war, he hoped to eke out a living through writing, and became involved in the Independent Labour Party, the Scottish Home Rule Association, the No More War campaign and the unemployed movement.

Despite that, after Mussolini and the Fascists took power in Italy in 1922, he wrote admiringly of them. He was looking at Italy through Scots eyes and believed the slogan 'Italy First' could be taken up at home as 'Scotland First'. Mistakenly, he believed Mussolini would move leftwards and champion the peasantry. The poet, literary critic and Communist John Manson points out: 'MacDiarmid was never a Fascist in the sense of a supporter of a right-wing dictatorship; he didn't belong to a Fascist group . . . he saw "a Scottish Fascism" as nationalist.'[84]

But his fascination with Mussolini does illustrate one weakness in MacDiarmid's politics: he saw the liberation of working people as being achieved through the actions of a 'great man'. Later, that would be Stalin.

In 1926, MacDiarmid, then living in Montrose, threw himself into the General Strike, and it showed in his poetry. In 1928, he was a founding member of the National Party of Scotland but was expelled four years later when it merged with the Scottish Party (disaffected Tories in the main) because his left-wing views were an obstacle to the unity that created today's SNP. The new party set its aim as securing a Scottish parliament, not independence, but for MacDiarmid there was no point in gaining Home Rule; he wanted a complete break with the United Kingdom.

He wrote after his forced exit:

> The Scottish Party headed by the Duke of Montrose and Sir Alexander MacEwan entirely consists of that sort of right wing moderate, and has as its sole object the confining of the Scottish Movement within the narrowest possible limits and with the least possible discomfort to the existing order. The National Party of Scotland had attempted, on the other hand, to stand pat on the few basic facts to a whole range of other considerations; but it has now abandoned even that effort and is fused with the Scottish Party.[85]

In 1934 MacDiarmid joined the Communist Party, but he could hardly hide his disdain of its central leadership in Scotland. A year after joining, he quoted Lenin: 'It would be a very serious mistake to suppose that one can become a Communist without making one's own the treasures of human knowledge.' He then added: 'My Scottish Communist comrades must forgive me if I am quite unable to recognise any of them in this description of what really constitutes a Communist.'

Later that year, in his journal, *New Scotland*, he raised the prospect of a new world war, arguing that Scotland should follow the lead of Ireland during the last conflict, and called for a 'proletarian and Republican' secession from the Empire.[86] This drew the ire of the Scottish Party leadership.

An exchange of letters followed, and by the beginning of the next year the Scottish leadership expelled him, but on appeal the leadership in London reinstated his membership. MacDiarmid's final expulsion, for 'nationalism', came in 1939 after he claimed that Scottish and Irish members of the International Brigades in Spain had refused to fight in the British Battalion because they could not fight alongside English volunteers. Despite his expulsion he continued to identify with communism and the Soviet Union, yet his full-blooded identification with Stalinism and the USSR luckily did not contaminate his poetry.

One huge service he did perform was keeping alive the memory and beliefs of John Maclean. In 1948, MacDiarmid and his fellow poet Sidney Goodsir Smith addressed a rally in Glasgow's St Andrew's Hall to mark the twenty-fifth anniversary of Maclean's death. Hamish Henderson wrote his famous song 'John Maclean March' for this meeting. MacDiarmid helped found the John Maclean Society in 1968 with Morris Blythman (Thurso Berwick).

In 1957 he re-joined the Communist Party in solidarity with the Soviet Union, which a year before had sent in tanks to crush the Hungarian Revolution, and at a time when it was losing members in protest. By the end of the decade, the poet was a supporter of the Campaign for Nuclear Disarmament and also joined the more radical, direct action Committee of 100. In 1964, he spoke along with Malcolm X at the Oxford Student Union.[87] He remained active on the Scottish left and in nationalist politics until his death.

MacDiarmid initially wrote poetry in English, but in the course of the 1920s began to use his own version of Lallans (or Doric, as he called it), using his own version for the simple fact that there are so many variations across Scotland. MacDiarmid set himself the task of carrying through the Scottish Renaissance, a rebirth of the culture that he believed had been destroyed by Anglicisation, Walter Scott and the subsequent kailyard movement. His task also involved rescuing Burns from tartanry and a sentimental portrayal of Scottish life. MacDiarmid also drew on Modernist influences, James Joyce being one of his heroes. All of this comes together in 'A Drunk Man Looks at the Thistle', surely his finest poem.

'A Drunk Man Looks at the Thistle' also reflects his own passionate involvement in the 1926 General Strike and a section of the long poem is entitled 'The Ballad of the General Strike'. He had joined the strike movement in Montrose, where he lived in the 1920s, and recalled:

> we had the whole area of Angus, Forfarshire; we had it sewn up. I was speaking when news came through of J.H. Thomas's [general secretary of the National Union of Railwaymen] betrayal of the strike. I was speaking to an audience of mainly railwaymen and they all broke down weeping. It was one of the most moving

experiences I have ever had – middle aged men most of them, weeping like children, you know. It was such a disappointment, because we knew, we knew we had it.[88]

Although typically in the poem the thistle has been considered the symbol of Scotland, writer John Baglow points out: '. . . the promise of the thistle eventually being transformed into a lovely flower represents on one level the aspirations and struggle of the working class to realise their potential.'[89]

The rose now bursts forth from the thistle:

> A rose loupt oot and grew, until
> It was ten times the size
> O' ony rose the thistle afore
> Had heistit to the skies.
>
> And still it grew until it seemed
> The hail! braid earth had turned
> A reid reid rose that in the lift
> Like a ball o' fire burned.

But the rose shrivels as hope gives way to bitter defeat:

> Syne the rose shrivelled suddenly
> As a balloon is burst;
> The thistle was a ghaistly slick,
> As gin it had been curst.
>
> Was it the ancient vicious sway
> Imposed itsel' again,
> Or nerve owre weak for new emprise
> That made the effort vain.

In the inter-war years the hopes of a Scottish Renaissance seemed to have been dashed. MacDiarmid was ekeing out a precarious existence and had fallen out badly with his friend Edwin Muir. In the post-war years his stock rose and a new generation of writers and artists celebrated his influence, which casts a long shadow over Scotland's cultural life.

Central to MacDiarmid's poetry is the very identity of Scotland, and that is what 'A Drunk Man Looks at the Thistle' returns to again and again. As his biographer Alan Bold points out: 'Much of his poetry is a dialogue between Chris Grieve, the postman's son, and Hugh MacDiarmid, the self-appointed saviour of Scotland.'[90]

There can be no denying his nationalism or that his view of the class struggle tended to identify the bourgeoisie as the *English* upper class, ignoring their Scottish allies. But for MacDiarmid freedom involves more than national independence. It is about human liberation, as he wrote in 'To Circumjack Cencrastus':

> For freedom means that a lad or lass
> In Cupar or elsewhaur yet
> May alter the haill o' human thocht
> Mair than Christ's altered it.
>
> I never set een on a lad or lass
> But I wonder gin he or she
> Wi' a word or deed'll suddenly dae
> An impossibility.

MacDiarmid's tombstone, in his hometown of Langholm, carries this extract from 'A Drunk Man Looks at the Thistle':

> I'll ha'e nae hauf-way hoose, but aye be whaur
> Extremes meet – it's the only way I ken
> To dodge the curst conceit o' bein' richt
> That damns the vast majority o' men.

There could be no finer epitaph.

TWELVE

World War II and After

Scotland's War

Thousands of Scots were on the front line during World War II, but Scotland itself was not. Even after Hitler overran Denmark and Norway in the spring of 1940, and then the Low Countries and France in May and June, Scotland was too far removed to be the object of sustained attack. Britain faced the threat of invasion that summer, with the crucial fight being over who controlled the skies above London and south-east England, the Battle of Britain. When the Luftwaffe failed to establish dominance they switched to the night bombing attacks of the Blitz, in a failed bid to demoralise the civilian population of the imperial capital.

But Scotland did not escape the bombing, nor horrific civilian deaths, though not on the scale of what London suffered. This does not mean that Scotland was not central to Britain's war effort. The Clyde was where the cross-Atlantic convoys that brought badly needed men, armaments, raw materials and food from North America were marshalled. The Orkneys was home to the Home Fleet, and Invergordon and Rosyth were important naval bases. Much of the exiled Polish army was based here before going to Italy and France, while the Highlands was used as a training ground for special forces and the Commandos. Scottish shipyards, factories, mines and farms worked at full stretch, and industry was working overtime to produce armaments. Above all, Scots served in every theatre of war.

For Scots, as for so many others in Britain and across the globe, Hitler had to be stopped. That made this war different from its predecessor. Some were aware that Churchill was fighting to preserve the British Empire, but they were, nevertheless, prepared to serve. Fifty thousand Scots were killed or wounded during World War II, whereas the casualty figure for the 1914–18 war totalled nearly 150,000. That is in part a reflection of the fact that the wartime government of Winston Churchill was aware that there could be no repeat of the horrendous casualty figures of twenty years before and did its utmost to avoid such high rates.

On 1 September 1939, children and their mothers were evacuated from Glasgow and Clydebank, Edinburgh, Rosyth and Dundee, fearful that the declaration of war would be followed by the carpet-bombing of strategic towns and cities. They were sent to rural areas and towns believed to be safe from bombing. The arrival of these children brought some of the realities of working-class life to the middle-class inhabitants of the communities that received them. In his history of Britain at war, Angus Calder recounts the story of one Glasgow mum who admonished her six-year-old for urinating, saying, 'You dirty thing, messing up the lady's carpet. Go and do it in the corner.' Calder points out: 'It throws light on the Glasgow tenements, where one broken-down lavatory might be shared (or ignored) by thirty people, and it was the cleanest families who refused to use the communal closets.'[1] He points out, too, that half the people of Glasgow did not have a bath.

Wartime food rationing, however, benefitted the poor. Access to a better diet meant the number of children dying in their first year fell by 27 percent during the war years and the average height of Glaswegian thirteen-year-olds increased by two inches. People were eating better because there were jobs and because incomes per head in Scotland doubled from £86 in 1938 to £170 in 1944.[2] Nevertheless, the reality of those conditions, which helped ensure class warfare on the home front, was never far away.

The fear of a repeat of the labour and rent strikes of the first war weighed heavily on the minds of the Churchill administration, and

Clydeside was an area of key concern. Accordingly, despite being a High Tory, Churchill was prepared to effectively cede control of the home front to his coalition partner, Labour, as well as once more relying on the trade union leaders to hold the cap on strikers. He appointed the former editor of *Forward*, Tom Johnston, as Secretary of State for Scotland. Johnston asked for and got approval to form a Council of State, and in 1942 he set up a broad-based Scottish Council of Industry, which helped boost the number of government contracts for Scotland.

When Johnston discovered that special hospitals in the Clyde Basin, built to treat casualties of aerial bombing, were lying unused, he ordered them to treat everyone for free; it was a nascent NHS. Later in the war he created the Hydro-Electricity Board, which used the waterpower of the Highlands to generate electricity.[3] Even before the landslide election victory that would return Labour to office in 1945, ushering in the welfare state, Johnston was putting many such measures in place.

Though Scotland was spared the worst of Hitler's air assault, there were still attacks on towns key to the British war effort. On the nights of 13 and 14 March 1941, German bombers attacked Clydebank, a major centre for shipbuilding and armaments. The first attack was made up of 260 bombers, dropping high-explosive bombs, incendiary bombs and landmines over a nine-hour assault. Much of the town was set alight and people were trapped in collapsed buildings. The following night, 200 bombers returned in a seven-and-a-half-hour attack. Over the two days, 528 civilians were killed, and more than 617 people were seriously injured. Out of Clydebank's 47,000 inhabitants, 35,000 were left homeless. One survivor recalled:

> What I'll never forget as long as I live was the noise and the screams and cries when I was taken to the First-Aid post . . . This was something you couldn't believe . . . the screams were terrible . . . people had lost arms and legs . . . some people were doing what they could to help but it was just too much for them. Oh . . . what a catalogue of injuries . . . people broken, smashed and burned . . . and others dead without so much as a scratch on their bodies . . . killed by blast.

Another survivor was in an air-raid shelter, playing cards with two pals, his brother, mother and father also there. He never heard the bomb that hit them: 'I felt the wall on my back . . . saw my brother being blasted through the door . . . my pals . . . blasted to bits . . . the concrete roof caved in smashing into my mothers chest . . . crushing my father.' He was buried in the rubble with the fire blazing and his dead friends on top of him for eight and a half hours before being dug out: 'I was paralysed from the waist down . . . my mother was killed . . . my friends were killed . . . my father and brother survived . . . all the other people in the adjoining shelters were killed'.[4]

On 7 May, the Luftwaffe hit Greenock, a key port for the wartime convoys. After a bomb hit a distillery, setting it ablaze, the flames acted as a beacon for the other bombers. An air-raid warden recalled that the whole town was ablaze. Bombs were still dropping in the early hours. That night, the civil authorities had to deal with more than 200 corpses as the warden recalled: 'At the mortuary at Princes Pier we had the unclaimed bodies of eight infants not any of them older than a year or eighteen months. We photographed them all. They were never claimed and we buried them privately in the Green-ock Cemetery.'[5]

Wartime Strikes

In the summer of 1940, Parliament passed Order 1305 outlawing strikes and setting up a National Arbitration Tribunal to resolve any industrial dispute. Although strikes were unlawful, the government took a much more *softly, softly* approach than in 1914–18. There were just thirty-eight wartime prosecutions under Order 1305 in England and Wales, but seventy-one in Scotland, mainly concerned with labour unrest on the Clyde.[6]

The temper there was evident in March 1940 when Beardmore workers walked out over the sacking of two men, and Albion Motors struck over the employment of a non-union worker.[7] Even as the Battle of Britain was reaching its climax that September, a major strike erupted over the sacking of the union convenor at British

Auxiliaries, lasting most of the month before the workers started drifting back.[8]

These strikes were both illegal under wartime legislation and unofficial because the trade union leaders had agreed to police those laws. The Labour Party in government from May 1940 onwards was utterly opposed to such actions. However, strikes were supported by the Communist Party until June 1941, when, following Hitler's invasion of the Soviet Union, they switched to opposing them, in line with Moscow's wishes that they help the war effort. The ILP and more radical groups continued to support workers taking action.

In 1942, a number of strikes in Glasgow occurred when boilermakers at the Queens Park works of North British Locomotives walked out and stayed out despite the best efforts of the Glasgow District Committee of the engineering union. Women workers at Rolls-Royce Hillington struck for union recognition. Two years later, workers at Albion Motors were out for six weeks.[9] Agnes MacLean, born in Scotland Street in Kinning Park, started at Rolls-Royce Hillington at the outset of war. Women were doing skilled work using sophisticated equipment but were denied equal pay with men doing the same or even less skilled work:

> . . . something had to be done about it, I mean we were really very angry about it, and in 1941 we did this big fight about it, the women's rate, and we were wanting at least the same grade as the unskilled, the labourer . . . so we fought for the male labourers rate, and and we didn't get it, of course, and we went on strike, and at that time there was law which stated that you can't go on strike because everybody was helping the war effort . . . it was really spontaneous and we just one day got on our coats and walked out and each department as it walked out was walking through each section, the girls just put on their coats and joined . . . we did put up a bit of a fight and eventually they had to look at it and they had to get some recognition for the male labourers' rate.[10]

In 1943, however, the women discovered that the company was not honouring the agreement. And so in July they threatened a strike.

The engineering union intervened (they had started to admit women into membership) and a Court of Inquiry was set up. In October, angry at the slow pace of negotiation, the women walked out, 'taking with them most of the men in the plant', as Agnes recalled, adding that 'the men were absolutely fantastic'.[11]

The strike involved some 16,000 workers, making it the biggest in wartime Britain, and lasted nearly a month, threatening to spread across Clydeside. Agnes MacLean was again involved, despite joining the Communist Party two years earlier. The strikers won though the settlement fell short of full equal pay.[12] Agnes MacLean succeeded in finally negotiating full equal pay in 1952, long before other plants in Scotland.[13]

In 1943, a strike at the Cardowan pit spread across Lanarkshire. The president of the Scottish miners' union, Abe Moffat, recalled that the colliers struck unofficially over the unfair transfer of a miner to another job. In response, the authorities took thirty-four miners to court, where some were fined but nine refused to pay and were jailed. The strike spread across the Lanarkshire coalfield.[14] Moffat arranged a meeting with the nine men in Barlinnie Jail, urging them to pay their fines in the interest of the war effort. Eventually they voted eight to one to do so. As Moffat said, 'I had to admire the lad who put his hand up against.'[15]

Under Tom Johnston's administration Labour must have felt any prospects of a nationalist revival had been dashed. Full employment was back, Johnston was putting welfare reforms in place and could reassure doubters that if this was not Home Rule, Scotland was governed from his office, the impressive new St Andrew's House on the side of Edinburgh's Calton Hill.

To add to this, the SNP suffered a split in 1942 when John MacCormick quit after he was outvoted over his proposal to launch a cross-party national convention to secure Home Rule. This had brought to a head the division between those who set the creation of a Scottish parliament as key, and those who wanted nothing but independence. That party conference voted in the pro-independence Douglas Young as chair. He was on bail after being sentenced to twelve months in jail for resisting conscription on the grounds that it was against the terms of the 1707 Treaty of Union. The party had already taken an anti-war stance prior to the outbreak of World War II hostilities. The dominant mood was one of pacifism, but there was also fringe nationalism that hoped a Nazi victory would bring Scottish independence.

Yet this anti-war stance did the SNP no harm. When Young contested the Kirkcaldy Burghs by-election in February 1944, he captured 42 percent of the vote. In another by-election the following year, the SNP gained its first MP in Motherwell – the Tories and Liberals did not stand, under a wartime agreement to give the sitting party a free run. The well-known scientist John Boyd Orr also took the Scottish Universities seat on a nationalist platform. It was a short-lived triumph because Labour re-took Motherwell that summer in their landslide Westminster general election win.[16] The nationalist revival had set down a marker for the future.

Post-War Reconstruction

The 1945 Westminster general election saw Labour returned with a landslide; however, the swing to Labour in Scotland was the lowest in the UK – 9.8 percent compared to 17.5 percent in London, 11.4 percent in Wales and a UK average of 12 percent.[17] That October, at the Scottish Labour conference in Musselburgh, Clement Attlee scolded the delegates for the party's poor performance in the general election.[18]

There was a long-term reason for this poor showing. Labour membership in Scotland was lower proportionally than in England, with party constituencies there averaging 754 members while Scottish ones averaged 410. In its Glasgow stronghold Labour was almost moribund at a grass-roots level. Its strength lay in the party machine, not in a mass membership – the party apparatus distrusted what members might vote for – with the result that the city had few left-wing MPs and none of any flair. That was less the case elsewhere in the country.[19]

There was little evidence of any significant improvement in the relationship between employers and their workers on Clydeside. A fresh wave of apprentices' strikes swept the Clyde in 1952 after a half-day stoppage on 7 February was followed by the suspension of some of the strikers. In response, apprentices in shipyards and engineering plants walked out. By March there was a full-scale strike. The *Glasgow Herald* reported on 21 March that 'Mr J. Reid' – Jimmy Reid – had successfully moved a resolution supporting the action at the engineering union's national youth conference. On 1 April, an employers' spokesman tried to blame the strike for holding up pay talks. Ten days later, apprentice delegates accepted a pay offer that fell short of their original claim. Once more they had gained a partial success.[20]

The last great apprentices' action was the biggest strike in 1960, with 60,000 out all over Britain. The Clyde Apprentices Committee organised what became a UK-wide strike, which began on 21 April. The strike committees organised collections and strike pay. 'Flying Squads' were sent to spread the strike to England. National delegate conferences were held. Employers, union officials and the press blamed the Communists and claimed intimidation was involved. The strike organisation continued until a national conference on 14 May called it off. The pay settlement that followed gave the workers less than they had aimed for, but was a still substantial step forward.[21]

The issue of equal pay for women had not been resolved during the war and remained a festering sore, particularly as greater numbers of women entered the workforce. Eventually, 1969 saw a fourteen-week strike by 1,000 women engineering workers at BSR (British Sound Recorders) in East Kilbride over the bonus system. Two of the strikers, the convenor, Annette Brownlie, and Margaret Milligan, a shop steward, decided after some weeks that things had gone 'flat' and something needed to be done to lift it and to stop strike-breakers. The next morning they led a sit-down in front of the buses bringing in the scabs: 'They brought in the riot police to drag us out of the way, but the thing snowballed and more people sat down. Then stones started to fly . . . Some of us wouldn't have said boo to a goose before the strike, but the things were done – fighting the police, painting the strikebreakers' houses "Scabs live here" . . .'

They returned to work having won equal pay, but management insisted on breaking up the women workers by forcing them to take on new and often menial tasks: 'One foreman said, "If I tell you to clean the toilets, that's what you'll do." So out we came again for another week, until we got our old jobs back. We got 100 percent trade unionism in our factory and union recognition.'[22]

By the end of the 1960s, Scottish workers were striking and demonstrating against the Labour government's attempts to introduce anti-union laws. The stage was set for further, bigger confrontations.

The post-war British governments, both Labour and Tory, actively intervened to provide badly needed jobs. They helped create the pulp and paper mill at Corpach, near Fort William, the car plants at Linwood outside Paisley and Bathgate, West Lothian. Government grants and cheap greenfield sites helped attract US multinationals, such as National Cash Register and Timex in Dundee, so that by 1973, 148 plants employing 14.9 percent of the total workforce were US-owned. Research and development remained, however, in the United States, and these plants proved very vulnerable when recession returned to stalk the global economy in 1973.[23] Between 1954 and 1960 the UK economy grew by 23 percent as world capitalism went through its great post-war boom, but Scotland's managed just 9 percent.[24] Unemployment topped 100,000 in 1959; between 1950 and 1970 more than half a million Scots voted with their feet and quit the country, and between 1951 and 1966, 476,000 emigrated, 89 percent of the population increase.[25] In the 1950s, 282,000 left, 142,000 of them for overseas.[26] Between 1961 and 1971, 215,000 left Scotland (55 percent for overseas), and of these 190,000 were from Clydeside. In those same years Glasgow's population fell by 165,000, 6.5 percent a year, twice that of Liverpool, in second place for population fall.[27] The population shift continued too. By 1951, 73.5 percent of Scotland's population lived in the central belt compared to 56.1 percent a century earlier.

During this period Scotland became renowned for having the worst housing conditions in Europe. The post-war housing crisis was particularly acute. Of 300,000 homes identified as slums in 1956, only 92,000 had been removed by 1963.[28]

At the end of World War II the housing shortage in Aberdeen led to a successful squatting movement led by left-wingers like Bob Cooney who took over the disused military camps at Torry Battery and Tillydrome. Blacklisted in Aberdeen, Cooney would go to work in Birmingham for twenty years, lodging with the Aberdonians David and Betty Campbell, all part of a thriving left-wing folk scene in the city. The Campbells' son and daughter, Ian and Isobel, were well-known artists, and their grandsons Ali and Robin helped form the band UB40 in the early 1980s. Bob Cooney was proud of these connections.[29]

In 1947, Harry McShane wrote a pamphlet pointing out that 98,000 Glasgow families were waiting for a council home, stating that they were trapped in 'insanitary accommodation suffering chronic overcrowding and infestation by vermin'. These conditions he blamed for the high rates of maternal and infant mortality in the Gorbals, which 'of thirty eight wards in the city . . . is either at the top, or second from the top, when each year, the figures relating to infant mortality are made known'.[30] The Housing (Repairs and Rents) (Scotland) Act of 1954, passed by a Tory government, forced local authorities to draw up plans for slum clearance. In the ten years following the passing of the Act, 32,000 homes in Glasgow were demolished. Many were moved to schemes on the city's edge, such as Easterhouse, Pollok, Castlemilk and Drumchapel, which had few amenities and required a costly trip into the city. The housing office in Easterhouse soon had a daily queue of tenants requesting a transfer. Others were rehoused in new towns such as East Kilbride and Cumbernauld, which had similar problems with lack of amenities and were far from old haunts in the city. Glenrothes in Fife was planned around the development of a new 'supper' pit at Rothes but it was forced to close almost immediately after opening because of flooding.

Within a decade and a half, 63 percent of housing in Glasgow, 57 percent in Dundee and 48 percent in Aberdeen was public, much of it high-rise building and new council estates, many on the periphery of the city. Similarly, Edinburgh saw much of its working class shunted off to schemes such as Wester Hailes, Niddrie and

Muirhouse. In his novel *Swing Hammer Swing*, Jeff Torrington writes of the new Gorbals emerging at the start of the 1960s: 'Whole tribes of Tenementers had gone off to the Reservations of Castlemilk and Toryglen or like, the bulk of those who remained had ascended into Basil Spence's "Big Stone Wigwam in the Sky".'[31] The last is a reference to the seventeen-storey high-rises built in the new Gorbals.

Successive local authorities in Glasgow developed an addiction for driving motorways through the city, something that has continued into the twenty-first century, despite the European Environment Agency's finding in 2012 that Glasgow was the most polluted city in the UK.[32]

There was hardship outside the cities as well. In the early 1930s, the Knoydart Estate was bought by the former Conservative MP and ex-Etonian Arthur Ronald Nall-Cain, Lord Brocket. Brocket was one of the most prominent supporters of Hitler and the Nazis, being personally invited to attend the Führer's fiftieth birthday celebrations in 1939. He fired most of the estate workers and evicted them from their homes to create a sporting estate for the enjoyment of himself and his upper-class pals. Gamekeepers were hired whose job it was to keep locals off the land.

As crofters returned from the war in 1945, hundreds across the Highlands applied for crofting land only to be told by the Department of Agriculture that no land was available. So on 9 November 1948, a group of seven young men, the Men of Knoydart, who had previously unsuccessfully applied for crofting land, decided to take matters into their own hands. Led by the local parish priest, Father Colin Macpherson, they occupied a small corner of Brocket's estate and began turning it into crofts.

Brocket took legal action and won. The land raiders had been told by their lawyers that they could expect to win the case and, accordingly, should end the occupation, which they mistakenly did.

The Labour Secretary of State for Scotland, Arthur Woodburn, who publicly boasted that he had never even set foot in Knoydart, refused to help the crofters and rejected the appeal lodged by them under the Land Settlement Act. Hugh MacDiarmid would turn his venom on Brocket and his like: 'There are far too many of these "business peers" swanking about, who are not worthy of a lance-corporal's stripe let alone a peerage – and far too many of them seem to have acquired vast Scottish estates in recent years. They ought to be expropriated.'[33]

Hamish Henderson's song 'The Men of Knoydart' ends thus:

> You may scream and yell, Lord Brocket,
> You may rave and stamp and shout
> But the lamp we've lit in Knoydart
> Will never now go out
> For Scotland's on the march again
> And we think it won't be long
> Roll on the day when the Knoydart way
> Is Scotland's battle song.[34]

Labour, Tories and Nationalists

In the aftermath of the war Labour dropped its historic support for Home Rule on 'compelling economic grounds'.[35] The experience of wartime coalition meant the Labour Party and trade union leaders looked to Westminster for direct investment and economic stimulus, as well as the new welfare state.

In October 1949, the veteran nationalist John MacCormick launched a covenant in support of Home Rule that attracted 1,250,000 signatures, a third of Scotland's adult population. It reached 2 million signatures in 1950, and 1,000 delegates came to a National Assembly in its support, but Labour was bitterly opposed and the SNP, from which MacCormick had resigned, stood aside. Instead, he negotiated an electoral agreement with the Tories and Liberals that alienated much of the support, and he failed to develop the momentum.[36] MacCormick would later become involved in more adventurous affairs like the removal of the Stone of Destiny from Westminster Abbey and its temporary return to Scotland.

In the 1951 general election, Labour polled 47.9 percent of the Scottish vote, although the Tories were returned at Westminster.[37]

Little did they know that this would be followed by a gentle but relentless decline in their support. Between 1945 and 1997 Labour's share of the vote north of the border was greater than in England in nine out of fourteen UK general elections, in 1950 the share was equal, and in 1955 Labour polled better in England.[38] It seems incredible today, but in the 1955 Westminster general election the Tories took slightly more than half the votes in Scotland. For a further decade the Tories were called the Conservative and Unionist Party on the ballot paper. In Glasgow, the Tories retained control of council seats such as Kinning Park, Whiteinch, Partick and Govanhill.[39]

Despite their high water mark in 1955, the Conservative and Unionist Party was in decline thereafter. In 1951, the Tories held eleven of Glasgow's Westminster constituencies, including Govan and Glasgow Central, to Labour's eight, and polled more than 270,000 votes. By 1964 they had just two Glasgow MPs and polled just over 180,000 votes in the general election of that year.[40]

The Tories were not the only ones seeing a decline in their fortunes. In 1950, membership of the Church of Scotland was 60 percent of the adult population, almost three times more than in England. By 1960 membership was in decline, the number falling by 1 percent each year during the subsequent decade, and by 2 percent between 1970 and 1974.[41]

The Kirk could not stop cinemas from opening on a Sunday in the 1960s, nor pubs from opening on the Sabbath in 1976. In the Western Isles and Highlands, the 'Wee Frees', strict Calvinists who had refused to join the re-united Church of Scotland, continued to block such moves.

After the rapid rise and fall of the Scottish Covenant movement, nationalism seemed sidelined but the SNP was able to win support from a younger layer of middle-class people concerned about the country's continuing decline. The SNP was able to make some impact, taking 18 percent of the poll in the November 1961 Bridgeton by-election, and in West Lothian a year later they came second to Labour.

There were warnings that the SNP could tap into discontent with Labour. The Nationalists saw further advances in 1967, coming second in the Glasgow Pollok by-election, taking 28 percent of the vote, and, in local elections, 18.4 percent nationally, returning sixty-nine councillors.

By May the Labour government of Harold Wilson was facing a run on the pound and to placate the markets was implementing austerity measures, creating bitterness among Labour voters. In the coalfields, more pits closed under Wilson than any other prime minister. In that month's Hamilton by-election, a Glasgow lawyer from an ILP background, Winnie Ewing, overturned a 16,000 Labour majority to win. In the following year's local election the SNP took 30 percent of the vote across the country.[42]

Ban the Bomb!

In 1961, the Tory government of Harold Macmillan agreed that the US Navy could base its nuclear submarine fleet, together with its Polaris missiles locked onto targets in the Soviet Union, at Holy Loch on the Clyde. Up to 10,000 people marched through Glasgow demanding that the government repudiate the agreement with the United States.[43]

One of the speakers at the march was the Rev. George Macleod, leader of the Iona Community, who warned his audience, 'You cannot spend a dollar when you are dead.' Folksong writer Morris Blythman (pen-name, Thurso Berwick) and John Mack Smith took up Rev. Macleod's words and adapted them in a song that would be sung at anti-Polaris protests and actions, 'Ding Dong Dollar':

> Ding dong dollar
> Everybody holler
> Ye canny spend a dollar when ye're deid.[44]

After these initial protests, the Direct Action Committee for Nuclear Disarmament (DAC) organised a campaign, warning President Kennedy by telegram that they intended to: '. . . occupy non-violently the submarines, the *Proteus* depot ship, and land installations. Our aim is to immobilize the base'.

The US proposed that the submarine tender, the *Proteus*, carrying the first missiles, should arrive on Saturday, 4 March, but the British authorities insisted they bring it forward to Friday the 3rd, in order to reduce the number of demonstrators. The Campaign for Nuclear Disarmament (CND) organised the protest on land while a group called the Glasgow Eskimos attempted to gather enough kayaks and rowboats to block the *Proteus*'s arrival.

On Friday, 3 March, the *Proteus* sailed up the Clyde and into the Holy Loch with her Polaris missiles. The peace campaigner Marion Blythman recalls that protesters came from all walks of life and from across Scotland by public transport, boat, car or by hitching a lift. At Ardnadam Pier they encountered American sailors waiting to be ferried out to naval vessels, and the protesters 'sang songs which aimed to get over the idea that Scotland was being pushed around and then, hammer it in. The words were balled into slogans like Ban Polaris – Hallelujah and Send the Yankees Hame . . .'[45]

The Glasgow Eskimos did not have enough boats to form a barrier across the loch as planned, having only three canoes and one dinghy. When *Proteus* anchored in Holy Loch, several members of the CND attempted to board it by climbing onto the anchor chains until they were forced off by US sailors. The *Proteus*'s Commander Lanin tried to write off the protesters as nothing but 'a bunch of Goddamn eskimos'.

Morris Blythman and co. set to work again, penning a new ditty to an Orange tune:

> We'll gaff the nyaff ca'ed Lanin
> We'll spear him whaur he blows
> For we are the Glesca Eskimos.

Blythman was not finished and produced one of his best songs in response to the attacks on the Glasgow Eskimos, 'The Eskimo Republic':

> Now fortune's wheel it is birlan roon
> An nation's rise that yince were doon,

So it's time tae sing a rebel tune
For the Eskimo Republic.

Chorus:
Whaur there is nae class, there is nae boss,
Nae kings nir queens, an damn the loss,
An ye get boozed up for a six months doss
In the Eskimo Republic.

When they mak a law, sure they aa agree,
For they aa sit on the com-mit-tee,
An they've got nae Lords an nae M.P.s
In the Eskimo Republic.

Now the Eskimo's no like me and you.
Every Eskimo has his ain i-ga-loo
An his mither-in-law has an i-ga-loo too
In the Eskimo Republic.

O, they flee aboot in thir wee kayaks
An they stick harpoons intae whales' backs.
Then they cut them up intae tasty wee snacks
For the Eskimo Republic.[46]

The protests continued through that spring around Holy Loch. On 21 May, a day of direct action was organised, with plans for a water blockade of the *Proteus* and also on land at the pier where personnel crossed to the base. Sixteen canoes, a launch and a houseboat serving as a floating hospital, with some 70 people, were there to greet *Proteus*. Some protesters managed to get on board the vessel, but were washed off with high-pressure hoses and then picked up by police boats. Nine canoeists were arrested and eight canoes impounded. Meanwhile, 200 people blocked Ardnadam Pier, and when police cleared a path for the American sailors thirty-two people were arrested.[47]

A few days later, the *Glasgow Herald* reported:

Three anti-Polaris demonstrators yesterday boarded the U.S. submarine Patrick Henry at the Holy Loch. Michael Nolan (26) made the most strategic approach by climbing up on top of the vessel's after-fin, jutting seven feet up into the air. US naval ratings offered him a cup of coffee if he would join them, but he politely refused and for three quarters of an hour remained cold and damp on his perch. A US naval launch with civil police on board then drew alongside and brought his escapade to an abrupt halt.[48]

That autumn, another attempt was made at blockading the base but the weather was so bad that 400 protesters were stranded aboard a ferry unable to dock at Dunoon. Those who could not get on a boat staged a march on the naval building in Greenock, but were blocked by police. At Ardnadam Pier there was a sit-down blockade: when American personnel appeared at the pier gate, protesters jeered at them, yelling 'Ban the bomb', 'Yankee filth' and 'Who dropped the first bomb?' Police cleared demonstrators by Saturday evening.[49] There were 351 protesters arrested.

In May 1962, the key speaker at Glasgow's May Day march and rally was the Labour leader Hugh Gaitskell, who was loudly booed. The previous autumn, he had succeeded in getting the party conference to reverse its vote of the year before to back nuclear disarmament, angering CND supporters. Gaitskell had to be escorted away by police, saying the hecklers were 'peanuts'. Morris Blythman was quick to respond:

> Ca' the folk peanuts
> When a'body kens,
> The only nut there was himsel[50]

The *Glasgow Herald* reported on 11 May 1962 that the executive committee of the Glasgow City Labour Party deplored the action of many Young Socialists on the May Day rally. The committee then ordered the Woodside constituency party to be investigated. The article mentioned that Communist Party members were being blamed for the heckling but quoted the CP's Glasgow District Committee's denial of responsibility for the protest. The paper then stated that the Federation of Young Socialists had discussed walking out of the rally and 'some branches' had agreed to this. Subsequently, the Labour Party disbanded the Glasgow Federation of Young Socialists.

Not only did the US base at Holy Loch stay until its eventual closure with the end of the Cold War, but the British nuclear base was built nearby at Faslane. Their presence meant the anti-nuclear protests would continue, and will continue until these weapons of mass destruction are removed.

The Folk Song Revival and the Edinburgh People's Festival

Song and music were a living part of social protest in Scotland in the 1950s, in a way that was not true south of the border. Some of the names already mentioned as penning protest songs were members of the folk song revival of that decade, and a larger attempt to create a Scottish popular culture.

Hamish Henderson not only collected songs but helped singers such as Jeannie Robertson, Jessie Murray and Jimmy MacBeath reach a wider audience. Norman Buchan, a future Labour MP, was a collector of folk songs, and he recalled his excitement at hearing them in concert, as well as his first meeting with Archie Fisher and Bobby Campbell, who wanted to know more about the songs he was making available.[51]

Central to the folk revival of the 1950s was Ewan MacColl. Though born in Salford, both his parents were part of a close Scottish exile community there, with MacColl recollecting that they 'spoke often of Scotland and their life there. They were exiles and still regarded themselves as visitors [to England] rather than settlers.'[52]

MacColl was involved after the war in the radical Theatre Workshop, headed by the playwright and actor Joan Littlewood, and he said of its reception in Scotland: 'Scotland was in the throes of a cultural renaissance; it was an exciting place to be and the poets, novelists, painters, composers and dramatists that we met greeted us with open arms.'[53]

Much later, in the 1970s, John McGrath of the radical 7:84 theatre group remembered: 'In Scotland people still come up to me after 7:84 Scotland shows and talk with clear and fond memories of "the Ewan MacColl" shows during the late forties. I am told they were *very* well attended, and I imagine there were very few Rolls-Royces outside the door.'[54]

A participant in the post-war folk revival, Corey Gibson, recalled:

Besides the politics of its form, the Folk-song Revival developed connections with the contemporary political climate. A defining event in the formation of the Revival was the first Edinburgh People's Festival of 1951 which was funded and organised in collaboration with the Labour Movement and trade unions. It was to offer a showcase of national art and folk-song, neglected by the Edinburgh International Festival since its inception in 1947 . . . the Edinburgh People's Festival during the three years of its existence had elements both literary and folk-based. It presented lectures and poetry recitations by MacDiarmid alongside the singing of ballads and broadsides by 'source-singers'.[55]

The festival was initiated by Hamish Henderson, Edinburgh Trades Union Council, the Miners' Union, the Labour and Communist parties, with the stated aim being: 'To initiate action designed to bring the Edinburgh Festival closer to the people, to serve the cause of international understanding and goodwill.'[56]

It succeeded in doing that: 'Highlights were Scots playwright Joe Corrie's "In Place of Strife" and Ewan MacColl's anti-nuclear play "Uranium 235". The climax to the week's celebration was a "People's Ceilidh". Singers, poets, performers and musicians from across the burgeoning Highlands and Islands folk scene were introduced by impresario Hamish Henderson himself.'[57]

The 1952 People's Festival was bigger, running for three weeks. It celebrated Hugh MacDiarmid's sixtieth birthday with poetry readings in English, Lallans and Gaelic by Sydney Goodsir Smith, Alexander Trocchi, Norman McCaig and Sorley McLean. A series of four Beethoven recitals, with explanations of the composer's life and work, was delivered in the unusual surroundings of George Heriot's School. The comments of miners, their wives and children in the newspapers reflect their glee at gaining access to the august corridors of Edinburgh's most prestigious fee-paying schools as much as their enjoyment of Beethoven. The grand finale was once again the Ceilidh, with performers from the Western Isles plus special guests from the West Indies, and a re-enactment of the trial speech of Thomas Muir, leader of the Scots radicals in the 1790s.[58]

Tragically, the then right-wing leadership of the STUC condemned the People's Festival as a 'Communist Front'. The Labour Party followed its lead. There was one more festival in 1953 but the steam had gone out of it. Its bastard offspring is today's Fringe, though its prices are beyond many of Edinburgh's citizens.

The post-war folk revival would see many of the major participants fall out, sometimes spectacularly. Hugh MacDiarmid fell out with both Hamish Henderson and Ewan MacColl over his refusal to accept that folk songs might be great poetry.[59] MacDiarmid attacked MacColl, saying he and his friends were 'left-wing advocates of regression to the simple outpourings of illiterates'.[60] MacDiarmid exempted Norman Buchan and Thurso Berwick from this category.

One of those influenced by the likes of Ewan MacColl was Bob Dylan. The two famously fell out when Dylan took up electrified instruments, but other key members of the folk revival were more open. Norman Buchan praised the skiffle movement of the late 1950s, made famous by the Glaswegian Lonnie Donegan. Ray and Archie Fisher and Bobby Campbell were influenced by blues and jazz, believing they were more relevant to city folk than some of the rural folk songs Hamish Henderson and Buchan were promoting.[61]

It was this post-war folk revival that laid the basis for a flowering of wider popular music in the 1960s and 1970s. By then a Scotland was emerging that would be different from the one dominated by Calvinism and the kailyard, albeit one that was nonetheless male-dominated.

REBEL LIVES: MARY BROOKSBANK

Mary Brooksbank was born in Shiprow, Aberdeen in 1897, in what she described as 'one of the worst slums in the city'. Her father, Alexander Soutar, was a dock labourer and union activist, and had a reputation of fighting for the union with his fists when necessary. Her mother, Roseann Gillan, worked as a domestic servant and fish gutter.[62] Later, Mary said that she hadn't a stitch when she was born: 'My mither had nothing for me – nothing. But all the neighbours rallied roon and gave her this and that. They rigged me oot.'[63]

Around 1907 the family moved to Dundee, where they lived at the foot of the Overgate and then in Blackness Road. Brooksbank recalled: '. . . we lost a beautiful baby brother, aged two and a half, a victim of diphtheria. No winder! The overcrowding was atrocious, as were the toilet facilities, or rather lack of them, for we had one WC between four tenants.'[64] At the age of eleven she left school to work in the Baltic jute mill. She would work in a series of mills, and in Craigie Mill from 1914 until 1920.

While carrying hot tea to her father at work in 1911 she witnessed the beginning of a carters' strike in the city: '. . . I saw a large crowd of carters, some of whom unyoked their horses and heaved their carts into the docks. I remember how the men faced the police who stood at attention with drawn batons.' It was the first time she heard 'The Red Flag', and when her mother heard her sing it a few days later she turned to her father and said, 'Dae ye hear that ane singin' a Protestant hymn.'[65]

The dockers were out too, and police reinforcements were rushed into Dundee. On 19 December, 300 men of the Black Watch arrived at the request of the Lord Provost. The strike ended on 24 December after the employers agreed to go to arbitration.

A year later, Mary Brooksbank was herself out on strike, demanding a pay rise. A young woman, dubbed 'The Lassie wi' the Green Felt Hat', was reported to be going around the mills with a half loaf tied around her neck, and blowing a whistle to pull women out on strike. The strikers then marched to other mills, pulling those out.

Brooksbank was appalled by the loss of friends during World War I and was drawn to those opposing the slaughter, and in 1917 was inspired by the Russian Revolution. In 1920, as wartime demand for jute dried up, she was made unemployed after standing up to an overseer. At the age of twenty-one, she joined the Communist Party, becoming active in the unemployed movement and helping spread the party's message in the city.[66]

By 1921 the soup kitchen at Constable Street baths was feeding 1,000 people a day. The unemployed movement organised a protest demanding 'work or full maintenance'; after it was attacked by police, three days of rioting followed. Brooksbank was charged with using 'seditious language' after telling a crowd, 'why die in the midst of plenty', when all that lay between them and food for their families was 'plate glass'. According to the press, she was repeating a remark of John Maclean, knowing full well he had been sent to jail for saying it.[67] She would serve the first of her three jail sentences.

In 1922, Mary received three months' training as a domestic servant on a government scheme. She was subsequently sent to Coldstream, in Berwickshire, as a maid in a hotel, and then moved to work as a domestic servant in Glasgow, where she attended one of the last meetings held by John Maclean, who left a deep impression on her. By 1924 she had returned to Dundee, where on 3 October that year she married Ernest Brooksbank, a widower, a journeyman tailor by trade.

In 1927, Mary Brooksbank attended a mass rally against Bolshevism in the city's Caird Hall. During a lull she demanded to know why the organisers had not protested the mass slaughter of 1914–1918. She was immediately grabbed by police and taken out to a police van. The next day, she was fined three guineas.[68]

Mary escaped prison when she and three male members of what was now the National Unemployed Workers Movement (NUWM) went as a delegation to the council but, after being told they'd be heard, were refused admittance. Angry, they burst into the council meeting only to be arrested by police. The men were fined and Mary was ordered to be kept under police observation for two weeks.

In September 1931, some 15,000 people joined a NUWM march to Albert Square over government benefit cuts. As it dispersed it was attacked by mounted police. Looking back, Brooksbank said, 'I still recall a woman cowering into the Exchange doorway, an old man lying with blood streaming from his head . . . I can still see the young mother cowering with her baby beneath the arches of the Albert Institute.'[69] She was one of six organisers arrested and kept in custody for three weeks. They were brought to trial only after the matter was raised in Parliament.

In court she was asked by Sheriff Malcolm to sit alongside him because he had heard she suffered from deafness. Typically, she is alleged to have replied: 'That'll be the last thing on earth I would do, sit wi' you.'[70] She was jailed in Perth Prison.

In October 1934, Brooksbank was one of the organisers of a NUWM march to Forfar to lobby the county council, with the Dundee marchers being joined by contingents from Blairgowrie, Montrose, Ferryden and Arbroath. A 25,000-strong rally in March 1935 waved off a Hunger March that had marched from Aberdeen, Fraserburgh and Peterhead on route to Glasgow under the slogan 'Down with the Slave Act'.

On her release she formed a branch of the Working Women's Guild, and her other activities included selling the *Daily Worker* and other party literature, picketing the parish council's poorhouse for better conditions and organizing street demonstrations against the Means Test investigators. In 1932, she was instrumental in launching the guild's 'charter', which included a demand for a reduction in rents. She twice stood in Dundee town council elections as a candidate for the Communist Party, but was not elected.[71]

Her disillusionment with the Communist Party came after listening to women party members who'd visited Russia. As a result she was labelled a 'Trotskyist' and expelled. Its doubtful she'd ever met a Trotskyist, but one of her former comrades who argued for her expulsion was later to claim in an interview, 'She was no Trotskyist, but she might as well have been one for all the trouble she caused.'[72]

Her husband died in 1943, by which time Mary Brooksbank had returned to the jute mills. A musician who could play the violin, in 1966 she had a book of her songs published. It included 'Oh Dear Me (The Jute Mill Song)'.

> Oh dear me, the mill's gannin' fast
> The puir wee shifters canna get a rest
> Shiftin' bobbins coorse and fine

They fairly mak' ye work for your ten and nine
Oh dear me, I wish the day was done
Rinnin' up and doon the Pass it is nae fun
Shiftin', piecin', spinnin' warp weft and twine
Tae feed and clad my bairnie affen ten and nine
Oh dear me, the warld is ill divided
Them that works the hardest are the least provided
I maun bide contented, dark days or fine
For there's nae much pleasure livin' affen ten and nine[73]

In the 1960s, when Ewan MacColl played a concert in Dundee, he complained of the lack of songs about the city. Brooksbank contacted him, and he included a number of her songs in his repertory. In the 1960s and '70s, she performed frequently in television and radio broadcasts in Scotland.

She wrote in the late 1960s regarding slum clerarance and re-housing:

The end of the Second World War saw an all out spurt, after a great deal of agitation . . . Big strides have been made in housing – agreed. Much has been done. Bit much more remains to be done. Higher standards will have to be achieved. Some of the houses in Fintry, Kirkton, Mid Craigie, Menzieshill and Charleston leave much to be desired. Many of the estates were built too hurriedly and with inferior materials. I myself have but recently been removed from a damp infested prefab which should have been demolished fifteen years ago.[74]

In 1970, at the age of seventy-three, Brooksbank went to Hanoi in Vietnam to tend to casualties of American bombing. She died in 1978. A library is named after her in Dundee, but she is best known for her songs. While active to her last – in the pensioners' campaign, for instance – the fact that Brooksbank had broken with Stalinism meant she was unfairly shunned by many who have recorded the history of the left in Scotland.

THIRTEEN

The 1970s: When Workers Won

By the close of the 1960s, action was being demanded by employers, international financial institutions and the financial press for government action to reduce labour costs and to roll back the trade unions. Despite the two-decades-long post-war boom, the UK lagged behind its competitors in terms of rates of growth, productivity and investment and suffered from a gap between imports and exports that would lead to periodic short economic crises.

In 1969, the Labour government of Harold Wilson introduced wage controls to limit rises and published a White Paper, 'In Place of Strife', that would seek to punish shop stewards for taking strike action. In a time when strikes for extra pay were growing, the government attack on shop stewards and limits on pay increases gave the actions a political edge.

For the first time since the defeat of the General Strike back in 1926, there occured a political strike against government policy when, on 1 May 1969, the unofficial Liaison Committee for the Defence of Trade Unions called for a stoppage against the government's initiative. Printers, engineers and dockers on Clydeside took part, with some 250,000 workers answering the call across Britain.[1]

The election of a Tory government led by Edward Heath in 1970 led to a further rise in working-class insurgency. At first the Heath government seemed to be doing well against the unions, but it came unstuck on the Clyde.

During the general election, the Tory government had said it would not use state funds to bail out 'lame ducks': companies that were in financial trouble. In February 1971, it responded to a request for a £6 million loan from Upper Clyde Shipbuilders by saying no and announcing that it would sell off the military shipbuilder Yarrow's. On 29 July, the government announced the closure of two out of four yards, with the loss of 6,000 jobs out of a total of 8,000. The shop stewards' committee announced a 'work-in' at the threatened yards in defence of 'the right to work'. The stewards' leader, Jimmy Reid, told a mass meeting: 'We are taking over these yards because we refuse to accept that faceless men can make these decisions . . . we want to work . . . there will be no hooliganism, there will be no vandalism, there will be no bevvying because the world is watching us.'[2]

John Taylor was a twenty-year-old apprentice electrician at the time, and looking back recalled: 'We were all shocked when Jimmy said to us in front of a TV camera that there would be no hooligan-ism or bevvying because the world was watching us, which seemed to imply that we were hooligans and alcoholics to the very same world he spoke about . . . The work-in idea caught everyone's imagination. When vast amounts of money at that time arrived for the fighting fund from all over the world to support the work-in, hope of the survival of the yards was given a serious boost, as was the morale of the workers.'[3]

The musician Jack Bruce, who had just left the group Cream, played two fund-raising gigs for UCS and John Lennon donated £5,000. When Jimmy Reid announced this at a mass meeting some-one shouted back, 'I thought Lenin was deid!'[4]

On 10 August, more than 12,000 shop stewards from across Scot-land and the north of England gathered in Glasgow and voted for a one-day solidarity strike and a national demonstration. The STUC held its first ever special one-day congress in support of the work-in, and on 18 August some 200,000 workers struck across Scotland, with 80,000 marching through Glasgow. Marchers chanted, 'Launch UCS, Sink Heath.'[5]

Strathclyde's chief constable, David McNee, warned London that he feared serious disturbances on the Clyde. A Tory cabinet minister, Peter Walker, later stated: 'There was a genuine feeling that unless some action was taken social disorder of a type not seen in this country could have taken place in the city.'[6] In February 1972, the government found £25 million to save three of the yards.

Looking back forty years later, the former shipyard engineer Jimmy Cloughley, one of the sit-in's coordinators, said: 'I think it's fitting that the [Scottish] parliament and the nation recall the achievements of Upper Clyde Shipbuilders. We were fighting a right-wing government who decided the shipyards were going to be closed. The most important aspect was that we fought for the right to work and our success can be measured in the 4,000 shipbuilding jobs still on the Clyde.'[7]

The success at UCS inspired occupations elsewhere. In 1970, the engineering firm Plessey bought the Royal Naval Torpedo works in Alexandria in the Vale of Leven, paying just £64,000, and promising to expand the workforce and develop production. Neither promise was kept. In May 1971, it made the first redundancies, and that summer announced it was closing the plant. The company had bought the plant not to make torpedoes but to strip it of its valuable machinery. Unemployment in the area was over 10 percent (a high figure in 1971) and there were no jobs on offer locally. On 6 September, the plant was due to close. Instead the workers held a mass meeting, marched through the works, locked the main gates and the Plessey flag was taken down and deposited on the manager's desk, with him being told, 'We have taken over'. Managers were admitted to the occupied factory only after agreeing to have their cars searched and having given certain satisfactory assurances to the workers. Any boss refusing this was locked out. The plant was barricaded and local families and some businesses supplied food and blankets.[8] The occupation lasted into 1972, when the plant was converted into a small industrial estate that provided some jobs.[9]

On 9 January 1972, miners began their first nationwide strike since 1926. The decisive battle would be at Saltley Gates in Birmingham, where engineering and car workers from across the city struck and marched on a key coal depot to join miner pickets in shutting it. The 'Battle of Saltley Gates' and the leader of the South Yorkshire miners, Arthur Scargill, that day became a legend in working-class history, but another key battle was also fought 300 miles north on the banks of the Forth. On Monday, 14 February, miners began arriving to form a mass picket outside Longannet Power Station on the upper Firth of Forth. The first to arrive at 4.30 a.m. were five coachloads from Ayrshire. They were met with a heavy police presence. Eventually 2,000 pickets faced 400 police.

Thirteen pickets were arrested and charged with 'mobbing and rioting'. The Scottish miners' president, Michael McGahey, who sustained a chipped leg bone from an 'accidental' – his word – kick from a policeman, told the *Glasgow Herald* that the mobbing and rioting charges were 'scurrilous' but unsurprising: 'there is no such thing as neutrality in society and the law is not neutral', he said, highlighting what he saw as the fundamental anti-working-class bias in the laws used to control pickets.[10]

The next day, the thirteen arrested appeared at Dunfermline Sheriff Court, were refused bail and taken in handcuffs to Edinburgh's Saughton Prison. After high-level talks involving senior government officials, the miners were brought back to the Dunfermline court and released on bail to be greeted by a thousand miners chanting, 'Easy, Easy'. On 16 June, amid further celebratory scenes, they were all acquitted.[11]

In the meantime, the fight at Longannet went on, with 1,500 pickets present on the Tuesday and 700 the next day, facing 600 police. On the Thursday, 1,500 pickets tried unsuccessfully to close Longannet and another six were arrested.[12] The collapse of the Tory government's resistance ensured a stunning victory for the miners. However, the behaviour of the police, using riot-control techniques, was not quickly forgotten.[13]

In the summer of the same year, a nationwide building strike erupted over pay and casual employment, in which Scotland was once again a centre of militancy. On 5 June, before nationwide selective strike action was called, every building site stopped work for half a day and 2,000 workers marched through the city.

By August selective strike action was replaced by all-out national action. In Scotland, union officials attempted to find a solution and agreed a deal with employers that fell far short of the workers' demands. A mass meeting of 4,000 Edinburgh building workers, on top of Calton Hill overlooking the city centre, voted it down.[14] In the end, the union leaders pushed through acceptance of local deals and the strike broke up as different companies settled.

At the same time, new groups of workers who had no tradition of taking industrial action had begun to strike and were winning: civil servants, teachers, council workers and lecturers. At the end of 1973, Glasgow firefighters took unofficial action. They had asked for £5 extra a week but Glasgow Corporation offered just £2.48, making an average weekly wage of £28. Over the previous decade, 27 firefighters had died on duty. On Friday, 26 October, only four of the city's 600 firefighters reported for duty. Across Britain, other firefighters worked to rule or responded only to emergency calls in solidarity. Two days after the strike began, the Fire Brigades Union's national conference made the strike official. By 5 November they'd won.[15]

Other groups beyond the traditional working class were also taking action for themselves. In 1926, Scottish students had scabbed on the General Strike. The vast majority still came from middle-class backgrounds in the 1970s but they were able to build links with the working-class movement. During the UCS sit-in, students had elected Jimmy Reid as Rector of Glasgow University in a show of solidarity. His speech on taking office was printed in full by the New York Times, which described it as the greatest speech since Abraham Lincoln's Gettysburg Address. In it, Reid talked about alienation famously saying, 'A rat race is for rats. We're not rats. We're human beings.'[16] In October 1973, when students marched through Glasgow for higher grants, Glasgow Trades Council and a number of other trade union bodies gave support.[17]

There had been growing discontent at the new Stirling University over the lack of facilities, and when the Queen came to open a new building there in October 1972 she was met by a protest over the amount lavished on her four-hour visit. The *Scotsman* reported, 'student mobs, drinking beer and cheap wine, shouted obscenities and threatened to engulf the Queen.'[18] One student offered the Queen a swig from his wine bottle. The writer seemed shocked that they were not drinking wine of the quality the Queen was used to. The chair of the Scottish Conservative Party, Sir William McEwan Younger, bemoaned that 'the damage done to Scotland's image is incalculable'.[19]

On the opening day of the disciplinary hearings that followed, The National Union of Students in Scotland called a rally that drew 4,000 people. Student union president Linda Quinn was suspended because she attended a planning meeting for the protest, failed to keep order at it and then drank from a bottle in the Queen's presence.[20] Students across Scotland began to make common cause with striking workers. Despite initially meeting with suspicion, the two groups gradually overcame reservations.

In another area of crisis, housing, the Heath government also implemented the Housing Financial Provisions Act, which demanded that local councils balance their books and end reduced rents for the poorest council tenants. Labour in Scotland pledged opposition but opposed extra-parliamentary action. Clydebank, Cumbernauld, Denny, Saltcoats, Whitburn, Alloa, Barrhead, Midlothian and Cowdenbeath councils refused to implement the act, holding out for a year.[21] But by the end of 1972 just five remained defiant, and by early January 1974 just Clydebank was left to stand alone.

Clydebank Council was made up of fifteen Labour, three Communist, two SNP and one independent. Threatened with legal action, the Labour group spokeswoman, Betty Brown, responded by saying, 'We aren't answerable to the Court of Session but to the people'. Several demonstrations were organised in conjunction with trades councils, individual unions and tenants' associations, but the issue was resolved at the Court of Session, which ordered the council to implement the Act in January 1973 and subsequently fined it £5,000 when it failed to do so. The council had a choice – defy the law and look to extra-parliamentary means, or accept the court's verdict and pay up. They chose the latter course. As soon as the fine had been paid, Gordon Campbell, the Tory Secretary of State for Scotland, asked the Court of Session for a final decree against the council.

Anticipating an even larger fine, on 6 March, Clydebank Council voted unanimously to implement the provisions of the Act.[22]

In the end, the council was forced to implement rent increases greater than those first proposed. Many tenants took part in rent strikes organised at grass-roots level – in Edinburgh's Pilton and Muirhouse estates, for instance – but without official support from Labour and the trade unions they were left to fight alone and faced eventual defeat.[23]

In 1974, a year after the military coup in Chile that brutally toppled the left-wing popular Unity government, killing President Salvador Allende and thousands of others, the Chilean submarine *O'Brien* docked in Greenock in order that its tailshafts could be repaired, protected and then sent back to South America as spares. When the tailshafts arrived at the Royal Navy Dockyard at Rosyth, the TGWU shop stewards in the stores organisation refused to release them and wrote to the Ministry of Defence, informing it that 'no future Chilean Navy work will be done in Rosyth dockyard until the fascist junta is removed and a freely, democratically elected government put in power and human rights restored in Chile'.

The blacking of work for the Chilean navy went on for four years until the MOD eventually agreed that no work would be carried out or supplies provided to the junta by the Rosyth dockyard.[24] Rolls-Royce workers at East Kilbride also refused to provide engines for the regime's airforce, including the British-built planes that had bombed Allende's presidential palace.

The election of a Labour government in 1974 did not end the strikes. Wage restraint under the new administration led to a spate of strikes over pay that autumn and winter, with some 40,000 out in October and November – bus workers, lorry drivers, Distillers' Company workers, refuse workers and engineering workers – but they were opposed by union leaders who wanted to maintain the 'Social Contract' with the prime minister, Harold Wilson, whereby they held down wages and were in return given some say over economic policy. Much of the left, including the Communist Party, followed suit, not wanting to break with the consensus.

SMT bus workers occupied the Transport Union HQ in Glasgow and sent a delegation to the London head office, but to no avail. On one occasion, five strike committees were meeting at the same time over the same issue in the Glasgow Trades Council offices but there was no co-ordination. This mini strike wave ebbed away.[25]

In 1976, cuts in education spending led to an occupation at Jordanhill College of Education in Glasgow, then at Moray House in Edinburgh and then at all Scottish teacher training colleges. The occupations spread south of the border and only the summer holidays brought them to an end.

In 1978–79 there was an explosion of strikes over low pay and the Labour government's wage controls, the 'Winter of Discontent', but there was not the same political edge of five years earlier. The stage was set for Labour's electoral defeat and the advent of Margaret Thatcher.

Oil and Devolution

Gas was first discovered in the North Sea in 1959, and it was hoped oil might be there too. Ten years later, a BP drilling rig struck pay dirt 150 miles east of Aberdeen. Oil was first brought ashore in November 1975. After the Queen pressed the button to start it flowing through a pipeline to the shore, Harold Wilson proclaimed it a 'turning point'. North Sea oil brought real changes, with the giant oil-rig yards like those at Nigg, Sullom Voe and Aberdeen becoming staging posts for workers going on and off the rigs.

At the ceremony opening the pipeline, Wilson had talked of 'our oil', but a growing number of Scots were beginning to think that it wasn't 'ours', that the benefits would not be used, in the main, to help Scotland. The SNP had already, two years before, come up with one of the great campaigning slogans, 'It's Scotland's Oil'. It could claim in one leaflet: 'How would you like your granny's pension doubled? With £825 million every year from Scotland's Oil, self-government will pay.'[26]

But the revenues were flowing to Whitehall and the oil companies. In response, a senior Treasury official wrote in a secret memo: 'The Scots have really got us over a barrel here . . . An independent

Scotland can go it alone.' There was a 'plausible case', one of his colleagues admitted, 'for arguing that [the oil] is Scottish'.[27] In May 2013, the Labour Chancellor, Denis Healey, admitted that the 1974–79 Labour government downplayed figures on Scotland's oil wealth to counter nationalism ahead of the 1979 devolution referendum.[28]

Norway, which had struck oil at the same time, put its oil revenues into a central Petroleum Fund, owned by its citizens and controlled by the Central Bank. When the UK energy minister Tony Benn proposed a similar oil fund it was rejected by the Labour cabinet. Earlier, Benn had established the British National Oil Corporation, which he wanted to use to control the oil fields and contract them out to the oil companies, but these companies threatened to scale back their North Sea operations, and Benn had to retreat.[29]

In 1973, the year of the huge hike in world oil prices, the SNP created a shock when Margo MacDonald overturned a 16,000 majority to win the Govan by-election, defeating Labour, which had just announced its opposition to Scottish devolution. Stung by the reverse in Govan, Harold Wilson ordered a U-turn over Home Rule.[30] Support for devolution was eventually won at a Scottish Labour Party conference in August 1974 on the basis of trade union votes.

In the February 1974 Westminster general election, called by the Heath government on the basis of 'who rules Britain, us or the miners', Labour scraped into government as the largest party. Its Scottish vote fell to 36.6 percent and its number of seats to forty. The key feature of the election was the SNP's success in winning seven seats. When Wilson called another election in order to gain an overall majority, in September of that year, the SNP took the second biggest share of the vote with 30.4 percent, won eleven seats, and came second in thirty-five constituencies.[31]

Many on the left of Labour opposed devolution, saying it would weaken the unity of the British working-class movement. In reality this all too often reflected a loyalty to the institution of Westminster and the British state. This reached a peak in 1979 when the Labour government held a referendum on whether Scottish and Welsh parliaments should be set up. Left-wing Labour MPs such as Robin Cook, Brian Wilson and Bob Hughes campaigned for a no vote. In the event, the Scottish result was a yes vote of 32.9 percent of eligible voters to a no vote of 30.8 percent, but Labour MPs had pushed through a parliamentary amendment that a majority of 40 percent or greater was needed. The yes vote fell short of that hurdle.[32] A study of the yes vote in 1979 showed it was 'heaviest among Labour and SNP voters, younger voters and the working class'.[33]

The SNP blamed the Labour government for not campaigning enough for a yes vote – the prime minister, Jim Callaghan, had made one brief visit during the campaign. After the referendum he proposed 'talks between the parties . . . to see if any accommodation could be reached on how to carry Devolution forward'. The SNP rejected this as not enough and moved a vote of no confidence in the government. Callaghan lost that vote and called a general election, which he lost to Margaret Thatcher.[34]

In Westminster it was widely believed that the 'Scottish question' was settled. How wrong they were.

Liberation Time

At the same time as the national question was becoming central, the women's movement also stirred in Scotland, and by the middle of the decade, Women's Liberation groups existed from Shetland to Galloway, with the main ones in the four big cities and on university campuses such as Stirling and St Andrew's. The first Scottish Women's Liberation Conference was held in 1972.[35] The Glasgow Women's Centre opened 'up a close' in Miller Street in 1975. At least two Scottish feminist magazines appeared, *Hen's Own* and *Nessie*.

Jenny Donaldson was a feminist and socialist active in Edinburgh at the time. She recalled: 'The Scottish womens' movement had a great deal to contend with. Like our English sisters, we were confronting issues and prejudices over women's role, and specifically over equal pay, abortion, nursery provision, and discrimination against women in employment[, which] was normal.'[36]

In 1967, the Abortion Act was introduced as a private member's bill by the Scottish Liberal MP David Steel, and came into force the following year. In order to receive an abortion, a woman needed the consent of two GPs, which was far from easy in the west of Scotland where many doctors opposed abortion on religious grounds (not just Catholics but many Presbyterians). The legislation came under attack in 1975 when the Labour MP for Glasgow Pollok, James White, introduced an abortion amendment bill that would lower the time limit for legal abortions. In response, the National Abortion Campaign was formed. In Edinburgh the NAC brought together a wide base of feminists, and was very active, as Jenny Donaldson recounts:

> Taking a page from the history of the suffragettes, the Edinburgh NAC group stormed and disrupted labour and militant political meetings demanding that our fellow male socialists discussed the issue of abortion as central to women's rights and did not brush it aside as a moral issue. At the time Robin Cook MP [Labour MP for Edinburgh Central] accused us of undermining the Scottish working class as given a choice working class women would not have so many children. We increasingly became involved in mass protests and demonstrations as the rise of the attacks on the 1967 Abortion Act took place.[37]

Along with others who described themselves as socialist feminists, Donaldson was also active in support of the Working Women's Charter, which campaigned for a wide range of social and economic demands in pursuit of women's liberation, and also pressed for greater involvement of women in the trade unions. The campaign was taken into factories, housing estates and community groups across Edinburgh, culminating in a large, well-attended conference by women active in trade unions and community groups.

The Scottish Women's Aid Federation was formed in 1976 and has been combating domestic violence and aiding women suffering abuse ever since. The extent of domestic violence was truly awful, with one survey carried out in 1980 finding that 25 percent of all serious assaults were carried out by men on their partners. It also found that while most women then left the home, a significant minority did not because of their economic dependence on the man or because of the stigma still associated with doing so.[38]

The Gay Liberation Front had a brief existence in Scotland. In 1972, the Scottish Minorities Group (later renamed the Scottish Homosexual Rights Group) was formed to campaign for the decriminalisation of homosexuality in Scotland (the law had been changed in England in 1967). In 1975, Edinburgh City Council refused permission for SMG to put up a name plate outside its newly bought premises in Broughton Street, stating that 'a homosexual colony might develop' and that it would drive 'normal people' out of the area.[39] At this stage the SMG was mainly made up of gay men but lesbians were beginning to organise, and eventually a conference in Partick, Glasgow, led to a Scotland-wide lesbian–feminist movement. Eventually, in 1980 the law banning sex between males over the age of 18 in Scotland was repealed.

Scotland was changing in the 1970s. Scottishness had been overwhelmingly male in the past; now that was changing. Not as fast as might be desired, but there was no going back.

FOURTEEN

The Thatcher Years

In 1987, the Proclaimers (twins Craig and Charlie Reid from Auchtermuchty) took 'Letter from America' to number three on the UK music chart. The duo were nationalists and the record sleeve featured a Highland couple at the time of the Clearances superimposed on the interior of the recently closed Gartcosh steel works. The lyrics list the factory closures, and compare the devastation of the Highland Clearances to job losses under Thatcherism. Though the analogy was stretching things a wee bit, it caught the mood of the times.

The list of closures in the 1980s included Singer in Clydebank, Goodyear in Glasgow, Monsanto in Ayrshire, Massey Ferguson in Kilmarnock, BSR in East Kilbride, Wiggins Teape pulp mill in Fort William, Peugeot Talbot's car plant in Linwood, the Invergordon aluminium smelter, Caterpillar in Uddingston, Burroughs in Cumbernauld, Plessey in Bathgate and Rowntree Mackintosh in Edinburgh.[1] Multinationals like Timex and Hoover shed thousands of jobs. In the first two years of the Thatcher administration Scotland lost a fifth of its workforce. There were still fifteen coal mines when she was first elected, just two when she left office. The jute industry in Dundee died, and with the closure of Ravenscraig in 1993 (under her heir, John Major) steelmaking came to an end.

From 1979 to 1983 the economy was in recession, but there was a growing belief among working people that Thatcher was prepared to see unemployment grow as a way to cow the trade unions and demoralise working-class communities. Sterling was kept at a high rate of exchange, which meant UK exports were more expensive, and interest rates too were high, meaning the cost of borrowing or servicing debt was also high. These combined factors hit industry hard. Thatcher made clear she wanted to see the survival of the fittest, with unprofitable firms being allowed to go to the wall, and that she was not concerned if the industrial sector shrank, because Britain's priority was in financial services.

Her free-market prescription for reversing Britain's long-term economic decline was music to the ears of big business. But she was also able to tap into considerable dissatisfaction with Labour's performance in office; the James Callaghan government oversaw a bigger fall in welfare spending than she achieved, as well as a greater fall in earnings.

In the 1979 general election, the Tory vote was not inconsiderable but Thatcher could not claim victory north of the border. Tories there took 31.4 percent of the vote (across the UK the figure was 43.9 percent), returning twenty-two MPs. Labour took the greatest percentage, 41.6 percent, giving them forty-four MPs.

There was considerable resistance to the jobs slaughter of the early 1980s across Scotland. Young unemployed Scots joined Right to Work protests and the People's March for Jobs, which were staged at Tory Party conferences in Brighton, Blackpool and elsewhere. The Labour Party called a march for jobs in Glasgow at the beginning of 1981 that drew 150,000 people. On 1 December 1981, Plessey announced the closure of its Bathgate plant. Unemployment in the town stood at 21.2 percent for men and 19 percent for women. The shop stewards led an occupation of the plant by the mainly female workforce.

A woman worker recalled: 'One of the achievements was that women were able to speak up for themselves, women that I would never have dreamt would have made a contribution at a union meeting, all had an opinion to give . . . it puts a backbone into people.'[2]

Commenting on the solidarity that saw £5,000–£6,000 raised each week in donations together with workplace and street collections, another woman worker commented: 'This is what gave the women the will to fight on . . . they felt that to stop fighting wasn't only letting themselves down, it was letting down that whole labour movement as well. If we'd been left on our own, I don't know if we would have lasted eight weeks.'[3] The plant was eventually sold by Plessey to a rival and kept open.

In February 1981, shop stewards sat down to meet management at the Lee Jeans plant in Greenock, owned by the giant American VF corporation. Despite full order books they were told the plant was to close. The owners wanted to switch production to Northern Ireland, where government grants were available. The union convenor, Helen Monaghan, recalled: 'They were very determined. We offered a three-day week or job sharing, just so that the work would stay in Greenock.'[4]

The workforce suspected something was up because orders were being rushed through. On being told of the closure, Monaghan put in place a plan to barricade the factory entrance. Margaret Wallace, then a twenty-year-old machinist, recalls the day the occupation began: 'There was a build up to it. We had an idea something was going to happen, but I don't think we expected what was to come. We were excited; it was just like a mission, and we just went along with it.'[5] Catherine Robertson, just nineteen during the occupation, said, 'It was very daunting. Just being so young and something like that happening. You didn't know things like this would happen; you didn't know it was going to be so big.'[6]

On that first evening they realised they had not arranged for any food. Margaret Wallace and a male colleague went onto the roof through a skylight and shinned down a drainpipe to go for fish and chips. On their return with 240 fish suppers they were stopped by police but allowed to carry on when they explained they were occupying the plant.

After that the workers got organised. For seven months the women, in shifts, remained in occupation. Machines were maintained and regularly oiled and the £1m worth of jeans in the factory were kept safe. Visitors and occupiers were searched as they left, to ensure nothing was taken. Meanwhile, Wallace and Robertson travelled the country, raising solidarity and much-needed money. At the Scottish TUC they received a standing ovation. Pat Clark was then a shop steward in the nearby shipyard:

> As platers' shop steward in the local Scott Lithgow shipyard I recall chairing a meeting on the morning of 6 February 1981 during which workers had little interest in the business of the meeting but were more concerned about what we should be doing to support 'the sit-in' . . . Having agreed in our yard to a weekly levy of 50p to support the occupation, we raised this with the joint shop stewards' committee and in virtually no time every shipbuilding and engineering worker in the Lower Clyde was having 50p stopped from their wages every week.[7]

He pointed out: 'It should never be forgotten that this took place after the defeat of the national steel strike. The traditionally militant Chrysler car plant at nearby Linwood closed at the same time with no fight. Thatcher was in the process of seeking to destroy the trade union movement. On 30 April 1981 thousands of shipyard workers downed tools and attended a rally at the factory. This was the date when the redundancy deal was to be confirmed and rumours spread that attempts would be made to forcibly end the occupation.'[8]

That did not happen and Helen Monaghan addressed the rally, saying, 'We didn't know when we occupied the factory where the help would come from, but we hadn't long to find out. Without the support of trade unionists we wouldn't have lasted this long and with your continued support we'll keep fighting.'[9]

In August 1981, after almost seven months, a management buy-out kept the factory open and the 140 workers still sitting-in won back their jobs. Thirty years on, Monaghan spoke of her pride in the way the action was carried out: 'We were determined. It wasn't easy, but it had to be done. We started it, and we were very determined we would be there until we heard something different.'[10] Margaret Wallace's message three decades on was 'You can win. Stick to your guns and don't be scared of the management.'[11]

The occupation at Lee Jeans was the exception: workers took industrial action against job losses and closure. More typically, announcements of closure would be met first by a protest but then a sullen acceptance that workers could not win against the free market and the power of multinationals. So on 8 April 1983, the *Edinburgh Evening News* reported:

> The entire workforce of the Henry Robb shipyard, threatened with more than 400 redundancies, marched through Leith on April 8, 1983 in a bid to raise public support for their fight to save jobs.
>
> In total, 850 workers marched from the gates of the yard – the only surviving shipbuilding yard on the Firth of Forth – to a rally at the Old State Cinema in Great Junction Street.
>
> They were led by union leaders who were appealing for solidarity in the fight against redundancies, which were threatened after British Shipbuilders said it wanted to shed 9000 jobs from its yards throughout Britain.

The picture accompanying the article shows young workers, likely apprentices, carrying placards saying, 'Don't Bring the 30s Back'.[12] Despite the march, the yard shut.

The Great Miners' Strike in Scotland

The 1984–85 miners' strike was the decisive confrontation of the Thatcher years. It was not entirely unexpected in Scotland, which lost 40 percent of its mining jobs between 1974 and 1984.[13] In the early 1980s, the National Coal Board's Scottish management took a hard line, closing pits and attacking union organisation. In early 1981, the NCB announced it was closing fifty pits across the UK because of the recession. Cardowan in Lanarkshire, and Highhouse and Sorn in Ayrshire were on that list.[14]

Miners across Scotland responded by walking out on strike. On 16 February, Mick McGahey said that pithead meetings should be convened to make the strike official. Within two days every Scottish pit was out – 19,000 miners in all. They were joined by 30,000 more in England and Wales.[15]

When the national executive of the NUM agreed unanimously to recommend a ballot of all members for a national strike, the government announced an unexpected U-turn that same day over the closures.[16] The miners had won that battle but there was more to come. In November 1982, the NCB produced a new hit list of fifty-five pits set for closure, of which five were in Scotland: Cardowan, Highhouse, Sorn and now Killoch in Ayrshire and Kinneil in West Lothian.[17]

The Scottish NCB director, Albert Wheeler, pushed through the closure of Sorn and Highhouse before turning on Cardowan in May 1983. The NUM delegate there simply declared, 'This is our Alamo'. When Wheeler arrived to announce the closure he was pinned against a wall and kicked and punched.[18] The Cardowan men went on strike but Mick McGahey argued that, following Margaret Thatcher's second electoral victory that year, they could not win.[19] The Cardowan miners – defending their 'Alamo' – fought on, in the face of a five-week lockout in July, before the campaign to preserve the pit was abandoned on 26 August.[20]

In September, management at Monktonhall offered voluntary redundancy to all miners over the age of fifty, without consulting the union as required. The NUM delegate, Davie Hamilton, called a union meeting, but when it ended management would not let the miners start work. That brought the pit to a halt as they walked out.[21] The strike lasted until November, with a Scotland-wide NUM one-day strike in solidarity in October.[22] At the Frances Colliery in Fife the NUM delegate was sacked after organising a collection for the Monktonhall strikers. Four hundred miners walked out and he was reinstated.[23]

When Albert Wheeler announced the closure of Kinneil in West Lothian just before Christmas 1982, the miners occupied the pit and sent out pickets across the Scottish coalfields. Area officials persuaded them to end the action, arguing that Scottish miners could not win on their own.[24]

At the beginning of 1984, Wheeler announced the closure of Polmaise Colliery in Stirlingshire. Two years earlier, Polmaise had

been described as the 'success story of the Scottish coalfield' by
Wheeler. It was also known as Scotland's most militant pit, which
many thought explained its closure. At the same time, management
also allowed Bogside in Fife to flood, then blamed the workforce for
its closure, adding to a growing sense of bitterness.[25] By March 1984,
when the national miner's strike began, roughly half of Scotland's
miners were involved in industrial action ranging from an overtime
ban to a strike.

The man chosen to head up the confrontation with the NUM was
a Scot. Ian MacGregor was appointed chair of the National Coal
Board in September 1983. He was born in Kinlochleven but
emigrated to the USA, where he became head of the mining giant
Amax, inflicting a major defeat on the mineworkers' union over the
closure of Belle Ayr Mine in Wyoming. Brought back to Britain by
the Labour government, he was appointed deputy chair of the state-
owned car maker British Leyland and played a key role in sacking the
union convener at the company's biggest plant, Longbridge in
Birmingham. The Tories made him chair of British Steel, where he
presided over the loss of 80,000 jobs.[26]

Later, when interviewed by the *Times* in June 1984, he explained
his outlook thus: 'I think the only thing the government is interested
in is seeing this business run properly . . . That's all the politics I
know of. I am not one of your local characters. I don't vote here
– I vote in Florida.'[27]

The Strike Begins

On 5 March 1984, Ian MacGregor announced that twenty 'uneco-
nomic pits' should close, with the loss of 20,000 jobs. Miners at
Cortonwood in South Yorkshire walked out on strike. The president
of the NUM, Arthur Scargill, encouraged them to picket other pits
in the region, and then across the country. Scargill then travelled to
Fallin Miners Welfare Club to address the Polmaise miners alongside
Mick McGahey in the miners' welfare club. The two leaders gave the
green light for the Polmaise miners to picket the Scottish coalfield.

Mick McGahey told a press conference: 'I want to emphasise the knock-on effects of the closure in pits and the loss of miners' jobs, the effect that will have on railways, the steel industry, engineering and electrical industries, because we don't only produce coal.'[28]

On 12 March, pickets brought out Killoch and Barony pits in Ayrshire. The next day, Polmaise miners assembled at Fallin before travelling to Bilston Glen in Midlothian to bring work there to a halt.[29] There would be criticism that Scargill and the NUM did not hold a national strike ballot. In March 1984, Mick McGahey replied to that: 'We are not dealing with niceties here. We shall not be constitutionalised out of a defence of our jobs.'[30] As Bobby Clelland recalls, Comrie Colliery initially voted against strike action in 1984, but once it was called out, it was solid in support: 'We just felt that, once you were called out, you then backed up your fellow miners.'[31]

One miner from Fife pointed out: 'The strike was not about wages and conditions – it was a struggle to defend the very existence of mining communities and it would be fought with bitter intensity to the very end.'[32]

On the first day of the strike, 12 March, Breakfast TV announced that Blairhall Colliery in Fife was working normally; however, it had closed in 1969. Whether accidental or deliberate, this would come to be seen as part of a concerted media drive to undermine the strike.[33]

The Scottish NUM had agreed to provide coal to the Ravenscraig steel mill to keep it working because the leadership feared it might be closed permanently if work stopped. Mick McGahey explained it was 'in the interests of Scotland's future'. In contrast, one Scottish miner argued: 'The only way to win the strike is by stopping people working.' Another prophesied: 'First they'll chop us, then they'll chop Ravenscraig.'[34]

Before the strike, Ravenscraig had received 4,000 tonnes of coal a day, when it needed just 900 to keep its furnaces going. The plant saw record production in April. When the miners and rail unions agreed to reduce the amount of coal, by allowing just one train a day to run from the Hunterston depot on the coast to Ravenscraig, management at the plant hired trucks to bring the coal in, paying £50 a journey.

On 4 May, the rail unions halted that one train in response to the use of lorry convoys. Three days later, a thousand miners clashed with police outside Ravenscraig as they tried to stop the convoys getting in. Fifty-two were arrested but fifty-eight trucks got in through the rear entrance. Mounted police were then used to attack pickets, sixty-five of whom were arrested. The next day, eight coach-loads of Fife miners were stopped en route to Ravenscraig. When the miners sat down on the road they were dragged off, with nearly three hundred being arrested. John McCormack from Polmaise recalls: 'I told the cops that we were all going on a seaside picnic to Largs. I showed him the pies and crisps in the back. But they wouldn't believe me. So I said to the guys to get off the buses and stand on the road as I thought they wouldn't arrest us all. But they did. More than 200 of us. Every police station in Glasgow was full of Polmaise miners.'[35]

On 8 May, 1,500 miners determined to shut down the coal supply dock at Hunterston faced 1,000 police and mounted units. John McCormack remembers that when the miners lined up on the picket line, mounted police charged. He was surprised no one was killed. His brother was knocked down by a police horse before being arrested, kept in a cell for ten hours and ended up being fined £150 for breach of the peace.[36]

The biggest single number of arrests in the strike occurred at the Lochgelly depot for open-cast coal, which Fife and Lothian miners tried to shut. Instead, 133 were arrested. In one instance, lorries carrying coal tried to access the depot via Ballingry. A local resident takes up the story:

> They were met by great hostility from pensioners, housewives and youngsters who poured abuse on them at every point along the road. The final straw for the lorry drivers came when well over 100 youngsters, between twelve and fourteen years, instead of going into school, marched out on the road down through the village to Lochore Miners' Institute singing and shouting and blocking the way of the worried lorry drivers. They never re-appeared.[37]

It was a rare victory in the year-long strike.

On 17 May, the Scottish NUM agreed to 18,000 tonnes of coal entering Ravenscraig each week, once more citing the national interest.[38] The plant kept running for the rest of the strike, so the miners failed to stop steel production.

A feature of previous miners' strikes had been the role of women in organising solidarity and joining the picket lines. That reached new heights in the 1984–85 strike. The first priority was to ensure the strikers and their families were fed and had some money to live on. In Fife, local miners' wives set up ten communal kitchens in the Dysart area, with the help of the local NUM. Cath Cunningham explains how women quickly wanted to contribute more: 'Soup kitchens and bingo nights soon became insufficient for many women . . . We started visiting factories and union meetings; we were invited to speak at meetings, a skill many of us acquired quite speedily. Wherever the men went to speak the women went too.'[39]

As the strike went on into the summer it was clearly becoming a war of attrition, as Margaret Cowie from Fallin, the daughter, mother and wife of a miner, recalled: 'In the beginning we thought it would be over in a few weeks but when we saw it wasn't going to be, the ladies got together to see what we could do. We needed to show the world that we were right behind the men.'

Initially, the main aim of the Women's Committee was to make sure that everyone, especially the children, had at least one hot meal a day. In many homes in the community there was no money coming in, so the Women's Committee was raising funds, collecting donations and addressing meetings. They had a caravan in nearby Stirling where people could donate food. There was a clear polarisation between those who supported the miners and those who took Thatcher's side, as Margaret Cowie recollects, 'Some people believed everything they said about us. We had a caravan in Stirling where people could bring food and sometimes folk would scream and shout and tell you to get back to work. But others were generous. Old ladies with nothing would give cash.'

As winter approached, such solidarity was key to ensuring the miners were not starved back to work. As the strike went into December it was crucial every striker and their family had a very merry Christmas. Margaret Cowie describes Christmas in Fallin: 'We had the room here stacked high with presents. And we sat up all night wrapping them and making sure there was something appropriate for everyone. No miner's child went without. Then we cooked the Christmas dinner.'[40]

Endgame

The miners were facing the full might of the state, hostility from most of the media and a government prepared to break their morale by any means. Tory ministers later admitted that the figures for strikers return-ing to work had been inflated to damage strikers' morale. The strike ended on 3 March 1985, nearly a year after it had begun. At a special conference the NUM voted, by a tiny margin, to return to work with-out any agreement with management. James Armitage remembers returning to work at Polmaise: 'The managers were lined up to sneer at us. But when they saw us with our heads held high, they slunk away.'[41]

The strike cast a dark legacy, not least for the mining communities and above all for those arrested and victimised during the strike: The Tories spent £26,000 per miner in defeating the NUM. We now know Thatcher came near to conceding defeat on at least two occasions but the miners were left to fight alone by the rest of the trade union move-ment and went down to a defeat that still casts its shadow today.[42]

Jim Finlayson was arrested at Bilston Glen, and was one of 170 local miners sacked. Speaking after Margaret Thatcher died in March 2013, he said: 'I feel, personally, she destroyed Scotland. You know, 250,000 workers were put out of work eventually and she got all the tax and revenue from the oil: she took that off us as well.'[43]

Caterpillar Occupation

At the Uddingston plant of the giant US corporation Caterpillar, the workforce left for the Christmas break in 1986 happy about the future of their jobs. The company had announced it would be expanding the factory. The trade union convener, John Brannan, recalled that the company laid on a party for the workforce and their families. That Christmas, the foundations were being dug for the expansion.[44]

Then, on 14 January, the multinational made a terse announcement of closure. The workers said the plant would remain open, and that afternoon they occupied it, telling management they could enter but only to collect their personal belongings.[45]

On 24 January, more than 100 shop stewards from engineering plants across Lanarkshire gathered in Motherwell to organise support. The Scottish TUC backed the occupation and support came from Caterpillar workers in France and Belgium. Whipping off the cloth cap he always wore, John Brannan told the meeting in Motherwell: 'Fill this bunnet and we'll not let you down.'[46] Substantial donations came from the workers at Hoover, UKC Laird, Rolls-Royce and Anderson Strathclyde.

As the campaign got under way solidarity began to flood in. Street collections, three times a week, were organised in Hamilton, Airdrie, Motherwell, Paisley, East Kilbride, Cumbernauld, Larkhall, Wishaw and Carluke, with more than £5,500 being collected in the first week, including £1,300 at a Rangers versus Aberdeen football match at Ibrox Park. Celtic supporters soon began competing as to who would donate more. As the collections spread they could total £17,000 a week.[47]

As the occupation went on, local shops sent food parcels, workers got free haircuts at local barbers – it seemed like all of Scotland wanted to help. The Labour leader Neil Kinnock, Shadow Scottish Secretary Donald Dewar and the former cabinet minister Tony Benn came to visit. The comic Andy Cameron was part of a star-studded troupe who staged shows at the plant.

Inside, security staff ceded control of the gates to the Joint Occupying Committee. Using materials left in the plant, combined with donated parts and supplies from outside, they built a tractor, painted it pink and announced to the world that they wanted to donate it to War on Want, which planned to send it to needy farmers in Nicaragua. The workers parked the Pink Panther in the middle of Glasgow's

George Square as a landmark for strike fund collections until a court order on behalf of Caterpillar prevented it going to Nicaragua.[48]

The then War on Want general secretary, and future Labour and Respect MP, George Galloway, said: 'The air was thick with talk of famine and there was a desperate need for the machinery they were making in the Third World. In the end the company defeated our bid to use the Pink Panther, but we got it to George Square where we guarded it twenty-four hours a day in the winter weather. It was a joy to behold.'[49] John Brennan added: 'The Americans couldn't believe what was going on, and that we were allowed to do this. At one of the meetings, one of them said that back home they would just shoot us.'

After three months, the numbers occupying the plant were falling. In the end, the men went back to work on 27 April, having been given improved redundancy payments. The plant closed in November.

The history of the occupation contrasts with the UCS sit-in a decade and a half before. The main difference was that in 1971 there existed a mass shop stewards' movement that had been blooded in struggle and alongside left-wing organisation within the workplace. By 1987, '. . . there was only a residual remnant of Broad Left stewards. There had been some experience of large-scale industrial battles, but there was no organized left to ensure cohesion within the workforce. The shop stewards movement outside the factory had been decimated by factory closure and the forces of the Left were divided and in disarray.'[50]

Those words still ring true today.

Direct Action Against Trident

The decision by Margaret Thatcher to lease long-range Trident nuclear missiles from the US, and to base them at Faslane on the Gare Loch, which leads into the Firth of Clyde, was met by widespread protest in Scotland. The Campaign for Nuclear Disarmament called a protest in Glasgow at Easter 1982 and a peace camp was set up outside the base. Faslane would become a scene of direct action, surpassing what took place at the Holy Loch two decades before.

Jim Ainslie served in the army for ten years before buying himself out because of his Christian beliefs. He went on to become a community minister in Glasgow's Easterhouse in 1986, where he joined CND and campaigned against the presence of Trident at Faslane. One incident he was involved in was a direct-action protest against the nuclear submarine *Victorious* as it returned to the base:

> Four or five of us were in canoes, but at one point three of us, more by chance and the flow of the current, were directly in front of it, about one hundred yards ahead. The Captain said afterwards he gave the order to stop engines, but with a few hundred yards to stop there's no way he could have stopped. What then happened was that the chap immediately to my side, who was a very good canoeist, was rammed and turned over. He was basically washed right over the front of my canoe, he was in the water. I canoed a wee bit away. I was capsized by the MoD police and that eventually came to court.[51]

Another CND activist, Brian Quail, was involved in 'Operation Braveheart' when fifty or sixty protesters near Hadrian's Wall, eight miles west of Newcastle, halted a nuclear weapons convoy heading to Faslane. Brian was one of those handcuffed to a transporter and recalled, 'The lovely thing about that, half of the people who were shouting "Scotland doesn't want Trident" were English, from Manchester and Durham and Newcastle. It was great to get that solidarity.'[52]

By August 1998 several hundred people had gathered outside the Faslane base to blockade it, with more than 100 being arrested. A year later, three women swam aboard a research vessel and dumped computers and files overboard, then tidied up and laid out anti-Trident pamphlets. They then called a press conference and, as a result, military police arrived. Looking at the tidy desks, they asked the women why they'd gone to such trouble to put out some pamphlets. It was only when staff arrived the next morning that they realised what had been done. The three women were arrested but subsequently acquitted.[53] Such action continues today and will until Trident and its successor are removed.

Nae Poll Tax Here

The Thatcher years were a pivotal moment in the history of Scotland. When she was first elected in 1979 there seemed no possibility of a Scottish parliament being achieved, support for the Scottish National Party had collapsed and the union seemed totally secure. Under Tory rule all changed utterly.

At the 1987 general election, the Tory share of the Scottish vote had fallen to 24 percent and they had lost eleven MPs, holding just ten Westminster constituency seats. Norman Stone, the Glaswegian Thatcherite academic, attributed the Scottish Tories' electoral annihilation to 'the decline of Imperial consciousness', observing with sadness and nostalgia for the days of the Empire that the Tories in Scotland were a 'foreign', 'patrician' group of outsiders.[54]

Something else had changed too. So far in this book, since the days of Thomas Muir in the late eighteenth century, Scottish workers mostly fought back alongside their Welsh and English sisters and brothers. In the 1970s, Scottish workers fought as part of a British movement. This had been true at the time of the Chartists, in the Great Unrest, during the Red Clyde years and in the 1930s. But now there was a divergence between the political situation in Scotland and that south of the border. The Tories never won a majority in Scotland under Thatcher, and by the time she quit they were facing annihilation.

Rejection of Thatcher and the Tories hardened into a belief that Scotland did not just reject the worst of her free-market values but that a consensus existed across the nation which put welfare first. In 1989, an opinion poll found that 77 percent agreed that Thatcher had treated the Scots as 'second class citizens'; a poll in 1987 had found that 75 percent regarded her as 'extreme'.[55] Increasingly, people believed that there was a democratic deficit, in that Scottish voters consistently rejected Thatcherism but still ended up with a Tory government.

In May 1988, Thatcher travelled to Scotland to address the General Assembly of the Church of Scotland. Her 'Sermon on the Mound' appeared to be an attempt to convince the Kirk that there was a theological justification for her political and economic policies, with her informing them: 'It is not the creation of wealth that is wrong but the love of money for its own sake.' She travelled on to Glasgow to attend the Scottish Cup final between Celtic and Dundee United, a diary date that could be explained only by her advisers' ignorance of Scotland. Thousands of supporters of both sides waved yellow cards at her.

This sense of alienation from the government in London and the Westminster system received a huge boost from the decision to implement the Community Charge – which became known as the poll tax – and to do so a year earlier than in England. The Tories fought the 1987 Westminster general election on the promise they'd implement the tax, claiming it was fair that 'the bishop and the brickie' would pay the same. A Scottish civil servant explained: 'The basis of the poll tax was the old ladies in Morningside living in six-bedroomed family houses who had no children at home and only had their bins emptied once a week.'[56] The General Assembly of the Church of Scotland condemned it as morally indefensible.

Thatcher ignored the fact that the Tories had returned only ten MPs out of seventy-two north of the border and pressed on, making the poll tax law in 1988 and announcing it would commence in Scotland in 1989. It was obvious she could enforce it on Scotland only with the votes of English Tory MPs.

Labour fought the 1987 Westminster general election on the promise that they would make the poll tax unworkable. *Scottish Labour Briefing* said, 'the policy was simple – Vote Labour to Stop the Poll Tax.'[57] One of the fifty Labour MPs elected in 1987, Brian Wilson, was clear in calling for extra-parliamentary action: 'No mandate exists for implementation of the poll tax in Scotland – the battle cannot be won in the House of Commons . . . I believe there should be a mass Scottish campaign outside Parliament to defeat the poll tax.'[58]

Labour and the trade unions took to the streets in a show of strength, but having argued the poll tax was unworkable, the party refused to break the law, so Labour councils proceeded to put in place measures for registering taxpayers and collecting payments. A Scottish Labour Party special conference, held in March 1988 in Glasgow, refused to back non-payment. This marked the end of official Labour opposition. The tag 'Feeble Fifty' was coined to describe the Scottish Labour MPs and it stuck.[59]

The SNP also promised they would obstruct the poll tax, and in November 1988 swept to a spectacular by-election victory in Glasgow Govan when Jim Sillars took the seat from Labour on an anti-poll-tax platform. The campaign made hay over Labour's failure to obstruct the poll tax, but in reality, the SNP-run council in Forfar went along with introducing the new tax.

At a grass-roots level, local Anti–Poll Tax Unions (APTUs) were being formed. One of the first was in Maryhill in north Glasgow. Activists went door to door, and by January 1988 had 2000 members. 'No Poll Tax Here' posters began to appear in windows across Scotland. The APTUs came together to form the Anti–Poll Tax Federation, chaired by Tommy Sheridan, who explained: 'We built the union through street meetings . . . bus stops, traffic islands, patches of spare ground all provided impromptu venues.'[60]

In March 1989, the Federation brought 15,000 people onto the streets of Glasgow in favour of non-payment. By 1 April, *Scotland on Sunday* calculated 850,000 people were not paying.[61] Speaking for the anti-poll-tax campaigners, Sheridan declared that 'non-payment in Scotland had become a deluge.'[62] When sheriff officers turned up to 'poind' (confiscate in order to sell) the belongings of a Rutherglen woman who had refused to register for the tax and then not paid the resulting fine, the APTUs mobilised 300 people to block them. It was the first of many such confrontations, with the local groups mobilising via 'telephone trees', each member undertaking to phone four or five other supporters.[63]

In addition, the *Glasgow Herald* reported on 14 November 1989 that anti-poll-tax campaigners had occupied the premises of the sheriff officers H. M. Love and Co. in Edinburgh's New Town to protest against warrant sales. 'As they spoke at the door to a member of staff more than thirty people, including some young children, and a dog with a cardboard placard round its neck appeared from behind some railings, rushed over the street and forced open the door.'

Police eventually broke up the occupation. The same day saw occupations of the premises of sheriff officers in Dundee and Galashiels, by Federation supporters. They wanted to deliver warning cards similar to those left by the officers. In Galashiels the occupation lasted two and a half hours before the sheriff officers agreed to take the card, and in Dundee one and a half hours.

In Glasgow, a group of about forty members of the Scottish Anti–Poll Tax Federation left their warning 'calling card' at the premises of the sheriff officers firm of Abernethy, McIntyre Co., in St Vincent Place. Tommy Sheridan said, 'We have done it to them before they did it to us.'[64]

Non-payment spread south of the border as the poll tax was introduced there, but the crucial event in its defeat was the biggest riot Central London had seen in a decade. On 31 March 1990, more than 200,000 people marched through the English capital, and when police attacked a sit-in outside Downing Street the protest erupted. Another 50,000 people demonstrated in Glasgow on the same day.

By November, Thatcher was gone, after backbenchers forced a leadership vote that she failed to win resoundingly enough. The poll tax went with her. Despite the Trafalgar Square riot and the spread of non-payment to England and Wales, the whole episode left a deep feeling that Scotland had been treated unfairly by a government that had no mandate to rule the people of Scotland. That sense would only grow as Tory rule at Westminster staggered on until 1997.

The journalist Ian MacWhirter points out: 'The poll-tax row finally persuaded Labour's ultra-cautious shadow Scottish secretary, Donald Dewar, to join the cross-party Scottish Constitutional

Convention in 1988 and sign its "Claim of Right" document, which called for a repatriation of Scottish sovereignty.'[65]

As a result of the poll-tax battle, Tommy Sheridan was elected to Glasgow City Council for Pollok in May 1992, despite being in Barlinnie Prison for defying a court order by attending a protest against the warrant sale of a non-payer's possessions. Scottish Militant Labour would form the Scottish Socialist Alliance with others on the left and then the Scottish Socialist Party. The basis for a major breakthrough by the radical left in the next decade had been laid.

The 1992 General Election and Scotland United

In 1992 the Tories under John Major won a Westminster general election they had been widely tipped to lose. Hopes were high that the nine Scottish Tory MPs would be wiped out. They actually won two extra seats. They had little time to celebrate, though.

Thousands flocked to Glasgow's George Square after a call went out from a new group, Scotland United, to hear speeches denouncing Tory rule as having no mandate and demanding a Scottish parliament. The initiative was begun by the leadership of the Scottish TUC, which quickly involved Labour MPs such as George Galloway and John McAllion plus the musicians Pat Kane of Hue and Cry and Ricky Ross of Deacon Blue. Importantly, the SNP decided to end a policy of not participating in broader groupings focusing on Scotland's constitutional position because they wanted nothing less than independence.[66]

On 14 April, the general secretary of the STUC, Campbell Christie, told the George Square rally they were there to 'tell the nation, to tell the Conservative government and to tell everyone throughout the world, that we in Scotland are not prepared to accept the election results. We representing the 75 percent in Scotland, we representing the 2.2 million electorate in Scotland who voted for constitutional change, are not prepared to allow the 23 percent, the 750,000 Tories to rule us.'[67]

The director of 7:84 Scotland theatre company, David Hayman, followed and posed a series of questions to the crowd and demanded an answer, it went thus:

'On Thursday April 9 did you vote Conservative?'
'No!'
'On Thursday April 9 did you vote for the destruction of our health service?'
'No!'
'On April 9 did you vote for the dismantling of our industry?'
'No!'
'Did you vote for the decay of our educational system?'
'No!'
'Did you vote for greed?'
'No!'
'Did you vote for selfishness?'
'No!'
'The English did, for the fourth election in a row. The people of England have voted for greed and selfishness, and I'll tell you something; there's fifty million of them and only five million of us, so we don't stand a snowball's chance in hell of ever having a parliament we deserve unless we have our own parliament. Right?'
'Yes!'
'Right?'
'Yes!'[68]

Hayman caught the mood. The rhetoric was light-years away from that of a decade and a half earlier at the time of UCS or when the miners had fought and won. Something fundamental had changed. Then the stress was on working-class unity across Britain. Now the stress was on the difference between values on either side of the border. The novelist William McIlvanney was cheered when, in response to attacks on it as being anti-English, he told a rally: 'Scottishness isn't some pedigree lineage, it's a mongrel tradition.'[69]

Despite the turnout, the Labour shadow Scottish secretary, Donald Dewar, attacked the Labour MPs taking part as being 'collaborators' with the SNP.

Opinion polls showed majorities of between 75 and 80 percent in favour of a Scottish parliament. With the SNP now prepared to work towards this, it was an unstoppable momentum. Later in the year, in December, the Nationalists organised a 25,000 strong rally in Edinburgh when the city hosted a European Union leaders' summit. Scotland United did not sustain itself or the protests but it did lay down a determination that Scotland should have Home Rule.

The Edinburgh writer, publisher and poet Kevin Williamson wrote of the hangover that followed the 1992 general election victory for the Tories: 'May Day 1992 was one of the bleakest in recent memory. Scotland had sunk into a collective despondency when the Tory Party . . . [was] re-elected to another five years in office. After thirteen years of divisive Tory rule – characterised by greed, privatisation, unemployment, strikes, riots, war and the Poll Tax – it didn't seem possible.'[70]

At the same time, Labour was rebranded as New Labour under the leadership of Tony Blair – educated at Fettes, Edinburgh's top private school – who took over upon the death of the Scot John Smith in 1994. He was committed to 'modernising' the party by accepting much of the Thatcher 'revolution' and dumping any hint of socialism. But despite his own misgivings he could not dump a commitment to creating a Scottish parliament.

Yet acceptance of devolution in the British ruling circles did not equate with any wish to loosen the Union. In 1995, the journalist George Rosie encountered a senior Whitehall civil servant in the mountains of Sutherland. Over a drink, he asked him why a London government would not want to see Scotland independent. The civil servant ticked off the reasons on the fingers of his hand:

One, oil. Two, gas. Three, fish. Four, water. Five, land. The oil and gas are self-explanatory, even now. Fish might not mean much to the British but it is a superb bargaining counter in Europe. Water will be important one day, I suspect. And as for all this [gesturing to the hills], well, this is our, how shall I say it, breathing space. That bit of elbow room that every country should have.[71]

Timex

The US multinational corporation Timex decided to break the union at its Dundee plant, announcing lay-offs just before Christmas in 1992. At the start of the new year, letters saying who would be sacked and who could stay were sent out by management. The workers refused to accept the letters and occupied the canteen. Management promised negotiations so they returned to work, although they voted overwhelmingly for action.

The negotiations never took place and the company refused a union offer to go to ACAS, the government conciliation service. So on 29 January 1993 the workers walked out on strike. A month later they returned ready to work en masse, only to be told they would have to accept a 10 percent wage cut and a reduction in pension. When they refused this offer they were locked out. Scabs were brought in to do their work, leading to mass pickets outside the plant with delegations of supporters travelling from across Britain to give support.

In April, several local workplaces stopped work to join demonstrators from NCR, Levi's, Ninewells Hospital and others who were marching to the factory gates to join pickets. A rally in a nearby park was attended by 6,000 people. On 17 May, 5,000 people from across the city, the rest of Scotland and south of the border joined in solidarity outside the factory gates, despite the police halting coaches bringing delegations to join the strikers. It took police over twenty minutes to force the scab bus through the picket line, and they simply gave up on trying to get scabs in cars and delivery trucks through.

In June 1993, the socialist journalist Paul Foot joined the picket line at Timex. His subsequent report is a gripping read. He interviewed Margaret Thompson, who had just returned from Norway, where she picketed the headquarters of the Olsen Line, eventual owners of Timex. She had already been to London, Manchester, Newcastle and Brighton to raise solidarity:

> I've been a shop steward for 20 years, but I never felt half what I feel today. I think it's because I realise my capabilities. I'm not just a worker at Timex, I've got a brain. If you do the same thing for 20 years, your brain goes soft. When I went into Timex as a girl, I was quiet as a lamb. Now I feel like a rottweiler. I think the best thing about this is you suddenly realise you have friends everywhere. At a factory in Newcastle they had exactly £110 in their coffers. After they heard us speak they gave us . . . £110, and I suddenly realised I was crying. They'd never met us, and they gave us everything.

Another striker, Jessie Britton, asked about leftists and others joining the picket lines. She responded: 'They are always complaining about outside agitators. But where would we be without the people from outside who support us? . . . we could never have got where we have without these young people selling papers and whipping up support for us.' Jessie also told Foot where she stood in relation to anti-union laws that attempted to restrict numbers on the picket lines, and the appeal from union leaders to respect the law: 'They are worried about their assets . . . but we aren't worried about our assets. We haven't got any. What use are union assets to us if we lose the strike and can't have a union?'

Foot writes that he 'asked gingerly' about the role of women in the strike. Jessie laughed and simply said, 'right here the men do the dishes and the women do the fighting.'

The report resounds with the wit and banter of the strikers, interrupted only when someone tries to cross the picket line. He sums up by quoting Debbie Osborne explaining, 'When I was in there [she said, giving a contemptuous jerk of the head at the factory gates] I felt like a nobody. Now I feel a somebody. In fact I feel ten times more important than anyone in there.'[72]

Eventually, in August 1993 the management, aware they could

not defeat the strikers, chose to walk away, closing the plant. The workers did not achieve victory but they did not feel defeated either.

Cultural Shift

Despite the damage inflicted on it, Scotland was experiencing a new cultural vibrancy during the Thatcher era. Novelists such as James Kelman, Alasdair Gray, William McIlvanney, Iain Banks and Irvine Welsh were international figures. A new generation of Glasgow painters made their mark: Ken Currie, Steven Campbell, Jenny Saville, Adrian Wiszniewski and Peter Howson. The classical composer James MacMillan had world renown. The folk music scene was engaged in all sorts of cross-overs, including with what is called 'World Music', a patronising term meaning non-Anglo-Saxon music. Scots were beginning to feel confident in a new identity that no longer centred on militarism and sport, and which was recognised elsewhere in the world.

Things were moving on from the start of the 1970s when Tom Nairn famously wrote, paraphrasing Denis Diderot, that 'Scotland will be free when the last Church of Scotland minister is strangled by the last copy of the *Sunday Post*.' The poet Iain Crichton Smith spoke similarly: 'When I see one of these Free Church ministers on the street in Lewis, I feel like walking across the road and hitting him in the face.'[73]

Kevin Williamson founded the magazine *Rebel Inc* in 1992, and argued that the period between then and the creation of a Scottish parliament in 1999 was 'the making of Scotland'. He launched the magazine on May Day 1992, just nine days after John Major's surprise general election victory, upstairs in a leading Edinburgh bookshop. He recalled, 'we had the bit between our teeth and we fought back.'

The backlash that followed was inevitable. He was invited onto BBC Radio Scotland's lunchtime arts show to defend himself against accusations of bad language, violence, filth and depravity. On that day technicians were on strike, and Kevin seized the moment when the presenter asked:

'So, Kevin, how do you defend your publication?'
'Well, Colin [Bell], I'd like to defend the magazine but as a trade unionist myself I'm going down to join the BECTU picket line outside'.[74]

It is easy to portray the cultural upsurge of the 1980s and '90s as simply a response to Thatcherism, but its roots were a lot deeper, and preceded the 1979 Westminster election. Alasdair Gray, Jeff Torrington and James Kelman wrote for more than a decade before finally having their books published in Scotland and England. Tom Leonard's *The Good Thief* appeared in the first issue of *Scottish International* in January 1968, but when he had tried to publish poems in *Glasgow University Magazine* the printer refused them because of the language. Later a typesetter wanted 'foreign language rates' for setting some of his poems. Kelman had been writing since about 1967 but his first collection of short stories, *An Old Pub Near the Angel*, was published only in 1973 in the USA and received little notice in Scotland or England.

Scottish International appeared between 1968 and 1974 and became a platform for these new writers. It published extracts from Alasdair Gray's *Lanark*, helping him secure a Scottish Arts Council grant to complete it. *SI* also published Alan Spence's stories. Its editor was Harry Tait, while two poets, Edwin Morgan and Robert Garioch, were members of its editorial board.

Lanark is, simply, a masterpiece. Gray's book is set in two places: the Glasgow where he grew up and lives, and the strange dystopian world of Unthank, a grey, oppressive place where Lanark, his hero, is trapped by emotional repression. Gray sees the novel, and much of his other writing, as an exploration of the ability of human beings to love and of the obstacles that inhibit that capacity.

Meanwhile, radical theatre came to Scotland in the 1970s when, for example, Billy Connolly starred in *The Great Northern Welly Boot Show*, based loosely on the UCS sit-in. The 7:84 theatre company had been set up in London in 1971, involving, among others, John McGrath, Elizabeth MacLennan and David MacLeanan (the title came from an *Economist* article that said just 7 percent of Britain's population owned 84 percent of the wealth), and in 1973 they formed 7:84 Scotland.

That year they took *The Cheviot, the Stag and the Black, Black Oil* on a tour of Scotland, travelling in a Transit van across the country. It was a rousing attack on the Clearances and much else. McGrath recalls that on its first performance they were 'staggered to see an Aberdeen audience stand up and cheer at the end'.[75] They moved on to the Highlands, performing in village halls and with a ceildh at the end of each show.

Their next play was *The Game's a Bogey*, centring on the figure of John Maclean. It opened at a miner's welfare club in Glenrothes and toured industrial Scotland, bringing Maclean to a whole new audience.[76] The Scottish TUC sponsored their later shows, as they did concerts of the Laggan, the left-wing folk group featuring the powerful voice of Arthur Johnstone.

Subsequently, what was most remarkable in all this was the sheer volume of first-class writing that came forth. Alasdair Gray and James Kelman met each other, and Tom Leonard and Liz Lochhead, for the first time in 1971 at a writers' group organised by Philip Hobsbaum, a lecturer in English at Glasgow University. What was equally remarkable was that the majority of this new writing reflected working-class experience and used everyday language, as spoken by ordinary Scots. James Kelman explains why:

> The establishment demands art from its own perspective but these forms of committed art have always been as suffocating to me as the impositions laid down by the British State, although I should point out of course that I am a socialist myself. I wanted none of any of it . . . How could I write from within my own place and time if I was forced to adopt the received language of the ruling class? Not to challenge the rules of narrative was to be coerced into assimilation, I would be forced to write in the voice of an imagined member of the ruling class. I saw the struggle as towards a

selfcontained world. This meant I had to work my way through language, find a way of making it my own.[77]

At the beginning of the 1980s, Peter Kravitz was working at the publisher Polygon. He recalled that if you asked about Scottish fiction in a bookshop you would be directed to historical romances. Publishers and bodies such as the Scottish Arts Council had little interest in encouraging new writers dealing with contemporary Scotland:

> When on behalf of Polygon I sent them [James] Kelman's second novel, *A Chancer*, they deemed it unworthy of a grant towards publication costs. They had received a complaint from a Conservative Member of Parliament, Alick Buchanan-Smith; one of his constituents had picked up Kelman's previous novel, *The Busconductor Hines*, in an Edinburgh bookshop, and was shocked that taxpayers' money was subsidising such language. Those who claimed to represent culture had lost their collective nerve.[78]

In December 1990, the *Scots Magazine* – a favourite read among Scots abroad – published an article by Maurice Fleming entitled 'Scotland the Depraved'. In it he called for a return to the values of the comic classics of Compton Mackenzie and more publicity for writers who could celebrate Scotland as opposed to those he labelled 'the terrible twosome': Kelman and Irvine Welsh, joined by Duncan McLean. He describes his targets as 'desperate to plumb even deeper depths of depravity'. These writers, he said, 'appear to view Scotland with undisguised and malicious disgust [portraying the place as] a nation of drunks, drug addicts and dropouts'.[79]

In 1992, the tabloid *Daily Record* ran a story under the headline 'Sex Shockers on School's Reading List', claiming 'dirty books' and 'classroom porn shockers' were in the library at Johnstone High School. As a result, five books were taken off the shelves: *A Chancer* and *Greyhound for Breakfast* by James Kelman; *The Color Purple* by Alice Walker; *The Cider House Rules* by John Irving; and *Perfume* by Patrick Süskind. Strathclyde Region's

Director of Education then ordered all post-1970 fiction to be removed and vetted.[80]

Kelman's first published novel, *The Busconductor Hines*, did not reach the prestigious Booker Prize shortlist. However, Richard Cobb (the chairman of the judges) did express his shock that 'one of the novels seemed to be written entirely in Glaswegian', as if that were enough to pass judgement on it. Anne Smith, editor of the (then Edinburgh-based) *Literary Review*, said of it, 'Who wants to read 300 pages about the life of a bus conductor where nothing much happens anyway?'[81]

Kelman's novel *How Late It Was, How Late*, published in 1994, was awarded the Booker Prize. The judges' decision was not unanimous, with Rabbi Julia Neuberger calling the decision a 'disgrace'.[82] She added it was 'just a drunken Scotsman railing against bureaucracy'. The English journalist Simon Jenkins described the author as an 'illiterate savage'.[83]

In his acceptance speech Kelman riposted:

There is a literary tradition to which I hope my own work belongs. I see it as part of a much wider process – or movement – toward decolonization and self-determination: it is a tradition that assumes two things: 1) The validity of indigenous culture; and 2) The right to defend it in the face of attack. It is a tradition premised on a rejection of the cultural values of imperial or colonial authority, offering a defence against cultural assimilation, in particular imposed assimilation. Unfortunately, when people assert their right to cultural or linguistic freedom they are accused of being ungracious, parochial, insular, xenophobic, racist etc.[84]

In response to similar critics of such uncouth language, Tom Leonard wrote:

right enuff
ma language is disgraceful
ach well
all livin language is sacred
fuck thi lohta thim

But not everyone followed this lead in writing in the vernacular. The Edinburgh-based crime writer Ian Rankin has said how impressed he was by Kelman's use of Scottish vernacular and how he enthusiastically showed Kelman's stories to his father. 'But he said he couldn't read it because it wasn't in English. Now, my dad is from the same working-class linguistic community as Kelman writes about. If he couldn't read it, but half of Hampstead was lapping it up, that to me was a huge failure and I decided then not to write phonetically.'[85]

The poet and playwright Liz Lochhead has also raised another issue: 'I do like Glasgow and the West of Scotland register, but that's only because its part of my own childhood and private register that I know intimately. I am certainly interested in Scottishness, but I feel that the territory that gets delineated is a macho William McIlvanney and Tom Leonard world and that's what Glasgowness feeds into.'[86]

But Lochhead did write, in *Lallans*:

It took me a long while to gain the courage to write in Scots, and the desire. Why's that? You can start to psychoanalyse yourself trying to answer that. But you'd be better off interrogating the Education System. 'Kidspoem' was a commission; the idea was to encourage kids to write in their 'home town' language. So I thought back to my own childhood, and remembered the words I still used, built a translation into the structure. Had fun . . .[87]

Leonard's *Radical Renfrew* was published in 1990, and he explains how he came to write it: 'While I was working in Paisley Central Library I saw behind the counter the local nineteenth century collection which no one had ever read and I wanted to read it. I thought that if there wasn't an anthology, I would make one, so I just read the collection and made an anthology from it . . . I had a distinct sense of audience: the audience would be the people who used the library.' In the introduction Leonard states that libraries are crucial to democracy.[88]

James Kelman is not just a novelist but a political activist, as reflected in collections of essays. In the 1980s, Kelman was part of the Workers' City group, which challenged Glasgow's designation as the 1990 European City of Culture. This was critical of the free-market ethos behind the festival, and the name was chosen in contrast to the renaming of part of the city centre as the Merchant City, something they said promoted the 'fallacy that Glasgow some- how exists because of . . . eighteenth century entrepreneurs and far-sighted politicians. [The merchants] were men who trafficked in degradation, causing untold misery, death and starvation to thou- sands.'[89] Subsequently, Kelman worked for Clydeside Action on Asbestos, fighting on behalf of victims of asbestosis refused compen- sation from contractors and local authorities.

Kelman, Gray, Leonard and Lochhead are very firmly West Coast writers. But the writer who gained the greatest international atten- tion came from the other side of the country. Irvine Welsh was born in Leith in 1961, before moving with his family at the age of four to Muirhouse, one of the many post-war council schemes that ring Edinburgh. Leaving school at sixteen, he worked in various jobs before leaving for London in 1978 to join the city's punk scene before getting a job with Hackney Council and then returning to Edin- burgh to study at Heriot-Watt University.

He has written fondly of his visits to his aunt and uncle's family in Southall in West London, as it began to be transformed into one of the centres of Britain's Asian community, and of his subsequent time living in London in the late 1970s and early 1980s. There is no petty nationalism here. Welsh, like Kelman, Leonard and other Scottish writers, has no animosity towards the English and clearly had good times in London.

Welsh published various stories in literary magazines. The first parts of what would become *Trainspotting* appeared in his friend Kevin Williamson's *Rebel Inc*, and as a result, in 1993 the book was published in London. A stage adaptation opened at Glasgow's Mayfest a year later, went on to the Edinburgh Festival and to tour the US. In Febru- ary 1996, Danny Boyle's film adaptation premiered, and Welsh enjoyed international fame of a sort few Scottish writers have achieved.

Trainspotting depicts a very different side of life in Edinburgh than was normally the case. As Welsh explained: 'That image was a lie: it was at best just a small constituent part of the culture of that city. That of the middle class festival city. Yet it had a hegemony over all the other images of this urban, largely working class but multi-cultural city. Other realities existed, had to be shown to exist.'[90]

Memorably, the anti-hero Renton gets to say these words:

Choose us. Choose life. Choose mortgage payments; choose washing machines; choose cars. Choose sitting oan a couch watching mind-numbing, spirit-crushing game shows, stuffing fuckin junk food into your mouth. Choose rotting away at the end of it all, pish and shiteing yersel in a home, a total fuckin embarrassment tae the selfish, fucked up brats ye've produced. Choose life. Well ah choose nae to choose life. If the cunts cannae handle that, its their fuckin problem.[91]

When Renton pays a visit to his dealer, he describes in passing the general economic stasis that now describes the landscape of Muir-house: 'Ah cross the dual carriageway and walk through the centre. Ah pass the steel-shuttered units which have never been let and cross over the car park where cars have never parked. Never since it was built. Over twenty years ago.'[92] This is a long way from the kailyard.

Renton chooses to be a supporter of Hibs (like Welsh), the team founded by Edinburgh's Catholic community, rather than Hearts, the Protestant team his brother Billy supports. In that way Renton and his pals are outsiders: Hearts have the bigger support and have been generally more successful. He and his pals are abused as 'Fenian cunts'. The choice is a rejection of Edinburgh's dominant Presbyterian culture, and that particular sense of Scottishness.

Billy joins the British Army and is killed in Northern Ireland. In the book Renton's grief will reappear but at the funeral his anger is on display, reinforced by the attendance of relatives from Glasgow, clearly Rangers supporters:

Ah cannae feel remorse, only anger and contempt. Ah seethed when ah saw that fuckin Union Jack oan his coffin, n watched that smarmy, wimpy cunt ay an officer, obviously oot ay his depth here, trying tae talk tae ma Ma. Worse still, these Glasgow cunts, the auld boy's side, are through here en masse. They're fill ay shite aboot how he died in the service ay his country n aw that servile Hun crap.[93]

Welsh lists George Eliot, Jane Austen and Charlotte Brontë as writers he admires, along with Walter Scott, Lewis Grassic Gibbon and James Hogg, whose 1824 *Confessions of a Justified Sinner* he describes as 'one of the best, most brilliant books ever written'. Of more recent Scottish writers, he says that reading James Kelman's *The Busconductor Hines* was a key moment ('Kelman was like Year Zero'), and of William McIlvanney's *Docherty*, 'this is a fucking great writer writing in his own voice, and it's like James Kelman, to me, is doing that but just taking it one stage further. And Alasdair Gray's taking it off in another direction.'[94] But he also draws a line between the West Coast writers and himself: 'A lot of the Glasgow writers are concerned with work and the alienation from work . . . Because of the industry in Glasgow there is a kind of machismo about work – that dignity of labour thing . . . I think work is a horrible thing. People should avoid it at all costs.'[95]

The author pinpoints the change that took place in Scotland during the Thatcher and John Major years:

> Like many Scots, I grew up saturated in something I assumed to be 'Britishness', and I loved it. *Steptoe and Son, The Likely Lads, Play for Today*, they were my cultural staples, and I was personally liberated by the welfare state, specifically the Butler Education Act. This meant that my college fees would be paid in full by the state, and I would also receive a full grant, which amounted to 2/3rds of my dad's wages. Now all that has gone . . .[96]

Alasdair Gray points to one reason crime fiction has taken off in Scotland in recent years: 'It's only been in the last twenty years that you have an awful lot of Scottish popular detective thrillers with Scottish settings and Scottish detectives and criminals. If you leave aside John Buchan, Scotland just wasn't interesting enough to have that kind of thing for most of the last century.'[97]

Topping the best-seller list for crime fiction is Ian Rankin, whose books are set in his adopted home, Edinburgh, and his native Fife (Rankin was born in Cardenden in the old coalfield).

These writers, in their different ways, have cut a path that others are following today. Rab Wilson worked as miner in his native

Ayrshire and in his poetry has continued to use Lallans in the new century, explaining, 'There is still a working class voice out there, but the powers that be don't want to publish it.'[98]

Reflecting on the damage done to working-class communities like his own in New Cumnock, he adds: 'The human spirit will always survive – if it can survive Auschwitz, it can survive call centres and Tesco. The problem is that modern work is so full on – it's not like Robert Burns working on a farm, when you had time to think. But maybe stacking shelves in Tesco is quite a conducive environment to be a poet. In fact, now that you mention it, I think I'll volunteer myself to work in Tesco for six months as their poet in residence.'

In 1985, Alexander Moffatt, head of painting at Glasgow School of Art, staged the exhibition *New Image*, featuring six 'Glasgow Boys', most of whom had been his pupils – Ken Currie, Peter Howson, Steven Campbell, Stephen Barclay, Stephen Conroy and Adrian Wiszniewski. (The original Glasgow Boys came to promini-nence in the 1880s and '90s and included James Guthrie, Arthur Melville, Joseph Crawhall, E. A. Walton, George Henry, John Lavery and E. A. Hornel. They were painting at a time when the city was at the peak of its prosperity.) Currie's *In the City Bar* was first shown in 1987, in the build-up to Glasgow being the 1990 European City of Culture. On its left a loyalist group are holding back a man in a vest, one of them with a Union Jack tattooed on his arm, while behind them a couple dance cheerlessly to a tartan-clad accordion player and a drummer[99] with the Stars and Stripes on his drum, a reference to the hold of a bastardised American culture. Off to the right an elderly worker downs another pint while Currie paints himself rolling up various plans for the future. But while he tarries in the bar a young girl strides purposely towards the door, and the future.

Currie said of his work in the 1980s and '90s: 'My paintings from that time were very stylized – mannered even – and very much . . . in the spirit of [Otto] Dix whose savage and melancholy social commen-tary on Weimar Germany seemed to resonate with my own concerns on the streets of my home city of Glasgow – a city utterly ravaged by Thatcher.'[100]

In that same year, 1987, he was commissioned to paint eight murals in Glasgow's People's Palace, to commemorate the 200th anniversary of the Calton Weavers' Massacre. These depict scenes from Glasgow's working-class history because, as he explains, 'I wanted to represent a cycle of images that showed the ebb and flow of an emergent mass movement, where the real heroines and heroes were the many unknown working class Scots who fought so selflessly for their rights'.[101]

In the course of the 1960s and '70s folk musicians in Scotland began to locate themselves in a wider European and global context. That coincided with an increased use of electrified instruments and an awareness that they could make a living from their music.

Archie Fisher recalled that the Robin Hall and Jimmie MacGregor duo opened a 'fork in the road' for musicians like him through their television success in the 1960s, which led them to being able to play bigger venues than folk clubs, increasing their earnings. Fisher was making £7 to £15 a night in folk venues in the 1970s, but when he became a backing musician for the successful Irish duo Tommy Makem and Liam Clancy he could make £140 a night on tour, plus food and accommodation.[102]

The Battlefield Band, like other 1970s acts such as Kentigern, the Clutha, Ossian, the Tannahill Weavers and Silly Wizard began playing acoustic music and performing traditional songs. The Battlefield Band was among the Scottish acts who regularly toured in Europe. The money was better than in Scotland or England. As they gained in popularity they decided to introduce the Scottish bagpipes, as Brian McNeill of the band recalls:

In 1979 . . . we realised that if we were going to do it properly we needed a piper and we went away and reformed the band . . . we took every German gig we could get. The money was better there, but also we got a much more sympathetic listening in Germany, simply in terms of the eclectic places we would play. [Having a piper] . . . gave us more of a platform for agents to book us in places like Germany and Belgium and Holland, because the booking platform wasn't, 'here's another band for a good night out', it was, 'here's a band that's got something unique and Scottish'. And so, to a certain extent you were expected to conform to that but by and large, that's where our tastes lay anyway and that's what we wanted to do.[103]

By the 1980s Runrig, Capercaillie, Ceolbeg and others were playing electric instruments and performing their own compositions. Donald Shaw was one of the founders of Capercaillie, at Oban High School in 1984, and says of their music: 'Capercaillie have been credited with being the major force in bringing Celtic music to the world stage, and their unique fusion of Gaelic culture and contemporary sound has always stretched boundaries in their quest to keep the music evolving.'[104] The band contributed seven tracks to the musical soundtrack of the 1995 Holywood film *Rob Roy*, with the singer Karen Matheson also appearing in it, performing unaccompanied.

Runrig was formed in April 1973 as a dance band but soon shifted to performing contemporary Gaelic songs. As their success grew, the record company encouraged them to include songs in English. That led to much criticism from their Gaelic fans but it meant commercial success followed. In 1989, their album *Searchlight* reached number eleven in the UK album chart, selling 60,000 copies in the first week.

Some Scottish artists moved on. Billy Connolly became part of the British establishment, a long way from his days mixing with the Young Socialists in Glasgow. In the late 1960s he had formed the Humbelbums with Gerry Rafferty, who also rose to international stardom. When Rafferty died in 2011 his former manager Michael Gray wrote: '. . . he retained a healthy scepticism not just about the music industry but about society, money and politics in general. His background was soaked in Scottish socialism and poverty, his mind sharp and his personality acerbic, and he wasn't going to be dazzled by the glamour of success.'[105]

That has been true for many of Scotland's great artists over the decades.

Thatcher's Legacy

In early 2012, when the Thatcher biopic *The Iron Lady* opened, the *Daily Record* sent a reporter to test the reaction to her in Motherwell. Carol Ann Perkins, a full-time carer, told them: 'My dad worked at Ravenscraig all his life. The closure was horrific. All these hard-working men were lost without jobs. My dad was very lucky to get another job but lots of men couldn't find work. People found it hard to feed their children. I just don't think people here will ever forgive Margaret Thatcher for what she did and how she did it.'

Firefighter Craig Reid, forty-one, said: 'There were so many jobs lost, especially among the people living around here. Even now, twenty years later, you can still see the aftermath. People don't recover quickly from losing their jobs and livelihoods. I don't think people will ever forgive what Thatcher did to us.'[106]

The response would have been similar in Liverpool, Newcastle, Doncaster or Coventry, but there was a different conclusion in Scotland. Thatcher had enjoyed no mandate in Scotland, people had not voted for her, and the response was a shift towards self-government (devolution) and, for some, independence. In the 1997 Westminster general election, the Tories were wiped out north of the border. Because of the proportional representation system they were able to maintain a presence in the forthcoming Holyrood parliament but only as a fringe party.

On a wider level, Christopher Harvie pointed to the demise of the Unionist cause by contrasting opposition to the creation of a Scottish parliament in 1997 and that to the 1932 Home Rule Bill:

Hundreds of grand, mainly Glasgow-based capitalists – shipbuilders, steelmakers, coal-owners – along with noblemen, clergy and university principals, had signed the notorious 'Ragman's Roll' [a reference to the Scottish nobles who capitulated to Edward I] protesting at any move toward a Scottish parliament. Sixty years later the grandson of one of the original signatories, Viscount Weir, could only get a dozen or so – including two elderly Tory clergymen, the novelist Alan Massie and the singer Moira Anderson – to declare against devolution.[107]

Something profound had happened during the Thatcher-Major years. The Tories had ceased to be a force in Scotland, which meant the political set-up and debate was very different to that in England. After protesting and striking, and failing to shift the 'Iron Lady', ordinary Scots had increasingly seized on a Scottish identity as a badge of resistance. This identity was seen not in terms of Empire and military glory but as representing a society with more social democratic values than that south of the border, while institutions once deemed the epitome of Britishness, such as the BBC, now added 'Scotland' to their title north of the border. Even the *Sun* had to describe itself as 'Scottish'.

The Labour leaders Tony Blair and Donald Dewar believed they could put a cap on this by creating a Scottish parliament and that a majority of Scots would accept devolution and reject independence. That would not prove to be the case. The years of Tory rule in the 1980s and '90s represented a fundamental break in Scottish politics and life. Prior to Thatcher, Scottishness for most was something restricted to the terraces of Hampden or Murrayfield. After her rule, it came to be seen by more and more Scots as something separate from Britishness.

Thatcher was a devout Unionist, yet she did more than any other British politician to undermine the unity of the British state.[108]

FIFTEEN

Twenty-First-Century Scotland

On 11 September 1997, 74 percent of Scottish voters said 'Yes' in a referendum on whether to establish a Scottish parliament, with 63 percent voting additionally to give it limited tax-raising powers. Tony Blair, elected as head of a New Labour UK government earlier that year, was no enthusiast for devolution and had been heard to say that a Scottish parliament would have no more powers than a parish council in England.[1] In the spring of 1997 he stated, 'Sovereignty rests with me as an English MP, and that's the way it will stay.'[2]

He had to swallow his beliefs because, first, he needed to be elected and every vote north of the border counted, and, second, all the main parties in Scotland and most of wider society now backed the creation of a parliament in Edinburgh. Blair was ressured by his Secretary of State for Scotland, Donald Dewar, that by granting devolution it would remove the rationale behind support for the SNP and independence. He was to be proved wrong about that, as were the architects of the new Scottish constitution in their design of the new political system.

The system of voting chosen for Holyrood elections, the additional member system, was designed to stop any one party gaining an overall majority. It combines first-past-the-post constituency MPs topped up by representatives elected on a proportional share of the vote across the wider regions of Scotland. It was described by Donald Dewar as 'the best example of charitable giving this century in politics,' meaning Labour would have expected a permanent majority on a simple first past the post. Instead, a party could get an overwhelming majority only if it polled more than half the total Scottish vote. However, that was introduced not to damage Labour but to stop an SNP victory, seen by the Westminster parties as a stepping stone to separation, and to ensure coalition governments.[3]

Labour would rule in Scotland, in coalition with the Liberal Democrats, from 1997 until 2007, when the SNP emerged from that year's elections as the largest party at Holyrood and Alex Salmond formed a minority government. In 2011, the unthinkable happened and the SNP won overall control of the Scottish Parliament. Labour had also lost overall control of local authorities outside Glasgow.

Nevertheless, the first major issue to impact on Scottish society was but the latest chapter in an old story.

We're Gonnae Stop the War!

The decision of the Blair government to participate in the US-led wars and occupations of Afghanistan and Iraq met with opposition from a majority of the Scottish people. On 15 February 2003, as US-led forces prepared to invade Iraq, Scotland was part of a global demonstration, initiated the previous autumn by the European Social Forum in Florence, which was attended by a strong Scottish delegation.

For the 15 February demonstration in Glasgow, the number of trains travelling to the city were doubled to cope with demand. People were still leaving the starting-point at Glasgow Green as marchers at the front reached the Scottish Exhibition and Conference Centre (SECC) car park two miles away. Protestors filled the streets along the length and breadth of the route. Some 150,000 people marched that day. More than 600 people marched through Lerwick in the Shetlands.

Tony Blair was due to address the conference but the Scottish Labour leadership re-arranged his speech so that he was in and out of Glasgow before the march started, let alone reached the SECC. Addressing the crowd, the city's Lord Provost, Alex Mosson, said: 'We are saying quite clearly, and we are the voice of the majority, that we don't want this war. If Tony Blair can't hear our voices from the SECC, then he will hear them in Downing Street.'

The Rev. Alan McDonald, convener of the Church of Scotland's Church and Nation committee, reported that parishes across Scotland were expressing 'horror' at the prospect of war. 'Our concern is for the ordinary people of Iraq, who are not "collateral damage", but are the men, women and children who will be underneath the incoming bombs and missiles. No matter how smart the weapons are, no matter how sophisticated the targeting is supposed to be, it is the children, women and men who will suffer and die, as they always do in modern war.'

The marchers included sixty-year-old Brenda King from Barnton in Edinburgh, who was accompanied by her husband, Alan. She said, 'I think the war is about oil. If they grew carrots, we would not bomb them. We have not been involved in a protest for a long time. But it is such a clear issue and we feel it is important.'

Sinclair Laird, forty-eight, from Hamilton, said: 'You can see the number of people that are against this war. This is the first time I have felt this animated in a long time. I think if we have a democratic government it will have to pay some attention to the public's opposition to this war, which is being echoed by protests around the world today.'[4]

One of the songs sung on that day, to the tune of the Italian resistance song 'Bella Ciao', went, 'George and Tony, dae ye know we're gonnae / Stop the War, Stop the War, Stop the War, War, War! / Tell George's crony, wee Berlusconi / That we're gonnae Stop the War'[5]

As the Stop the War Coalition became established in Scotland, it was able to develop new alliances that included not just the trade unions, the broader left and sections of the Labour Party, but sections of the SNP, the Green Party and representatives of the Muslim community as well. The opposition of the SNP leaders to the invasion of Iraq (but not Afghanistan) and to the 'anti-terror' laws put through by Westminster meant the nationalists were able to win significant support among the younger generation of Scottish Muslims, whose parents had traditionally voted Labour.

While Scots were demonstrating in huge numbers against one war, others would die in Afghanistan and Iraq. Rose Gentle from Pollok in Glasgow helped found Military Families Against War after her son was killed by a roadside bomb outside Basra in Iraq: 'Gordon was a nineteen-year-old, he had no idea where Iraq was, he thought he was going for peacekeeping . . . He wasn't killed by weapons of mass destruction, which is why he was sent.'[6]

The Longest Industrial Action Since 1984–85

The longest strike in Scotland since the miners' strike of 1984–85 involved nursery nurses across Scotland taking action. It ended with the last group of nurses in Glasgow going back to work after fourteen weeks of all-out strike.

The strike was the final chapter in a fight for decent pay that had been going on for over two years. Prior to the strike, the top rate of pay for a nursery nurse was £13,800. Despite increased responsibilities, they had not been regraded for sixteen years. The strike became a battle for national pay and conditions after the Labour-dominated association of local authorities in Scotland (Cosla) told the nurses that new deals would have to be settled with individual councils. These three bodies were all Labour-controlled. Carol Ball, a nursery nurse and the union convenor said, 'the employers are desperate not to come to a national agreement. The support for the strike among nursery nurses is as strong as ever. The message we have got from national delegates' meetings and from local mass meetings is that people want a decent national regrading and pay deal. Getting that is now all about solidarity.'[7]

The strike action was very solid, with the strikers throwing up new and innovative tactics. More than 4,000 marched in Glasgow at the beginning of the strike. Over 2,000 demonstrated at the Scottish

Parliament in Edinburgh. When Cosla refused to come to the negotiating table to discuss a national deal, more than 2,000 nursery
nurses marched, with a table, to the Cosla offices. Over 1,000
marched through Ayr during the Easter holidays. In Glasgow there
were unofficial demonstrations where strikers were joined by parents
and supporters. The majority of parents refused to cross picket lines,
and many were involved in picketing and raising support. The strike
challenged New Labour's drive to break up national pay structures
and to introduce performance-related pay.

'Other workers know what is at stake,' reported Jill McNaughton,
a striker from Dundee, 'that's why wherever we have gone to get
support it has been forthcoming. And the level of involvement in the
strike through picketing, marches and sending out delegations means
we deserve to win.'[8]

Liz McCulloch, a striker from East Ayrshire, explained: 'At root
this is about New Labour at Westminster, the Scottish Parliament
and in local authorities trying to bully low paid-workers out of what
is rightfully ours.'[9]

In the end, the union leadership of Unison decided a national
agreement was not possible, to the anger of many strikers, and
went for local deals. The Glasgow nursery nurses in particular felt
they were left to fight alone. Kate, a Glasgow nurse with eight
years' experience, stated: 'We wanted social justice over pay and
working conditions. What we got instead was being starved back
to work.'

Others were angrier still, as another Glasgow nursery nurse, Janice,
made clear: 'I think that Unison should hang their heads in shame.
Many of us made big sacrifices to go on strike but they pulled the rug
from under us. We were committed to win but they gave in too
easily. I don't know why this happened but I do know that they were
not at all happy when we voted to stay on strike in Glasgow.'[10]

Nursery nurses were left with pay offers that varied widely between
councils, with a gap as far apart as £8.76 and £10.46 per hour in
some cases. Most of the offers made by local authorities were at the
lower end of the scale. The unions largely remained tied to Labour
and all too often put loyalty to the party before the interests of their

own members. One union official, not wanting to be identified, admitted: 'The reality is that when the chips are down Scotland's union leaders put the Labour Party's interests first.'[11]

When the SNP took charge of the Scottish executive in 2007, one senior trade union official admitted that the new administration bent over backwards to consult with the unions and contrasted that with Labour, which effectively shunned them.

The World's Leaders Visit Scotland

For five days in 2005, the sun shone on Edinburgh as protesters gathered in the capital to counter the G8 gathering of world leaders, including George W. Bush, at the luxury Gleneagles Hotel. They were supposedly discussing reducing poverty in Africa but the protesters had heard their promises before.

On 2 July, some quarter of a million people from across Scotland and Britain gathered for a Make Poverty History march and rally. It was organised by a broad coalition of NGOs, religious bodies, youth organisations, trade unions and more. Many protesters carried banners emphasising one or other key issue – 'Drop the Debt', 'Fight Poverty Not War' or 'Stop Climate Chaos'.

Tracy Sabatini from Glasgow brought her two children, Stephano, nine, and Louisa, seven, on the march. 'The children understand people in Africa are dying,' she said. 'Hopefully, after experiencing an event like this, when they reach adulthood they will know how to fight for justice.' Rebecca Njeri's group Stand Up for Africa works for just that, by raising funds and campaigning. The sixth-former from London said the day had been 'lovely'. 'We've met people from different places and the support from the people of Edinburgh has been wonderful. All we're saying to the world leaders is we all have the same feelings; let's treat people equally.'[12]

The singer-songwriter Billy Bragg won over his audience when he sang, 'You know where you are with the New World Order – right up the arse of the USA.' Earlier he had told the crowd, 'If in a year's time nothing has changed, you know who to blame . . . It will be the fault of those eight men – the leaders of the G8. We need to send a message to those eight men – "We know where you live".'[13]

The next day saw 5,000 people attend the G8 Alternatives counter-summit in the Usher Hall to discuss alternatives to neo-liberalism and hear a wide range of anti-capitalist campaigners from across the globe.

Sunday 3 July also saw the Stop the War Coalition organise a march down the Mound and to the top of Calton Hill, where they staged a 'Naming of the Dead' ceremony, with protesters taking turns to read out the names of Iraqis and Afghanis killed in the US-led wars. A Glasgow teacher, Linda O'Mahaney, took part explaining: 'These people are being forgotten, the Iraqi dead aren't even being counted. There are a number of people whose children have died up there and we wanted to go with them. It seems to me it is absolutely incredible that in a city like Edinburgh you can't even join a march up a road. We're going to try to catch them up though.'[14]

Other protest actions during this time included a protest at the Dungavel detention centre, housing refugees facing deportation, and a blockade at the Faslane Trident base.

Five days of protest against the G8 culminated on 6 July with a march from Auchterarder to Gleneagles Hotel. At 9 a.m. the organisers, G8 Alternatives, were told by police that the march had been cancelled because of 'public safety' concerns. Police roadblocks sought to stop transport reaching Auchterarder. The organisers meanwhile had telephoned an array of MSPs, MPs, trade union and community leaders to get them to protest. The STUC and the Fire Brigades Union lodged protests. The police backed down initially by saying 2,000 could march, and then caved in completely.

Gill Hubbard of G8 Alternatives said, 'I'm sure all of you will agree that this would have been a travesty of democracy if we were not allowed to protest against the warmongers. We're on this side of the fence, they're on that side of the fence. Which side are people on? The people of Scotland are on our side, we are going to march and we are delighted about that.'[15]

The march set off with police filming participants, and reached the security fence inside which world leaders had gathered. A group simply pushed past the fence and entered the secure zone, eventually being charged at by riot police. Overhead, a Chinook helicopter brought in further riot police. The protest was effective, getting within sight and earshot of Gleneagles Hotel, but non-violent on the part of the protesters, with just two arrests being made.

The people of Auchterarder were supportive too, despite being fed horror stories about demonstrators wrecking the village. People had put up posters in different languages saying 'Welcome to Auchterarder'. They waved at protesters from their windows and some participated in the march.

Ian Rankin's penultimate Inspector Rebus crime thriller, *The Naming of the Dead* (named after the Stop the War protest), is set during the protests and is dedicated 'to everyone who was in Edinburgh on 2 July 2005'.

For a Nuclear-Free Scotland

The United Kingdom is one of nine states that officially admit to possessing nuclear weapons. The Trident missiles currently based at the UK's sole nuclear base, Faslane, are capable of killing 225 million civilians. They cost British taxpayers £2 billion a year.

Currently, all the major Westminster parties are agreed on spending £100 billion on a new generation of weapons of mass destruction to replace Trident. Like Trident and its predecessor Polaris, these will effectively be leased from the US and could be used only with Washington's permission. In April 2013, as campaigning for the independence referendum was under way, thousands marched through Glasgow demanding nuclear missiles be removed from Scotland and the billions scheduled to be spent replacing Trident be allocated to welfare.

One of the march organisers, Brian Larkin, co-ordinator of the Edinburgh Peace and Justice Centre, said Trident should be scrapped and the money put into 'human needs' instead. 'We want the resources that go into Trident to fund disability benefits, create jobs, scrap the bedroom tax, fund the NHS, fund education and fund welfare.'[16] Yet as Brian Quail, an executive member of Scottish CND, points out: '. . . now [in 2013] we see all the opposition parties in Scotland united in supporting this British WMD, Trident. There is a perverse logic to this situation. Labour, like the Tories and LibDems, is a Unionist party. This means that they are a nationalist party – i.e. British nationalist. Trident is the ultimate symbol of Britishness. This is our national fetish, the sacrosanct totem of our great power status. And it has ever been so.'[17]

The peace campaigner Isobel Lindsay explains: 'All of the UK's nuclear weapons capacity is based at Faslane/Coulport. If a Scottish government insists that no nuclear warheads be allowed in Scottish waters or land (as New Zealand did), we could disarm Trident very quickly. We would have to agree to store the warheads (disabled) at Coulport for a short period until another storage facility could be built (or hopefully a decommissioning process). If nuclear-armed Trident submarines are not allowed to use Scottish waters or land, there is no other site for them in England or Wales that has the physical requirements and the infrastructure.'[18]

In 2012, though the SNP conference voted with the party leadership to reverse the party's longstanding commitment to quit NATO, that does not remove the fact that Scotland has no interest in this war-making alliance. This goal does not require a revolution: it is very easy and very possible to achieve. Further, we could withdraw from NATO, which is an aggressive alliance pursuing US interests and a neo-liberal programme, and insist that Scottish troops will not take part in any more imperialist wars.

Being Working Class in Today's World

In the course of the new century the numbers of people taking part in protests and social movements has grown, globally as well as in Scotland. This contrasts with the lack of strike action by workers and the relative decline of the trade unions. Among New Labour it became fashionable to talk of the working class as a declining and spent force and to regard trade unions, in similar ways to the Tories, as dinosaurs (although that did not stop them taking union money).

There is no question that since the 1980s there has been a restructuring of the workforce in Scotland, as in other developed economies, but does that equate to the disappearance of the working class? The numbers of people employed in call centres today is comparable to those once employed in shipbuilding or engineering. The jobs are very different but call centre workers still face exploitation in the real sense of the word, as outlined in a Trades Union Congress report, 'Calls for Change', published in April 2001. It highlighted the following complaints: extreme monitoring of work, staff timed over how often they go to the toilet and how long they spend there, staff having to ask permission to go to the toilet and being hauled in front of bosses to explain why they go so often, inadequate or no breaks, stress and other health problems.[19]

A major study into working conditions and attitudes at Scottish call centres published in 2007 makes fascinating reading. Monitoring was so claustrophobic at the Holstravel call centre that team leaders would systematically listen in to agents' internal as well as external calls. On one occasion, a worker called a friend in another team to let her know that she had a job interview the following day and was going 'to pull a sickie'. The next day, the team leader, having heard this conversation, phoned the agent's home several times demanding to speak with her.

At Holstravel, 'Mission Control', a centrally located circular pen of computers, monitored performance among other tasks and detected irregular patterns of call activity, which would lead to phone calls to team leaders, alerting them to a worker's deviation from their allotted workload.[20]

One woman who worked as a travel consultant at Holstravel explained that workloads were subject to regular speed-ups while rewards for meeting increased targets were being cut: 'At first when we started, like in October, November and December, they were offering you really good money . . . Now they [the targets] are unrealistic . . . For your call conversion reaching, your stretch target they offer you eighty quid. For the same time last year for people in my team, they were offering six hundred quid.'[21]

A female customer adviser at the Moneyflow centre complained: '. . . when I started it was more customer service orientated so you had to give good service to your customer, take time. But now you feel you have just got to get the customer off the phone. So again you are working harder, you are taking more calls, you feel you can't go for a break because you feel eyes are on you to be there on the phone taking calls.'[22] She complained she was often asked to work overtime, meaning working as many as twelve hours a day, sometimes being informed of this by a note left on her desk. She complained, too, that while management wanted workers to be 100 percent flexible, they were not themselves so flexible in return.[23]

A female software engineer at Beta City Telecommunications had a similar complaint: 'I know if I do two long twelve hour days in a row then my brain is mince for the rest of the week because I'm just exhausted. I don't like that. It's not on. It's not healthy.'[24]

More than half (59 percent) of call centre employees, and more than a quarter (29 percent) of those in software, stated that they attached some degree of importance to the right to independent representation, and instrumental collectivist approaches to union membership are evident in the following quotations. One female customer service advisor at Entcomm call centre said, 'I'd never have advocated unions in the past . . . I have actually made inquiries about the communications union because I was a bit concerned about my contract . . . they are kind of shoving it out the door now and changing bits of it, and we are scared to sign things away . . . I would take a union line now and I can't believe I'm saying this, because I was never like that.'[25]

A male software engineer at Beta explained he'd like the union to be more active: 'There is still a place for union representation. The union were taking a very active role in [a voluntary redundancy exercise]. They've not done so much since then but, at the time, it was good to know that they were behind you and that they were there if you needed them, and it was one of the first things I did when I joined Beta was join the union . . . [T]hey do take a minimal role in our pay but I think they should take a more active role.'

There are, of course, real differences between working in a call centre and in a shipyard or engineering factory. The nature of the latter ensured there was a collective identity, if not across the whole yard or plant, at least among particular sections, most obviously skilled workers. They had real power and could stop production almost instantly.

Call centre and software engineering companies go to great lengths to prevent that, and to create a corporate identity. But these workers are making profits for their company and its clients. They too can hit their employer where it hurts, in the pocket, and they come from communities where class remains a strong identity and where there is a living tradition of resistance. Those shipyards and engineering plants were not always bastions of trade union organisation. They had to be organised, issues like sectarianism had to be overcome, and this generally took place through the common experience of struggle.

Sarah Collins is a young trade unionist, active in Unison in Ayrshire and currently an elected member of the STUC youth committee. She is well aware of the realities of organising at work in a neo-liberal age:

> Just over 25 per cent of the British workforce is in a trade union in the UK today. Proportionately, that's 20 per cent less than 30 years ago. At the last count, only five per cent of workers aged 16 to 20 were members of a trade union in Scotland, growing to just 11 per cent for 16–24 years olds. When asked how much they know about trade unions, 42 per cent of the young people responded that they knew nothing at all whilst a further 44 per cent said that they didn't know very much. Despite this, research demonstrates that 63 per cent of employees under 30 believe strong trade unions are needed to protect the working conditions and wages of employees and only nine per cent of young people have unfavourable attitudes towards trade unions.[26]

Yet she also points out: 'Between 2000 and 2005 over three million people took part in protests against the government. Over a third of these protesters were between twelve and twenty-five, yet this group formed only 17 per cent of the UK population in 2005. This is far higher in terms of figures and percentages than the late 1960s and early 1970s.'[27]

These are figures for the UK as a whole but they translate to Scotland.

Her prescription for the unions is: target politicised young people; break with the Labour Party; work with young people who identify themselves on the left and even the far left; demand from the Scottish government rights for young people facing precarious work (temporary and part-time employment).

The mantra of Labour politicians and many trade union leaders in the run-up to the 2014 independence referendum is to stress the tradition and benefits of class unity across the UK (despite the fact that the former have been abusing any notion of class resistance for two and a half decades). But there are now some fundamental differences between Scotland and England, and that divergence cannot simply be wished away.

Scots are more likely to identify themselves as working class and to support policies that aim to re-distribute wealth from top to bottom. In many ways, that is not different from working people in the north of England, who also do not vote for Tory governments. But there is a difference, as Michael Keating, professor of politics at Aberdeen University, explains:

> It seems that in the course of the 1980s and 1990s, *Scottish* national identity was rebuilt around themes of resistance to *neo-liberalism*, including a substantial section of the middle classes. To some degree, *Scottish* identity fills the role in sustaining social solidarity previously played (if only partly) by class. This resource is not available in the northern regions of England, where social democratic values are denied a territorial outlet.[28]

Two-thirds of Scots regard themselves as working class, and the Scottish Election Survey in 2007 found that those who identified as working class saw themselves as more Scottish than the middle class did, reinforcing the politics of class and nation.[29] Scottish politics is dominated by a contest between the SNP and Labour. While both support neo-liberal social and economic policies, they operate in a very different context to that in Westminster.

As I write this, the main parties seem transfixed by the apparent rise of the United Kingdom Independence Party, and following a UKIP by-election victory and a good vote in local elections, have responded by claiming they too are tough on immigration and support a referendum on EU membership. In England, the UKIP leader Nigel Farrage is a constant presence in the media, where he is lauded as the voice of the common people. Yet on a visit to Edinburgh in May 2013 he was reduced to looking like a bumbling upper-class toff who clearly knew little or nothing about Scottish politics and the views of the majority of Scots.

In Scotland there is currently no pressure from the right, but there is the shadow of the left. Indeed the SNP has proved more astute at seeming to espouse 'Old Labour' values, because in 2007 it took the radical left vote in large part after the implosion of the SSP. The party is aware that the Greens are a presence on its left, and that if the radical left got its act together they could win back a large part of those votes.

Land Ownership

'Scotland continues to have the most inequitable distribution of land ownership in Europe.' Those are the words of a former New Labour minister, Brian Wilson, in 2012.[30] The figures are truly staggering. In 2010, more than 83 percent of rural land in Scotland (94 percent of our total land mass) was privately owned. Just 969 individuals owned 60 percent of it. The vast majority of 5.2 million Scots owned none.[31]

Scotland's land-ownership pattern is the most concentrated in Europe today and one of the more concentrated systems in the world. Much is still owned by great landed families, but a growing percentage by corporations; between 22 and 25 percent is held in offshore or beneficial ownership with little information available as to who the income accrues, with widespread tax avoidance.[32] The writer and broadcaster Lesley Riddoch argues: 'The single biggest obstacle to the transformation of Scottish rural communities is their lack of control over land . . . the Big Society in Scotland will remain forever blocked by the power of the Big Landowners – whoever wins at Holyrood.'[33]

As Shelter notes in a report on housing in rural Scotland: '. . . the huge concentration of land in a small number of hands can distort access to land. And housing investment, just like any other form of investment with long payback periods, may not be helped by the volatile and unregulated land market in Scotland.'[34] For example, 25 percent of estates over 1,000 acres have been held in the same family for over 400 years. In the Highlands, 50 percent haven't been put up for sale since World War II.[35]

As Bryan MacGregor argues, the primary motivation for many of the frequently absentee landlords – which may comprise as many as 66 percent of the owners – is simply sport and private enjoyment, not the needs of the community as a whole.[36]

In 1993, Assynt crofters succeeded in buying the North Lochinver Estate in Sutherland, on which they lived and worked, after the Scandinavian property developer that owned the 21,000-acre estate went bust. This inspired other communities to follow, including the islanders of Eigg (1997) and Gigha (2002), and the people of the Knoydart peninsula (1999), as well as the North Harris Estate (2003).

New Labour did give crofting communities the right to buy their land, abolishing the feudal system and guaranteeing freedom to roam. The 2003 Scottish Land Reform Act made it easier for communities to gain ownership of the land on which they live and work. The Act has been criticised, however, as the right to buy comes into effect only when a landowner is willing to sell. Half of Scotland has not been on the market for over 100 years.

In 2012, Corporatewatch cast a light on one community suffering under a corporate absentee landlord:

The Blackford estate, right next to the Gleneagles estate, represents many of the problems which occur when land is owned by a foreign absentee landlord purely for its commercial value. The estate is home to the Highland Spring company – the second biggest bottled water company in the UK. It is privately owned by a series of holding companies believed to terminate in Mohammed Mahdi al-Tajir, the former Ambassador to the United Arab Emirates to Great Britain and billionaire businessman who made his fortune in oil and property.

Once a thriving rural community, locals claim that the owners have systematically allowed Blackford to fall into disrepair, letting farms lie empty rather than replace new tenants. There is nothing the locals can do except watch their community disintegrate, as all rights lie with the unreachable landowner. This is not an isolated example.[37]

Farther south, another landlord, this time a Scot, has blighted another community:

> In South Lanarkshire the Earl of Home, owner of 30,000 acres, permitted Scottish Coal to open a fifth opencast coal mine within a 5km area near Douglas and Uddington. Here, the nearby communities (who sent over 700 letters of objection to the plan, out of a population of 1000) will be subject to increased noise, a constant stream of Heavy Goods Vehicles, destruction of the local environment and, it is alleged, an increased risk of illness due to poisoned ground water and coal dust. The project spawned a seven month long protest camp which was ultimately evicted by Scottish Coal.'[38]

Scotland is losing huge sums of money in tax avoidance schemes benefitting landowners. In some cases, the real beneficiaries of land take refuge in legal black holes. For example, in 1995 the Duke of Buccleuch had his wealth re-evaluated from £300 million to £40 million in the *Sunday Times* Rich List because his estate was owned by a company in which he did not own any shares. The shares, it turned out, were owned by four Edinburgh lawyers and were worth £4. The money is ultimately held in a trust, and the beneficiaries are unknown.[39]

As Andy Wightman writes: '. . . over 22 per cent and perhaps as much as 25 per cent of the privately owned rural land in Scotland is held in some form of offshore or beneficial ownership where, to varying degrees, the beneficiaries are unknown and tax is being avoided.'[40]

In an investigation undertaken in 2003, Andy Wightman and Torcuil Crichton analysed 500 estates and estimated that the annual loss of tax revenue was around £72 million due to offshore ownership, noting that 'The true figure would be much more if it were possible to survey all of Scotland'.

At the beginning of the last century, Thomas Johnston made this appeal in *Our Scots Noble Families*:

> Show the people that our Old Nobility is not noble, that its lands are stolen lands – stolen either by force or fraud; show people that the title-deeds are rapine, murder, massacre, cheating, or court harlotry; dissolve the halo of divinity that surrounds the hereditary title; let the people clearly understand that our present House of Lords is composed largely of descendants of successful pirates and rogues; do these things and you shatter the Romance that keeps the nation numb and spellbound while privilege picks its pocket.[41]

As late as 1938, Johnston was moving a private member's bill in the Westminster Parliament, which would have nationalised the land.[42] Why not in the twenty-first century? This is a basic right that needs to be revived. Land should be nationalised and controlled by the people who live and work on it.

It Is Our Oil (and Wind, and Waves, and . . .)

In May 2013, the former Labour Chancellor Denis Healey told *Holyrood* magazine that an independent Scotland would 'survive perfectly well' due to North Sea reserves and that the rest of the UK would 'just need to adjust'. He also admitted that the money from North Sea oil in the 1980s had not been used to benefit ordinary people: 'Thatcher wouldn't have been able to carry out her policies without that additional 5 per cent on GDP from oil. Incredible good luck she had from that. It's true we should have invested the money in things we needed in Britain . . .'[43]

BBC Scotland's main morning news programme, *Reporting Scotland*, gave fifteen seconds to this story, despite it being front-page news in that morning's *Scotsman* and the previous day's *Sunday Post*. In contrast, the UK Treasury report into the viability of an independent Scotland's financial sector dominated headlines throughout the day on BBC Scotland and was repeated in regular news bulletins on TV and radio.[44]

Margo MacDonald MSP responded angrily: 'Westminster politicians, in all parties, lied and misinformed about the oil revenues, size of the oilfields and for how long they would produce oil . . . Scots were lied to, the secret Cabinet papers recording that the books had been cooked to make it look as though an independent Scotland would be a poorer place to live . . .'[45]

North Sea oil accounted for 10 percent of the UK government's budget in the 1980s. It was frittered away: 'The government of Margaret Thatcher supported a policy of rapid extraction, making the UK a net oil exporter and generating substantial tax revenues . . .'[46]

The revenue from North Sea oil allowed Thatcher to drive up interest rates and the value of sterling. Both damaged manufacturing by increasing the cost of exports and burdening companies with higher interest rates. She used these measures to sacrifice the 'lame ducks' in order to, supposedly, create a leaner, fitter industrial sector. In reality, it profited the City of London and the finance sector.[47] Now the central UK state is about to do the same, rushing to let corporations exploit natural resources at knock-down prices, in search of a quick inflow of money to the Treasury in Whitehall.

In March 2013, Moray Offshore Renewables (MOR) was given exclusive rights to build the world's biggest offshore wind farm in the Moray Firth. It is hoped it will supply electricity to between 800,000 and 1 million homes, a substantial proportion of Scotland's housing. MOR is a joint venture involving the Spanish oil company Repsol, the Portuguese power group EDP, and China's Three Gorges group, which is wholly owned by the Chinese state. Who gave MOR exclusive rights? The answer is the Crown Estates, a London-based body that controls, on behalf of the House of Windsor, all of the sea bed in Scotland's territorial waters.

Writing in *Scottish Left Review*, Gordon Morgan points out:

MOR pays the Crown Estate a commercially negotiated rent for its rights. No figures are available for this, however, the income from marine rents in 2010/2011 of the Crown Estate for the whole of the UK was £46.5 million. The right to commercially exploit our natural resources does not seem highly valued. The Scottish

Government justifiably wishes devolution of the Crown Estate powers in Scotland.[48]

You might think that in this day and age the land, waters and seabed of a country would belong not to a monarch but to the citizens of that country. If we took control of these natural assets, they could be used in an environmentally friendly way to benefit the people and the country.

A Woman's Place

If any decent society can be judged by its treatment of women, then Scotland today falls short. It would be good to report progress, but it remains a society scarred by sexism and negative images of women. We have got a serious problem affecting the everyday lives of countless women right at home. According to Amnesty International, there is an incident of domestic violence recorded every ten minutes in Scotland, with one woman in five experiencing such abuse in her lifetime. One in three young women who are in a relationship will suffer an unwanted sex act.[49] The report found: 'twenty six percent of Scots surveyed in 2007 thought that a woman bore some responsibility for being raped if she wore revealing clothing.'[50]

In 2009–10 there were 884 cases of rape reported in Scotland. Of these, ninety-two were prosecuted, resulting in forty-one convictions. In 2008–09 the conviction rate was 3 percent of reported rapes.[51]

Between 1997–98 and 2006–07 there was a 90 percent increase in the daily sentenced female population and an 83 percent increase in the number of women jailed on remand. But 56 percent of the adult women admitted to jail were serving sentences under six months.[52]

Women still bear the responsibility for bringing up our children. Childcare costs across the UK are among the highest in Europe, and are a barrier to mothers who choose to return to work. Speaking prior to a debate on childcare in the Scottish Parliament in May 2013, Eileen Dinning, Chair of the Scottish Trades Union Congress (STUC) Women's Committee, argued:

Free childcare would boost the economy and support families to lift them out of poverty, as evidenced by the report by the Institute for Public Policy Research (IPPR) 'Making the Case for Universal Childcare'. Making childcare free at the point of use would be good for families and for public finances as universal childcare would bring a net return to the government of £20,050 over four years for every woman who returned to work after one year of maternity leave.[53]

In 2013, full-time female workers in Scotland earned 14 percent less than male workers, while for part-time jobs the difference is a full 35 percent. The findings were revealed in a report compiled for Glasgow Caledonian University by Emily Thomson, Co-Director of Women in Scotland's Economy Research Centre (WISE), and Morag Gillespie, Senior Research Fellow, Scottish Poverty Information Unit. Thomson concluded: 'While we found some evidence of employers considering the issue of equal pay in their workforce, there was much less evidence of action being taken to make equal pay a reality. This was particularly acute in the private sector.'[54]

In the summer of 2013 it was revealed that fewer than 0.3 percent of apprentices are disabled and fewer than 2 percent were from an ethnic minority. Meanwhile, only 1 percent of construction apprentices were women, according to research for the Equality and Human Rights Commission (EHRC) in Scotland. A total of 11,381 women began an apprenticeship in 2011–12, with women totalling 43.1 percent of all new apprentices.

But the research, by Heriot-Watt University in Edinburgh, said that compared with England, Wales and Northern Ireland, 'Scotland is the only country in which the number of female starts is persistently lower than male starts' and that the other countries had 'succeeded in correcting previous trends of female under-representation in terms of starts'.[55]

The outlook for women, faced with the Westminster austerity drive, is not a happy one, as Mhairi McAlpine outlines:

The austerity currently being imposed is starting to make its presence felt. Attacks on benefits and cut backs in public sector jobs have seen the cuts fall most heavily on women. An estimated 70% of the cuts come directly out of women's pockets, but even this underestimates the burden that is likely to fall on women. With youth unemployment growing, cuts to housing benefit and skewed disability assessments it is likely that many women will be pushed back into caring roles and expected to provide financial, practical and housing support to vulnerable family members who find themselves falling through the holes in the social safety net . . . As benefits is a reserved matter together with legal aid, Scottish women have limited opportunity to challenge these Westminster taken decisions . . . while the NHS sell off in England is likely to see cuts to women's services, many of them time-critical, undermining women's autonomy and reproductive control. While part of the union, we may well see challenges under EU competition legislation to undermine the Scottish NHS, leading to the same issues being replicated up here. Protective legislation which secures workers rights is being systematically diminished . . .[56]

In any discussion regarding a new and better Scotland, the position of women should take centre stage. McAlpine argues:

The women of Scotland must actively engage in the independence debate . . . We have a unique opportunity to redefine our destiny, far too important an opportunity to be left to men in suits dictating from on high, or indeed to be the sole preserve of our male comrades. We must highlight the needs of women and ensure that they come to the fore in any constitutional change. We do not need a woman as the head of state; we don't need any head of state. What we need is women at the head of the destruction of the UK state.[57]

Islamophobia in Scotland

Since the 9/11 attacks in the USA, we have been subjected to a constant barrage of Islamophobia from the media and politicians. It is the ideology of the US-led and UK-backed 'war on terror'. Across Europe, it has seen the return of the politics of exclusion, with bans on the wearing of the niqab and the burqa and on the construction of minarets. It has become commonplace to hear that there is a 'clash of civilisations', between an enlightened West and an Islamic world stuck in a feudal era.

The language and the targeting of individual Muslims, mosques, Islamic schools and cultural centres parallels pre-war anti-Semitism. Yet the divergence between Scottish and English politics finds expression in the current level of Islamophobia in both countries.

In May 2013, a young soldier was hacked to death on the streets of Woolwich, south London, by two men claiming to be acting in the name of Islam. There, Faith Matters, which monitors anti-Muslim hatred, reported that the number of incidents in the six days following the awful murder had risen to 193, including ten assaults on mosques – a fifteen-fold increase in such attacks.[58] I could find no reports of any such attacks in Scotland.

Back in 2005 a survey found that 65 percent of respondents had some degree of favourability towards Muslims. When asked if Muslims were loyal to Scotland, 46 percent said yes. The survey also found evidence of a desire among Muslims to become 'mainstream', while both Muslims and non-Muslims viewed integration in Scotland as 'easier' than in England. 'Scottishness' was identified with friendliness, sociability and having a welcoming disposition.[59]

There were some negatives. Non-Muslims cited the fact that Muslims did not drink alcohol as a barrier to integration into Scottish life, and nearly half of non-Muslims believed further Muslim immigration would dilute the Scottish identity. But it was particularly noteworthy that nearly 70 percent of young Scottish Muslims aged eighteen to twenty-four regarded themselves as integrated into Scottish society.

In 2005, it was found that more than half of Scotland's Pakistani communities had experienced ethnic harassment, but they also reported that they found it easier to identify with Scotland. Scottish Pakistanis felt there was less conflict between Muslims and non-Muslims in Scotland compared with England and that they had become more strongly bound to Scotland since 9/11 and the 2003 invasion of Iraq.[60]

This is not to say Islamophobia and racism do not exist in Scotland and do not scar the land. In May 2013, the *Scotsman* reported:

Hijab headscarves were torn off two Muslim women during one of a spate of racist attacks in Edinburgh by children as young as eight, police said yesterday. The women, in their early twenties, are said to have been 'traumatised' by the incident which happened last week, in which two children hurled racial abuse at them before ripping off the hijabs. The culprits are believed to be aged eight and fourteen. There has been a recent spike in hate crimes against Polish and Muslim residents at Wester Hailes Park in Edinburgh.[61]

In the same month *STV News* reported:

Increased levels of Islamophobia and negative attitudes towards Polish people could be behind a 20 percent rise in racist incidents in Scotland, experts have said. Every day in Scotland, seventeen people are abused, threatened or violently attacked because of the colour of their skin, ethnicity or nationality. 20.4 percent from the 5123 racist incidents recorded in 2008-09. The figures, revealed in a freedom of information request to Scotland's eight police forces, come despite there only being a 13 percent increase over the previous five years.[62]

One white male resident of Glasgow's South Side, when asked about his attitude to Muslims, responded: 'I like to think I have a very humanist outlook on life, I like to judge people as I see them. But September 11th and the press are fighting continually to change my view and I feel as though they are winning a wee bit. It's not for the want of me trying not to fight against that but I feel as though the terrorists involved in September 11th . . . the whole point of their idea was to crystallise world opinion and to a certain extent I think it worked.'[63]

Islamophobia has been a constant presence in our lives since 9/11, and Scots are not immune to the scapegoating of migrants. But the situation is different from that in England. The English Defence League is a real concern, the Scottish Defence League thus far insignificant. The fascist British National Party has failed to impact on Scotland, gaining no electoral success. In England, it has been a different story.

CONCLUSION:

Our Destiny Is In Our Hands

The people of Scotland are no better or worse than the people of any other country. Like them, we have our share of villains and those who have committed wrong towards their fellow human beings. But Scotland has also contributed more than its fair share of rebels, those women and men who have championed the downtrodden, the victims of injustice and the oppressed. Today Scotland is scarred by a deep divide between those enjoying great wealth and those who live in fear of poverty, with many already struggling to feed their family or heat their home.

Let us start with those who live not simply in comfort but who possess extraordinary wealth. As in every other country, the last three decades of unbridled free-market capitalism has led to a growing imbalance in society, with an explosion of wealth at the top. Far from that 'trickling down' to the great majority below, their lives have become more insecure.

At the top ring of society, Scotland, proportionally, has the highest number of millionaires in the UK outside London and the southeast. Between 2008 and 2010 the number increased by 18 percent, from 34,000 to 40,000. This is predicted to grow by 38 percent by 2020, the second-fastest rate of any UK region.[1] The number of Scots among Britain's wealthiest people reached a ten-year high in 2013 with the *Sunday Times* Rich List finding that 78 people based in Scotland had joined its ranks.

The number of Scottish billionaires has grown from two to six in two years, with Mahdi al-Tajir, head of the Highland Spring mineral water firm, named as Scotland's richest person, worth £1.65 billion. The eighty-one-year-old former UAE ambassador to the UK has a 24,000-acre estate near Gleneagles, Perthshire, and splits his time between there and London. He is the forty-fourth-richest person in the UK and has interests in metal, oil and gas trading and a large property portfolio, as well as running Highland Spring.

He is joined on the list by the Grant and Gordon whisky family, worth £1.4 billion; the oil tycoon Sir Ian Wood, £1.2 billion; the Thomson family, whose DC Thomson publishing company is valued at £1.1 billion; Alastair Salveson and his family, who have a £1.05 billion share of Aggreko, the Glasgow plant-hire firm; and the businessman Jim McColl, worth £1 billion. The combined wealth of Scotland's 100 richest people amounts to a record £21.1 billion, almost double the level in 2004.[2]

The country also has the distinction of having the highest proportion of Michelin-starred restaurants per millionaire, and this number is rising. Scotland has a luxury appetite, or at least some Scots have, together with the highest incidence of high-end car dealerships per millionaire and the second-highest in the UK of luxury retail stores.[3] One in four children in Edinburgh attends a fee-paying school; in north-east Glasgow, 35 percent leave school with no qualifications.[4]

Iain McWhirter notes: 'You could scarcely think of a less socialist city than Edinburgh, where 25 percent of school children go to private schools and average house prices are ten times Scotland's median wage.'[5]

The vast majority of these wealthy people owe their position to inherited wealth and a privileged upbringing. Few began trading from a market barrow and climbed up the pole to found a multinational corporation. The Scottish upper class has always formed an integral part of the British ruling class – it is not the case that since 1707 we have been under English rule: they must take responsibility for the crimes of Empire and of British imperialism, and the crimes they committed against their own. Who better to hold them to account than the people of Scotland?

In September 2014, the Scottish people will have a unique opportunity when they will be asked in a referendum to vote Yes or No in favour of Scottish independence. In the official debate on that choice, discussion centres on Scotland's constitutional position, whether it will maintain sterling and so on. But let's pose the question differently. The people of Scotland are being asked if they would like to create a new state, and that could be a very different place – one based in pursuing the interests of the many, not the few.

Yes, Scotland is blighted by the growing extremes of wealth and poverty, but that has been exacerbated by our membership of the United Kingdom, the fourth most unequal nation in the developed world, and it's getting worse. This has been true for the last thirty years. We pay the price in terms of child poverty, ill health, low educational achievement and much more. Back in 2008 the average income of the richest 10 percent of earners in the UK was almost twelve times that of the bottom 10 percent, up from eight times in 1985. The annual average income in the UK for the top 10 percent in 2008 was just under £55,000; the bottom 10 percent averaged £4,700.[6]

Since the financial crash of 2008 and the recession that followed, matters have got worse because rather than blunting the neo-liberal offensive of the previous three decades, the crash has intensified it. Our pensions are under attack, privatisation continues, the numbers in insecure work grow, and there is a government drive to remove the disabled and the sick from benefits and much more.

Since 2010, this has been taking place under a Westminster government, a coalition of the Tories and Liberal Democrats, that once more has no mandate in Scotland. The Labour opposition accuses them of implementing their austerity programme too fast, but accepts the need to cut welfare and public spending in order to pay off a budget deficit largely caused by using £1.3 billion to bail out the banks in 2008 – despite their responsibility for the implosion of the financial system. Prior to that, under Thatcher and then Tony Blair, British governments enjoyed a tragic love affair with the City of London and the financial services centred there.

The result is a massive economic imbalance within the United Kingdom. It can boast the greatest distance between rich and poor regions than any other state in Europe. Back in 1989, London produced just over 150 percent of the average for the UK economy. By 2009 that was up to 175 percent. In the autumn of 2013, it was revealed that after five years of austerity and cuts, London's economy was doing even better than at the height of the boom which preceded the 2008 financial crash – in contrast, nearly every other part of the UK has seen its economy shrink. London and the south-east were racing away from the rest of the UK.[7] During the boom from 1997 to 2006, the south-east was responsible for 37 percent of the UK's growth in output. Since the crash of 2007, however, its share has rocketed to 48 percent.[8] It should be added that the great majority of the people of London suffer from a shocking imbalance between rich and poor.

In other words, the financiers and bankers based in London helped drive the global and UK economy to the wall, but rather than being punished they have continued to coin it in at our expense. Writing in the spring of 2012, the editor of *Scottish Left Review*, Robin MacAlpine, reminds us of the problems facing the UK economy, and Scotland's as a consequence of our membership of that state:

> Low productivity, low pay, inequality, inherent economic instability, weak real exports, lack of investment in research and development and all the rest are much more to do with the structure of the labour market. We have pointlessly high wages at the top, unacceptably low wages at the bottom, nothing much in between and no link between economic growth and individual prosperity. Just to remind you, the last ten pre-crash years of economic growth in the UK lifted average wages by zero . . . The real failure of the UK economic policy is the failure to stimulate industrial production. Between 1990 and 2011, the following are the rates of change in industrial production: Austria 99 per cent, Canada 35 per cent, Finland 83 per cent, USA 50 per cent, Germany 32 per cent, Sweden 54 per cent, the UK –1.2 per cent. Could the UK's economic failure be summed up more concisely?[9]

Failure to invest has been one of the features of the UK economy since the close of the nineteenth century. British capitalists preferred investing abroad or in financial speculation than at home, while high levels of military spending meant low levels of spending on education, transport and the country's infrastructure.

In May 2013, the *Guardian* revealed that this problem has not gone away: 'According to an analysis by the House of Commons library, Britain invests a lower percentage of GDP than any other of the leading western industrial nations. The figures . . . show that while most G8 countries have increased investment as a proportion of national income since 2010, Britain suffered the biggest fall of any G8 country apart from Italy.'[10]

On a wider front, membership of the United Kingdom means being trapped in a state that despite austerity is willing to spend billions earmarked to replace Trident in order to cling to its position as a world power. Maintaining that great-power status, despite the UK's relentless economic decline, means clinging to the coat tails of the United States – the cost of which is that the UK is a country virtually permanently at war. Far from bringing any benefits, it means that across the globe millions of people who have been militarily occupied, subject to drone attacks and bombing or simply had a pro-Western dictatorship foisted on them hate the United Kingdom in second place to the United States.

Where does Scotland stand today? For the vast majority of working people real poverty and economic distress were the reality for their grandparents or great-grandparents. It was only in the mid-1950s that living standards rose so that people could afford some of the comforts of life, that decent housing was made available and a welfare state came into existence that could offer a safety net for those forced out of work.

The sad truth is that the two or three post-war decades, which coincided with the longest economic boom in capitalist history, were the exception in our history. Like many, I was assured by my parents in the 1960s that I would not have to live through what had blighted their youth – mass unemployment, fascism and war. I was the first in my family to go to university and the future seemed assured. But economic bad times returned in the mid-1970s, and have never been far away since. Today, the consensus among our rulers and across wider society is that far from things getting better for our children, future generations can expect a fall in living standards and less job security. If they go to university they will not get the sort of grant I received from the state, they will have to borrow money to live on and leave college with a debt. Few in current circumstances will be able to afford to buy a house, and unlike in the 1950s, 1960s and 1970s there are few council homes available – precariousness in housing will be added to precariousness in work. Added to this, they are being told they will have to work into their late 60s and will have to pay more than their parents did if they want a half-decent pension.

It's not a cheery picture, but it's one that's common across Europe and North America. It is one of the fundamental reasons we have seen powerful movements challenge neo-liberalism and the free-market policies shared by governments whether of the centre right or centre left. Hopefully working people in Scotland will continue to resist as they did in huge numbers in 2003 over the invasion of Iraq, in 2005 over global poverty and more recently against austerity.

And there are good reasons people should take to the streets and vote to exit austerity in September 2014. This is a snapshot of where Scotland stands in the autumn of 2013:

- As the Westminster government proclaims an economic recovery, unemployment in Scotland is over 7 percent.[11]
- Youth unemployment was over 22 percent in August 2013, with 96,000 16–24-year-olds jobless, a 27 percent increase since 2009.[12]
- 160,000 children are living in poverty, 16 percent of our youth. That figure is widely expected to rise as a result of the Coalition government's austerity measures.[13]
- One third of Scottish families and 56 percent of pensioners are affected by fuel poverty, with gas and electricity prices increasing further, this in an energy-rich country; 28,000 people died of cold in the 2011–12 winter. The UK mortality rate from inadequate heating is one of the highest in Europe, and deaths in Scotland exceed those in England and Wales.[14]

Aberdeen, because of oil wealth, is one of the wealthiest cities in the UK. Barry Douglas is the minister of Kings Community Church in the city's Seaton district, where 29 percent of the local people live below the poverty line. He runs a food bank distributing food to those in need. He described one couple who'd turned up after the man had a heart attack and was forced to give up work. This man had never claimed benefits in his life and was trying to make ends meet as he waited for the paperwork to get sorted: 'They'd worked all their lives and never once looked for or needed charity. But they came to us completely starving and at their wits' end. It was heartbreaking. We ended up giving them five bags of food.'

He also related how the church stepped in when a young mum had her money stopped because she was a few minutes late for her benefits' appointment: 'She was very vulnerable and very frightened. She was a couple of minutes late and they stopped her benefits. She did not have a single penny to buy food for herself or her children.'[15]

Life expectancy in Scotland for both women and men is poor compared to the rest of the United Kingdom, standing at 75.8 years for males and 80.3 years for females. This was the lowest among the UK countries. The figures for the UK were 78.1 for men and 82.1 for women.[16] Elsewhere in northern and western Europe, it's between three and five years lower than in Denmark, Norway, Iceland, Finland and Ireland.[17]

Huge differences remain between the death rates of the richest and poorest people living in Scotland. Scottish Public Health Observatory (ScotPHO) figures revealed that in 2011 there were 424 deaths per 100,000 people from the most affluent 10 percent of the population. But this rate more than doubled to 1,014 per 100,000 in the least-well-off group.[18]

In Glasgow, male life expectancy in Dalmarnock, Calton, Kinning Park and Townhead is below sixty: Britain, as a country, passed this mark during World War II. While poverty is concentrated in the East End of Glasgow, inequality exists across Scotland. The difference in life expectancy between the best and worst postcode areas is twenty-two years in Edinburgh, seventeen years in Paisley, fifteen years in Perthshire and nine years in the Highlands.[19]

A child born in Calton, in the East End of Glasgow, is three times as likely to suffer heart disease, four times as likely to be hospitalised and ten times more likely to grow up in a workless household than a child in the city's prosperous western suburbs.

In contrast, Scotland's top neighbourhoods (in the west of Scotland, Bearsden, Milngavie, Lenzie, Clarkston and Kilmacolm) offer an outstanding quality of life, with high salaries, reasonable house prices and a life expectancy longer than the average for any country in the developed world. This is the reality of life in one of the world's richest countries, a country with enormous resources of oil, renewable energy and water. If those resources were used for the benefit of the many, all of these ills could be reversed. But that cannot happen within the United Kingdom. We saw how successive Westminster governments frittered away the revenues from North Sea oil, and lied about the possible benefits they could bring a Scotland in charge of its own finances. Today we do not even control the sea bed around our land, and cannot ensure that the benefits of wind and tidal farms are not spent on war, nuclear missiles and tax breaks for the rich. It is not revolutionary to demand, for example, a programme of job creation, aimed at creating real skills.

The message from the Tories, Labour and Liberal Democrats at Westminster is that we have to accept austerity for the foreseeable future. But we are not 'all in it together' as David Cameron claims. We are picking up the bill while those at the top party on.

An independent Scotland should refuse to foot the bill for bailing out the global financial system – in solidarity with the people of Greece, Spain, Portugal and Ireland whose lives have been dealt a body blow by even harsher austerity programmes imposed on them undemocratically by the European Union and the International Monetary Fund. As for two of the biggest recipients of bail-out largesse, the Royal Bank of Scotland (RBS) and HBoS – the largest elements of Scottish big business – they could and should be taken entirely into public hands and run democratically in the public interest.

The objection to independence is that this is far from the vision of Scotland being offered by the SNP government. The First Minister, Alex Salmond, was quite willing to condemn the 'casino capitalism' of the City of London but would not say a word against his former employers at RBS, undoubtedly among the most foul and disreputable elements of British capitalism.[20] The SNP government's vision for Scotland is one complete with the Queen, NATO, the pound and neo-liberalism – which makes it imperative that there has to be a radical vision of what Scotland could be.

The forecast for what's on offer from Westminster is more austerity, more war and more free-market measures. Westminster is addicted to war and in love with the City of London. Over three decades that's beggared the lives of millions of us. It's time for change, surely? Further, it trails behind the USA in any war or human rights violation in a desperate effort to maintain the supposed 'special relationship'.

If the vote in September 2014 is about the creation of a new state then it should be one that benefits the people of Scotland. One that is more democratic than the UK state, more equal and committed to the needs and welfare of its people.

Surely the road to that better Scotland would be less rocky in an independent country, and possibly make it that bit easier to deal with our supposed rulers. Scotland is a class-divided country no better or worse than any other but we have a chance to take control of our destiny. There's nothing guaranteed, but surely we can deal with our own rapacious ruling class and move on to a better society than this.

The United Kingdom is an obstacle to radical change for all its inhabitants, in thrall to its own past – witness the endless royal and state occasions growing as the economic situation worsens for the vast bulk of us.

The Scottish people have a chance to escape. Some of our sisters and brothers in Liverpool, Newcastle and Doncaster say 'Don't leave us in Tory hands!' But if you were offered the chance for your prison wing to escape you would not insist on staying to suffer alongside the rest. You'd hope your example would inspire them, and organise to help them from the outside.

If we can create a more just and equal Scotland it could help refute the idea popularised by Thatcher that 'there is no alternative' to the free market. Some of us are thinking further, to Maclean's idea of a

Workers' Republic, a dream we hold in our hearts and minds. Many more look back to the legacy of 'Old Labour' and the creation in 1945 of the welfare state. The best way of ensuring that it survives is to break with the policies of successive Westminster governments, which have eroded it relentlessly.

The Glaswegian novelist Alasdair Gray has written of how, post-war, he benefitted from a decent, low-cost council home and from free education. He states simply: 'We do not want an independent Scotland because we dislike the English, but because we want separation from that union of military, financial and monarchic establishments calling itself the United Kingdom.'[21]

Throughout this book we have heard the voices of ordinary Scots who have stood up and put themselves on the line in pursuit of justice, equality and the greater good. Come referendum day we know what some of them – John Maclean, James Connolly, Harry McShane and Jimmy Reid, for instance – would have said, which is to say yes to independence. They supported that because they were internationalists and democrats.

I think it's a safe bet to say that the bulk of those voices heard in this book would say, 'It's time to go.' If we can take control of our destiny and the wealth of this country in our own hands the Scottish people can go forward to make a far better chapter in their history.

Acknowledgements

I have been lucky to know some of the people I have written about and quoted in this book. As a young student I had to pick up Harry McShane to bring him to a student meeting in Edinburgh and could not believe I was in the same car as someone who had been John Maclean's right-hand man. I was in Hamish Henderson's company at Sandy Bells and Morris and Marion Blythman's daughter Joanna took me to meet them over dinner and good malt afterwards.

Mike Davis and Tariq Ali suggested I write this book and for that I am grateful but also owe them a debt for the inspiration they have given me over the years.

My engagement with Scotland's national question began some four decades ago. The late Neil Williamson wrote on independence as part of a debate among members of the International Marxist Group to which I belonged in both Edinburgh and Glasgow in the 1970s. In the following decade my own clumsy attempts to write on it were superseded by those of Neil Davidson who's *Discovering the Scottish Revolution, 1692–1746* I would urge everyone to read.

James Foley and Pete Ramand were writing their own book on the Scottish question at the same time as me, and far from being rivals I learned much from them, and I hope they too learned a wee bit from me. Marion Blythman and Jenny Donaldson also commented on what I wrote about the Women's Liberation Movement in Scotland.

I owe thanks to Jonathon Shafi, key organiser of the Radical Independence Campaign, as well as thanks to all the comrades of the International Socialist Group in Scotland.

My editor at Verso, Leo Hollis, was my best critic and a tower of strength. Thanks to him and all the team at Verso.

Lastly, apologies to my partner, Carmela, and to our two sons, Malcolm and Leonardo, for the time this project took away from them and for keeping the boys off the computer; double apologies to them for lumping them in with supporting Hibs – as well as Arsenal and Roma. No apologies that they can choose to be Italian or Scots or both – a great choice.

Any mistakes or faults are my responsibility. Whether the analysis is right, we can debate.

Notes

1. Scotland Emerges

1 '10,000 Years Old: World's Oldest Calendar Found in Scottish Field', *Herald*, 15 July 2013
2 Friedrich Engels, *The Origins of the Family, Private Property and the State*, Resistance Books, 2004, p. 67
3 Gordon Menzies (ed.), *Who Are the Scots and the Scottish Nation?*, Edinburgh University Press, 2002, p. 9
4 A. P. Fitzpatrick, 'The Submission of the Orkney Islands to Claudius: New Evidence?' *Scottish Archaeological Review* 8, 1989, pp. 123–29
5 Neil Oliver, *History of Scotland*, Weidenfeld and Nicolson, 2009, pp. 36–37
6 Chris Wickham, *The Inheritance of Rome: A History of Europe from 400 to 1000*, Allen Lane, 2009, p. 154
7 Ibid.
8 Ian Johnston, 'The Truth About the Picts', *The Independent*, 6 August 2008
9 N. J. Higham, *The Convert Kings: Power and Religious Affiliation in Early Anglo-Saxon England*, Manchester University Press, 1997, pp. 255–60; William Douglas Simpson, *The Historical Saint Columba*, Oliver & Boyd, 1963, p. 46
10 James Earle Fraser, *From Caledonia to Pictland: Scotland to 795*, Edinburgh University Press, 2009, p. 215
11 Neil Oliver, *History of Scotland*, pp. 56–57
12 G. W. S. Barrow, 'Anglo-French Influences', in Gordon Menzies (ed.), *Who Are the Scots and the Scottish Nation?*, pp. 89–90
13 Robert Bartlett, *The Making of Europe: Conquest, Colonization and Cultural Change, 950–1350*, Penguin, 1994, pp. 54–55
14 T. C. Smout, *A History of the Scottish People: 1560–1830*, Fontana Press, 1987, pp. 27–28

15 Thomas Johnston, *The History of the Working Classes in Scotland*, Forward Publishing (no date), pp. 21–22
16 Ibid., p. 73

2. The Wars of Independence

1 The Society of Ancient Scots, *Lives of Scottish Poets*, Volume 1, T. Boys, 1821–22, made available by David Hill Radcliffe (ed.), Centre for Applied Technologies in the Humanities, Virginia Tech, pp. 51–52, http://scotspoets.cath.vt.edu/select.php?select=Wyntoun._Andrew, accessed 17 September 2012
2 Thomas Johnston, *The History of the Working Classes in Scotland*, p. 32
3 Patrick Fraser Tytler, *History of Scotland*, William Tait, 1828, p. 122
4 Andy King and David Simkin, *England and Scotland at War, c.1296–c.1513*, Brill, 2012, p. 43
5 A. D. M. Barrell, *Medieval Scotland*, Cambridge University Press, 2000, pp. 127–28
6 Neil Oliver, *A History of Scotland*, pp. 89–90
7 Hector MacMillan, *Handful of rogues: Thomas Muir's enemies of the people*, Argyll, 2005, p. 248
8 G. W. S. Barrow, *Robert the Bruce and the Community of the Realm of Scotland*, Edinburgh University Press, 2005, pp. 113–16
9 Andy King and David Simkin, *England and Scotland at War, c.1296–c.1513*, pp. 49–50
10 G. W. S. Barrow, *Robert the Bruce and the Community of the Realm of Scotland*, pp. 132–35
11 Thomas Johnston, *The History of the Working Classes in Scotland*, p. 23
12 G. W. S. Barrow, *Robert the Bruce and the Community of the Realm of Scotland*, pp. 177–79
13 Ibid., p. 179
14 A. D. M. Barrell, *Medieval Scotland*, p. 113
15 Ibid., p. 117
16 Christopher Harvie, *Scotland and Nationalism: Scottish Society and Politics, 1707–1977*, George Allen and Unwin, 1977, p. 23
17 A. D. M. Barrell, *Medieval Scotland*, p. 135
18 Katie Stevenson, *Chivalry and Knighthood in Scotland: 1424–1513*, Boydell Press, 2006, p. 152
19 Neil Davidson. 'Marx and Engels on the Scottish Highlands', *Science & Society* 65 (2001), no. 3, p. 314
20 T. C. Smout, *A History of the Scottish People 1560–1830*, p. 38
21 Neil Davidson, 'Marx and Engels on the Scottish Highlands', p. 317
22 Neil Oliver, *A History of Scotland*, p. 132

3. Reformation and the War of the Three Kingdoms

1 Neil Davidson, *Discovering the Scottish Revolutions: 1692–1746*, Pluto Press, 2003, p. 24
2 Thomas Johnston, *The History of the Working Classes in Scotland*, p. 44
3 Gordon Donaldson, *Scotland: James V to James VII*, Oliver and Boyd, 1971, pp. 215–28, 284–90
4 Ross Cowan, 'Lairds of the Battle', *Military History Monthly*, 32 (2013), May
5 Victor Kiernan, 'Banner with a Strange Device: The Later Covenanters', in Terry Brotherstone (ed.), *Covenant, Charter and Party: Traditions of Revolt and Protest in Modern Scottish History*, Aberdeen University Press, 1989, p. 25
6 Thomas Johnston, *The History of the Working Classes in Scotland*, p. 146
7 Edward J. Cameron, 'Andrew Fletcher and the Scottish Radical Political Tradition', in P. H. Scott (ed.), *The Saltoun Papers: Reflections on Andrew Fletcher*, Saltire Society, 2003, p. 161
8 John Coffey, *Politics, Religion and the British Revolution: The Mind of Samuel Rutherford*, Cambridge University Press, 1997, p. 35
9 I. J. Gentiles, *The English Revolution and the Wars in the Three Kingdoms, 1638–1652*, Pearson, 2007, p. 6
10 Rev. W. P. Breed, *Jenny Geddes or Presbyterianism and Its Great Conflict with Despotism*, Philadelphia Presbyterian Board of Publication, 1869, pp. 18–19
11 Ralph Lownie, *Auld Reekie: An Edinburgh Anthology*, Random House, 2011, p. 137
12 Professor John Stuart Blackie, 'The Ballad of Jenny Geddes', 1842, http://grantian.blogspot.co.uk/2005/04/ballad-of-jennie-geddes.html, accessed 26 April 2013
13 Victor Kiernan, 'Banner with a Strange Device: The Later Covenanters', p. 31
14 I. J. Gentiles, *The English Revolution and the Wars in the Three Kingdoms, 1638–1652*, p. 3
15 T. C. Smout, *A History of the Scottish People: 1560–1830*, p. 153
16 Christopher Hill, *Reformation to Industrial Revolution*, Penguin, 1971, pp. 165–66
17 Neal Ascherson, *Stone Voices: The Search for Scotland*, Granta Books, 2003, pp. 278–79
18 Richard L. Greaves, *Enemies Under His Feet: Radicals and Nonconformists in Britain, 1664–1677*, Stanford University Press, 1990, pp. 66–74
19 Ibid., p. 78
20 Neal Ascherson, *Stone Voices: The Search for Scotland*, p. 280
21 Peter Hume Brown, *A History of Scotland to the Present Time*, Oliver and Boyd, 1908, pp. 323–25
22 Edward J. Cameron, 'Andrew Fletcher and the Scottish Radical Political Tradition', p. 162
23 Neil Oliver, *A History of Scotland*, p. 238
24 Lewis Grassic Gibbon, *A Scots Quair*, Penguin, 1986, p. 464
25 T. C. Smout, *A History of the Scottish People: 1560–1830*, pp. 165–66

4. Union, Jacobites and Popular Unrest

1 Winnie Ewing, *Stop the World: The Autobiography of Winnie Ewing*, Birlinn, 2004, p. 291

2 Neil Davidson, *Discovering the Scottish Revolution, 1692–1746*, Pluto, 2003, p. 109

3 http://www.robertburns.org/works/344.shtml, accessed 26 April 2012

4 T. M. Devine, *The Scottish Nation 1700–2000*, Allen Lane, 1999, p. 32

5 John Leonard Roberts, *Clan, King, and Covenant: A History of the Highland Clans from the Civil War to the Glencoe Massacre*, Edinburgh University Press, 2000, pp. 187–94

6 Ibid., pp. 233–35

7 T. C. Smout, *A History of the Scottish People 1560–1830*, pp. 184–85

8 Karen J. Cullen, *Famine in Scotland: The 'Ill Years' of the 1690s*, Edinburgh University Press, 2010, pp. 50–51

9 T. C. Smout, *A History of the Scottish People 1560–1830*, p. 201

10 Neil Davidson, *Discovering the Scottish Revolution, 1692–1746*, p. 99

11 Christopher A. Whatley and Derek J. Patrick, *The Scots and the Union*, Edinburgh University Press, 2006, p. 11

12 'How Was This Kingdom United?' *Socialist Worker*, 2 October 2004, accessed 27 April 2013

13 Christopher Harvie, *Scotland and Nationalism: Scottish Society and Politics 1707–1977*, George Allen and Unwin, 1977, p. 64

14 Christopher A. Whatley and Derek J. Patrick, *The Scots and the Union*, pp. 11–12

15 Ibid.

16 Neil Davidson, *The Origins of Scottish Nationhood*, Pluto Press, 2000, p. 54

17 T. M. Devine, *The Scottish Nation 1700–2000*, p. 14

18 Rosalind Mitchison, *Lordships to Patronage: Scotland 1603–1745*, Edinburgh University Press, 1983, pp. 154–55

19 Neil Davidson, *Discovering the Scottish Revolution*, p. 216

20 Alistair Livingston, 'The Galloway Levellers: A Study of the Origins, Events and Consequences of their Actions', a dissertation submitted to the Faculty of Arts, University of Glasgow, for the degree of M. Phil. (Research) in History, May 2009, p. 7, http://theses.gla.ac.uk/874/01/2009livingstonmphil.pdf, accessed 16 October 2012

21 Ibid., p. 55

22 Chris Bambery, 'The "Nineteen" – The Forgotten Jacobite Rebellion of 1719', *Military History Monthly*, June 2012

23 Alistair Livingston, 'The Galloway Levellers', p. 7

24 Neil Davidson, *Discovering the Scottish Revolution*, p. 257

25 Alistair Livingston, 'The Galloway Levellers', p. 65

26 Ibid., p. 86

27 Peter Aitchison and Andrew Cassell, *The Lowland Clearances, Scotland's Silent Revolution*, Tuckwell, 2003 p. 49

28 Christopher A. Whatley, *Scottish Society 1707–1830: Beyond Jacobitism, Towards Industrialisation*, Manchester University Press, 2000, pp. 154–56

29 Ibid., pp. 189–92

30 Ibid., p. 192
31 Ibid., pp. 167–68
32 Ibid., p. 197
33 Ibid., pp. 197–98
34 Ibid., p. 198
35 Ibid.
36 Murray Pittock, *The Myth of the Jacobite Clans*, Edinburgh University Press, 1995, p. 60
37 Stephen Brumwell, *Paths of Glory: The Life and Death of General James Wolfe*, Continuum, 2006, pp. 53–54
38 Ibid.
39 Ibid.
40 John Prebble, *Culloden*, Penguin, 1996, p. 301
41 Ian Gilmour, *Riot, Rising and Revolution: Governance and Violence in 18th Century England*, Hutchinson, 1992, pp. 105
42 Neil Davidson, *Discovering the Scottish Revolution*, pp. 244–47

5. Enlightenment and Capitalism

1 Sir Walter Scott, *Waverley*, Claire Lamont (ed.), Oxford University Press, 2008, p. 34
2 Fernand Braudel, *The Perspective of the World: Civilisation and Capitalism, 15th–18th Century*, vol. 3, Phoenix Press, 2002, p. 372
3 Ibid.
4 Austin Cramb, *Fragile Land: The State of the Scottish Environment*, Edinburgh University Press, 1998, p. 194
5 Neil Davidson, *The Origins of Scottish Nationhood*, p. 110
6 Linda Colley, *Britons: Forging the Nation 1707–1837*, Yale, 1992, p. 130
7 Neil Davidson, *The Origins of Scottish Nationhood*, pp. 94–95
8 Rosalind Mitchison, *Lordships to Patronage: Scotland 1603–1745*, Edinburgh University Press, 1983, p. 162
9 Hugh John Massingberd, *The Great Houses of Scotland*, Laurence King, 1997, pp. 83–91
10 Michael Fry, *The Dundas Despotism*, Edinburgh University Press, 1992, p. 1
11 Ibid., p. 4
12 A. P. W. Malcolmson, *The Pursuit of the Heiress: Aristocratic Marrriage in Ireland 1740–1840*, Ulster Historical Foundation, 2006, pp. 222–24
13 T. C. Smout, *A History of the Scottish People: 1560–1830*, pp. 299–300
14 Arthur Herman, *How the Scots Invented the Modern World: The True Story of How Western Europe's Poorest Nation Created Our World & Everything in It*, Crown Publishers, 2001, pp. 20–21
15 T. C. Smout, *A History of the Scottish People: 1560–1830*, p. 215
16 Neil Oliver, *A History of Scotland*, 2009, p. 307
17 T. C. Smout, *A History of the Scottish People: 1560–1830*, p. 246
18 Christopher Harvie, *Scotland and Nationalism: Scottish Society and Politics 1707–1977*, p. 128
19 Adam Smith, *The Works of Adam Smith: The Nature and Causes of the Wealth of Nations*, T. Cadell, 1812, p. 6

20 Ibid., p. 7
21 Ibid., p. 88
22 Adam Ferguson, *An Essay on the History of Civil Society*, Edinburgh University Press, 1966, p. 187
23 Adam Hochschild, *Bury the Chains: The British Struggle to Abolish Slavery*, Macmillan, 2005, pp. 25–27
24 Ibid., pp. 170 and 202
25 Ibid., p. 228 Robert Crawford, *The Bard*, Random House, 2011, p. 383
26 Jock Morris, 'The Patriot Bard', in Chris Bambery (ed.), *Scotland, Class and Nation*, Bookmarks, 1999, p. 149
27 Alexander Wilson, *The Chartist Movement in Scotland*, Manchester University Press, 1970, p. 88

6. Radicals and Chartists

1 Iain Gray, 'Six Strikers Who Wove a Legend: The Calton Weavers', scottishrepublicansocialistmovement.org/Pages/SRSMArticlesSixStrikerswhowoveaLegend.aspx, accessed 25 March 2013
2 H. W. Meikle, *Scotland and the French Revolution*, Frank Cass, 1969, p. 64
3 Iain Gray, 'Six Strikers Who Wove a Legend: The Calton Weavers'
4 Ibid.
5 Donnie Fraser, 'The Dawn of Republicanism', scottishrepublicansocialistmovement.org/Pages/SRSMTheDawnofRepublicanism.aspx, accessed 23 April 2013
6 Samuel Bernstein, *Essays in Political and Intellectual History*, Ayer, 1969, p. 42
7 John McGowan, *Policing the Metropolis of Scotland: A History of the Police and Systems of Police in Edinburgh & Edinburghshire, 1770–1833*, Turlough Publishers, 2010, p. 92
8 Rosalind Mitchison, *A History of Scotland*, Routledge, 1985, p. 363
9 Alternative Perthshire, 'Friends of the People and the United Scotsmen', alternative-perth.co.uk/frdspeople.htm, accessed 24 September 2012
10 Donnie Fraser, 'The Dawn of Republicanism'
11 H. W. Meikle, *Scotland and the French Revolution*, pp. 96–97
12 Thomas Johnston, *The History of the Working Classes in Scotland*, p. 219
13 Kenneth J. Logue, *Popular Disturbances in Scotland 1780–1815*, John Donald, 1979, p. 14
14 Ian Bell, *Robert Louis Stevenson: Dreams of Exile*, Mainstream Publishing, 1992, p. 34
15 John Hostettler, *Dissenters, Radicals, Heretics and Blasphemers: The Flame of Revolt That Shines Through English History*, Waterside Press, 2012, p. 142
16 Carl B. Cone, *The English Jacobins: Reformers in Late 18th Century England*, Transaction Publishers, 2010, p. 185
17 Peter Mackenzie, *The Life of Thomas Muir, Esq. Advocate, Younger of Huntershill, Near Glasgow*, W. R. McPhun, 1831, p. 107
18 Thomas Johnston, *The History of the Working Classes in Scotland*, p. 219
19 Thomas Alfred Jackson, *Trials of British Freedom: Being Some Studies in the History of the Fight for Democratic Freedom in Britain*, Ayer Publishing, 1940, p. 39

20 Ibid., pp. 43–45
21 Thomas Johnston, *The History of the Working Classes in Scotland*, p. 226
22 J. M. Bumsted, *Lord Selkirk: A Life*, University of Manitoba Press, 2008, p. 54; and Edward Royle, *Revolutionary Britannia: Reflections on the Threat of Revolution in Britain, 1789–1848*, Manchester University Press, 2000, p. 20
23 Christopher A. Whatley, *Scottish Society 1707-1830: Beyond Jacobitism, Towards Industrialisation*, Manchester University Press, 2000, p. 289
24 W. Hamish Fraser, *Scottish Popular Politics: From Radicalism to Labour*, Edinburgh University Press, 2000, p. 20
25 Thomas Johnston, *The History of the Working Classes in Scotland*, p. 230
26 Ibid.
27 Alternative Perthshire, 'Friends of the People and the United Scotsmen', alternative-perth.co.uk/frdspeople.htm, accessed 24 September, 2012
28 H. W. Meikle, *Scotland and the French Revolution*, Frank Cass, 1969, pp. 152–53
29 Rosalind Mitchison, *A History of Scotland*, p. 363
30 David R. Ross, *A Passion for Scotland*, Luath Press, 2003 p. 123
31 Gordon Pentland, 'The French Revolution, Scottish Radicalism and the "People Who Were Called Jacobins"', in Ulrich Broich, H. T. Dickinson, Eckhart Hellmuth and Martin Schmidt (eds), *Reactions to Revolution: The 1790s and Their Aftermath*, Lit Verlag, 2007, p. 99
32 Ibid., p. 100
33 Ibid., p. 101
34 Linas Eriksonas, *National Heroes and National Identities: Scotland, Norway, and Lithuania*, Peter Lang, 2004, p. 141
35 Dick Gaughan Song Archive, 'Thomas Muir of Huntershill', dickgaughan.co.uk/songs/texts/thommuir.html, accessed 1 May 2013
36 T. M. Devine, *The Scottish Nation 1700–2000*, Allen Lane, 1999, pp. 222–23
37 John McGowan, *Policing the Metropolis of Scotland: A History of the Police and Systems of Police in Edinburgh & Edinburghshire, 1770–1833*, p. 202
38 Ibid., p. 214
39 *Edinburgh Magazine*, 19 September 1837, in *The Edinburgh Magazine*, vol. 5, July–December 1819, Archibald Constable, 1819, p. 276
40 T. Clarke and T. Dickson, 'Class and Class Consciousness in Early Industrial Capitalism, Paisley 1770–1850', in T. Dickson (ed.), *Capital and Class in Scotland*, John Donald, 1982, p. 38
41 Linas Eriksonas, *National Heroes and National Identities: Scotland, Norway, and Lithuania*, p. 142
42 T. M. Devine, *The Scottish Nation 1700–2000*, p. 226
43 Rosalind Mitchison and G. W. S. Barrow, *Why Scottish History Matters*, Saltire Society, 1997, p. 86
44 James Brown, *From Radicalism to Socialism: Paisley Engineers 1890-1920, Our History*, History Group of the Communist Party, 1980, p. 2
45 Rosalind Mitchison and G. W. S. Barrow, *Why Scottish History Matters*, p. 86
46 T. M. Devine, *The Scottish Nation 1700–2000*, p. 227
47 Alexander Somerville and John Carswell, *The Autobiography of a Working Man*, Turnstile Press, 1848, pp. 22–23
48 Michael Fry, *Edinburgh: A History of the City*, Pan, 2010, p. 250

49 Thomas Johnston, *The History of the Scottish Working Classes*, pp. 244–45
50 Alternative Perthshire, '1832 Reform Act and Associated Agitation in Perth', alternative-perth.co.uk/1832reformact.htm, accessed 24 September 2012
51 Anna Clark, *The Struggle for the Breeches: Gender and the Making of the British Working Class*, University of California Press, 1997, p. 206
52 Ibid.
53 Ibid., p. 205
54 T. M. Devine, *The Scottish Nation 1700–2000*, p. 276
55 Tomas Phelan, 'James McNish and the Glasgow Cotton Spinners Union', *United Scotsman*, vol. 2, no. 5, scottishrepublicansocialistmovement.org/Pages/SRSMArticlesJamesMcNishandtheGlasgowCottonSpinnersUnion.aspx, accessed 2 May 2012
56 Ibid.
57 Dorothy Thompson, *The Chartists: Popular Politics in the Industrial Revolution*, Wildwood House, 1986, pp. 221–23
58 W. Hamish Fraser, 'The Scottish Context of Chartism', in Terry Brotherstone (editor), *Covenant, Charter and Party: Traditions of Revolt and Protest in Press*, 1989, p. 67
59 John Charlton, *The Chartists: The First National Workers Movement*, Pluto Press, 1992, p. 17
60 Dorothy Thompson, *The Chartists: Popular Politics in the Industrial Revolution*, p. 223
61 Robert Duncan, 'Chartism in Aberdeen: Radical Politics and Culture 1838–1848', in Terry Brotherstone (ed.), *Covenant, Charter and Party: Traditions of Revolt and Protest in Modern Scottish History*, p. 87
62 Dorothy Thompson, *The Chartists: Popular Politics in the Industrial Revolution*, pp. 284–85
63 Alexander Wilson, *The Chartist Movement in Scotland*, Manchester University Press, 1970, pp. 192–94
64 Robert Duncan, *The Mineworkers*, Birlinn, 2005, pp. 134–36
65 W. W. Knox, *An Industrial Nation: Work, Culture and Society in Scotland, 1800–Present*, Edinburgh University Press, 1999, p. 68
66 Thomas Johnston, *The History of the Scottish Working Classes*, p. 276
67 Dorothy Thompson, *The Chartists: Popular Politics in the Industrial Revolution*, p. 320
68 Alexander Wilson, *The Chartist Movement in Scotland*, p. 218
69 Ibid., pp. 217–21
70 Ibid., p. 226
71 Thomas Johnston, *The History of the Scottish Working Classes*, pp. 254–55
72 Malcolm Chase, *Chartism: A New History*, Manchester University Press, 2007, p. 316
73 Alexander Wilson, *The Chartist Movement in Scotland*, p. 222
74 Ibid., pp. 235–39
75 Louise Yeoman, 'Helen McFarlane – the radical feminist admired by Karl Marx', BBC Radio Scotland, 26 November 2012

7. The Highland Clearances and Resistance

1 Murray Pittock, *The Invention of Scotland: The Stuart Myth and the Scottish Identity, 1638 to the Present*, Taylor and Francis, 1991, pp. 107–8
2 T. M. Devine, *The Scottish Nation 1700–2000*, p. 187
3 J. M. Bumsted, *The People's Clearance: Highland Emigration to British North America 1770–1815*, University of Manitoba Press, 1982, pp. 44–45
4 Eric Richards, *A History of the Highland Clearances: Emigration, Protest, Reasons,* Taylor and Francis, 1985, p. 306
5 Alexander Mackenzie, *The History of the Highland Clearances*, P. J. O'Callaghan, 1883, pp. 17–18
6 Eric Richards, *A History of the Highland Clearances: Emigration, Protest, Reasons*, p. 53
7 Laurence Gourievidis, *The Dynamics of Heritage: History, Memory and the Highland Clearances*, Ashgate, 2012, p. 22
8 Robert Knox, *The Races of Men*, Henry Renshaw, 1850, p. 378
9 T. C. Smout, *A Century of the Scottish People 1830–1950*, p. 65
10 Alexander Mackenzie, *The History of the Highland Clearances*, p. viii
11 Neil Davidson, *The Origins of Scottish Nationhood*, p. 148
12 'Farming and Clearance', Ross and Cromarty Roots, rosscromartyroots. co.uk/index.asp?pageid=54211, accessed 9 May 2013
13 'Western Isles History – The Bernera Riot', Virtual Hebrides, virtualheb. co.uk/bernera-riot-western-isles.html, accessed 8 May 2013
14 Tom Gallagher, *Glasgow, the Uneasy Peace*, Manchester University Press, 1987, p. 66
15 Ibid.
16 Murray Pittock, *The Invention of Scotland: The Stuart Myth and the Scottish Identity, 1638 to the Present*, p. 109
17 Alastair MacIntosh Gray and William Moffat, *A History of Scotland: Modern Times*, Oxford University Press, 1999, p. 28
18 Ibid.
19 Eric Richards, *A History of the Highland Clearances: Emigration, Protest, Reasons*, p. 342
20 Florence S. Boos (ed.), *Working-Class Women Poets in Victorian Britain: An Anthology*, Broadview Press, 2008, p. 173
21 Sorley MacLean, 'Maírí Mhor nan Oran', *Calgacus*, Winter 1975
22 Tom Gallagher, *Glasgow, the Uneasy Peace*, p. 66
23 Ian Murdoch MacLeod MacPhail, *The Crofters War*, Acair, 1989, p. 100

8. Scotland in the Nineteenth Century

1 Gordon T. Stewart, *Jute and Empire: The Calcutta Jute Wallahs and the Landscapes of Empire*, Manchester University Press, 1998, pp. 171–73
2 Christopher Harvie, *Scotland and Nationalism: Scottish Society and Politics 1707–1977*, p. 74

3 Ray Burnett, 'Scotland and Antonio Gramsci', *Scottish International* 9, November 1972

4 Michael Lynch, *Scotland – A New History*, Pimlico, 1992, p. 358

5 Tom Nairn, 'The Three Dreams of Scottish Nationalism', *New Left Review* 49, May-June 1968, p. 7

6 Neil Davidson, 'In Perspective – Tom Nairn', *Socialist Review*, March 1999

7 T. M. Devine, *The Scottish Nation 1700–2000*, p. 287

8 Christopher Harvie, *Scotland and Nationalism: Scottish Society and Politics 1707–1977*, pp. 33–34

9 Ibid, pp. 107–8

10 T. C. Smout, *A Century of the Scottish People 1830–1950*, p. 41

11 T. M. Devine, *The Scottish Nation 1700–2000*, p. 258

12 William Knox, *Industrial Nation: Work, Culture and Society in Scotland 1800–Present*, p. 132

13 J. J. Smyth, *Labour in Glasgow 1896–1936: Socialism, Suffrage, Sectarianism*, Tuckwell Press, 2000, pp. 19–21

14 T. C. Smout, *A Century of the Scottish People 1830–1950*, pp. 8–9

15 Richard Rodger, *The Transformation of Edinburgh: Land, Property and Trust in the Nineteenth Century*, Cambridge University Press, 2001, p. 18

16 T. C. Smout, 'Scotland 1850–1950', in Francis Michael Longsteth Thompson, *The Cambridge Social History of Britain, 1750–1950*, Cambridge University press, 1993, p. 217

17 Ian R. Mitchell, 'The Garngad: Heaven and Hell', glasgowwestend.co.uk/whatson/thegarngadheavenandhell.php, accessed 8 May 2013

18 Ibid.

19 Ibid.

20 Ibid.

21 Michael Fry, *Edinburgh: A History of the City*, Pan, 2010, pp. 242–43

22 Robert Duncan, *The Mineworkers*, p. 74

23 Harry McShane, *Glasgow District Trades Council Centenary Brochure 1958–1958: A Hundred Years of Progress*, Civic Press, 1958, p. 7

24 Lanarkshire Communities, 12 April 2012

25 Bla'an'tir's Ain Website, 'The Ejection of the Blantyre Widows', blantyrebiz/The-Ejection-of-the-Blantyre-Windows.html, accessed 12 April 2013

26 T. C. Smout, *A Century of the Scottish People 1830–1950*, p. 33

27 Seán Damer, 'State Class and Housing: Glasgow 1885–1919', in Joseph Melling (ed.), *Housing, Social Policy and the State*, Taylor and Francis, 1980, p. 85

28 T. C. Smout, *A Century of the Scottish People 1830–1950*, p. 103

29 Ibid., p. 35

30 Ibid., p. 150

31 T. M. Devine, *The Scottish Nation 1700–2000*, pp. 263–64

32 Tom Gallagher, *Edinburgh Divided: John Cormack and No Popery in the 1930s*, Polygon, 1987, pp. 10–11

33 T. C. Smout, *A Century of the Scottish People 1830–1950*, p. 240

34 Ibid., p. 242

35 Christopher Harvie, 'Before the Breakthrough, 1886–1922', in Ian Donnachie, Christopher Harvie and Ian S. Wood (eds), *Forward! Labour*

Politics in Scotland 1888–1988, Polygon, 1989, p. 12; and Tom Gallagher, *Glasgow, the Uneasy Peace*, p. 71

36 Bernard Aspinwall and John McAffret, 'A Comparative View of the Irish in Edinburgh in the Nineteenth Century', in Roger Smith (ed.), *The Irish in the Victorian City*, Taylor and Francis, 1985, p. 132

37 Tom Gallagher, *Glasgow, the Uneasy Peace*, p. 7

38 Elaine McFarland, *Protestants First: Orangeism in 19th Century Scotland*, Edinburgh University Press, 1990, p. 49

39 Tom Gallagher, *Glasgow, the Uneasy Peace*, p. 29

40 J. E. Handley, *The Irish in Modern Scotland*, Cork University Press, 1947, p. 44

41 Tom Gallagher, *Glasgow, the Uneasy Peace*, p. 32

42 Elaine McFarland, *Protestants First: Orangeism in 19th Century Scotland*, p. 66

43 Tom Gallagher, *Glasgow, the Uneasy Peace*, p. 29

44 Ibid., p. 14

45 Ibid., pp. 26–27

46 Elaine McFarland, *Protestants First: Orangeism in 19th Century Scotland*, pp. 143–44 and 186

47 Ibid., p. 145

48 Ibid., pp. 148–49

49 Ibid., pp. 166–67

50 Ibid., pp. 192–93

51 'The Jewish Community in Scotland', Education Scotland, educationscotland. gov.uk/higherscottishhistory/migrationandempire/experienceofimmigrants/ jewish.asp, accessed 1 October 2012

52 Nathan Abrams, 'Jute, Journalism, Jam and Jews: The Anomalous Survival of the Dundee Hebrew Congregation', bangor.ac.uk/creative_industries/docu-ments/JUTE, JOURNALISM,JAMANDJEWS.pdf, accessed 1 October 2012

53 Andrew Nash, *Kailyard and Scottish Literature*, Rodopi B.V, 2007, p. 183

54 Richard Zumkhawala-Cook, *Scotland as We Know it: Representations of National Identity in Literature, Film and Popular Culture*, McFarland, 2008, p. 29

55 James Veitch, *George Douglas Brown*, H. Jenkins, 1952, pp. 153 and 156

56 T. M. Devine, *The Scottish Nation 1700–2000*, pp. 260–61

57 Eleanor Gordon, *Women and the Labour Movement in Scotland 1850–1914*, Clarendon, 1991, p. 141

58 William M. Walker, *Juteopolis: Dundee and Its Textile Workers 1885–1923*, Scottish Academic Press, 1979, pp. 86–87

59 Lynne Abrams, *The Making of Modern Women: 1789–1918*, Pearson, 2002, p. 112

60 Eleanor Gordon, *Women and the Labour Movement in Scotland 1850–1914*, p. 192

61 Robert Duncan, *The Mineworkers*, p. 142

62 Ibid.

63 T. C. Smout, *A Century of the Scottish People 1830–1950*, p. 106

64 Christopher Harvie, 'Before the Breakthrough, 1886–1922', in Ian Donnachie, Christopher Harvie and Ian S. Wood (eds), *Forward! Labour Politics in Scotland 1888–1988*, p. 9

65 James J. Smyth, 'The ILP in Glasgow: The Struggle for Identity', in Alan

McKinlay and R. J. Morris (eds), *The ILP on Clydeside 1893–1932: From Foundation to Disintegration*, Manchester University Press, 1991, p. 26

66 Ibid., p. 22
67 Christopher Harvie, 'Before the Breakthrough, 1886–1922', p. 10
68 W. Hamish Fraser and Clive Lee, *Aberdeen 1800–2000: A New History*, Dundurn, 2000, p. 192
69 Ibid., p. 194
70 David Howell, *British Workers and the Independent Labour Party, 1888–1906*, Manchester University Press, 1984, p. 170
71 James Connolly, *James Connolly: Selected Writings*, Pluto Press, 1998, p. 32
72 C. Desmond Greaves, *The Life and Times of James Connolly*, Lawrence and Wishart, 1976, pp. 30–31
73 Kieran Allen, *The Politics of James Connolly*, Pluto Press, 1990, p. 6
74 C. Desmond Greaves, *The Life and Times of James Connolly*, p. 48
75 Kieran Allen, *The Politics of James Connolly*, p. 10

9. The Clyde Runs Red

1 T. M. Devine, *The Scottish Nation 1700–2000*, p. 309
2 T. C. Smout, *A Century of the Scottish People 1830–1950*, p. 267
3 Christopher Harvie, 'Before the Breakthrough, 1886–1922', p. 21
4 'Compulsory Military Service, Should the Working Class Support it?', Socialist Labour Press, 1918, p. 15.
5 William Kenefick, *Red Scotland! The Rise and Fall of the Radical Left, 1872 to 1932*, Edinburgh University Press, 2007, p. 134
6 Gordon Brown, *Maxton*, Collins Fontana, 1988, pp. 58–59
7 Iain McLean, *The Legend of the Red Clydeside*, John Donald, 1983, pp. 21–22
8 Rob Duncan, 'Independent Working Class Education and the Formation of the Labour College Movement in Glasgow and the West of Scotland, 1915–1922', in Robert Duncan and Arthur McIvor (eds), *Militant Workers: Labour and Class Conflict on the Clyde 1900–1950, Essays in Honour of Harry McShane 1891–1988*, John Donald, 1992, p. 107
9 Ann and Vincent Flynn, 'We Shall Not Be Removed', in Laurie Flynn (ed.), *We Shall Be All*, Bookmarks, 1978, p. 22
10 Seán Damer, 'State Class and Housing: Glasgow 1885–1919', in Joseph Melling (ed.), *Housing, Social Policy and the State*, Taylor and Francis, 1980, p. 104
11 Trish Caird, 'Women and the Left: Mary Barbour', http://internationalsocialist.org.uk/index.php/2013/03/women-on-the-left-mary-barbour/, accessed 24 March 2013
12 William Gallacher, *Revolt on the Clyde*, Lawrence & Wishart, 1990, p. 51
13 John McHugh, 'The Clyde Rent Strike, 1915', *Scottish Labour History Society* 12 (1978) p. 58
14 Ann and Vincent Flynn, 'We Shall Not Be Removed', p. 24
15 William Gallacher, *Revolt on the Clyde*, p. 52
16 *Glasgow Herald*, 29 October 1915
17 William Gallacher, *Revolt on the Clyde*, p. 53
18 Trish Caird, 'Women and the Left: Mary Barbour'

19 Seán Damer, 'State Class and Housing: Glasgow 1885–1919', p. 94
20 Tom Bell, *Pioneering Days*, Lawrence and Wishart, 1941, p. 110
21 *Forward*, 27 November 1915
22 William Gallacher, *Revolt on the Clyde*, p. 57
23 Ann and Vincent Flynn, 'We Shall Not Be Removed', p. 28
24 Seán Damer, 'State Class and Housing: Glasgow 1885–1919', p. 98
25 Iain McLean, *The Legend of Red Clydeside*, John Donald, 1983, p. 41
26 James Hinton, *The First Shop Stewards' Movement*, George Allen and Unwin, London, 1973, p. 296
27 Ibid.
28 Iain McLean, *The Legend of Red Clydeside*, p. 10
29 Tony Cliff and Donny Gluckstein, *Marxism and Trade Union Struggle: The General Strike of 1926*, Bookmarks, 1986, p. 67
30 James Hinton, *The First Shop Stewards Movement*, p. 138
31 Ibid., p. 140
32 Gordon Brown, *Maxton*, p. 61
33 Ibid., pp. 61–62
34 James Hinton, *The First Shop Stewards Movement*, p. 140
35 Iain McLean, *The Legend of Red Clydeside*, p. 63
36 James Hinton, *The First Shop Stewards Movement*, p. 145
37 Ibid.
38 Christopher Harvie, 'Before the Breakthrough, 1886–1922', p. 23
39 Rob Duncan, 'Independent Working Class Education and the Formation of the Labour College Movement in Glasgow and the West of Scotland, 1915–1922', p. 115
40 James Hinton, *The First Shop Stewards Movement*, p. 257
41 Ibid., p. 250
42 Gordon Brown, *Maxton*, p. 83
43 Ibid.
44 John Leopold, 'Forty Hours Strike', in Laurie Flynn (ed.), *We Shall Be All: Recent Chapters in the History of Working Class Struggle in Scotland*, Bookmarks, 1978, pp. 34–35
45 Ibid., p. 36
46 Ibid., p. 37
47 Ibid.
48 Ibid., pp. 37–38
49 Ibid., p. 39
50 Ibid.
51 Ibid., p. 40
52 John Foster, 'Strike Action and Working Class Politics on Clydeside 1914–1919', *International Review of Social History* 35:1, (1990) p. 55
53 R. A. Leeson, *Strike: A Live History 1887–1971*, George Allen and Unwin, 1973, p. 61
54 Iain McLean, *The Legend of Red Clydeside*, p. 133
55 Ibid., p. 125
56 J. T. Murphy, *Preparing for Power*, Pluto Press, 1972, pp. 176–77
57 William Gallacher, *Revolt on the Clyde*, p. 220
58 Nan Milton (ed.), *John Maclean: In the Rapids of Revolution*, Allison and Busby, 1978, p. 14

59 Ibid., p. 77
60 Nan Milton, *John Maclean*, Pluto Press, 1973, p. 99
61 B. J. Ripley and J. McHugh, *John Maclean*, Manchester University Press, 1989, p. 106
62 Nan Milton (ed.), *John Maclean: In the Rapids of Revolution*, p. 101
63 Nan Milton, *John Maclean*, p. 180
64 Tom Gallagher, *Glasgow, the Uneasy Peace*, Manchester University Press, 1987, p. 88; and Nan Milton, *John Maclean*, p. 203
65 Nan Milton, *John Maclean*, p. 238
66 Nan Milton (ed.), *John Maclean: In the Rapids of Revolution*, p. 178
67 Ibid., p. 233
68 Ibid., p. 225
69 Ibid., pp. 247–48
70 Ibid., p. 234
71 Ibid., p. 253

10. The 1920s: Economic Decline and General Strike

1 Michael S. Moss and John R. Hume, *Shipbuilders to the World: 125 Years of Harland and Wolff, Belfast 1861–1986*, Blackstaff Press, 1986, p. 192
2 C. E. V. Leser, 'Manufacturing Industry', in Alec Cairncross (ed.), *The Scottish Economy: A Statistical Account of Scottish Life*, Cambridge University Press, 1954, p. 121
3 Marjory Harper, *Emigration from Scotland between the Wars: Opportunity or Exile?* Manchester University Press, 1998, pp. 10–11
4 'Tarbrax Village', Museum of the Scottish Shale Industry, scottishshale.co.uk/GazVillages/TarbraxVillage.html, accessed 14 May 2013
5 Michael Anderson, 'The Demographic Factor', in T. M. Devine and Jenny Wormald (eds), *The Oxford History of Modern Scotland*, Oxford University Press, 2012, p. 52
6 T. C. Smout, 'Scotland 1850–1950', in Francis Michael Longsteth Thompson, *The Cambridge Social History of Britain, 1750–1950*, Cambridge University press, 1993, p. 260
7 T. C. Smout, *A Century of the Scottish People 1830–1950*, pp. 75–76
8 Roger Hutchison, *The Soap Man: Lewis, Harris and Lord Leverhulme*, Berlinn, 2003, p. 126
9 James Hunter, *The Making of the Crofting Community*, John Donald, 2006, p. 272
10 Paul Richard Thompson, Tony Walley and Trevor Lums, *Living the Fishing*, Routledge, 1983, p. 305
11 Ibid., p. 306
12 Marjory Harper, 'Crofter Colonists in Western Canada', in Philip Buckner and R. Douglas Francis (eds), *Canada and the British World: Culture, Migration and Identity*, University of British Columbia Press, 2006, pp. 198–205
13 William Kenefick, *Red Scotland! The Rise and Fall of the Radical Left, 1872 to 1932*, Edinburgh University Press, 2007, p. 133
14 Christopher Harvie, 'Before the Breakthrough, 1886–1922', p. 24

15 Ibid., p. 25
16 Ibid., pp. 27–28
17 Ibid., p. 26
18 William Knox, '"Ours Is Not an Ordinary Parliamentary Movement": 1922–1926', in Alan McKinlay and R. J. Morris (eds), *The ILP on Clydeside 1893–1932: From Foundation to Disintegration*, Manchester University Press, 1991, p. 154
19 Ibid., p. 159
20 Gordon Brown, *Maxton*, pp. 145–46
21 William Knox, '"Ours Is Not an Ordinary Parliamentary Movement": 1922–1926', p. 159
22 Ibid., p. 161
23 Gordon Brown, *Maxton*, p. 154
24 Ibid.
25 Ibid., p. 161
26 J. J. Smyth, *Labour in Glasgow 1996–1936: Socialism, Suffrage, Sectarianism*, Tuckwell Press, 2000, pp. 109–10 and 185–87
27 Annemarie Hughes, *Gender and Political Identities in Scotland 1919–1939*, Edinburgh University Press, 2010, p. 123
28 Gordon Brown, *Maxton*, p. 101
29 Tom Gallagher, *Glasgow, the Uneasy Peace*, pp. 88–89
30 Ibid., p. 90
31 Máirtín Ó Catháin, '"A Winnowing Spirit": Sinn Fein in Scotland, 1905–38', academia.edu/4725333/A_Winnowing_Spirit_Sinn_Fein_in_Scotland_1905-38, accessed 13 October 2013
32 Tom Gallagher, *Glasgow, the Uneasy Peace*, p. 91
33 'Folk Singer Reader's Relative Ferried Arms for IRA', *Belfast Newsletter*, 1 October 2013, accessed 15 October 2013
34 Tom Gallagher, *Glasgow, the Uneasy Peace*, p. 91
35 Bill Kelly, *Sworn to be Free: The Complete Book of IRA Jailbreaks 1918–1921*, Anvil Books, 1971, pp. 126–28
36 Tom Gallagher, *Glasgow, the Uneasy Peace*, pp. 95–96
37 Ibid., p. 94
38 Catriona Burness, *The Making of Scottish Unionism 1886–1914*, Routledge, 2002, p. 31
39 Colin Kidd, *Union and Unionism: Political Thought in Scotland*, Cambridge University Press, 2008, p. 15
40 Callum G. Brown, *Religion and Society in Scotland Since 1707*, Edinburgh University Press, 1997, p. 141
41 Stewart J. Brown, 'Presbyterians and Catholics in Twentieth Century Scotland', in Stewart J. Brown, George M. Newlands and Alexander C. Cheyne (eds), *Scottish Christianity in the Modern World: In Honour of A. C. Cheyne*, T. and T. Clark, 2001, p. 265
42 Ibid.
43 Ibid., p. 268
44 Séan Damer, '"The Clyde Rent War!" The Clydebank Rent Strike of the 1920s', in Gerry Mooney (ed.), *Class Struggle and Social Welfare*, Routledge, 2000, p. 76
45 'Jane Rae', west-dunbarton.gov.uk/tourism-and-visitor-attractions/museums-and-

galleries/collections/people-and-personalities/people-and-personalities
-clydebank/individuals-clydebank/jane-rae/, accessed 18 September 2012

46 'Jenny Hislop', grahamstevenson.me.uk/index.php?option=com_content&vi
ew=article&id=293:jenny-hyslop-&catid=8:h&itemid=109, accessed 18
September 2012

47 Bert Moorhouse, Mary Wilson and Chris Chamberlain, 'Rent Strikes, Direct
Action and the Working Class', in Ralph Miliband and John Saville (eds),
Socialist Register 1972, Merlin, 1972, p. 137

48 Ibid.

49 *Glasgow Herald*, 14 July 1924

50 *Barrier Miner*, 31 December 1924

51 *Barrier Miner*, 5 February 1925

52 *Independent*, 14 August 1992, accessed 24 September

53 Jock Kane with Betty Kane, 'No wonder we were all rebels – an oral history',
grahamstevenson.me.uk/index.php?option=com_content&view=article&id
=697&itemid=63, accessed 24 September 2012

54 Roy A. Church and Quentin Outram, *Strikes and Solidarity: Coalfield Conflict
in Britain, 1889–1966*, Cambridge University Press, 2002, p. 81

55 Mary Docherty, *A Miner's Lass*, Lancashire Community Press, 1992, p. 35

56 Ibid., p. 37

57 *Independent*, 14 August 1992

58 'Perthshire and the 1926 General Strike', Alternative Perthshire, accessed 13
May 2013

59 Ibid.

60 Laurie Flynn, 'The People's Republic', in Laurie Flynn (ed.), *We Shall Be All:
Recent Chapters in the History of Working Class Struggle in Scotland*, p. 10

61 James Klugmann, 'Marxism, Reformism and the General Strike', in Jeffrey
Skelley (ed.), *The General Strike, 1926*, Lawrence and Wishart, 1976, p. 88

62 Laurie Flynn, 'The People's Republic', p. 11

63 James Klugmann, 'Marxism, Reformism and the General Strike', p. 88

64 Tony Cliff and Donny Gluckstein, *Marxism and Trade Union Struggle: The
General Strike of 1926*, Bookmarks, 1986, p. 235

65 Chris Farman, *May 1926, The General Strike, Britain's Aborted Revolution?*
Granada, 1974, p. 205

66 Tony Cliff and Donny Gluckstein, *Marxism and Trade Union Struggle: The
General Strike of 1926*, p. 196

67 Ibid., p. 199

68 Ibid.

69 Ibid., p. 226

70 Paul Carter, 'The West of Scotland', in Jeffrey Skelley (ed). *The General Strike,
1926*, p. 116

71 Ibid.

72 J. J. Smyth, *Labour in Glasgow 1896–1936: Socialism, Suffrage, Sectarianism*,
p. 107

73 Paul Carter, 'The West of Scotland', p. 133

74 Chris Farman, *May 1926, The General Strike, Britain's Aborted Revolution?*,
p. 239

75 Paul Carter, 'The West of Scotland', p. 123

76 Chris Farman, *May 1926, The General Strike, Britain's Aborted Revolution?*, p. 158

77　Ian MacDougall, 'Edinburgh', in Jeffrey Skelley (ed.), *The General Strike, 1926*, p. 150
78　Ibid., pp. 150–51
79　Chris Farman, *May 1926, The General Strike, Britain's Aborted Revolution?*, p. 232
80　Annemarie Hughes, *Gender and Political Identities in Scotland 1919–1939*, Edinburgh University Press, 2010, p. 99
81　J. J. Smyth, *Labour in Glasgow 1896–1936: Socialism, Suffrage, Sectarianism*, p. 107
82　'Perthshire and the 1926 General Strike', Alternative Perthshire, accessed 13 May 2013
83　Ibid.
84　Laurie Flynn, 'The People's Republic', p. 12
85　Tony Cliff and Donny Gluckstein, *Marxism and Trade Union Struggle: The General Strike of 1926*, pp. 252–53
86　Laurie Flynn, 'The People's Republic', pp. 112–13
87　Robert Duncan, *The Mine Workers*, pp. 230–31
88　R. A. Leeson, *Strike: A Live History 1887–1971*, p. 105
89　Jock Kane with Betty Kane, 'No wonder we were all rebels – an oral history' accessed 24 September 2012
90　J. J. Smyth, *Labour in Glasgow 1996–1936: Socialism, Suffrage, Sectarianism*, p. 108
91　Robert Duncan, *The Mine Workers*, p. 233
92　Ibid., p. 234
93　'Helen Crawfurd – Political Activist, Suffragette and Red Cydesider', Alternative Perthshire, alternative-perth.co.uk/helencrawfurd.htm, accessed 11 May 2013
94　Kevin Morgan, Gideon Cohen and Andrew Flinn, *Communists and British Society 1920–1991*, Rivers Oram Press, 2007, p. 154
95　Ibid.
96　Graham Stevenson, 'Communist Biogs: Helen Crawfurd', grahamstevenson. me.uk/index.php?option=com_content&view=article&id=128:helen-craw-furd-anderson&catid=3:c&Itemid=99, accessed 11 May 2013
97　Seán Damer, 'State Class and Housing: Glasgow 1885–1919', p. 92
98　William Kenefick, *Red Scotland!: The Rise and Fall of the Radical Left, 1872 to 1932*, p. 148
99　Esther Breitenbach and Eleanor Gordon, *Out of Bounds: Women in Scottish Society 1800–1945*, Edinburgh University Press, 1992, p. 181
100　Andy Thorpe, *The British Communist Party and Moscow: 1920–43*, Manchester University Press, 2000, p. 35
101　Jill Liddington, *The Road to Greenham Common: Feminism and Anti-Militarism in Britain Since 1820*, Syracuse University Press, 1989, p. 131
102　Graham Stevenson, 'Communist Biogs: Helen Crawfurd'
103　Mary Davis, *Sylvia Pankhurst: A Life in Radical Politics*, Pluto Press, 1999, p. 93
104　Graham Stevenson, 'Communist Biogs: Helen Crawfurd'
105　Ibid.

11. The Great Depression: Suffering and Resistance

1 T. C. Smout, *A Century of the Scottish People 1830–1950*, p. 115
2 Ibid., p. 114
3 William Knox, *Industrial Nation: Work, Culture and Society in Scotland 1800–Present*, p. 190
4 T. C. Smout, *A Century of the Scottish People 1830–1950*, pp. 114–15
5 Edwin Muir, *Scottish Journey*, Mainstream, 1996, p. 139
6 William Knox, *Industrial Nation: Work, Culture and Society in Scotland 1800–Present*, p. 192
7 Ibid.
8 Richard Croucher, *We Refuse to Starve in Silence: A History of the National Unemployed Workers Movement 1920–1946*, Lawrence and Wishart, 1987, pp. 18–21
9 Ibid., pp. 48–49
10 George Rawlinson, 'Mobilising the Unemployed: The National Unemployed Workers' Movement in the West of Scotland', in Robert Duncan and Arthur McIvor (eds), *Militant Workers: Labour and Class Conflict on the Clyde 1900–1950, Essays in Honour of Harry McShane (1891-1988)*, John Donald, 1992, p. 185
11 Ibid., p. 189
12 Ibid., p. 190
13 Ibid., p. 187
14 Ian MacDougall, *Voices from the Hunger Marches: Personal Recollections by Scottish Hunger Marchers of the 1920s and 1930s*, vol. 1, Polygon, 1990, p. 147
15 Ibid., p. 130
16 Ian MacDougall, *Voices from the Hunger Marches: Personal Recollections by Scottish Hunger Marchers of the 1920s and 1930s*, vol. 2, Polygon, 1991, p. 282
17 Richard Croucher, *We Refuse to Starve in Silence: A History of the National Unemployed Workers Movement 1920–1946*, p. 158
18 Ibid., p. 166
19 Ibid., pp. 192–93
20 J. J. Smyth, *Labour in Glasgow 1896–1936: Socialism, Suffrage, Sectarianism*, p. 148
21 Tom Gallagher, *Edinburgh Divided: John Cormack and No Popery in the 1930s*, Polygon, 1987, p. 111
22 Ibid., p. 39
23 Ibid., pp. 51–53
24 Ibid., p. 123
25 Ibid., p. 145
26 Tom Gallagher, *Glasgow, the Uneasy Peace*, p. 155
27 Ibid., p. 153
28 Stephen M. Cullen, 'The Fasces and the Saltire: The Failure of the British Union of Fascists in Scotland, 1932–1940', *Scottish Historical Review* LXXXVIII, 2, 224 (October 2008), pp. 314–15
29 Ibid., p. 312
30 Stephen Dorril, *Blackshirt: Sir Oswald Mosley and British Fascism*, Penguin, 2007, pp. 293, 453

31 Martin Pugh, '*Hurrah for the Blackshirts': Fascists and Fascism in Britain Between the Wars*, Jonathan Cape, 2005, p. 231
32 Ibid., pp. 312, 315
33 Henry Maitles, 'Blackshirts Across the Border', *Socialist Review*, 172 (February 1994)
34 Ibid.
35 Ibid.
36 Ian McDougall (ed.), *Voices from the Spanish Civil War*, Polygon, 1986, p. 241
37 'The Leader in Scotland', *The Blackshirt*, 8 June 1934
38 Ian MacDougall (ed.), *Voices from the Spanish Civil War*, p. 33
39 'Fascist Meeting Sequel', *The Scotsman*, 6 June 1936
40 Daniel Gray, *Homage to Caledonia*, Luath Press, 2008, p. 26
41 Colin Cross, *The Fascists in Britain*, St Martin's Press, 1963, p. 108
42 Juliet Gardiner, *The Thirties: An Intimate History*, HarperCollins, 2011, p. 406
43 'The Amazing Life Of Bob Cooney Part 2 – Fighting Fascism', 18 July 2011, http://aberdeenvoice.com/tag/brigade/, accessed 6 October 2012
44 'Blackshirts in Red Scotland', http://afaarchive.files.wordpress.com/2012/06/blackshirts-in-red-scotland.pdf8, accessed 5 October 2012
45 Nathan Abrams, *Caledonian Jews: A Study of Seven Small Communities in Scotland*, McFarland, 2009, p. 28
46 Henry Maitles, 'Blackshirts Across the Border'
47 Daniel Gray, *Homage to Caledonia*, p. 19; and Ian MacDougall, 'Scots in the Spanish Civil War 1936–1939', in Grant G. Simpson (ed.), *The Scottish Soldier Abroad, 1247–1967*, Rowman & Littlefield, 1992, p. 146
48 Ian MacDougall, 'Scots in the Spanish Civil War 1936-1939', pp. 132–33
49 Ibid., p. 134
50 Daniel Gray, *Homage to Caledonia*, p. 100
51 Ibid., p. 51
52 Ibid., p. 52
53 Ibid., pp. 23–24
54 Ibid., p. 25
55 Ibid., p. 106
56 Mary Docherty, *A Miner's Lass*, Lancashire Community Press, 1992, p. 140
57 Daniel Gray, *Homage to Caledonia*, pp. 111–15
58 Margery Palmer McCulloch, *Scottish Modernism and Its Contexts 1918–1959: Literature, National Identity and Cultural Exchange*, Edinburgh University Press, 2009, p. 108
59 Daniel Gray, *Homage to Caledonia*, pp. 137–39
60 Ibid., p. 203
61 Julie Arnot, 'Women Workers and Trade Union Participation in Scotland 1919–1939', pp. 297–301, http://theses.gla.ac.uk/3086/01/1999arnotphd.pdf, accessed 9 October 2012
62 Ibid.
63 Ibid.
64 Ibid.
65 Richard Croucher, *Engineers At War 1939–1945*, Merlin, 1982, pp. 13–14
66 Ibid., p. 45

67 Ibid., pp. 49–50
68 Nina Fishman, *The British Communist Party and the Trade Unions 1933–1945*, Scolar Press, 1995, pp. 95–96
69 Richard Croucher, *Engineers At War 1939–1945*, pp. 51–52
70 Ibid., p. 52
71 Nina Fishman, *The British Communist Party and the Trade Unions 1933–1945*, pp. 95–96
72 Richard Croucher, *Engineers At War 1939–1945*, p. 71
73 Nina Fishman, *The British Communist Party and the Trade Unions 1933–1945*, p. 201
74 Clive Howard Lee, *Scotland and the United Kingdom: The Economy and the Union in the Twentieth Century*, Manchester University Press, 2005, p. 18
75 T. M. Devine, *The Scottish Nation 1700–2000*, p. 325
76 Ian Donnachie, 'Scottish Labour in the Depression: The 1930s', in Ian Donnachie, Christopher Harvie and Ian S. Wood (eds), *Forward! Labour Politics in Scotland 1888–1988*, p. 55
77 Tim Pat Coogan, *Wherever Green Is Worn*, Palgrave Macmillan, 2002, pp. 229–30
78 Dr. Robert D McIntyre, 'The Scottish National Party in the Nineteen Thirties', electricscotland.com/history/mcintyre/chap5.htm, Accessed 19 October 2012
79 *Parliamentary Debates: Official Report*, vol. 272, His Majesty's Stationary Office, 1933, pp. 285–6.
80 Attila Dosa, *Beyond Identity: New Horizons in Modern Scottish Poetry*, Rodopi, 2009, p. 87
81 Rebecca Wilson, Gillean Somerville-Arjat (eds), *Sleeping With Monsters: Conversations with Scottish and Irish Women Poets*, Polygon, 1990, p. v
82 Hugh MacDiarmid, 'The Politics and Poetry of Hugh MacDiarmid', in *Selected Essays of Hugh MacDiarmid*, University of California Press, 1970, p. 22
83 Hugh MacDiarmid and Alan Bold (ed.), *The Thistle Rises: An Anthology of Poetry and Prose*, Hamish Hamilton, 1984, p. 289
84 Allan Armstrong, 'The Republic of the Imagination', *Emancipation and Liberation*, 14 (2006), http://republicancommunist.org/blog/2007/03/13/the-republic-of-the-imagination/, accessed 4 December 2013
85 Hugh MacDiarmid and Lewis Grassic, *Scottish Scene or the Intelligent Man's Guide to Albyn*, Jarrods, 1934, p. 11
86 John Manson, 'Hugh MacDiarmid: The Poet and the Party', *Communist History Network Newsletter*, 12 (Spring 2002), socialsciences.manchester.ac.uk/chnn/CHNN12P.html, accessed 24 October 2012
87 Jeremy Matthew Glick, *'Taking Up Arms Against a Sea of Troubles': Tragedy as History and Genre in the Black Radical Tradition*, ProQuest, 2007, p. 2
88 Hugh MacDiarmid and Alan Bold, *The Thistle Rises*, p. 282
89 John Baglow, *Hugh MacDiarmid: The Poetry of Self*, McGill-Queen's Press, 1987, p. 77

12. World War II and After

1 Angus Calder, *The People's War*, Granada, 1982, p. 49
2 T. M. Devine, *The Scottish Nation 1700–2000*, pp. 550–51
3 Angus Calder, *The People's War*, p. 342
4 Tom McKendrick, 'The Clydebank Blitz', tommckendrick.com/code/blitzpage1.html, accessed 17 May 2013
5 'Greenock Corporation and the Blitz', *WW2 – A People's War*, 23 March 2004, bbc.co.uk/history/ww2peopleswar/stories/34/a2453834.shtml, accessed 26 November 2012
6 Angus Calder, *The People's War*, p. 457
7 Richard Croucher, *Engineers At War 1939–1945*, p. 85
8 Ibid., pp. 102–4
9 Nina Fishman, *The British Commnist Party and the Trade Unions 1933–1945*, pp. 317–18
10 Transcript of interview with Agnes McLean, *A People's War* (Thames TV / Channel 4), pp. 4–10, 21–25, keele.ac.uk/history/currentundergraduates/tltp/WOMEN/SUMMERFI/TEXT/SUMER263.HTM#Title, accessed 2 October 2012
11 Penny Summerfield, 'Women and War in the Twentieth Century', in June Pervis (ed.), *Women's History: Britain 1850–1945*, Routledge, 1995, p. 274
12 Geoffrey G. Field, *Blood, Sweat, and Toil: Remaking the British Working Class, 1939–1945*, Oxford University Press, 2011, p. 105
13 Esther Breitenbach, 'Scottish Women's Organisations and the Exercise of Citizenship, c1900–c1970', in Pat Thane (ed.), *Women and Citizenship in Britain and Ireland in the Twentieth Century*, Continuum, 2010, p. 64
14 R. A. Leeson, *Strike: A Live History 1887–1971*, p. 161
15 Ibid.
16 Christopher Harvie, 'The Recovery of Scottish Labour: 1939–1951', in Ian Donnachie, Christopher Harvie and Ian S. Wood (eds), *Forward! Labour Politics in Scotland 1888–1988*, p. 73
17 Ibid., p. 77
18 Bob McLean, 'Labour in Scotland Since 1945: Myth and Reality', in Gerry Hassan (ed.), *The Scottish Labour Party*, Edinburgh University Press, 2004, p. 34
19 Christopher Harvie, 'The Recovery of Scottish Labour: 1939–1951', p. 69
20 Farquhar McLay (ed.),*Workers' City: The Real Glasgow Stands Up*, Clydeside Press, 1988, citystrolls.com/workers-city/sandy.htm, accessed 17 July 2012
21 Ibid.
22 R. A. Leeson, *Strike: A Live History 1887–1971*, p. 233
23 Christopher Harvie, *Scotland and Nationalism: Scottish Society and Politics, 1707–1977*, pp. 174–76
24 Michael Keating, 'The Labour Party in Scotland: 1951-1964', in Ian Donnachie, Christopher Harvie and Ian S. Wood (eds), *Forward! Labour Politics in Scotland 1888–1988*, p. 87
25 Frances Wood, 'Scottish Labour in Government and Opposition 1964–1979', in Ian Donnachie, Christopher Harvie and Ian S. Wood (eds), *Forward! Labour Politics in Scotland 1888–1988*, p. 101

26　Michael Anderson, 'The Demographic Factor', in T. M. Devine and Jenny Wormald (eds), *The Oxford History of Modern Scotland*, Oxford University Press, 2012, p. 52

27　Vincent Cable, 'Glasgow: Area of Need', in Gordon Brown (ed.), *The Red Paper on Scotland*, EUSPB, 1975, pp. 232 and 239

28　Frances Wood, 'Scottish Labour in Government and Opposition 1964–1979', p. 101

29　*Aberdeen Voice*, 21 October 2011, http://aberdeenvoice.com/tag/fascism/, accessed 1 October 2012

30　Harry McShane, 'Glasgow's Housing Disgrace', in Robery Duncan and Arthur McIvor, *Labour and Class Conflict on the Clyde 1900–1950*, John Donald, 1992, p. 28

31　Jeff Torrington, *Swing Hammer Swing*, Harcourt Brace, 1994, p. 14

32　'Glasgow Has Highest Level of Toxic Pollution in UK', road.cc, 25 September 2012, http://road.cc/content/news/67317-glasgow-has-highest-level-toxic-pollution-uk, accessed 25 October 2013

33　Hugh MacDiarmid, 'Knoydart Land Seizures', *The National Weekly*, 1 (10) (20 November 1948)

34　'The Men of Knoydart', Dick Gaughan's Song Archive, dickgaughan.co.uk/songs/texts/knoydart.html, accessed 23 April 2013

35　Michael Keating, 'The Labour Party in Scotland: 1951–1964', p. 91

36　Christopher Harvie, 'The Recovery of Scottish Labour: 1939–1951', pp. 80–82

37　Ibid., p. 66

38　David McCrone, *Understanding Scotland: The Sociology of a Nation*, Routledge, 2001, p. 107

39　Tom Gallagher, *Glasgow, the Uneasy Peace*, p. 269

40　Frances Wood, 'Scottish Labour in Government and Opposition: 1964–1979', p. 89

41　Christopher Harvie, *Scotland and Nationalism: Scottish Society and Politics, 1707–1977*, p. 204

42　Frances Wood, 'Scottish Labour in Government and Opposition: 1964–1979', pp. 105–7

43　Global Non Violent Action Database, 'Scots and Peace Activists Protest US Navy Ba'se at Holy Loch, Scotland, 1960–61', http://nvdatabase.swarthmore.edu/content/scots-and-peace-activists-protest-us-navy-base-holy-loch-scotland-1960-61, accessed 24 April 2013

44　Marion Blythman, 'We Were on the Side of Anything That Made the Americans Mad', in *Nuclear Free Scotland*, 50th Anniversary Edition, May 2008, 'Then and Now: 50 Years of Struggle for a Better World', google.co.uk/url?sa=t&rct=j&q=morris%20blythman%20thurso%20berwick&source=web&cd=43&cad=rja&ved=0CDwQFjACOCg&url=http%3A%2F%2Fwww.banthebomb.org%2Fhistory%2FNFSapr08.pdf&ei=RfJ3Uam6A8KX0AWcqIHQDQ&usg=AFQjCNFJelboE3iVHHE1zrhiZQntAcPWdw&bvm=bv.45580626,d.d2k, downloaded 24 April 2013

45　Ibid.

46　'Thurso Berwick (1919–81)', http://citystrolls.com/a-real-peoples-history/thurso-berwick-1919-1981, accessed 18 May 2013

47　Marion Blythman, 'We Were on the Side of Anything That Made the Americans Mad'

48 *Glasgow Herald*, 28 March 1961
49 Marion Blythman, 'We Were on the Side of Anything That Made the Americans Mad'
50 Ibid.
51 'The Govan Billiard Hall Song', Tobar an Dualchais, tobarandualchais.co.uk/en/fullrecord/79164/4;jsessionid=23D351023CDC10AC5DF42CEF867C F3DD, accessed 25 October 2013
52 Ewan MacColl, *Journeyman*, Sidwick and Jackson, 1990, p. 21.
53 Ibid., p. 265
54 John McGrath, *Naked Thoughts that Roam About: Reflections on Theatre, 1958–2001*, Nick Hern Books, 2002, p. 47
55 Corey Gibson, 'Hamish Henderson's Conception of the Scottish Folk-song Revival and Its Place in Literary Scotland', p. 56, academia.edu/539708/Hamish_Hendersons_conception_of_the_Scottish_Folk-song_Revival_and_its_place_in_literary_Scotland, accessed 9 October 2012
56 Ibid.
57 Colin Fox, 'Time for a People's Festival', *Frontline*, 5 (2001), redflag.org.uk/frontline/five/05festival.html, accessed 9 October 2012
58 Ibid.
59 Raymond Williams, *Keywords*, Oxford University Press, 1985, p. 237
60 Dave Harker, *Class Act: The Cultural and Political Life of Ewan MacColl*, Pluto Press, 2007, p. 192
61 Tobar an Dualchais, 'The Govan Billiard Hall Song'
62 Mary Brooksbank, *No Sae Lang Syne: A Tale of This City*, Dundee Printers Ltd (no date), p. 5
63 'Hey Donal Donal', http://sangstories.webs.com/heydonalhodonal.htm, accessed 26 May 2013
64 Mary Brooksbank, *No Sae Lang Syne: A Tale of this City*, p. 6
65 Ibid., p. 10
66 Ibid., p. 9
67 Annmarie Hughes, *Gender and Political Identities in Scotland: 1919–1939*, Edinburgh University Press, 2010, p. 192
68 Mary Brooksbank, *No Sae Lang Syne: A Tale of this City*, p. 30
69 Ibid., p. 35
70 Graham Stevenson, 'Communist Biogs: Mary Brooksbank', grahamstevenson.me.uk/index.php?option=com_content&view=article&id=70:mary-brooksbank&catid=2:b&Itemid=98, accessed 30 April 2013
71 'Mary Brooksbank – Revolutionary, Poet and Songwriter', Alternative Perthshire, alternative-perth.co.uk/marybrooksbank.htm, accessed 30 April 2013
72 Ibid.
73 Ibid.
74 Mary Brooksbank, *No Sae Lang Syne: A Tale of This City*, p. 27

13. The 1970s: When Workers Won

1 Ralph Darlington, *Glorious Summer: Class Struggle in Britain, 1972*, Bookmarks, 2001, p. 17

2 Colin Nicholson, *Edwin Morgan: Inventions of Modernity*, Manchester University Press, 2002, p. 76

3 'There will be no hooliganism. There will be no vandalism. There will be no bevvying, because the world is watching us', *Evening Times*, 28 July 2011, eveningtimes.co.uk/features/features-editors-picks/jimmy-reid-1971-there-will-be-no-hooliganism-there-will-be-no-vandalism-there-will-be-no-bevvyin, accessed 20 May 2013

4 Harry Shapiro, *Jack Bruce: Composing Himself*, Jawbone, 2010, pp. 146–47

5 Colin Nicholson, *Edwin Morgan: Inventions of Modernity*, p. 77

6 Ralph Darlington, *Glorious Summer: Class Struggle in Britain*, p. 22

7 'UCS work-in veterans celebrate 40th anniversary of famous dispute . . . and this time there WAS bevvying'; *Daily Record*, 16 September 2011, dailyrecord.co.uk/news/real-life/ucs-work-in-veterans-celebrate-40th-1081953, accessed 20 May 2013

8 *Socialist Worker*, 11 September 1971

9 'Industry in the Vale of Leven', valeofleven.org.uk/valeindustry4.html, accessed 4 July 2012

10 Jim Phillips, 'The 1972 Miners' Strike: popular agency and industrial politics in Britain', *Contemporary British History* 20 (2) (2006), pp. 187–88

11 Ibid., p. 188

12 Ralph Darlington, *Glorious Summer: Class Struggle in Britain*, 1972, p. 64

13 Jonathan Winterton and Ruth Winterton, *Coal, Crisis, and Conflict: The 1984–85 Miners' Strike in Yorkshire*, Manchester University Press, 1989, p. 165

14 Ralph Darlington, *Glorious Summer: Class Struggle in Britain, 1972*, p. 201

15 Gordon Honeycombe, *Red Watch: A True Story*, Jeremy Mills Publishing, 2007, pp. 16–24

16 Jimmy Reid, Rectorial Address, Scottish Left Review, scottishleftreview.org/li/index.php?option=com_content&task=view&id=336, accessed 4 December 2013

17 Caroline Hoefferie, *British Student Activism in the Long Sixties*, Routledge, 2013, p. 188

18 Robert Crawford, 'The Crown', in Caroline McCracken-Flesher (ed.), *Culture, Nation and the New Scottish Parliament*, Bucknell University Press, 2007, p. 241

19 Ibid.

20 Caroline Hoefferie, *British Student Activism in the Long Sixties*, p. 198

21 Leslie Sklair, 'The Struggle Against the Housing Finance Act', in Ralph Miliband and John Saville (eds), *Socialist Register*, Merlin, 1975, p. 258

22 Ibid., p. 261

23 Frances Wood, 'Scottish Labour in Government and Opposition: 1964–1979', p. 113

24 Neil Davidson, 'In Perspective: Tom Nairn', *Socialist Review*, March 1999, http://pubs.socialistreviewindex.org.uk/isj82/davidson.htm, accessed 19 May 2013

25 Dave Sherry, 'The Present Is History', in Laurie Flynn (ed.), *We Shall Be All: Recent Chapters in the History of Working Class Struggle in Scotland*, Bookmarks, 1978, pp. 50–52

26 Andy Beckett, *When the Lights Went Out: Britain in the 1970s*, Faber and Faber, 2009, p. 196

27 Ibid., p. 197

28 *Scotsman*, 20 May 2013

29 Andy Beckett, *When the Lights Went Out: Britain in the 1970s*, p. 200
30 Frances Wood, 'Scottish Labour in Government and Opposition: 1964–1979', pp. 114–15
31 Ibid., pp. 115–18
32 Ibid., pp. 120–29
33 William Knox, *An Industrial Nation: Work, Culture and Society in Scotland, 1800–Present*, Edinburgh University Press, 1999, p. 304
34 Andy Beckett, *When the Lights Went Out: Britain in the 1970s*, pp. 502–5
35 Esther Breitenbach, 'Feminist Politics in Scotland from the 1970s to 2005', in Pat Thane and Esther Breitenbach (eds), *Women and Citizenship in Britain and Ireland in the 20th Century: What Difference Did the Vote Make?*, Continuum, 2010, p. 154
36 Private correspondence, October 2013
37 Ibid.
38 Mark Kirby et al., *Sociology in Perspective*, Heinemann, 2000, p. 86
39 Roger Davidson and Gayle Davis, *The Sexual State: Sexuality and Scottish Governance, 1950–80*, Edinburgh University Press, 2012, p. 75

14. The Thatcher Years

1 T. M. Devine, *The Scottish Nation 1700–2000*, p. 594
2 'Fighting Plant Closure – Women in the Plessey Occupation 1982', http://libcom.org/history/fighting-plant-closure-women-plessey-occupation-1982, accessed 9 October 2012
3 Ibid.
4 Reevel Alderson, 'Lee Jeans Women Remember Seven-Month Sit-in Success', BBC News Scotland, February 2011, bbc.co.uk/news/uk-scotland-12366211, accessed 1 October 2012
5 Ibid.
6 Ibid.
7 Pat Clark, 'The 1981 Lee Jeans Occupation: Women Showed How to Win, *Socialist Worker*, 26 March 2005
8 Ibid.
9 Ibid.
10 Reevel Alderson, 'Lee Jeans Women Remember Seven-Month Sit-in Success'
11 Ibid.
12 'Nostalgia: Henry Robb Shipyard Strike', scotsman.com/edinburgh-evening-news/features/nostalgia/nostalgia-henry-robb-shipyard-strike-1-2881055, accessed 23 April 2013
13 Andrew Taylor, *The NUM and British Politics*, Ashgate, 2005, p. 188
14 *Times*, 11 and 19 February 1981
15 *Scottish Miner*, February 1981
16 *Economist*, 21 February 1981
17 *Times*, 24 and 27 November 1982
18 *Glasgow Herald*, 14 May 1983
19 *Times*, 21 June 1983.
20 Terry Brotherstone and Simon Pirani, 'Were There Alternatives? Movements

from Below in the Scottish Coalfield, the Communist Party, and the Development of Thatcherism, 1981–1985', *Critique*, 36 (2005), p. 110

21 *Glasgow Herald*, 15 September 1983

22 *Glasgow Herald*, 16 and 21 September 1983; *Scotsman*, 14 October 1983

23 *Glasgow Herald*, 24 September 1983.

24 Alex Callinicos and Mike Simons, *The Great Strike: the Miners' Strike of 1984–5 and Its Lessons*, Socialist Worker Publications, 1995, p. 43

25 Ibid., p. 46

26 Ibid., p. 41

27 Ibid., p. 109

28 'Miners Strike over Threatened Pit Closures', BBC *On This Day*, 12 March 1984, http://news.bbc.co.uk/onthisday/hi/dates/stories/march/12/newsid_2540000/2540175.stm, accessed 22 May 2013

29 Martin Adeney and John Lloyd, *The Miners Strike 1984–1985: Loss Without Honour*, Routledge, 1988, p. 96

30 Jon Winterton and Ruth Winterton, *Coal, Crisis and Coalfield: The 1984–1985 Miners Strike in Yorkshire*, p. 70

31 '25 Years On: Miners' Strike Changed Course of My Life', *Glasgow Herald*, 9 March 2009, heraldscotland.com/25-years-on-miners-strike-changed-course-of-my-life-1.904570

32 Robert Duncan, *The Mine Workers*, p. 259

33 Alex Callinicos and Mike Simons, *The Great Strike: The Miners' Strike of 1984–5 and Its Lessons*, p. 15

34 Ibid., p. 88

35 Joan Burnie, 'The pits are gone . . . but the ghosts from 1984 still haunt Fallin', *Daily Record*, 4 March 2004, thefreelibrary.com/The+pits+are+gone+..+but+the+ghosts+from+1984+still+haunt+FALLIN.-a0113890069, accessed 20 May 2013

36 Robert Duncan, *The Mine Workers*, p. 265

37 Ibid.

38 Alex Callinicos and Mike Simons, *The Great Strike: The Miners' Strike of 1984–5 and Its Lessons*, pp. 86–92

39 Robert Duncan, *The Mine Workers*, p. 263

40 Joan Burnie, 'The pits are gone . . . but the ghosts from 1984 still haunt Fallin'

41 Ibid.

42 Alex Callinicos and Mike Simons, *The Great Strike: The Miners' Strike of 1984–5 and Its Lessons*, p. 9

43 *Guardian*, 17 April 2013

44 *Los Angeles Times*, 22 March 1987, http://articles.latimes.com/1987-03-22/news/mn-14818_1_plants-workers-occupy, accessed 8 October 2012

45 Ibid.

46 Charles Woolfson and John Foster, *Track Record: The Story of the Caterpillar Occupation*, Verso, 1988, pp. 115–16 and p. 50

47 Ibid., pp. 50–51

48 Ibid., pp. 115–16

49 '25 Years On: Workers Look Back on Caterpillar Factory Sit in', http://concretehelper.com/25-years-on-workers-look-back-on-caterpillar-factory-sit-in/, accessed 22 May 2012

50 Charles Woolfson and John Foster, *Track Record: The Story of the Caterpillar Occupation*, p. 264

51 Bernadette Meaden, *Protest for Peace*, Wild Goose Publications, 1999, p. 30

52 Ibid., pp. 32–33

53 Mary-Wynne Ashford, *Enough Blood Shed: 101 Solutions to Violence, Terror and War*, New Society Publishers, 2006, pp. 80–81

54 Norman Stone, 'Can the Tories Govern Scotland?', *Sunday Telegraph*, 14 June 1987

55 Ewen Cameron, *Impaled Upon a Thistle: Scotland Since 1880*, Edinburgh University Press, 2010, p. 322

56 Ibid.

57 Michael Lavalette and Gerry Mooney, '"No Poll Tax Here": The Tories, Social Policy and the Great Poll Tax Rebellion', in Michael Lavalette and Gerry Mooney (eds), *Class Struggle and Social Welfare*, Routledge, 2013, p. 213

58 Ibid.

59 Ibid., p. 217

60 Ibid., p. 218

61 Ibid., p. 219

62 Ibid.

63 Ibid.

64 *Glasgow Herald*, 14 November 1989

65 Ian MacWhirter, 'That Bloody Woman', *New Statesman*, 26 February 2009

66 Ian MacWhirter, 'Will Scotland Rise Up Against "English" Tory Rule?' 10 October 2009, http://iainmacwhirter2.blogspot.co.uk/2009/10/will-scotland-rise-up-against-english.html, accessed 23 May 2013

67 Stephen Reicher and Nick Hopkins, *Self and Nation*, SAGE, 2001, p. 194

68 Ibid., p. 195

69 Neal Ascherson, 'The Warnings That Scotland's Patient Nationalism Could Turn Nasty', *Independent on Sunday*, 21 November 1993, independent.co.uk/voices/the-warnings-that-scotlands-patient-nationalism-could-turn-nasty-1505824.html, accessed 23 May 2013

70 Kevin Williamson, 'Rebel Inc: 20 Years On & Ready For More', *Bella Caledonia*, 2 May 2012, http://bellacaledonia.org.uk/2012/05/02/rebel-inc-20-years-on-ready-for-more/

71 Richard Zumkhawala-Cook, *Scotland as We Know it: Representations of National Identity in Literature in Literature, Film and Popular Culture*, McFarland, 2008, p. 16

72 Paul Foot, 'Seize the Time', *Socialist Review*, 165 (June 1993), pp. 10–11, marxists.org/archive/foot-paul/1993/06/timex.htm, accessed 25 March 2013

73 Michael Gardiner, *Modern Scottish Culture*, Edinburgh University Press, 2005, p. 182; and James Campbell, *Invisible Country: A Journey Through Scotland*, New Amsterdam, 1990, p. 107

74 Kevin Williamson, 'Rebel Inc: 20 Years On & Ready For More' John McGrath, *Naked Thoughts That Roam About: Reflections on Theatre, 1958–2001*, Nick Hern Books, 2002, p. 65

75 Ibid., pp. 73–74

76 James Kelman, *And the Judges Said . . .*, Secker and Warburg, 2002, p. 40

77 Peter Kravitz, 'Essay: As It Never Was', *Variant*, 13 (Summer 2001), variant.org.uk/13texts/Peter_Kravitz.html, accessed 24 October 2014

78 Peter Kravitz (Introduction), *The Vintage Book of Contemporary Scottish Fiction*, Vintage, 1997, p. xxi

79 Ibid.
80 Ibid., p. xxiii
81 *Independent*, 13 October 1994, independent.co.uk/voices/highly-literary-and-deeply-vulgar-if-james-kelmans-booker-novel-is-rude-it-is-in-good-company-argues-robert-winder-1442639.html, accessed 29 October 2013
82 Scott Hames, 'Eyeless in Glasgow: James Kelman's Existential Milton', *Contemporary Literature*, 50 (3) (Fall 2001)
83 James Kelman, Booker Prize Acceptance Speech, citystrolls.com/z-temp/z-pages/kelman.htm, accessed 29 October 2013
84 Tom Leonard, *Intimate Voices: Selected Work 1965–1983*, Vintage, 1995, p. 120.
85 Simon Kövesi, *James Kelman*, Manchester University Press, 2007, p. 7
86 Ian Brown, 'Processes and Interactive Events: Theatre and Scottish Devolution', in Steve Blandford (ed.), *Theatre and Performance in Small Nations*, Intellect, 2013, p. 37
87 'Liz Lochhead – The SRB Interview', *Scottish Review of Books*, 7 (4) (2011), scottishreviewofbooks.org/index.php/back-issues/volume-seven-2011/volume-seven-issue-four/442-liz-lochhead-the-srb-interview, accessed 29 October 2013
88 Attila Dosa, *Beyond Identity: New Horizons in Modern Scottish Poetry*, p. 183
89 James Kelman *Some Recent Attacks: Essays Cultural and Political*, AK Press, 1992, pp. 1–4.
90 Aaron Kelly, *Irvine Welsh*, Manchester University Press, 2005, p. 20
91 Ibid., p. 45
92 Irvine Welsh, *Trainspotting*, Vintage, 2004, p. 18
93 Ibid., p. 218
94 Aaron Kelly, *Irvine Welsh*, pp. 11–12
95 Ibid., pp. 84–85
96 Irvine Welsh, 'Scottish Independence and British Unity', *Bella Caledonia*, 10 January 2013, http://bellacaledonia.org.uk/2013/01/10/irvine-welsh-on-scottish-independence-and-british-unity/, accessed 28 October 2013
97 Anna Burnside, 'Alasdair Gray: "Self-rule for Scotland would make us grow up"', *Independent*, 8 August 2011, independent.co.uk/arts-entertainment/books/features/alasdair-gray-selfrule-for-scotland-would-make-us-grow-up-2333613.html, accessed 28 October 2013
98 James Foley, 'Radical Lallans Poet: Rab Wilson', *Communiqué*, 28 July 2011, http://internationalsocialist.org.uk/index.php/2011/07/radical-lallans-poet-rab-wilson/#sthash.w1KrFY2o.dpuf, accessed 28 October 2013
99 Grant Pooke, *Contemporary British Art: An Introduction*, Routledge, 2012, p. 87
100 Ibid., p. 88
101 The Glasgow History Mural, mediamatters.co.uk/media/kcurrie.html, accessed 30 October 2013
102 Simon McKerrel, 'Modern Scottish Bands (1970–1990): Cash as Authenticity', *Scottish Music Review*, 2 (1) (2011)
103 Ibid.
104 Ibid.
105 Michael Gray, 'Death of Gerry Rafferty', http://bobdylanencyclopedia.blogspot.co.uk/2011/01/death-of-gerry-rafferty.html, accessed 21 May 2013

106 'Margaret Thatcher Is Back but Should Scots Ever Forgive the Iron Lady?', *Daily Record*, 8 January 2012
107 Christopher Harvie, *Scotland and Nation: Scottish Society and Politics 1707 to the Present*, Routledge, 2004, p. 228
108 Ian MacWhirter, 'That Bloody Woman', *New Statesman*, 26 February 2009

15. Twenty-First-Century Scotland

1 Thomas Zittel and Dieter Fuchs, *Participatory Democracy and Political Participation: Can Participatory Engineering Bring Citizens Back In?* Taylor and Francis, 2006, p. 83
2 Anthony Seldon, *Blair's Britain 1997–2007*, Cambridge University Press, 2007, p. 492
3 Ibid., p. 491
4 'Organisers Hail Anti-war Protests', BBC Scotland News, 15 February 2003, http://news.bbc.co.uk/1/hi/scotland/2765093.stm, accessed 25 May 2013
5 Alistair Hulett, 'Scottish Struggles Created a Rich Tradition of Radical Song', *Socialist Worker*, 20 August 2005, socialistworker.co.uk/article.php?article_id=7144, accessed 25 March 2013
6 Lyn Smith, *Voices Against War: A Century of Protest*, Mainstream, 2009, p. 283
7 Gerry Mooney and Tricia McCafferty, '"Only looking after the weans"? The Scottish Nursery Nurses' Strike, 2004', http://strathprints.strath.ac.uk/1375/1/strathprints001375.htm, accessed 24 April 2013
8 Ibid.
9 Ibid.
10 Ibid.
11 Mark Irvine, 'Scotland, Labour and the Trade Union Movement: Partners in Change or Uneasy Bedfellows', in Gerry Hassan (ed.), *The Scottish Labour Party*, Edinburgh University Press, 2004, p. 230
12 'Poverty Marchers Call for Justice', BBC News, 2 July 2005, http://news.bbc.co.uk/1/hi/uk/4645251.stm, accessed 23 April 2013
13 Online report, socialistworker.co.uk/art/6701/A+coalition+against+the+new+global+order, 3 July 2005
14 'Naming the Dead', Guardian Blog, 4 July 2005, guardian.co.uk/news/blog/2005/jul/04/namingthedead1, accessed 23 April 2013
15 BBC, 'Protesters Breach G8 March Route', 6 July 2005, http://news.bbc.co.uk/1/hi/scotland/4654767.stm, accessed 23 April 2013
16 'Thousands of Anti-nuclear Protesters Attend Glasgow March against Trident', *Daily Record*, 13 April 2013, dailyrecord.co.uk/news/scottish-news/thousands-anti-nuclear-protesters-glasgow-march-1828754, accessed 15 April 2013
17 'The Constitution Page: Defence', *Scottish Left Review*, 72, (September-October 2012), scottishleftreview.org/feature/the-constitution-page-defence/, accessed 28 May 2013
18 Ibid.
19 'Call Centre Staff Angry at Intrusive Monitoring, Claims TUC', personneltoday.

com/articles/05/04/2001/5448/call-centre-staff-angry-at-intrusive-monitoring-claims.htm, accessed 30 May 2013

20 Chris Baldry et al., *The Meaning of Work in the New Economy*, Palgrave MacMillan, 2007, p. 67

21 Ibid., p. 71

22 Ibid., p. 78

23 Ibid., pp. 141–42

24 Ibid., p. 146

25 Ibid., p. 214

26 Sarah Collins, 'Our Generation Is Your Friend', *Scottish Left Review*, 75, (March/April 2013)

27 Ibid.

28 Michael Keating, *The Government of Scotland: Public Policy Making After Devolution*, Edinburgh University Press, 2010, p. 49

29 L. Paterson, F. Bechhofer and D. McCrone, *Living in Scotland: Social and Economic Change since 1980*, Edinburgh University Press, 2004, p. 99; R. Johns, D. Denver, J. Mitchell and C. Pattie, *Voting for a Scottish Government: The Scottish Parliament Election of 2007*, Manchester University Press, 2010, pp. 81–82.

30 Brian Wilson, 'System of Land Ownership – Worst in Europe', *West Highland Free Press*, 14 March 2012, localpeopleleading.co.uk/policy-talk/policy-articles/1347/, accessed 13 May 2013

31 Andy Wightman, *The Poor Had No Lawyers: Who Owns Scotland and How They Got It*, Birlinn, 2010, p. 106

32 Andy Wightman, *Scotland: Land and Power – the Agenda for Land Reform*, Luath Press, 1999, p. 30

33 Lesley Riddoch, 'Big Landowners Biggest Obstacle to the Big Society in Rural Scotland', 25 February 2011, lesleyriddoch.co.uk/2011/02/, accessed 13 May 2013

34 Gavin Corbett and Andy Wightman, *Housing, Homelessness and Land Reform*, Shelter Scotland, 1998, p. 2

35 Andy Wightman, *The Poor Had No Lawyers: Who Owns Scotland and How They Got It*, p. 256

36 Bryan D. MacGregor, 'Owner Motivation and Land Use on Landed Estates in the North-west Highlands of Scotland', *Journal of Rural Studies*, 4 (4) (1988), pp. 389–404

37 'Scottish PLC: Land Ownership in Scotland', corporatewatch.org/?lid=1308, accessed 13 May 2012

38 Joseph Ritchie, 'Introducing the Land Issue Part 2: Why it Matters and How it Can Change', Bright Green Scotland, http://brightgreenscotland.org/index.php/2011/07/introducing-the-land-issue-part-2-why-it-matters-and-how-it-can-change/, accessed 13 May 2013

39 Jimmy Reid Foundation, 'Quick Note: Who Owns Scotland?' http://reidfoundation.org/portfolio/quicknote-who-owns-scotland/, accessed 14 May 2013

40 Andy Wightman, *Scotland: Land and Power – the Agenda for Land Reform*, pp. 46–47

41 Thomas Johnston, *Our Scots Noble Families*, Forward Publishing Company, 1909, p. x

42 *Glasgow Herald*, 15 December 1938

43 *Scotsman*, 20 May 2013
44 'Anger at BBC Scotland virtual news blackout of Healey North Sea Oil admission', http://newsnetscotland.com/index.php/scottish-news/7414-anger-at-bbc-scotland-virtual-news-blackout-of-healey-north-sea-oil-admission, accessed 24 May 2013
45 Margo MacDonald, 'We Were Lied to Over Oil Money', scotsman.com/news/margo-macdonald-we-were-lied-to-over-oil-money-1-2939440, accessed 24 May 2013
46 Nathaniel O. Keohane and Sheila M. Olmstead, *Markets and the Environment*, Island Press, 2007, p. 218
47 David Torrance, *'We in Scotland': Thatcherism in a Cold Climate*, Birlinn, 2009, p. 65
48 Gordon Morgan, 'Its Scotland's Wind', *Scottish Left Review*, 76 (May–June 2013), scottishleftreview.org/article/it%E2%80%99s-scotland%E2%80%99s-wind/, accessed 28 May 2013
49 Amnesty Scotland, 'Why Do We need International Women's Day in Scotland?', 8 March 2013, http://www2.amnesty.org.uk/blogs/scottish-human-rights-blog/why-do-we-need-international-womens-day-scotland, accessed 24 May 2013
50 Ibid.
51 Colette Douglas Home, 'For Some, Sexual Equality Is Still in the Dark Ages', *Herald*, 28 May 2013, heraldscotland.com/comment/columnists/for-some-sexual-equality-is-still-in-the-dark-ages.21196607, accessed 28 May 2013
52 Scotland Future's Forum, 'Women, Punishment and Human Rights, 2011', scotlandfutureforum.org/assets/library/files/application/Women,_Punishment_and_Human_Rights_-_final_report.pdf, accessed 24 May 2013
53 STUC Women's Committee on Scottish Parliament Childcare Debate, May 8th 2013, stuc.org.uk/news/998/stuc-women-s-committee-on-scottish-parliament-childcare-debate
54 Catriona Stewart, 'Women in Scotland Losing Out in Battle for Equal Pay', *Evening Times*, 17 July 2013,eveningtimes.co.uk/news/women-in-scotland-losing-out-in-battle-for-equal-pay-130699n.21624793, accessed 31 July 2013
55 'Equality and Human Rights Commission: Scottish Government Not Maximising Potential of All Scotland's People', *Herald*, 31 July 2013, heraldscotland.com/news/home-news/equality-and-human-rights-commission-scottish-government-not-maximising-potential-of-all-scotlands-people.1375287, accessed 31 July 2013
56 Mhairi McAlpine, 'A Woman's Place Is in the Independence Movement', *Second Council House of Virgo*, 3 June 2012, 2ndcouncilhouse.co.uk/blog/2012/06/03/a-womans-place-is-in-the-independence-movement/, accessed 25 May 2013
57 Ibid.
58 Cahal Milmo and Nigel Morris, 'Woolwich Attack: Number of Islamphobic Incidents Continues to Rise with Ten Attacks on Mosques Since Murder of Soldier Lee Rigby', *Belfast Telegraph*, 28 May 2013, belfasttelegraph.co.uk/news/local-national/uk/woolwich-attack-number-of-islamophobic-incidents-continues-to-rise-with-ten-attacks-on-mosques-since-murder-of-soldier-lee-rigby-29300306.html, accessed 28 May 2013
59 Amy Homes, Chris McLean and Lorraine Murray, Ipsos MORI Scotland, British Council, 'Muslim Integration in Scotland', July 2010, britishcouncil.

　　org/scotland-society-muslims-integration-in-scotland-report.pdf,　accessed 25 May 2013

60　Asifa Hussain and William Miller, *Devolution Briefings, Towards a Multicultural Nationalism?* Anglophobia and Islamophobia in Scotland Briefing No. 24, March 2005, devolution.ac.uk/pdfdata/Briefing%2024%20-%20Hussain-Miller.pdf, accessed 25 May 2013

61　'Edinburgh: Headscarves Torn Off Two Muslim Women', *Scotsman*, 6 May 2013, scotsman.com/news/racial-attack-on-muslim-women-1-2921652, accessed 25 May 2013

62　'Racism on the Rise in Scotland', STV News, 11 February 2011', http://news.stv.tv/scotland/227562-racism-on-the-increase-in-scotland/,　accessed 25 May 2013

63　Satnam Virdee, Christopher Kyriakides and Tariq Modood, 'Codes of Cultural Belonging: Racialised National Identities in a Multi-ethnic Scottish Neighbourhood', *Journal of Ethnic and Migration Studies*, 35 (2) (February 2009), pp. 289–308

Conclusion: Our Destiny Is In Our Hands

1　Barclays Wealth, '2011 UK Wealth Map', p. 36

2　STV News, 'Six Billionaires Among Ranks of Scots Dominating British Rich List', 21 April 2013, http://news.stv.tv/scotland/222270-six-billionaires-among-ranks-of-scots-dominating-sunday-times-rich-list/, accessed 13 May 2013

3　Barclays Wealth, '2011 UK Wealth' Map, p. 36

4　James Foley, *Britain Must Break: The Internationalist Case for Independence*, ISG, 2012, p. 19

5　Ibid.

6　STV News, 'Six Billionaires Among Ranks of British Rich List'

7　James Meadway, 'Breaking Free of London-Focused Growth', New Economics Foundation, 23 May 2013, neweconomics.org/blog/entry/Breaking-free-of-London-focused-growth, accessed 25 May 2013

8　Aditya Chakrabotty, 'London's Economic Boom Leaves Rest of Britain Behind', *Guardian*, theguardian.com/business/2013/oct/23/london-south-east-economic-boom, accessed 2 November 2013

9　Robin MacAlpine, 'Economy Plan Chained by Convention', *Scotsman*, 24 May 2013, scotsman.com/the-scotsman/opinion/comment/robin-mcalpine-economy-plan-chained-by-convention-1-2942502, accessed 30 May 2013

10　Phil Inman, 'UK Investment Fall Among Worst in G8', *Guardian*, 23 May 2013, theguardian.com/business/2013/may/23/concerns-health-uk-ecoomy-gdp-growth-ons, accessed 3 November 2013

11　'Economic Recovery Not Certain, Warns Think-Tank', *Herald*, 31 October 2013,　heraldscotland.com/business/markets-economy/economic-recovery-not-certain-warns-think-tank.22560739, accessed 31 October 2013

12　Scottish Government, 'Labour Market Monthly Briefing Summary Tables October 2013', scotland.gov.uk/Resource/0043/00436901.pdf, accessed 31 October 2013

13　'MSPs to Investigate Problem of Child Poverty', *Scotsman*, 31 October 2013, scotsman.com/news/politics/top-stories/msps-to-investigate-problem-of-child-poverty-1-3161755, accessed 31 October 2013

14 Scottish Government, 'Fuel Poverty Evidence Review: Defining, Measuring and Analysing Fuel Poverty in Scotland, 2012', scotland.gov.uk/Resource/0039/00398798.pdf, accessed 31 October 2013

15 James Moncur, 'Aberdeen's First Food Bank Is Helping Dozens of Needy People', *Daily Record*, 23 May 2013, dailyrecord.co.uk/news/scottish-news/aberdeens-first-food-bank-helping-1905723, accessed 30 May 2013

16 *Daily Record*, 18 October 2013, dailyrecord.co.uk/news/scottish-news/scots-most-productive-workers-uk-2464919, accessed 31 October 2013

17 Pedro Morago, 'Health and Health Inequalities', in Steve Hathersall and Janine Bolger (eds), *Social Policy for Social Work, Social Care and the Caring Professions: The Scottish Perspective*, Ashgate, 2010, p. 209

18 'Death Rates Point to Scotland Wealth Split, *Scotsman*, 27 March 2013, scotsman.com/news/health/death-rates-point-to-scotland-wealth-split-1-2859611, accessed 28 March 2013

19 'A Nation Still Divided by Poverty and Inequality', *Scotsman*, January 4 2006, http://news.scotsman.com/health.cfm?id=11972006 , accessed 28 May 2013

20 Pete Ramand, 'Austerity, the Left and Independence', 25 July 2011, http://internationalsocialist.org.uk/index.php/2011/07/austerity-the-left-and-scottish-independence/, accessed 29 May 2013

21 Rodge Glass, *Alasdair Gray: A Secretary's Biography*, Bloomsbury, 2012, p. 277

INDEX

Torrington, Jeff, 230, 280
Torryburn, 53–4
Trades Union Congress (TUC), 179–87
Tranent, 90, 183
Trevelyan, Charles, 112
Trevlyn, Valda, 214
Trotter, Alexander, 84
Tyneside, 123, 124, 157
Tytler, James, 87

Uddingston Caterpillar occupation, 266
Uddington, 308
Ulaid, 8
Ullapool, 108
Ulster, 8
Union, Act of, 56–9, 69–70
Union of the Crowns, 39
United Scotsmen, 90–1

Victoria, Queen, 117, 121, 133
Vikings, the, 11, 12
Voltaire, 75

Wade, General, 63, 64
Wales, 7
Wallace, Margaret, 258–9
Wallace, William, 18, 20–3, 24
Wallace Monument, 120
Wallacestone, the, 92
Watkins, Peter, 67
Watson, the Rev. John, 133
Watson, Stuart, 211
Watt, Robert, 91
Watters, George, 202
Wedderburn, Robert, 32–3
Weir, William, 123, 147, 149, 150
Welsh, Irvine, 279, 282, 285–7
West Calder, 187

West Lothian, 129
West of Scotland Female Powerloom
    Weavers Association, 98
Wester Ross, 2, 11
Western Isles, the, 12
Whatley, Christopher, 63
Wheatley, John, 127, 161, 168–9, 170,
    174, 180, 212
Wheeler, Albert, 261–2
Whitby, Synod of, 9–10
White, James, 254
White, Rev. John, 173–4
Wightman, Andy, 308–9
Wilkes, John, 72
Wilkinson, Ellen, 190
William III, 49–50, 52, 55
William IV, King, 98
William the Conqueror, 13
William the Lion, King, 13, 15
Williamson, Kevin, 276, 279–80
Wilson, Brian, 253, 271–2, 306
Wilson, Harold, 233, 244, 250, 251, 252
Wilson, James, 95–96, 96
Wilson, Rab, 287–8
Wishart, Bishop of Glasgow, 20
Wishaw, 193
Wood, Sir Ian, 317
Woodburn, Arthur, 230
Woods, William, 125
Worker, The, 150
World War I, 142–3, 151, 153, 159–60,
    166, 190, 215, 240
World War II, 165, 220–6, 243

Yeoman, Louise, 106
Young, Bob, 185
Young, Douglas, 225–6